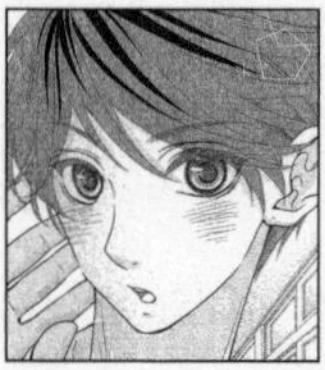

KAI ICHINOSE

A lover of women and the most popular boy in school. High school first-year. He and Takanashi fight like cats and dogs, but...!?

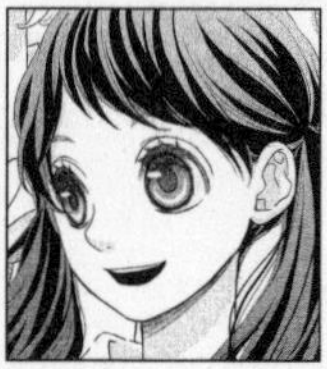

RIKO TAKANASHI

A heroic girl. Classmate of Kai's since elementary school who has absolutely no interest in him. Currently has a crush on Suwa-sensei.

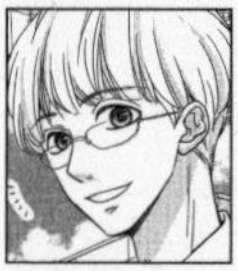

SATOSHI SUWA

The assistant teacher of Kai and Riko's class. Like an older brother to Riko.

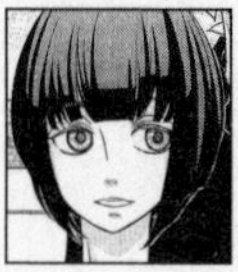

AKEMI

Suwa-sensei's girlfriend. Like an older sister to Riko.

Kai's Friends

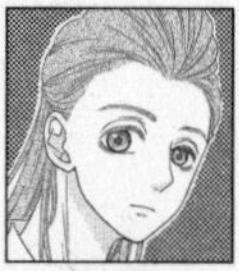

TAROU TORAMARU

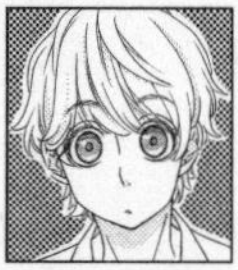

MIKI KIRITANI

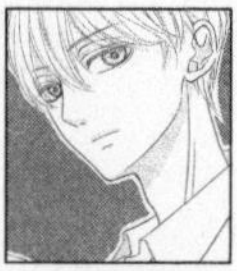

TAKAYA MISAKI

Riko's Friends

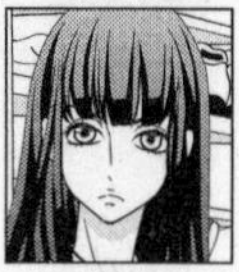

KAGURA TATSUNAMI

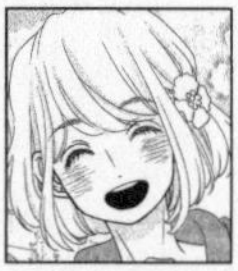

KIYO OOSHIMA

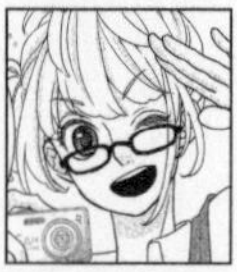

AYUMI SHIMURA

STORY

● Kai, the school's most popular playboy, learns that violent and short-tempered Riko Takanashi has a crush on Suwa-sensei. This first glance at her girlish side causes a strange emotion to grow in him.

● One day, Riko falls ill and Kai takes her home and looks after her. This is when Kai finally realizes that his feelings for her are love.

● Kai also learns that Suwa-sensei has a girlfriend, whom Riko has known for most of her life, and that she has kept her feelings to herself out of consideration for the two people who mean so much to her. Kai denounces her crush as empty, and Riko, accepting his criticism, attempts to move past her feelings by getting close to another boy.

● Kai senses that Riko is forcing herself and in the heat of the moment declares, "There's a guy who really loves you!" confessing his true feelings...!?

Thank you very much
for picking up HATSU * HARU
Volume 4.

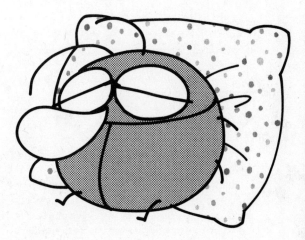

CHAPTER 13

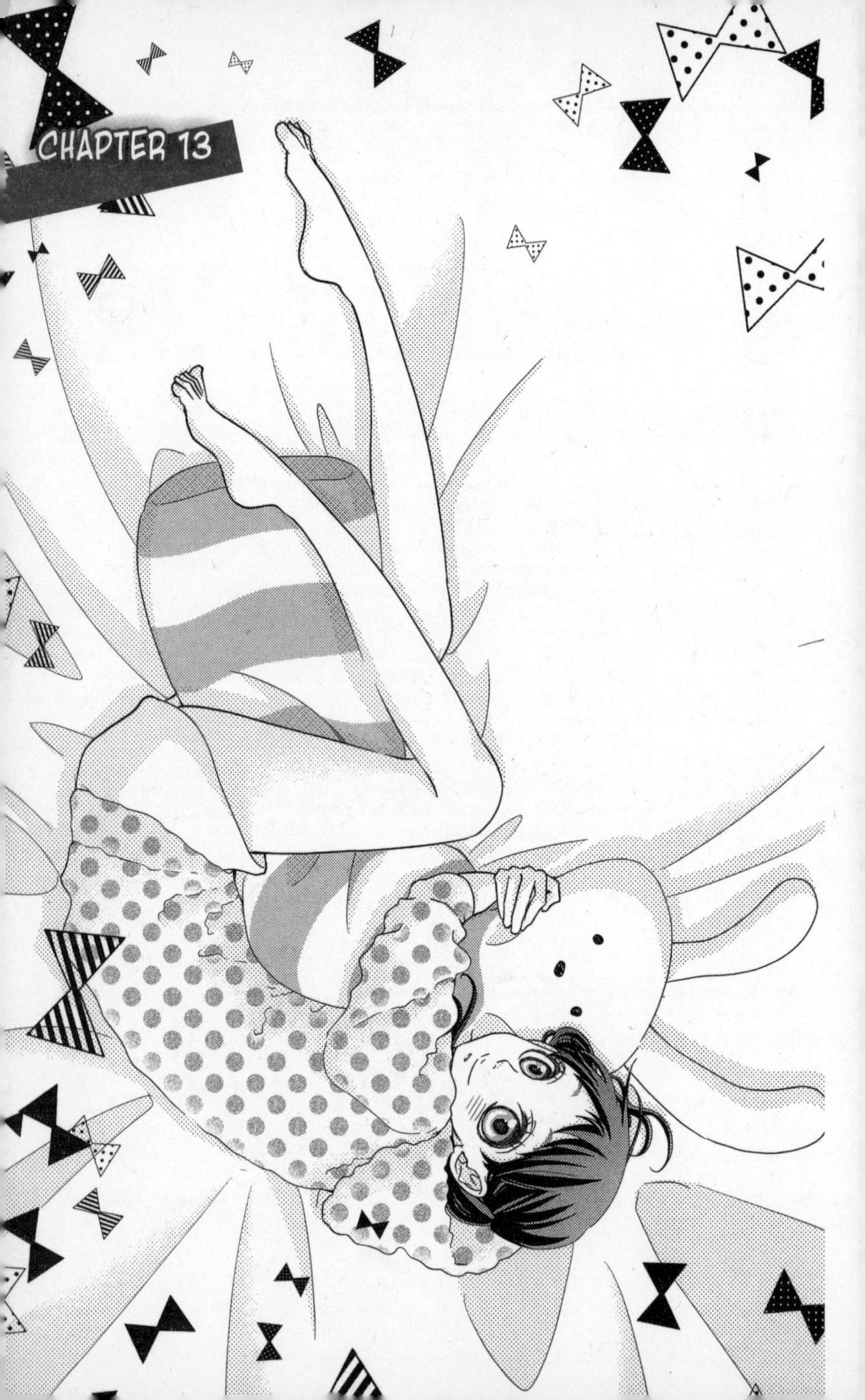

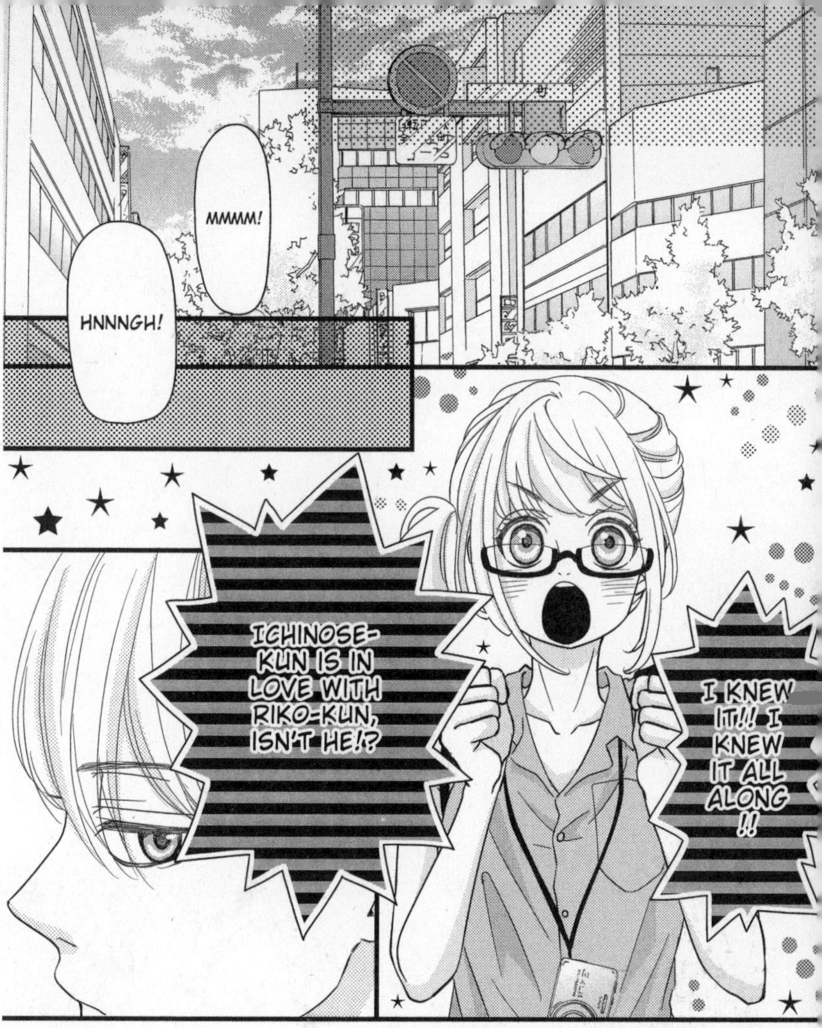
MMMMM!
HNNNGH!
ICHINOSE-KUN IS IN LOVE WITH RIKO-KUN, ISN'T HE!?
I KNEW IT!! I KNEW IT ALL ALONG!!

hatsu haru

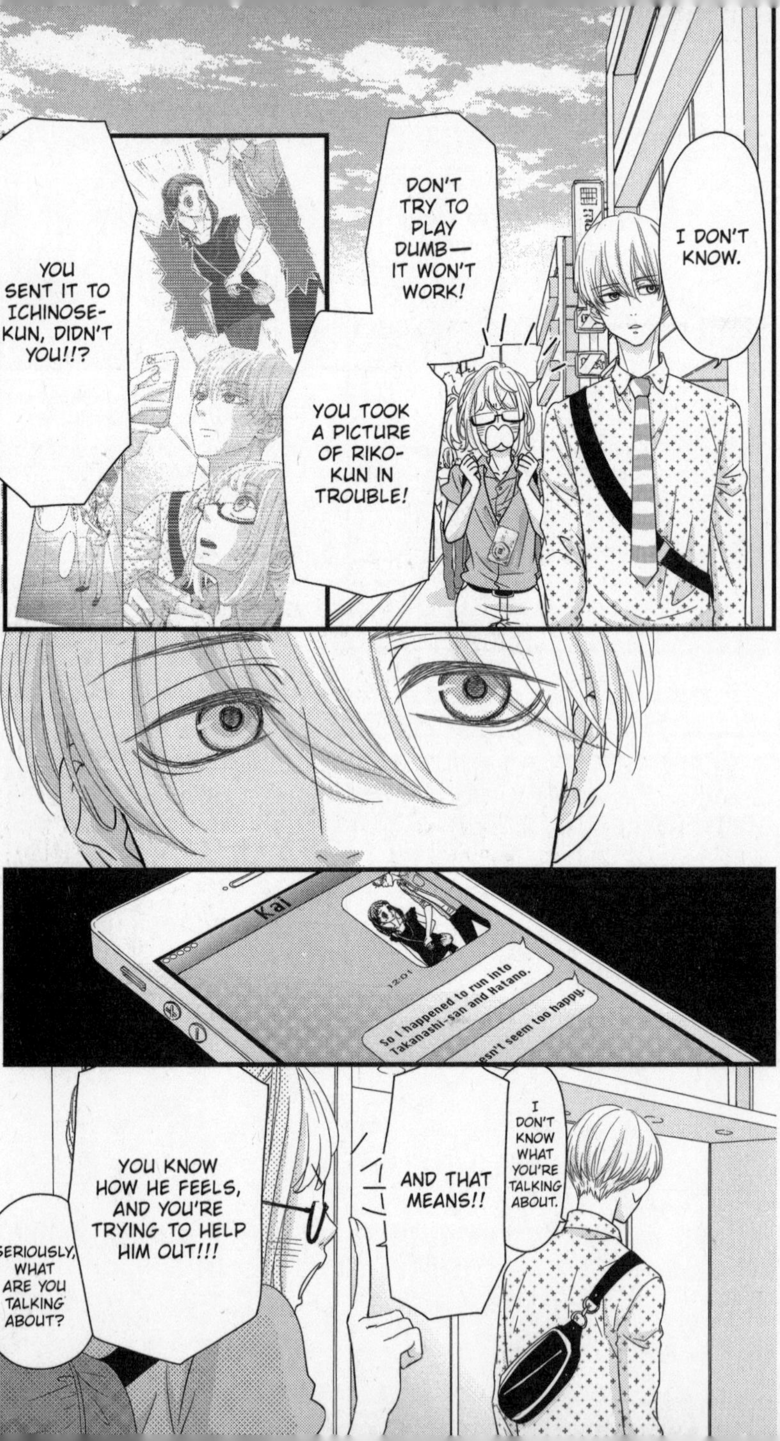
I DON'T KNOW.
DON'T TRY TO PLAY DUMB—IT WON'T WORK!
YOU TOOK A PICTURE OF RIKO-KUN IN TROUBLE!
YOU SENT IT TO ICHINOSE-KUN, DIDN'T YOU!!?
Kai
12:01
So I happened to run into Takanashi-san and Hatano.
esn't seem too happy.
I DON'T KNOW WHAT YOU'RE TALKING ABOUT.
AND THAT MEANS!!
YOU KNOW HOW HE FEELS, AND YOU'RE TRYING TO HELP HIM OUT!!!
SERIOUSLY, WHAT ARE YOU TALKING ABOUT?

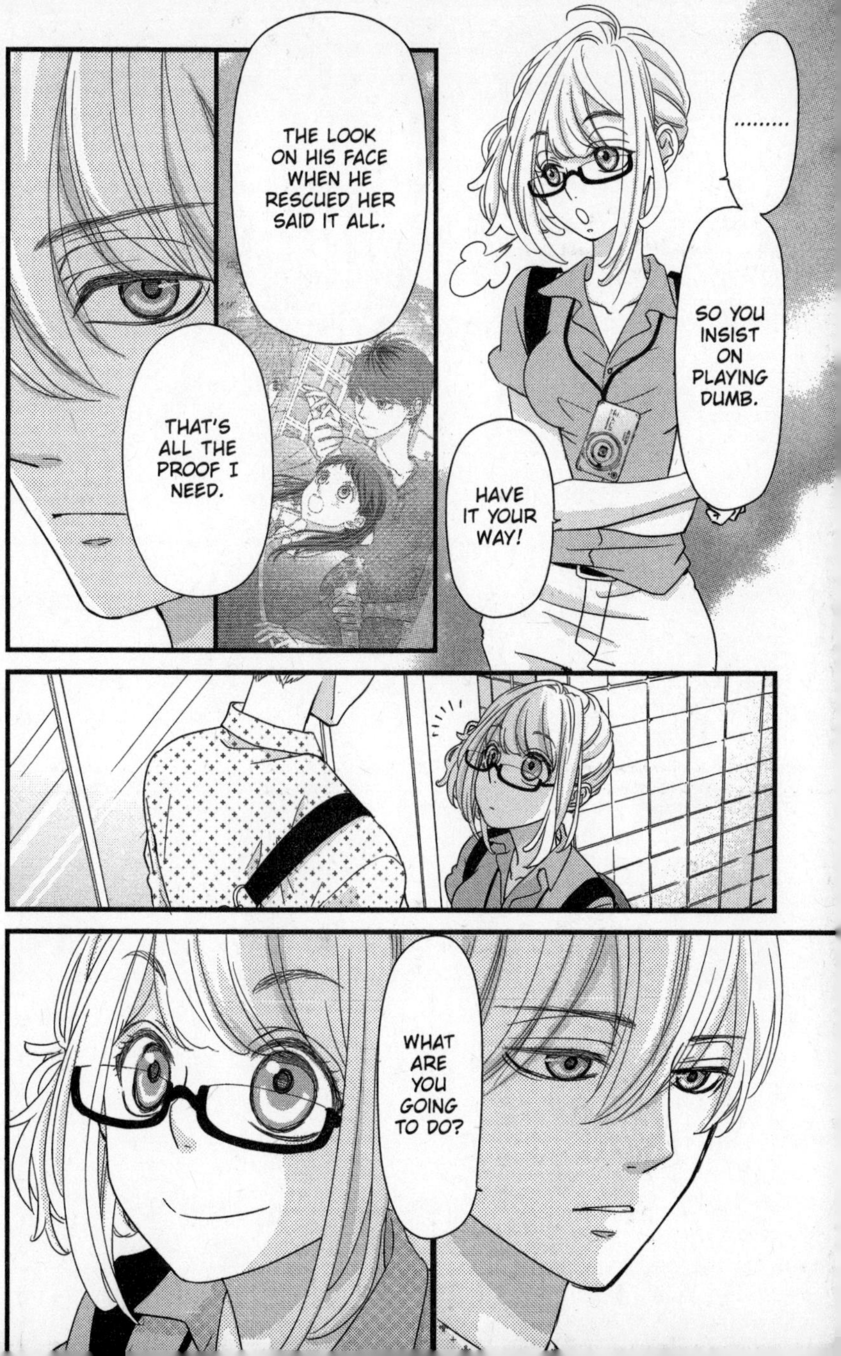
....
SO YOU INSIST ON PLAYING DUMB.
HAVE IT YOUR WAY!
THE LOOK ON HIS FACE WHEN HE RESCUED HER SAID IT ALL.
THAT'S ALL THE PROOF I NEED.
WHAT ARE YOU GOING TO DO?

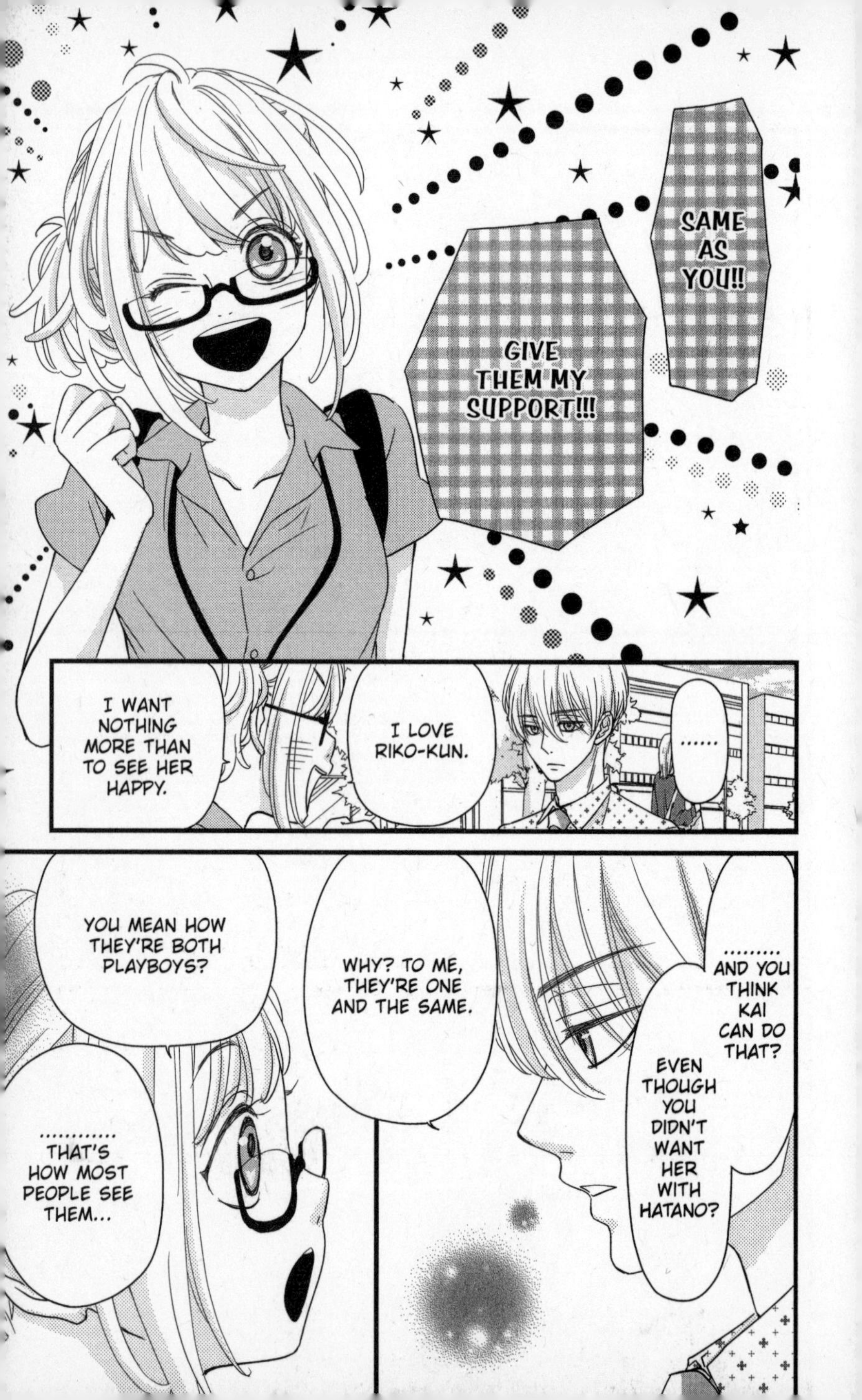
SAME AS YOU!!
GIVE THEM MY SUPPORT!!!
......
I LOVE RIKO-KUN.
I WANT NOTHING MORE THAN TO SEE HER HAPPY.
.... AND YOU THINK KAI CAN DO THAT?
EVEN THOUGH YOU DIDN'T WANT HER WITH HATANO?
WHY? TO ME, THEY'RE ONE AND THE SAME.
YOU MEAN HOW THEY'RE BOTH PLAYBOYS?
.... THAT'S HOW MOST PEOPLE SEE THEM...

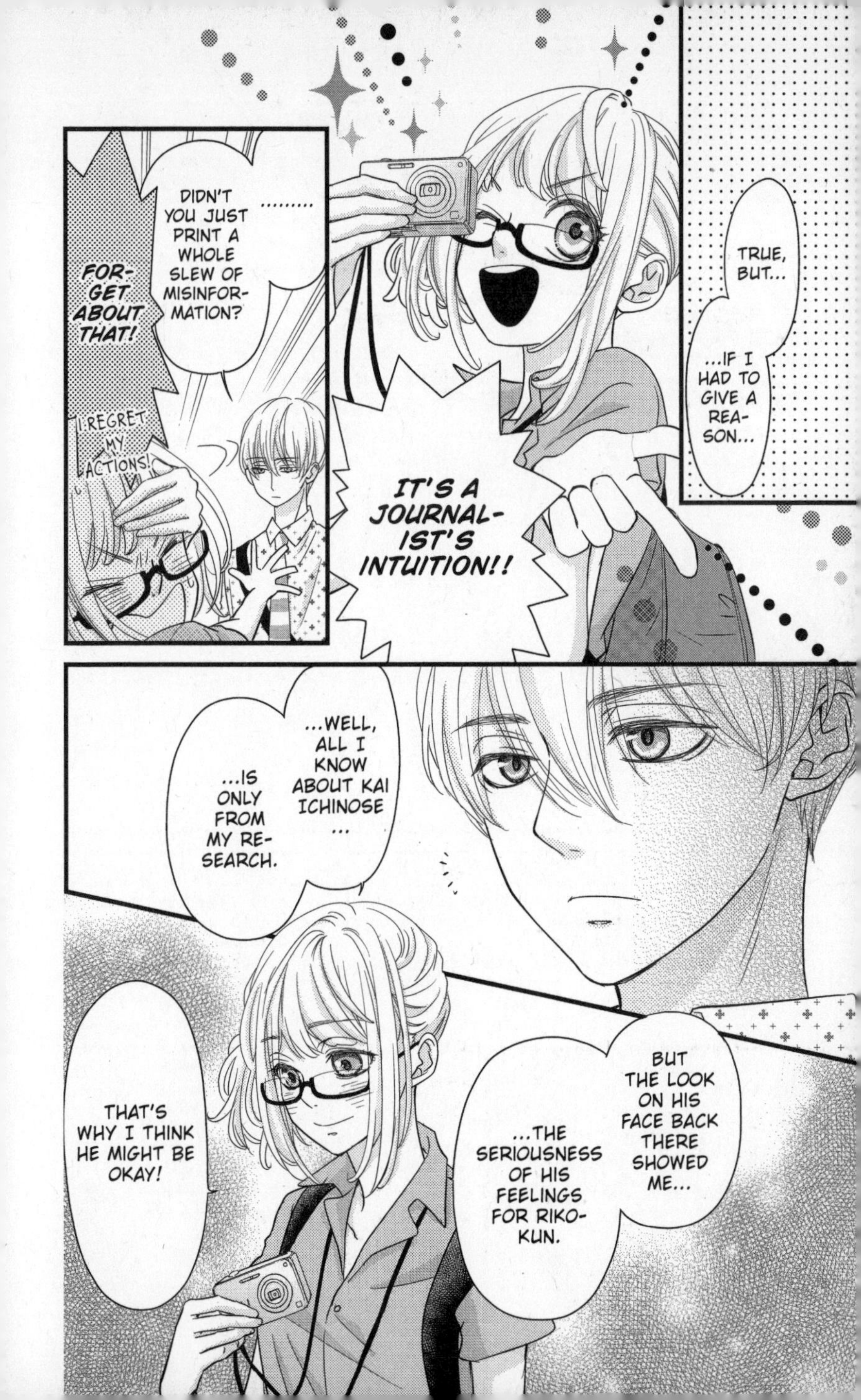
TRUE, BUT...
...IF I HAD TO GIVE A REASON...
IT'S A JOURNALIST'S INTUITION!!
....
DIDN'T YOU JUST PRINT A WHOLE SLEW OF MISINFORMATION?
FORGET ABOUT THAT!
I REGRET MY ACTIONS!
...WELL, ALL I KNOW ABOUT KAI ICHINOSE...
...IS ONLY FROM MY RESEARCH.
BUT THE LOOK ON HIS FACE BACK THERE SHOWED ME...
...THE SERIOUSNESS OF HIS FEELINGS FOR RIKO-KUN.
THAT'S WHY I THINK HE MIGHT BE OKAY!

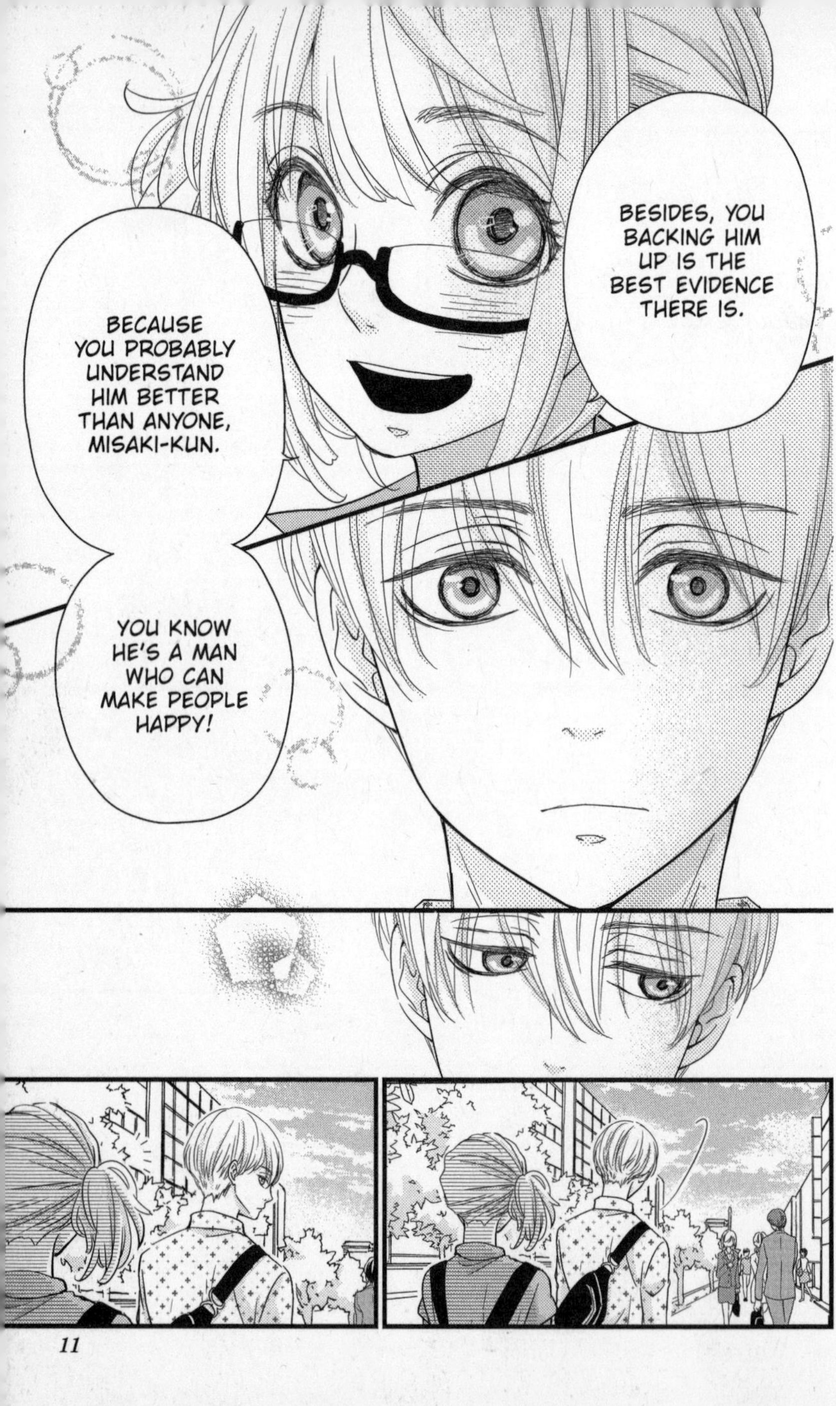
BESIDES, YOU BACKING HIM UP IS THE BEST EVIDENCE THERE IS.
BECAUSE YOU PROBABLY UNDERSTAND HIM BETTER THAN ANYONE, MISAKI-KUN.
YOU KNOW HE'S A MAN WHO CAN MAKE PEOPLE HAPPY!

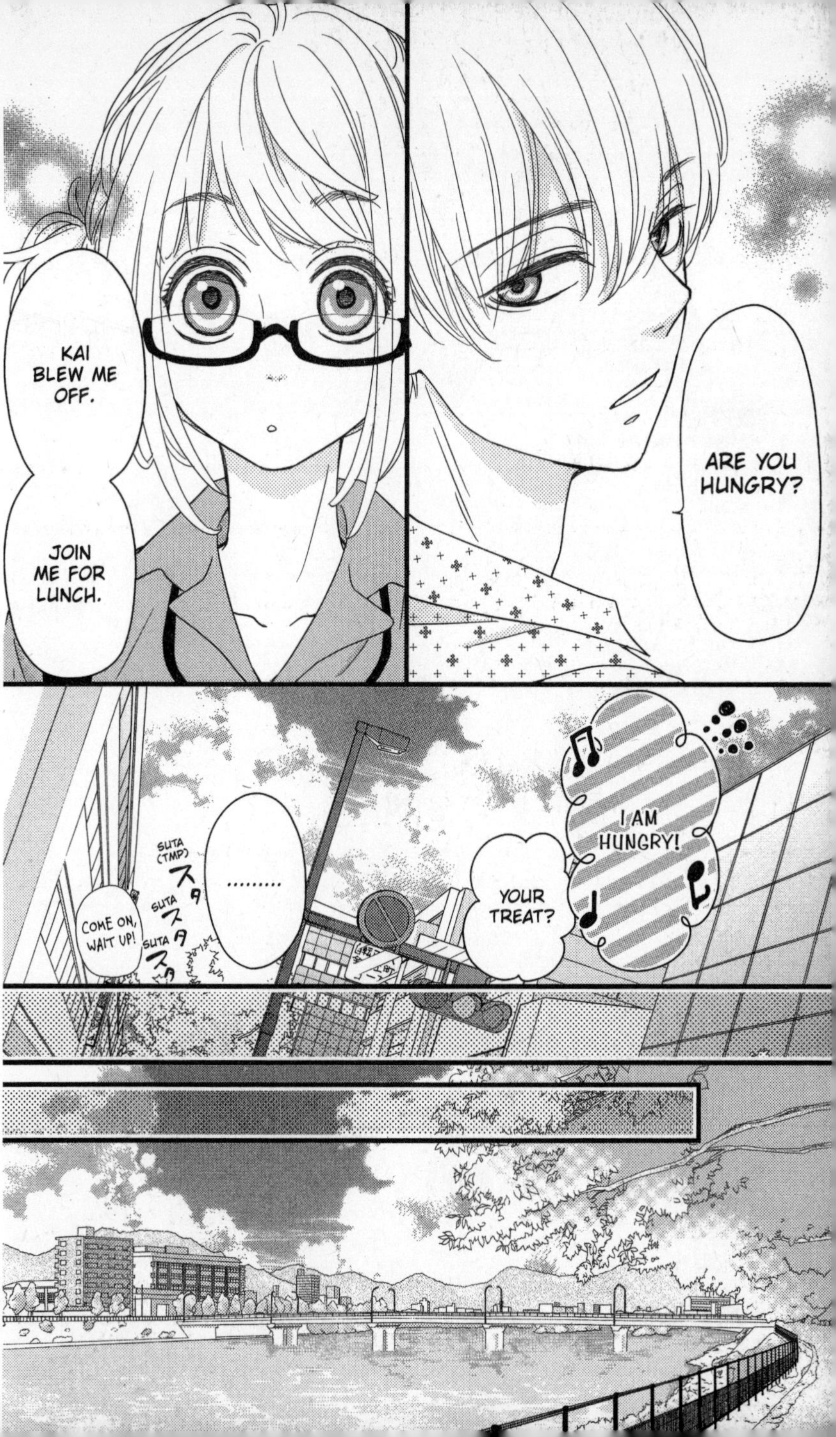
ARE YOU HUNGRY?
KAI BLEW ME OFF.
JOIN ME FOR LUNCH.
I AM HUNGRY!
YOUR TREAT?
....
SUTA (TMP) スタ
SUTA スタ
SUTA スタ
COME ON, WAIT UP!

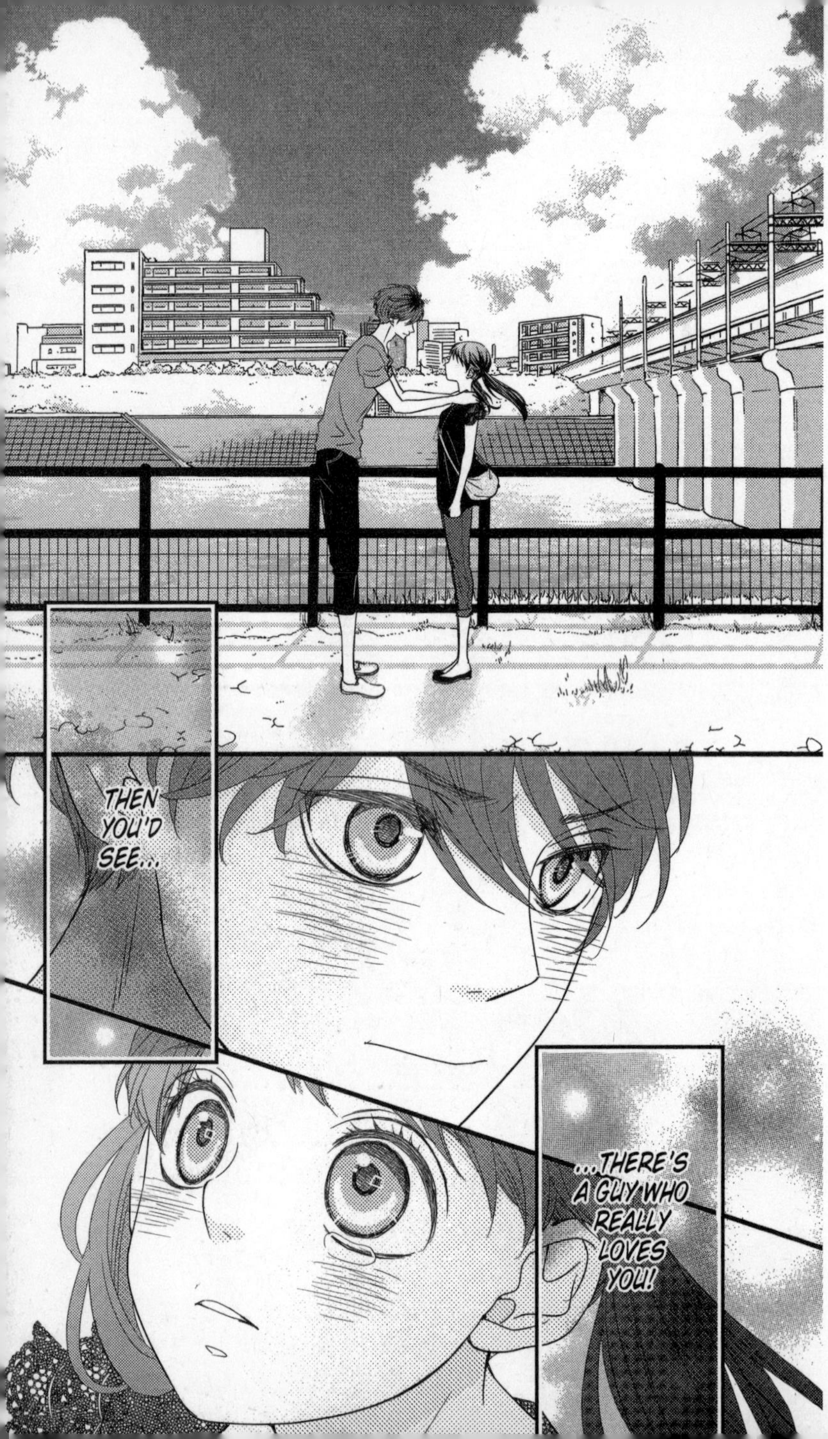
THEN YOU'D SEE...
...THERE'S A GUY WHO REALLY LOVES YOU!

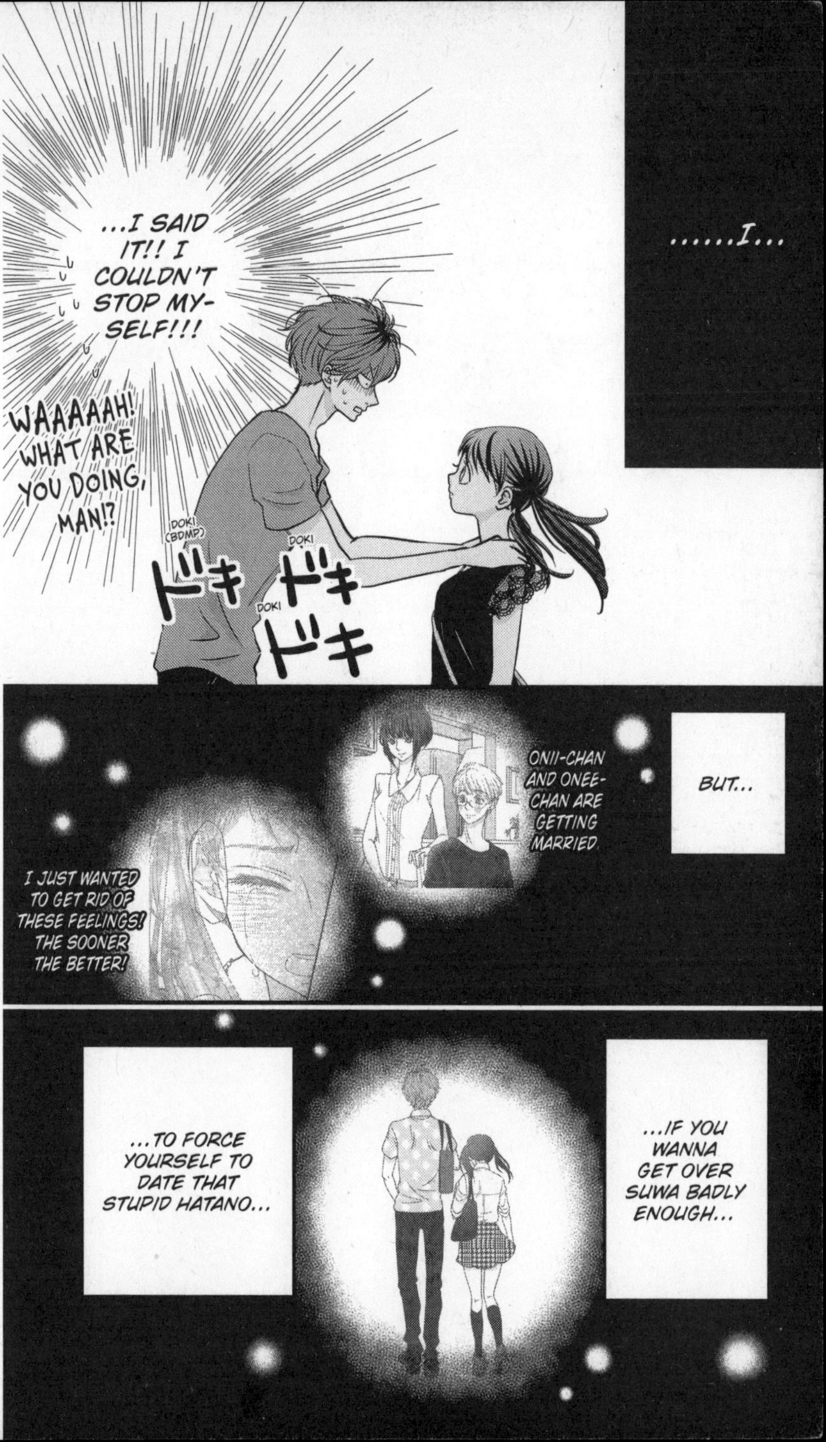
......I...
...I SAID IT!! I COULDN'T STOP MY-SELF!!!
WAAAAAH! WHAT ARE YOU DOING, MAN!?
DOKI (BDMP)
ドキ
DOKI
ドキ
DOKI
ドキ
BUT...
ONII-CHAN AND ONEE-CHAN ARE GETTING MARRIED.
I JUST WANTED TO GET RID OF THESE FEELINGS! THE SOONER THE BETTER!
...IF YOU WANNA GET OVER SUWA BADLY ENOUGH...
...TO FORCE YOURSELF TO DATE THAT STUPID HATANO...

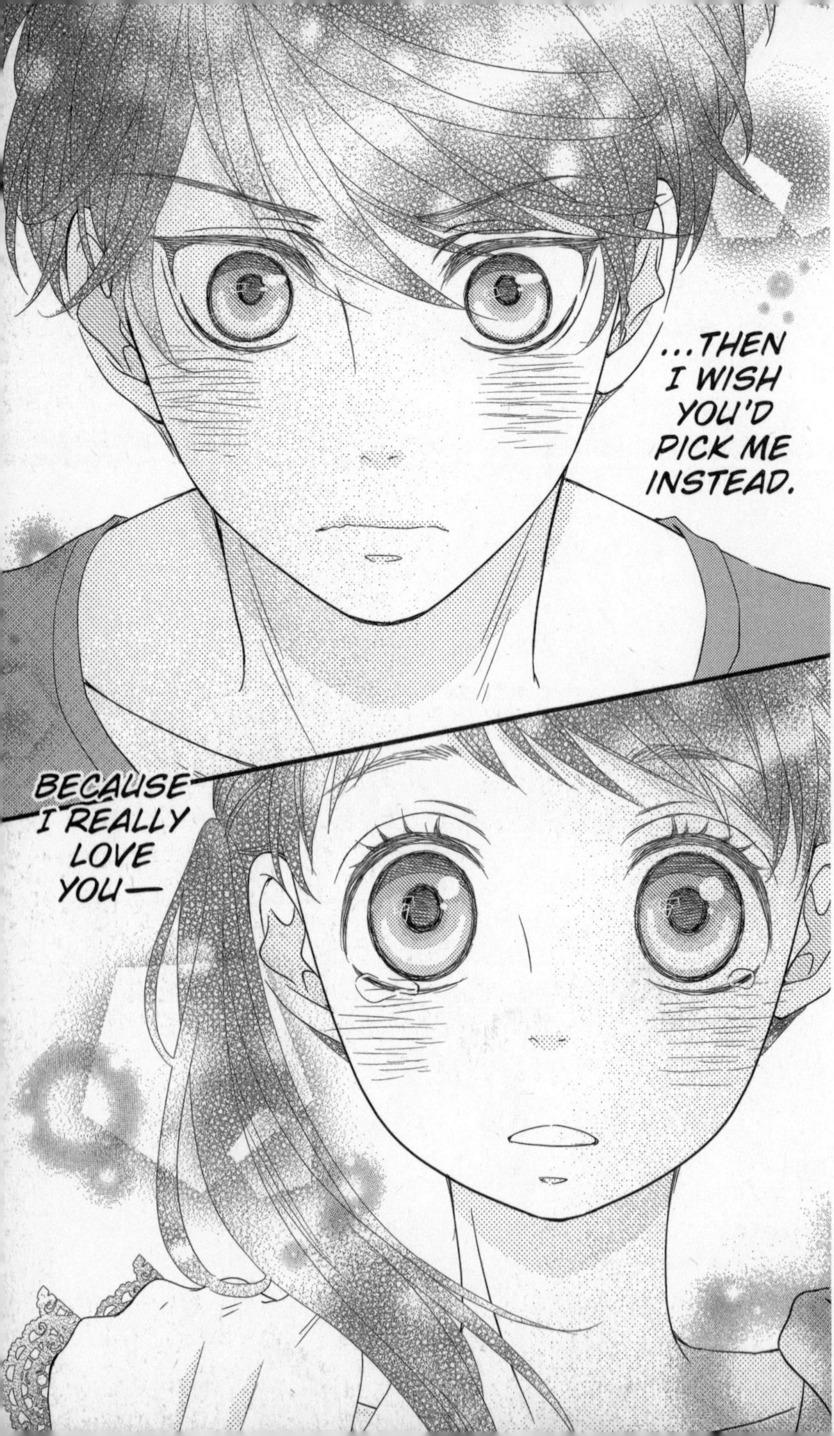
...THEN I WISH YOU'D PICK ME INSTEAD.
BECAUSE I REALLY LOVE YOU—

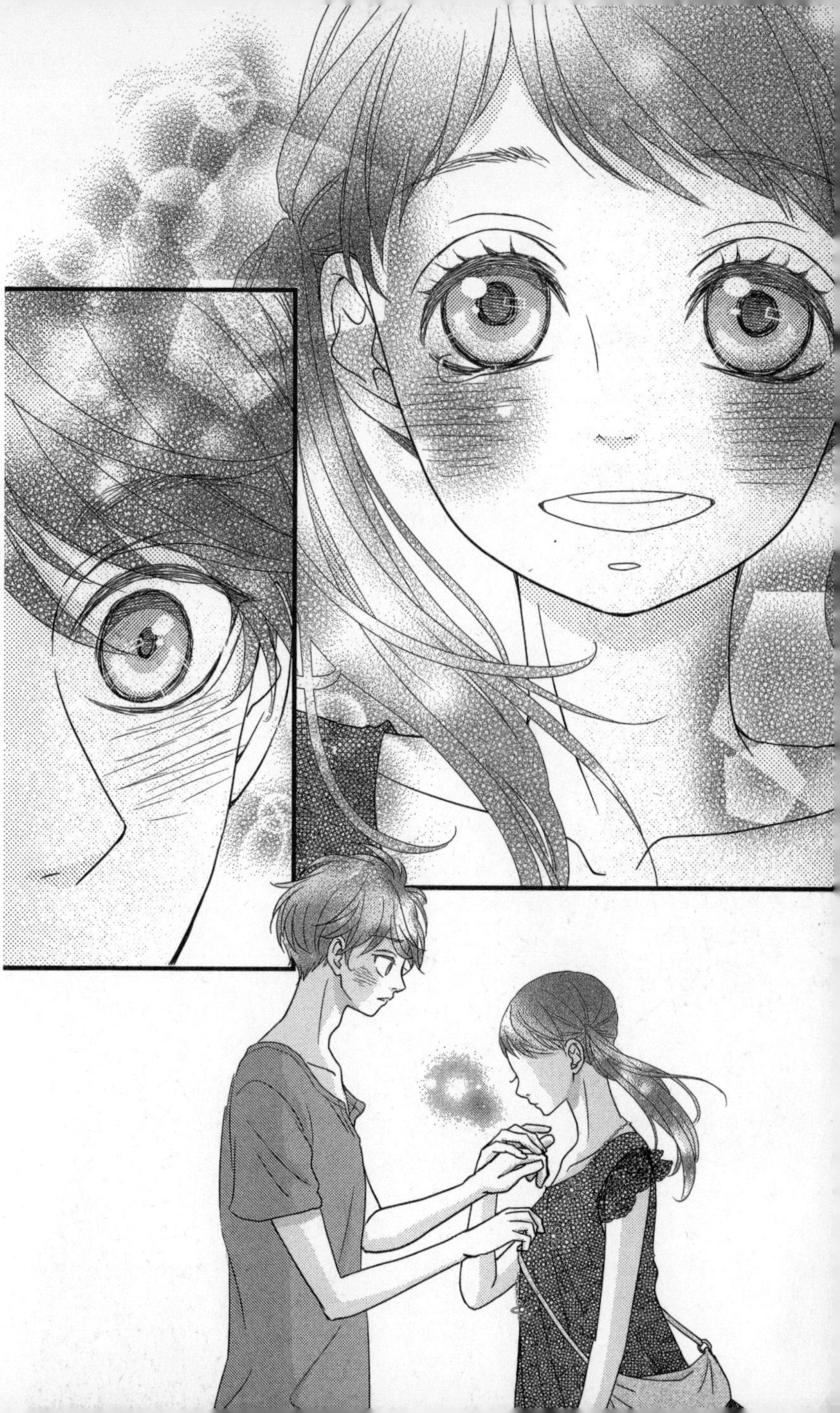

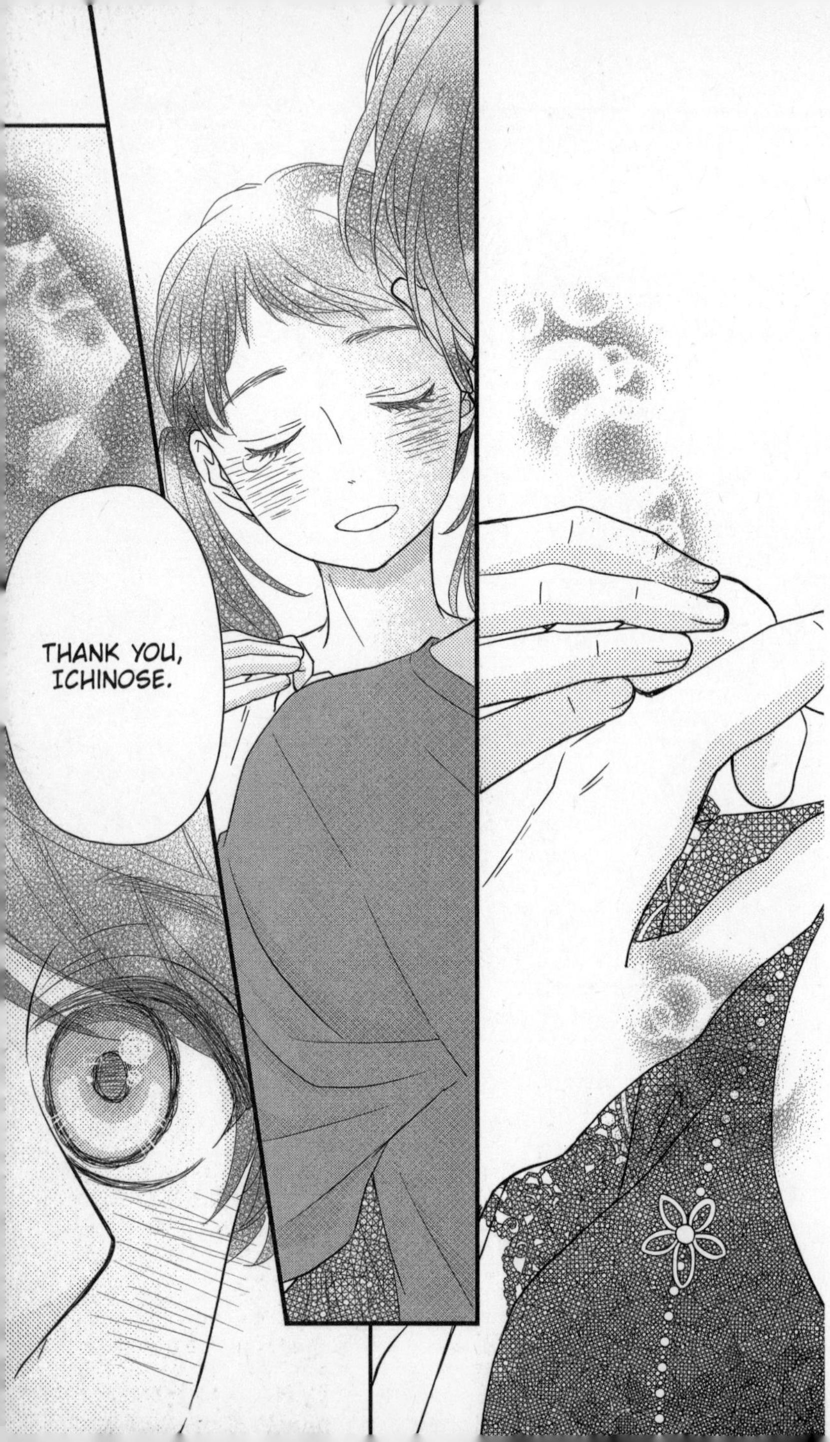
THANK YOU, ICHINOSE.

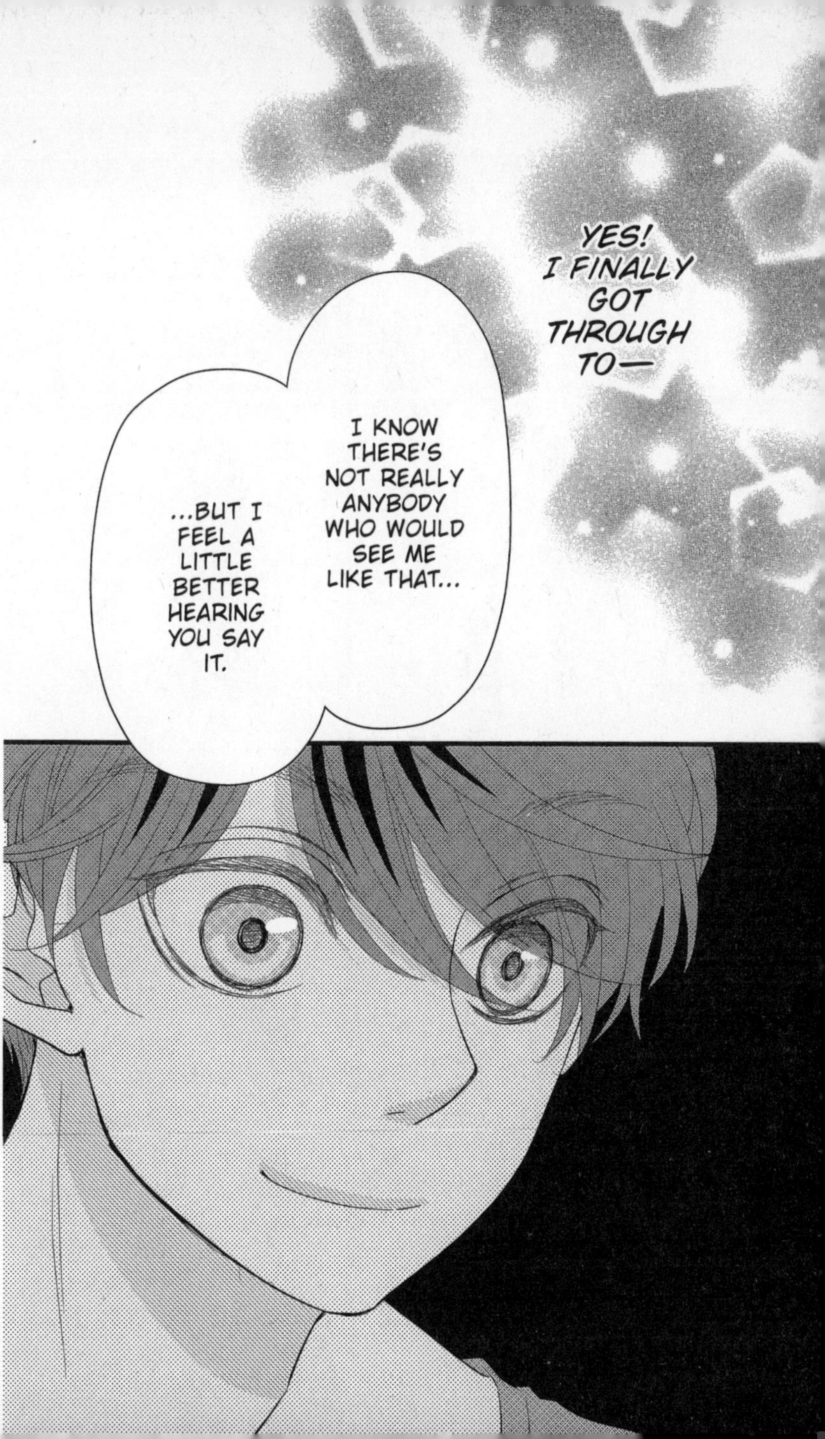
YES! I FINALLY GOT THROUGH TO—
I KNOW THERE'S NOT REALLY ANYBODY WHO WOULD SEE ME LIKE THAT...
...BUT I FEEL A LITTLE BETTER HEARING YOU SAY IT.

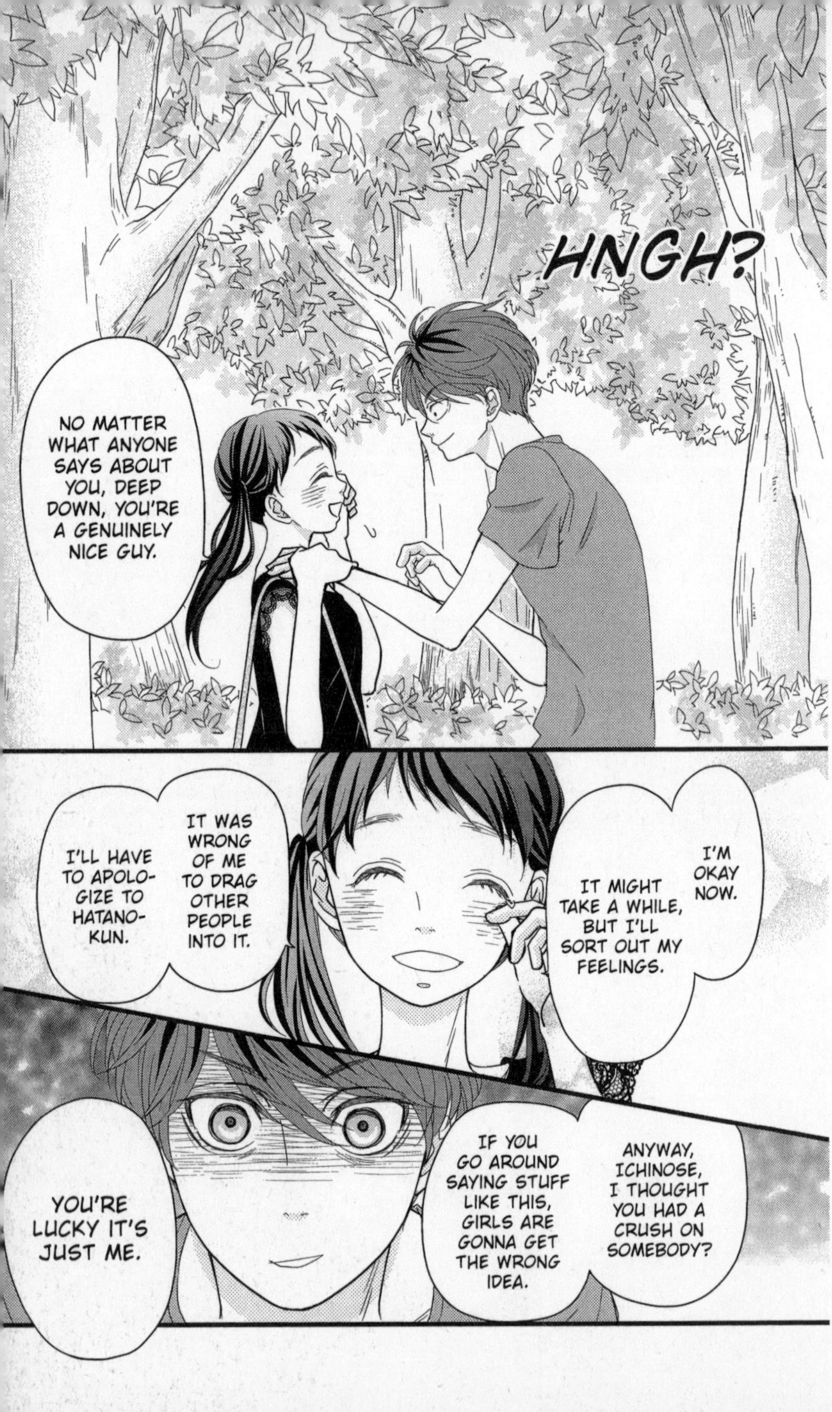
HNGH?
NO MATTER WHAT ANYONE SAYS ABOUT YOU, DEEP DOWN, YOU'RE A GENUINELY NICE GUY.
I'M OKAY NOW.
IT MIGHT TAKE A WHILE, BUT I'LL SORT OUT MY FEELINGS.
IT WAS WRONG OF ME TO DRAG OTHER PEOPLE INTO IT.
I'LL HAVE TO APOLO-GIZE TO HATANO-KUN.
ANYWAY, ICHINOSE, I THOUGHT YOU HAD A CRUSH ON SOMEBODY?
IF YOU GO AROUND SAYING STUFF LIKE THIS, GIRLS ARE GONNA GET THE WRONG IDEA.
YOU'RE LUCKY IT'S JUST ME.

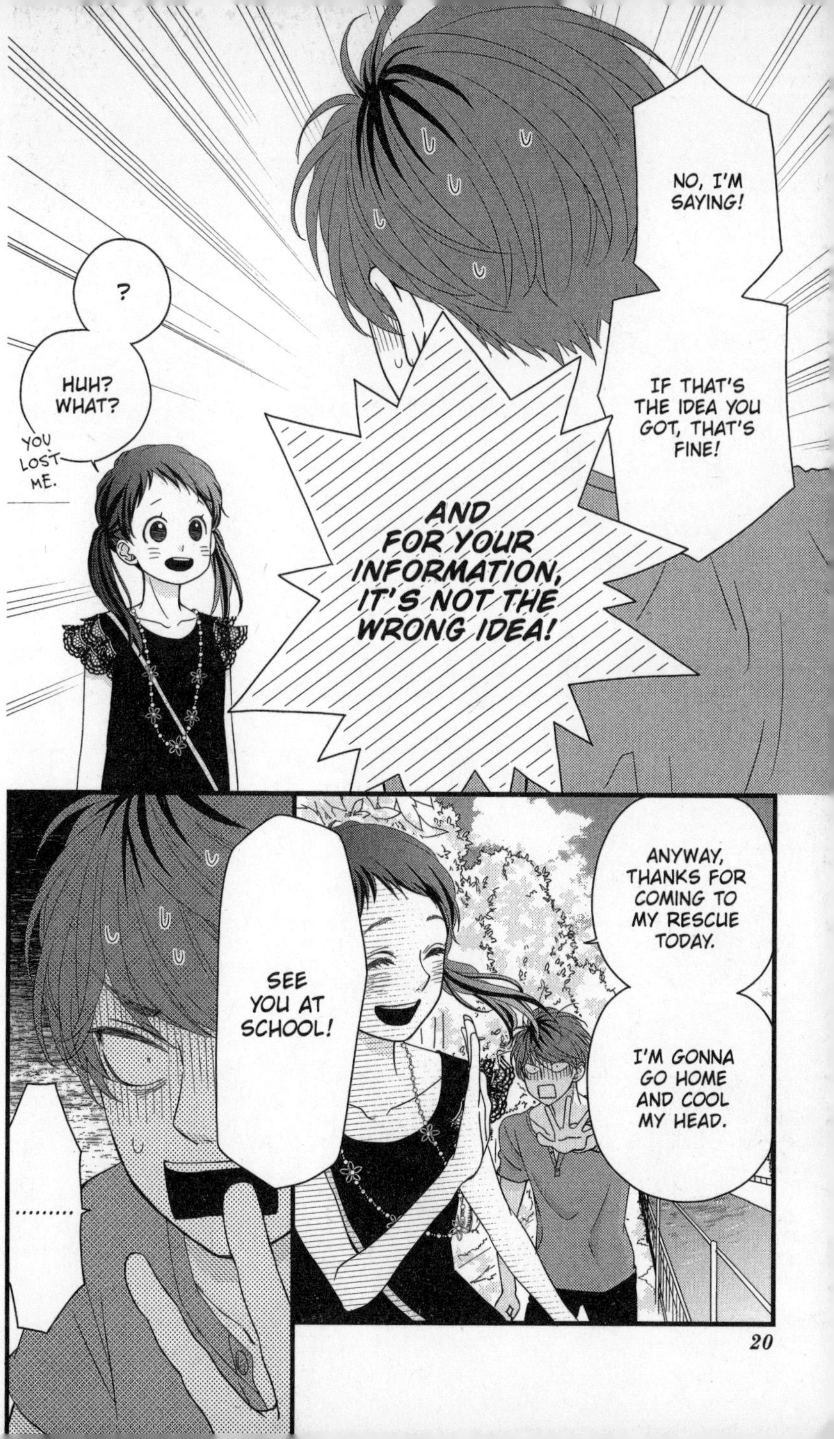
NO, I'M SAYING!
IF THAT'S THE IDEA YOU GOT, THAT'S FINE!
AND FOR YOUR INFORMATION, IT'S NOT THE WRONG IDEA!
?
HUH? WHAT?
YOU LOST ME.
ANYWAY, THANKS FOR COMING TO MY RESCUE TODAY.
I'M GONNA GO HOME AND COOL MY HEAD.
SEE YOU AT SCHOOL!
....

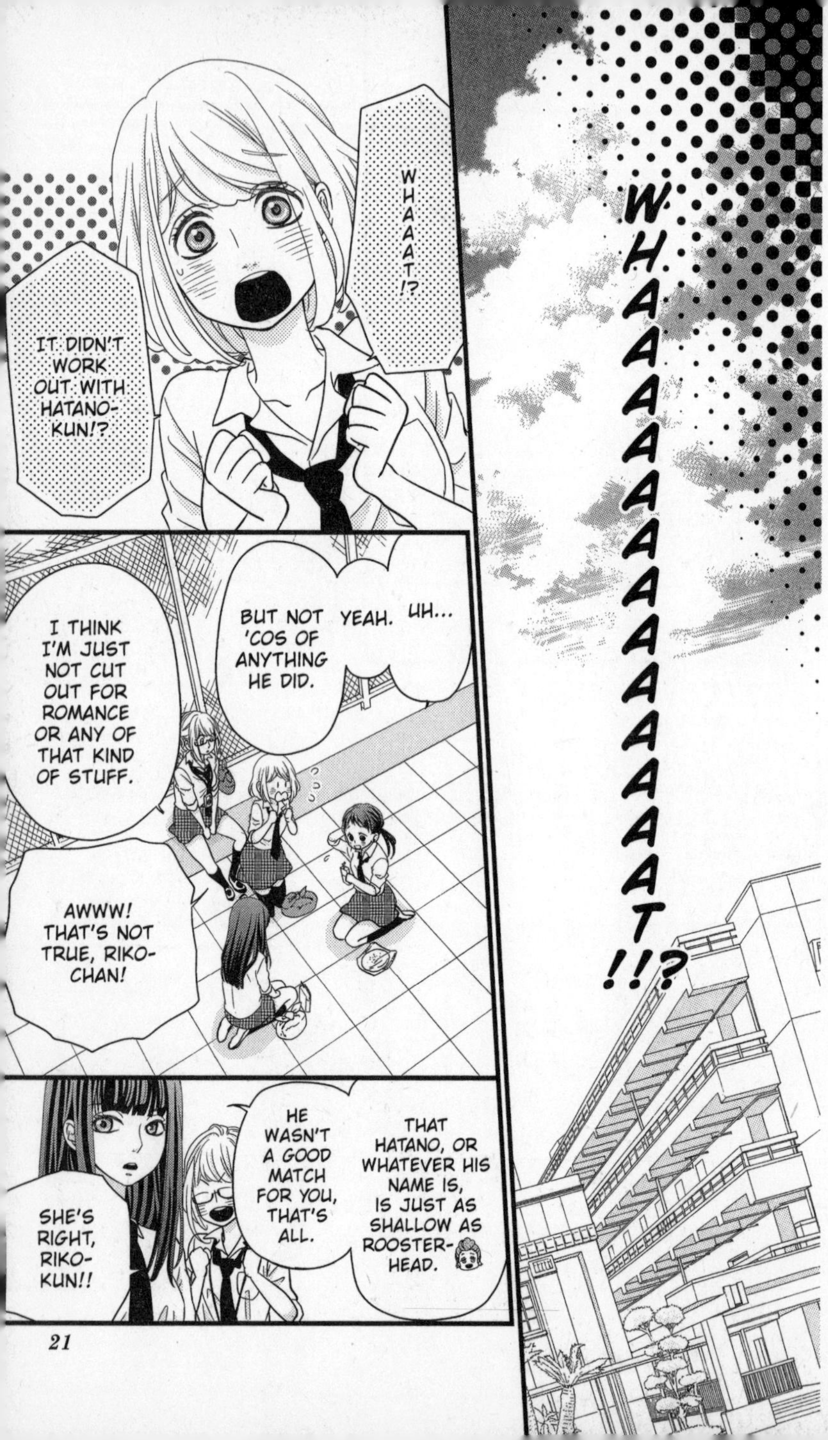
WHAAAAAAAAAAAAAAT!!?
WHAAAT!?
IT DIDN'T WORK OUT WITH HATANO-KUN!?
UH...
YEAH.
BUT NOT 'COS OF ANYTHING HE DID.
I THINK I'M JUST NOT CUT OUT FOR ROMANCE OR ANY OF THAT KIND OF STUFF.
AWWW! THAT'S NOT TRUE, RIKO-CHAN!
THAT HATANO, OR WHATEVER HIS NAME IS, IS JUST AS SHALLOW AS ROOSTER-HEAD.
HE WASN'T A GOOD MATCH FOR YOU, THAT'S ALL.
SHE'S RIGHT, RIKO-KUN!!

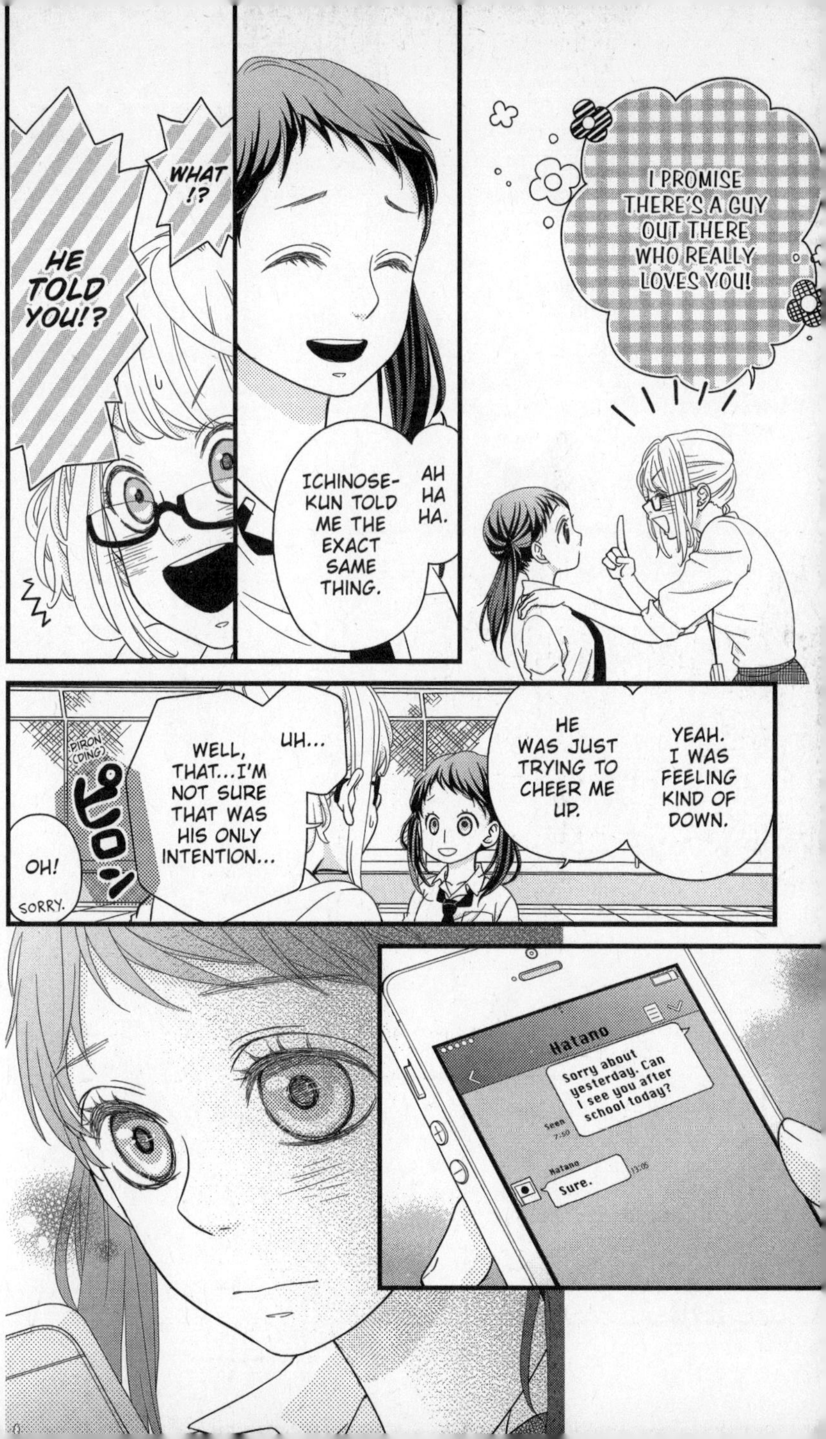
I PROMISE THERE'S A GUY OUT THERE WHO REALLY LOVES YOU!
AH HA HA.
ICHINOSE-KUN TOLD ME THE EXACT SAME THING.
WHAT!?
HE TOLD YOU!?
YEAH. I WAS FEELING KIND OF DOWN.
HE WAS JUST TRYING TO CHEER ME UP.
UH...
WELL, THAT...I'M NOT SURE THAT WAS HIS ONLY INTENTION...
PIRON (DING)
OH!
SORRY.
Hatano
Sorry about yesterday. Can I see you after school today?
Seen 7:50
Hatano 13:05
Sure.

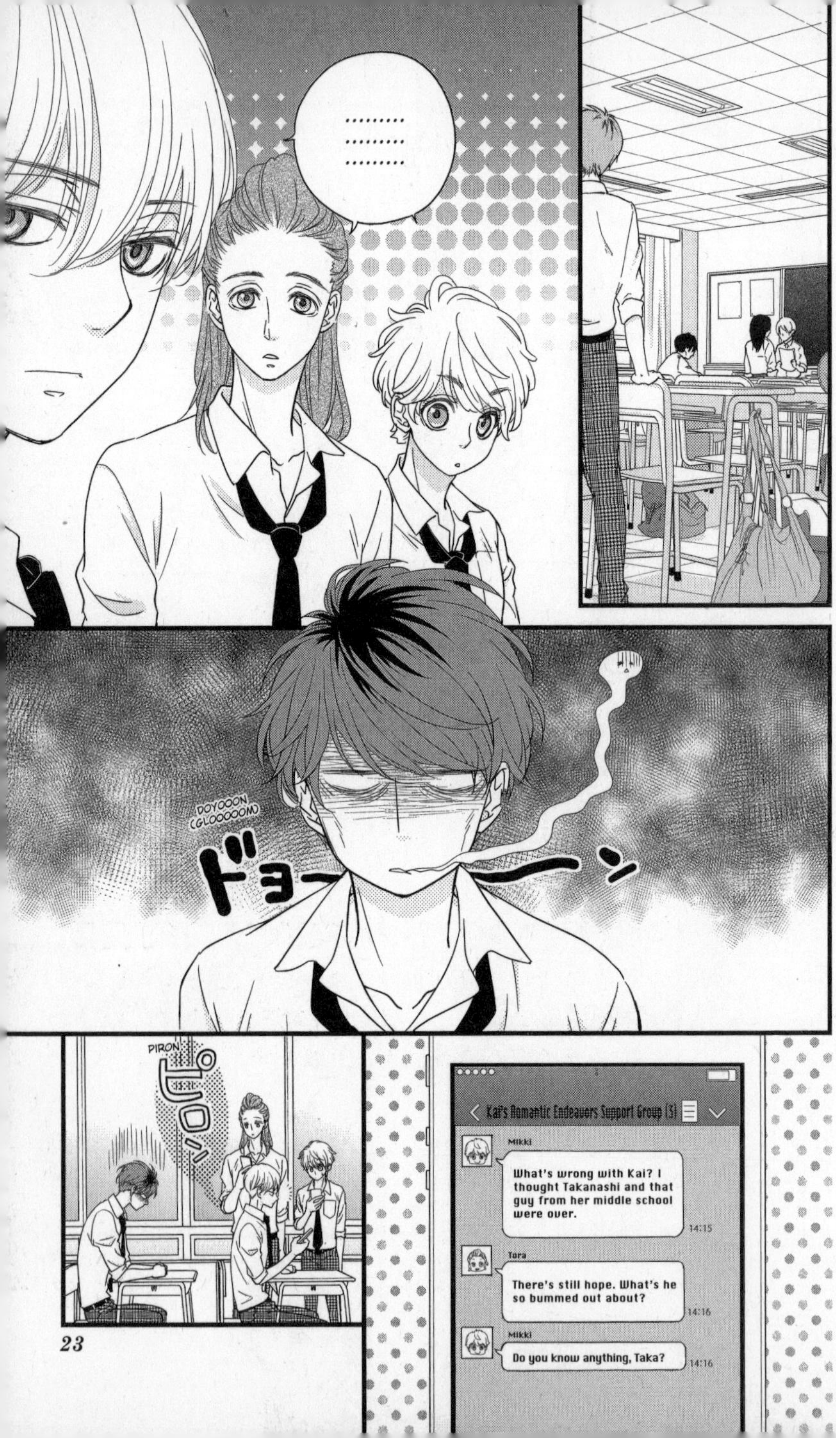
....
....
....
DOYOOON (GLOOOOOM)
ドヨーーン
Kai's Romantic Endeavors Support Group (3)
Mikki
What's wrong with Kai? I thought Takanashi and that guy from her middle school were over.
14:15
Tora
There's still hope. What's he so bummed out about?
14:16
Mikki
Do you know anything, Taka?
14:16
PIRON
ピロン

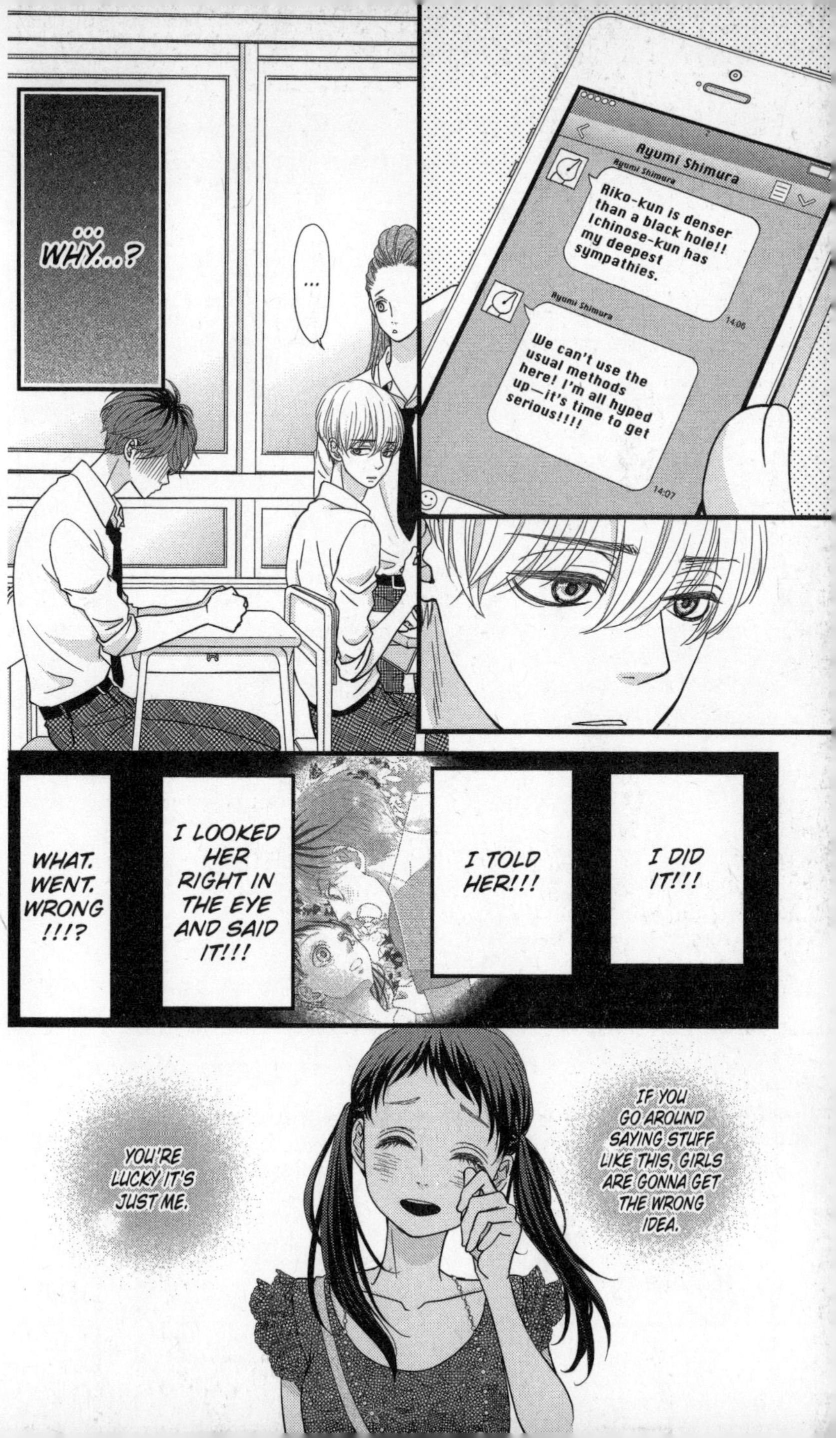

Ayumi Shimura
Ayumi Shimura
Riko-kun is denser than a black hole!! Ichinose-kun has my deepest sympathies.
14:06
Ayumi Shimura
We can't use the usual methods here! I'm all hyped up—it's time to get serious!!!!
14:07
...
...WHY...?
I DID IT!!!
I TOLD HER!!!
I LOOKED HER RIGHT IN THE EYE AND SAID IT!!!
WHAT. WENT. WRONG!!!?
IF YOU GO AROUND SAYING STUFF LIKE THIS, GIRLS ARE GONNA GET THE WRONG IDEA.
YOU'RE LUCKY IT'S JUST ME.

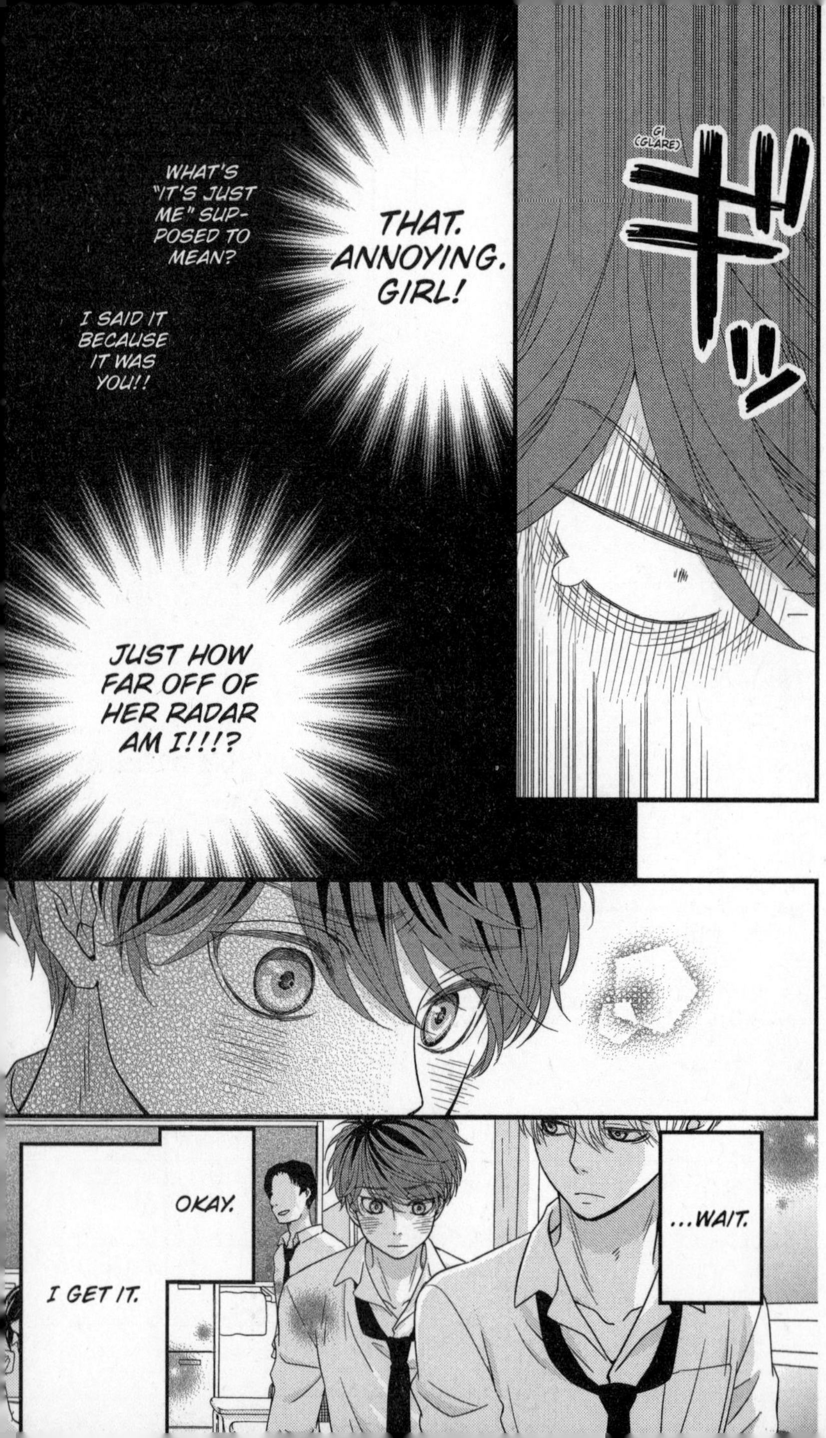
GI (GLARE)
THAT. ANNOYING. GIRL!
WHAT'S "IT'S JUST ME" SUP-POSED TO MEAN?
I SAID IT BECAUSE IT WAS YOU!!
JUST HOW FAR OFF OF HER RADAR AM I!!!?
...WAIT.
OKAY.
I GET IT.

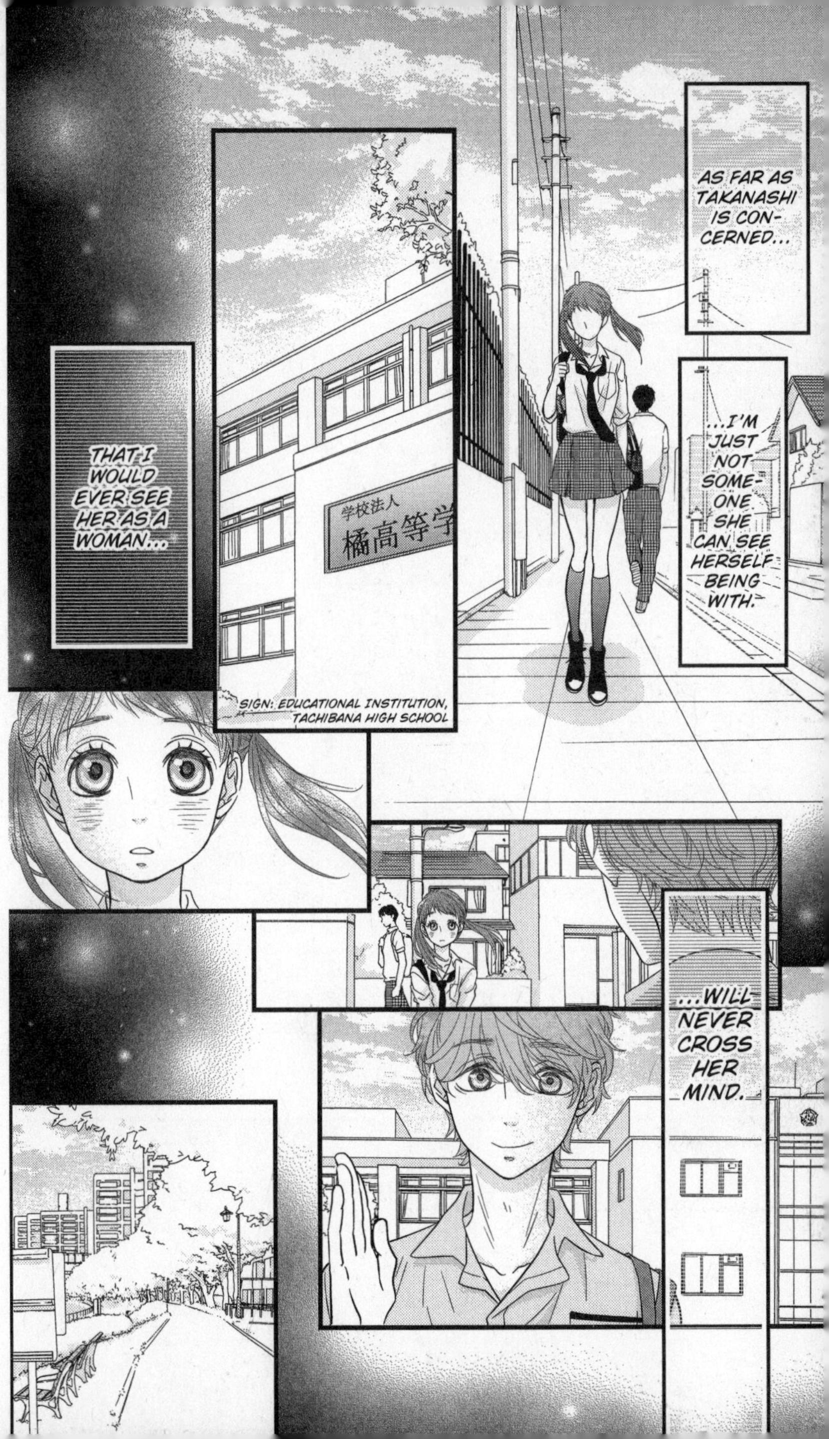
AS FAR AS TAKANASHI IS CONCERNED...
...I'M JUST NOT SOMEONE SHE CAN SEE HERSELF BEING WITH.
学校法人
橘高等学
SIGN: EDUCATIONAL INSTITUTION, TACHIBANA HIGH SCHOOL
THAT I WOULD EVER SEE HER AS A WOMAN...
...WILL NEVER CROSS HER MIND.

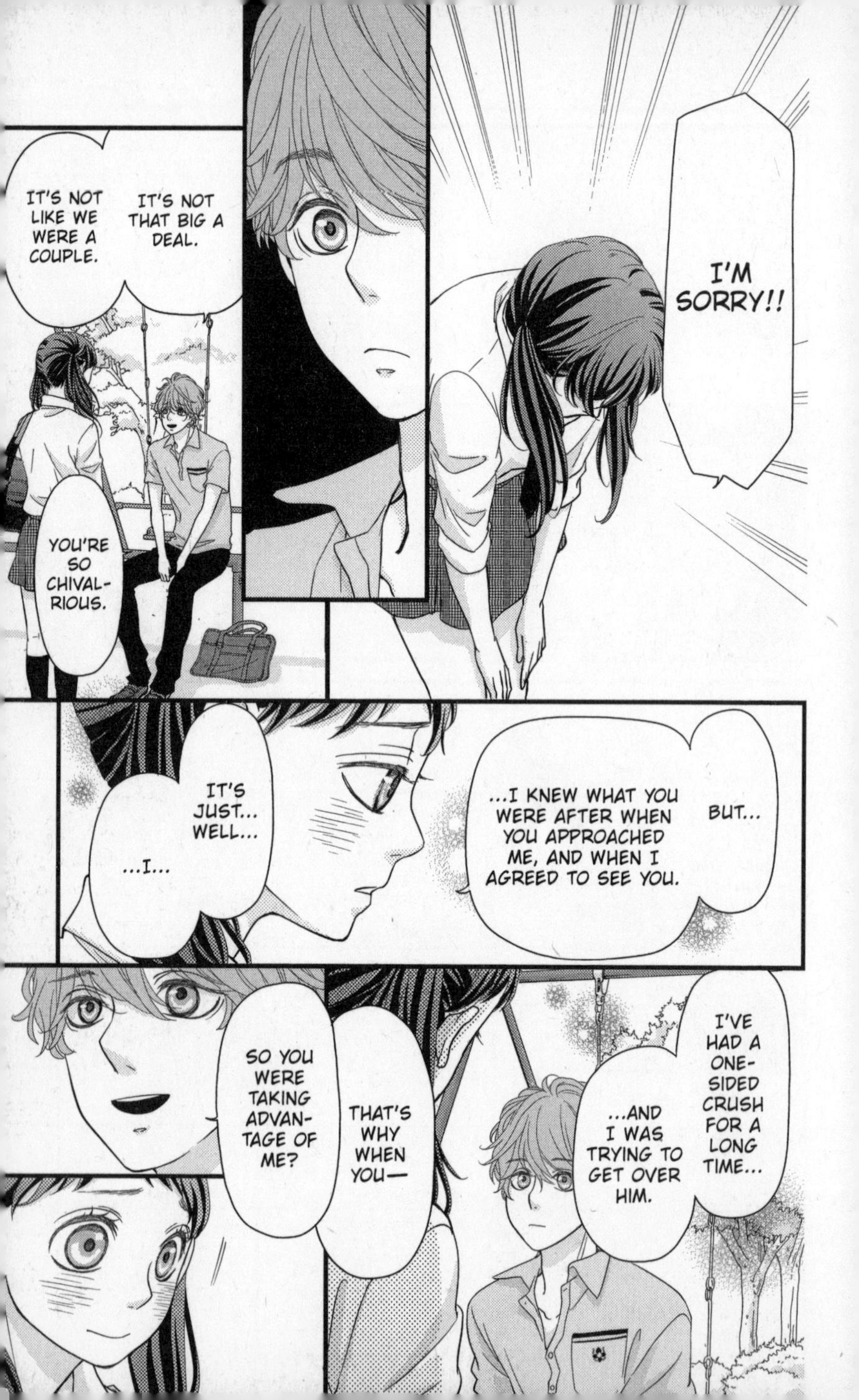
I'M SORRY!!
IT'S NOT THAT BIG A DEAL.
IT'S NOT LIKE WE WERE A COUPLE.
YOU'RE SO CHIVAL-RIOUS.
BUT...
...I KNEW WHAT YOU WERE AFTER WHEN YOU APPROACHED ME, AND WHEN I AGREED TO SEE YOU.
IT'S JUST... WELL...
...I...
I'VE HAD A ONE-SIDED CRUSH FOR A LONG TIME...
...AND I WAS TRYING TO GET OVER HIM.
THAT'S WHY WHEN YOU—
SO YOU WERE TAKING ADVAN-TAGE OF ME?

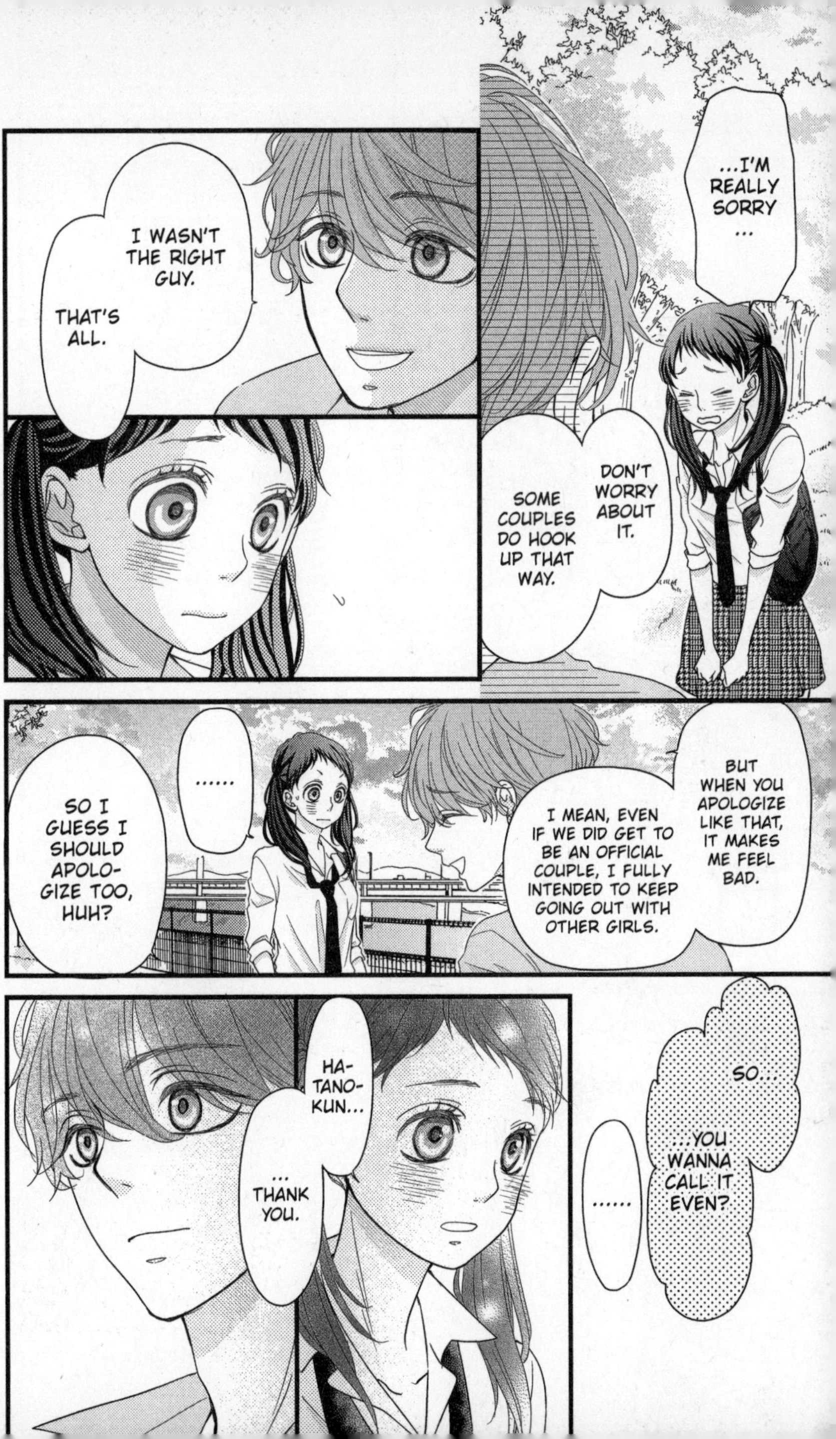
...I'M REALLY SORRY ...
DON'T WORRY ABOUT IT.
SOME COUPLES DO HOOK UP THAT WAY.
I WASN'T THE RIGHT GUY.
THAT'S ALL.
BUT WHEN YOU APOLOGIZE LIKE THAT, IT MAKES ME FEEL BAD.
I MEAN, EVEN IF WE DID GET TO BE AN OFFICIAL COUPLE, I FULLY INTENDED TO KEEP GOING OUT WITH OTHER GIRLS.
......
SO I GUESS I SHOULD APOLOGIZE TOO, HUH?
SO...
...YOU WANNA CALL IT EVEN?
......
HATANO-KUN...
...THANK YOU.

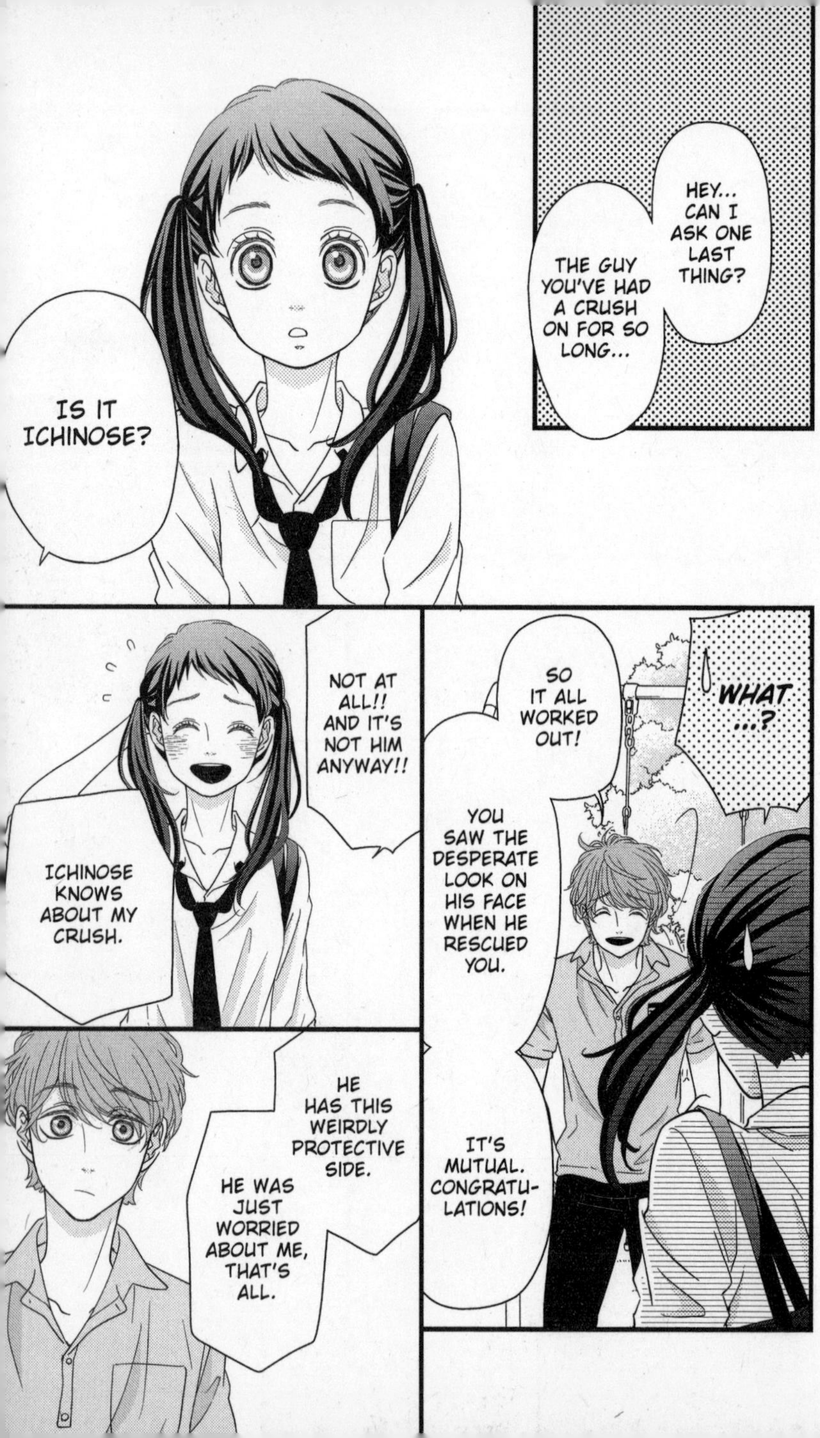
HEY... CAN I ASK ONE LAST THING?
THE GUY YOU'VE HAD A CRUSH ON FOR SO LONG...
IS IT ICHINOSE?
WHAT ...?
SO IT ALL WORKED OUT!
YOU SAW THE DESPERATE LOOK ON HIS FACE WHEN HE RESCUED YOU.
IT'S MUTUAL. CONGRATU-LATIONS!
NOT AT ALL!! AND IT'S NOT HIM ANYWAY!!
ICHINOSE KNOWS ABOUT MY CRUSH.
HE HAS THIS WEIRDLY PROTECTIVE SIDE.
HE WAS JUST WORRIED ABOUT ME, THAT'S ALL.

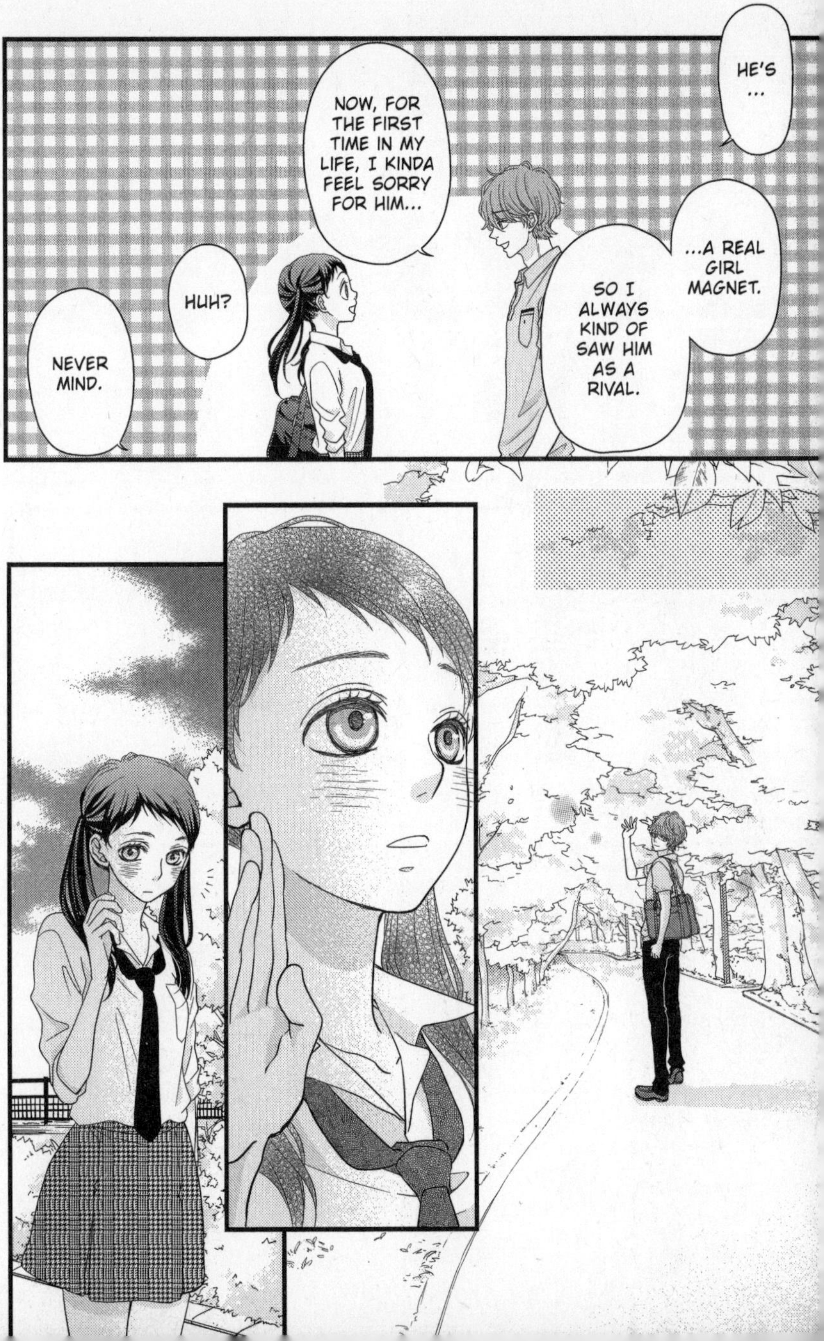
HE'S...
...A REAL GIRL MAGNET.
SO I ALWAYS KIND OF SAW HIM AS A RIVAL.
NOW, FOR THE FIRST TIME IN MY LIFE, I KINDA FEEL SORRY FOR HIM...
HUH?
NEVER MIND.

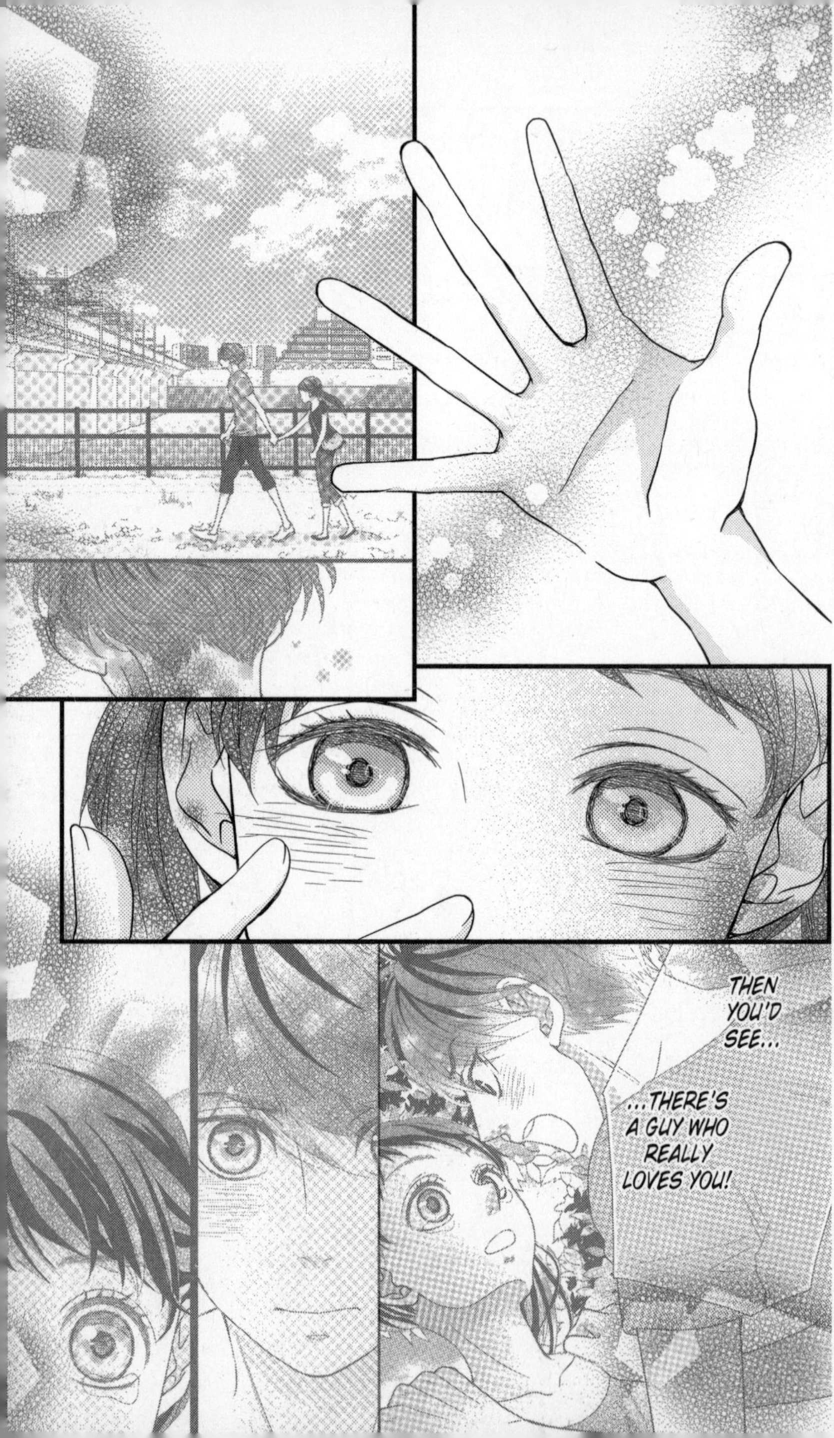
THEN YOU'D SEE...
...THERE'S A GUY WHO REALLY LOVES YOU!

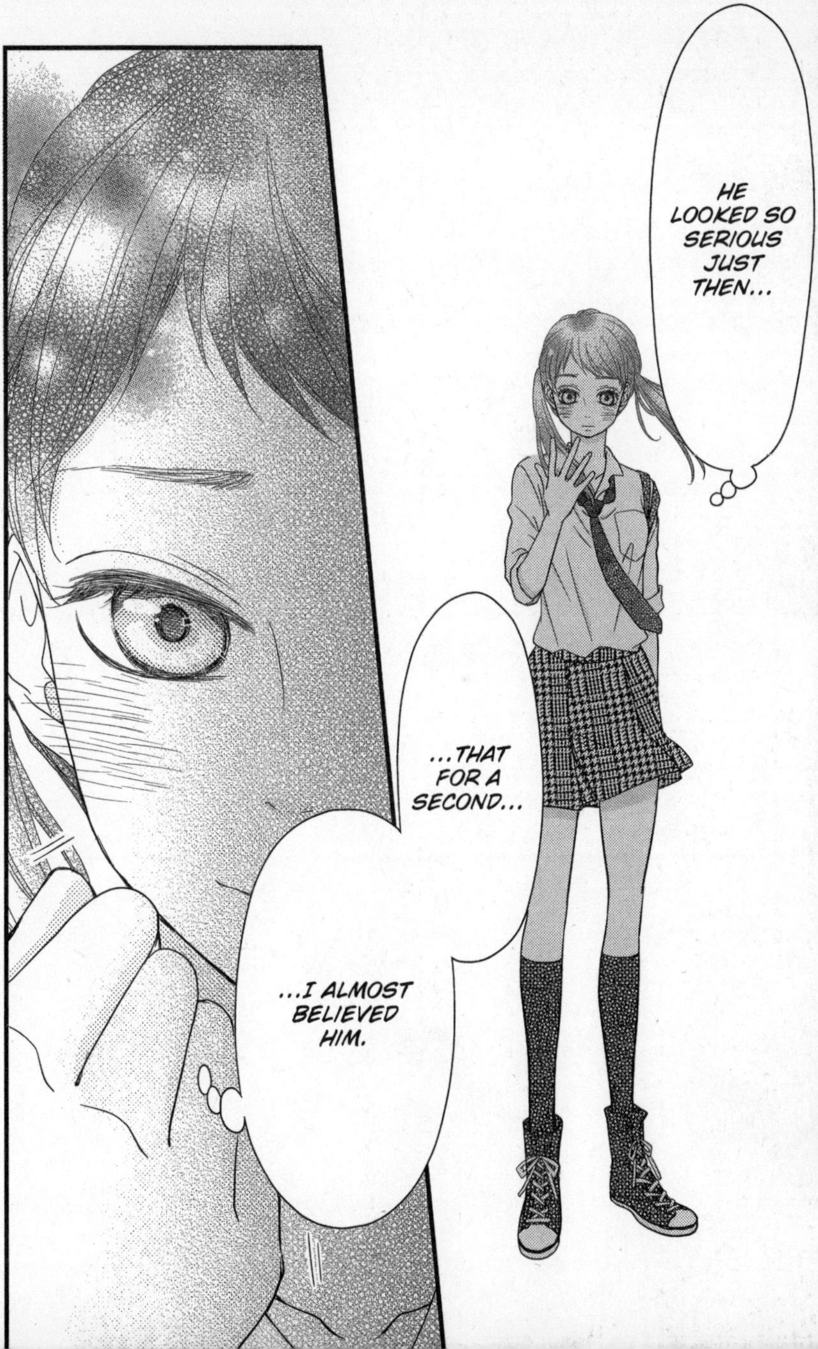
HE LOOKED SO SERIOUS JUST THEN...
...THAT FOR A SECOND...
...I ALMOST BELIEVED HIM.

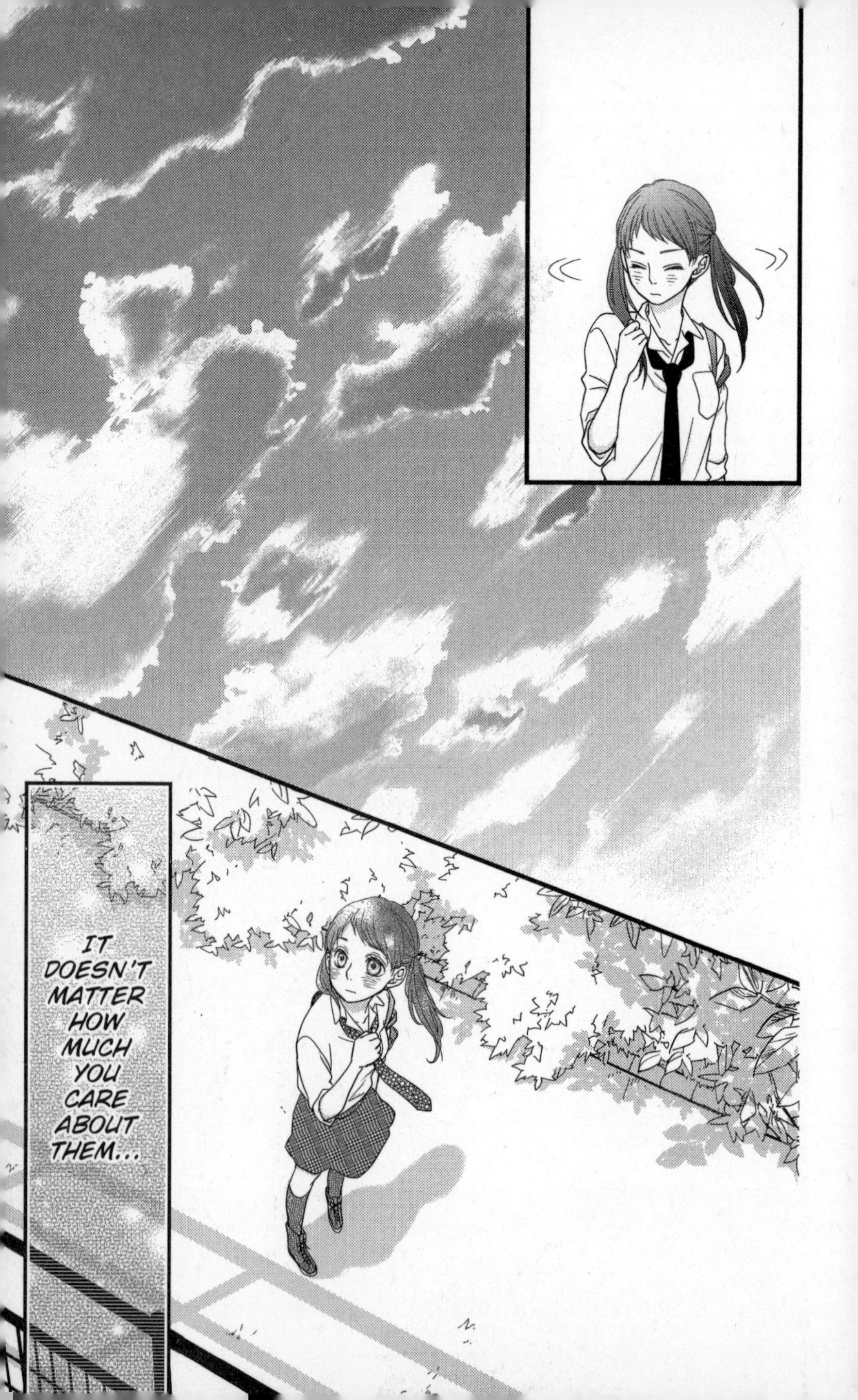
IT DOESN'T MATTER HOW MUCH YOU CARE ABOUT THEM...

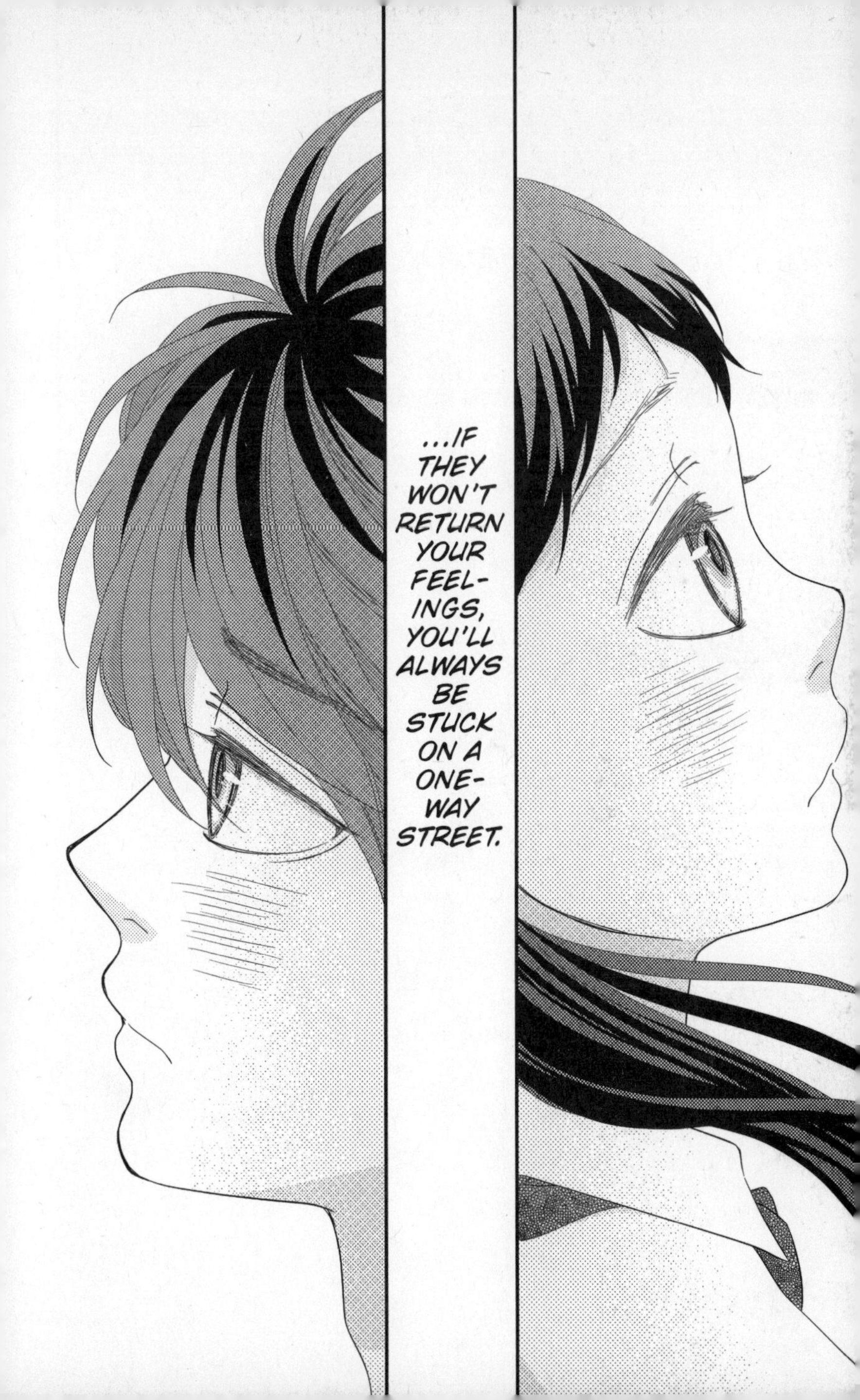
...IF THEY WON'T RETURN YOUR FEELINGS, YOU'LL ALWAYS BE STUCK ON A ONE-WAY STREET.

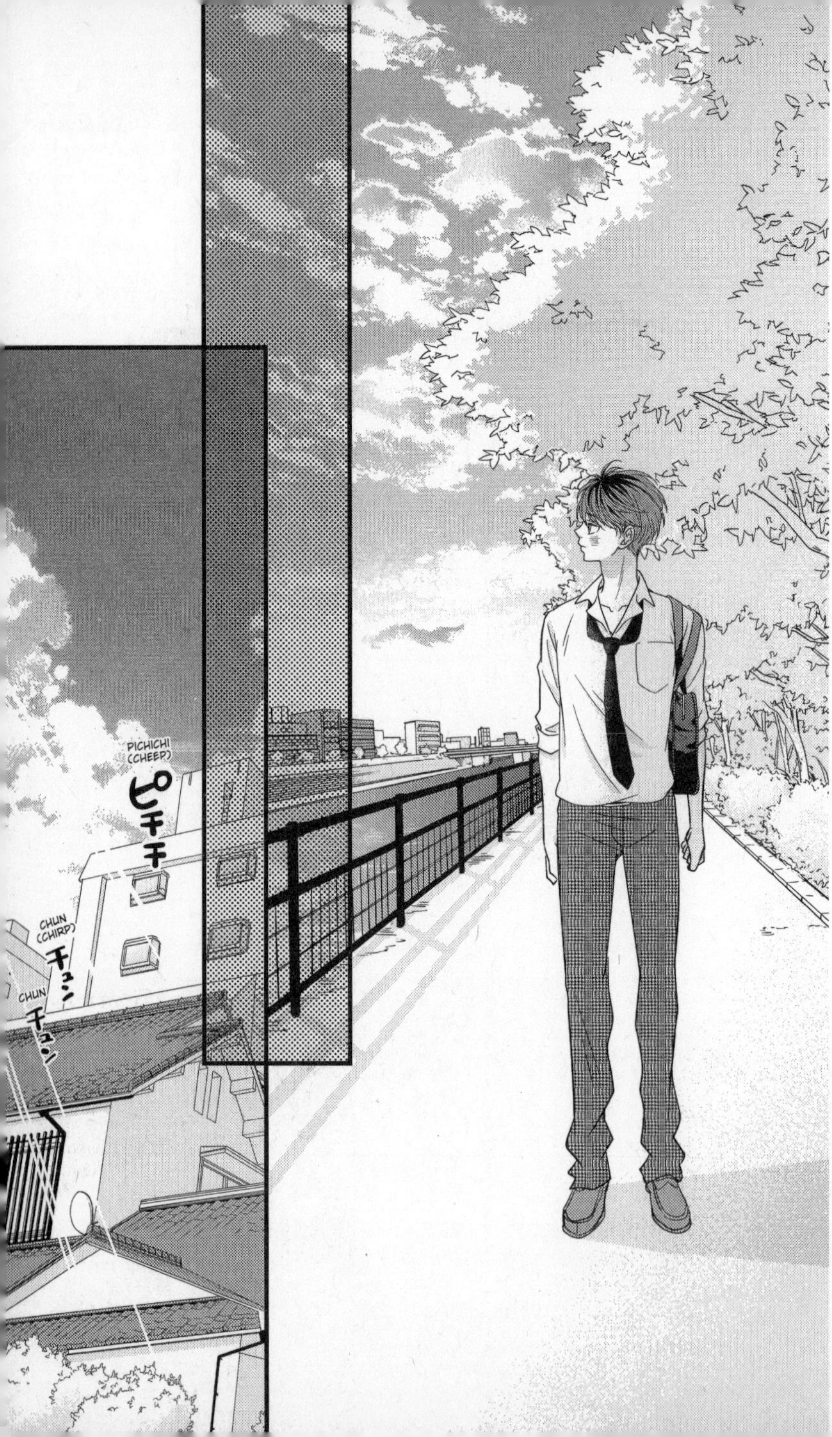
PICHICHI (CHEEP)
ピチチ
CHUN (CHIRP)
チュン
CHUN
チュン

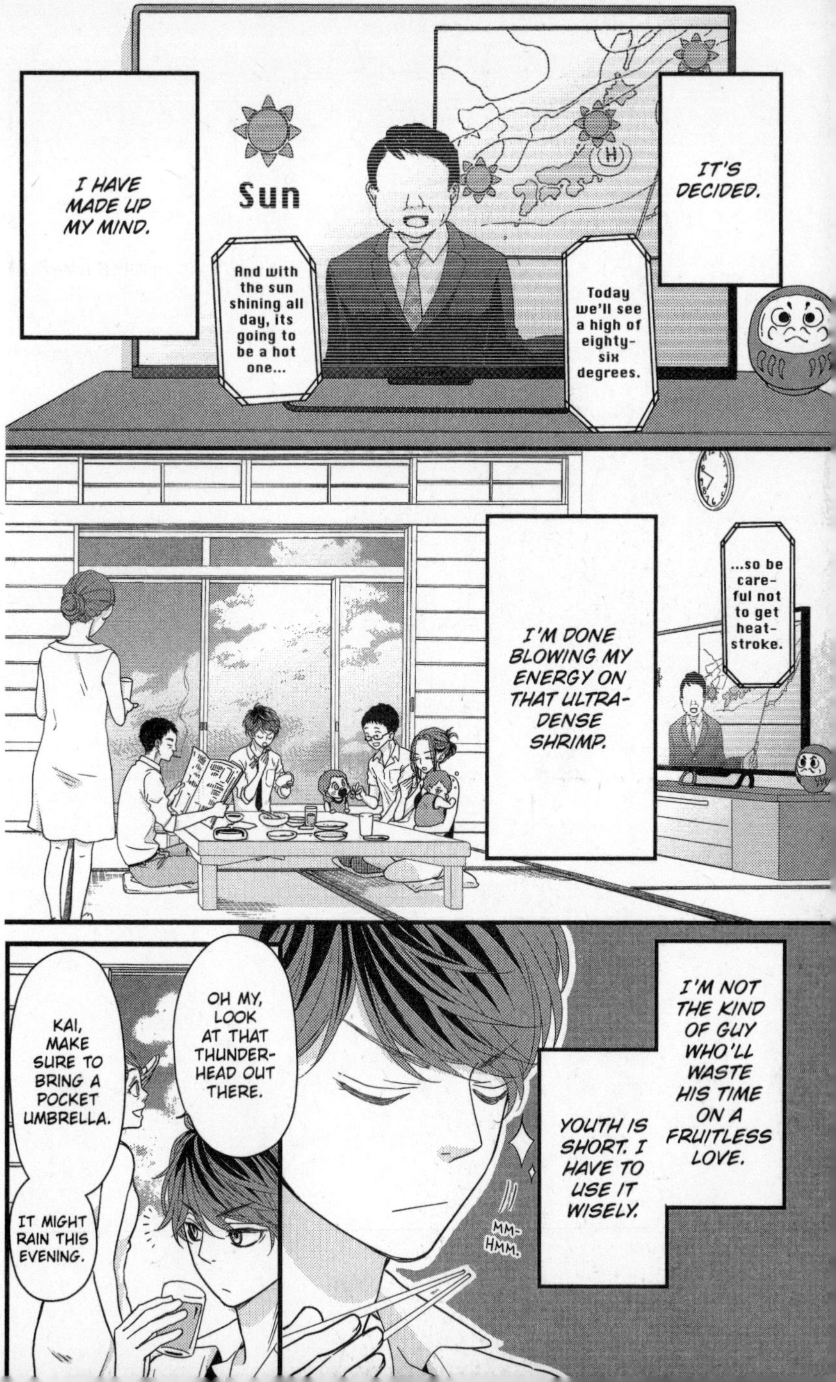
IT'S DECIDED.
Today we'll see a high of eighty-six degrees.
Sun
And with the sun shining all day, its going to be a hot one...
I HAVE MADE UP MY MIND.
...so be care-ful not to get heat-stroke.
I'M DONE BLOWING MY ENERGY ON THAT ULTRA-DENSE SHRIMP.
I'M NOT THE KIND OF GUY WHO'LL WASTE HIS TIME ON A FRUITLESS LOVE.
YOUTH IS SHORT. I HAVE TO USE IT WISELY.
MM-HMM.
OH MY, LOOK AT THAT THUNDER-HEAD OUT THERE.
KAI, MAKE SURE TO BRING A POCKET UMBRELLA.
IT MIGHT RAIN THIS EVENING.

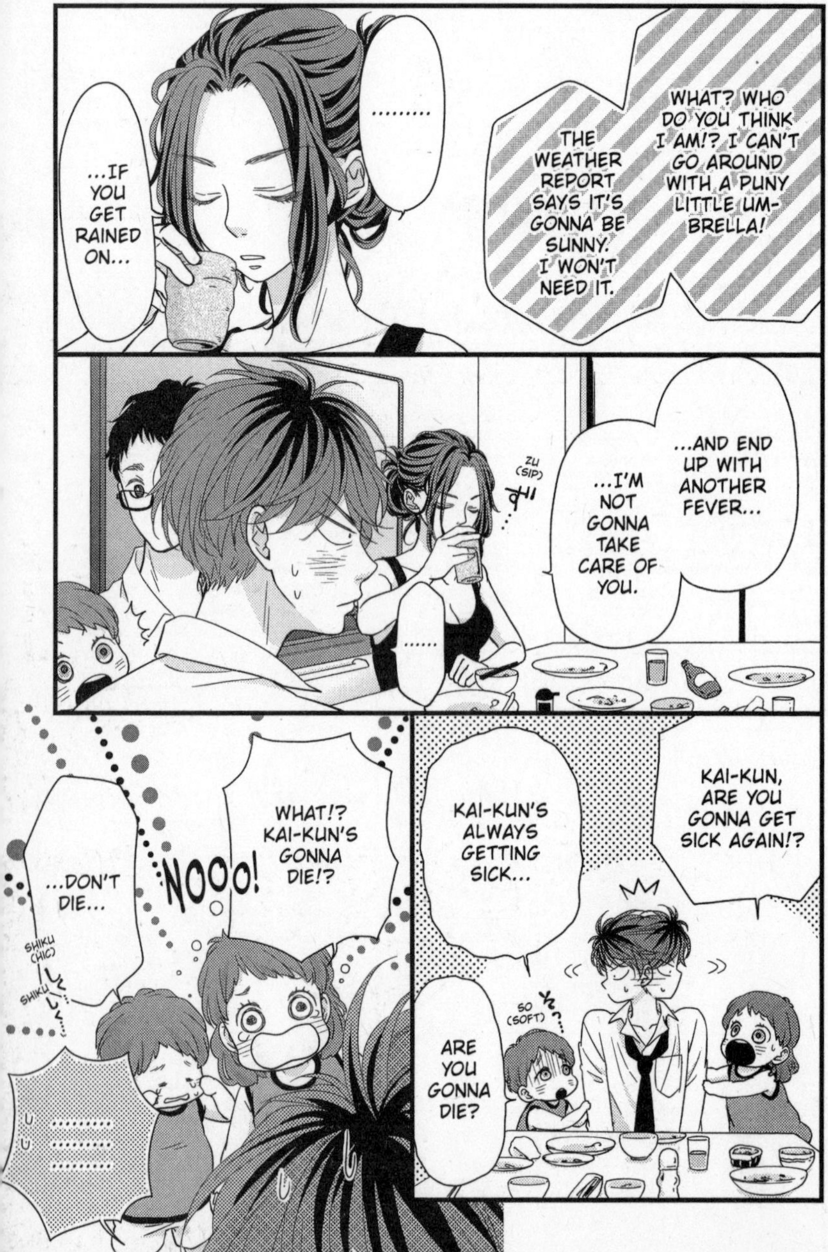
WHAT? WHO DO YOU THINK I AM!? I CAN'T GO AROUND WITH A PUNY LITTLE UM-BRELLA!
THE WEATHER REPORT SAYS IT'S GONNA BE SUNNY. I WON'T NEED IT.
....
...IF YOU GET RAINED ON...
...AND END UP WITH ANOTHER FEVER...
...I'M NOT GONNA TAKE CARE OF YOU.
ZU (SIP)
......
KAI-KUN, ARE YOU GONNA GET SICK AGAIN!?
KAI-KUN'S ALWAYS GETTING SICK...
SO (SOFT)
ARE YOU GONNA DIE?
WHAT!? KAI-KUN'S GONNA DIE!?
NOOO!
...DON'T DIE...
SHIKU (HIC)
SHIKU
U ....
U ....
....

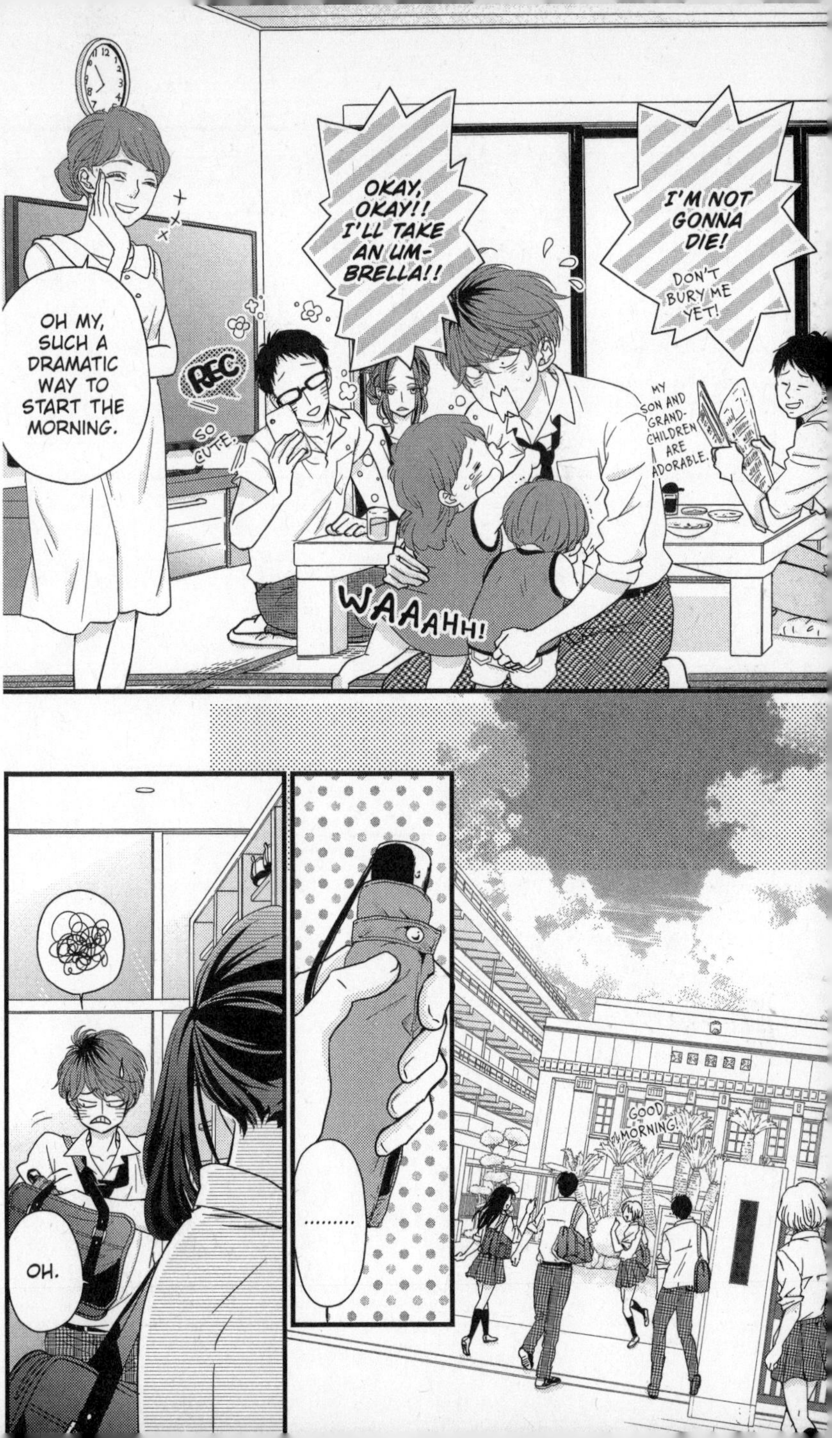

I'M NOT GONNA DIE!
DON'T BURY ME YET!
MY SON AND GRAND-CHILDREN ARE ADORABLE.
OKAY, OKAY!! I'LL TAKE AN UM-BRELLA!!
REC
SO CUTE.
OH MY, SUCH A DRAMATIC WAY TO START THE MORNING.
WAAAHH!
GOOD MORNING!
....
OH.

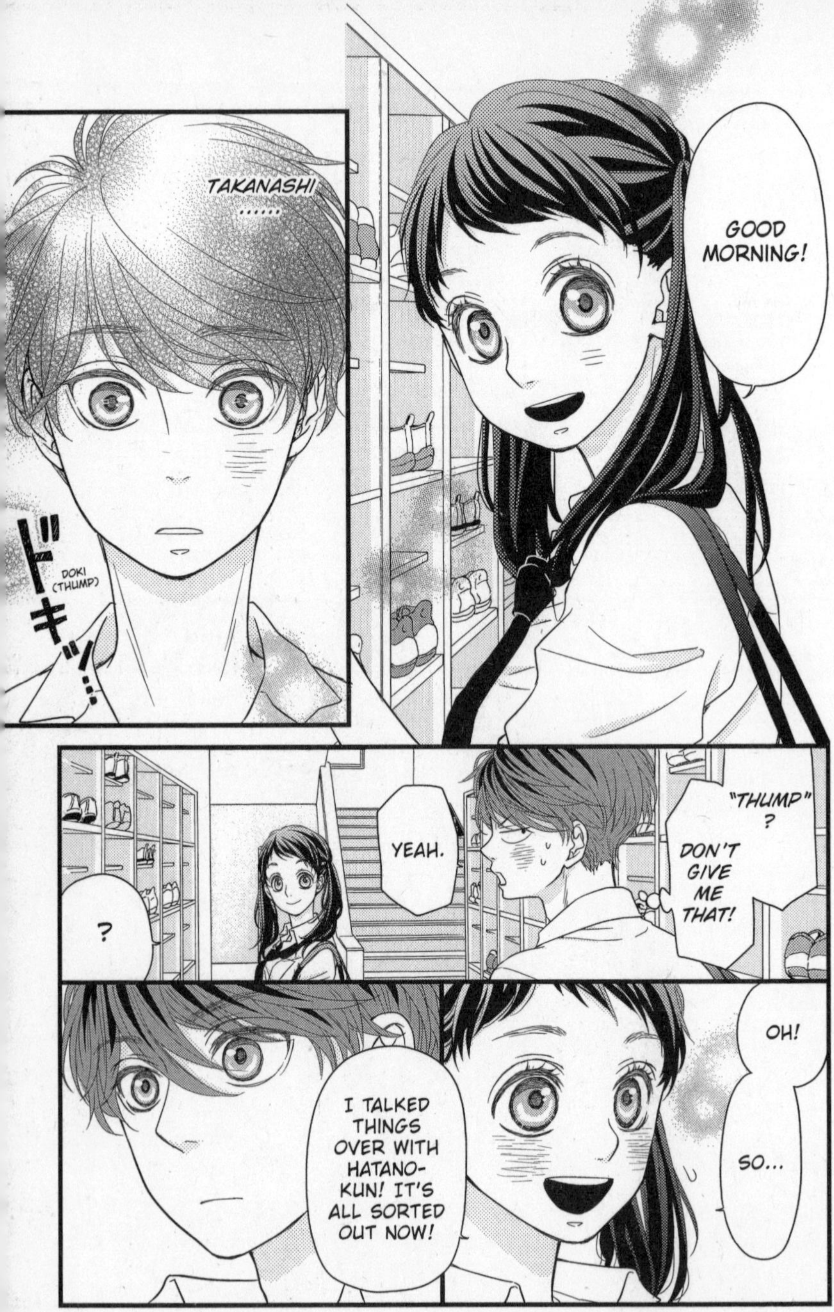
GOOD MORNING!
TAKANASHI ......
ドキッ...
DOKI (THUMP)
"THUMP"?
DON'T GIVE ME THAT!
YEAH.
?
OH!
SO...
I TALKED THINGS OVER WITH HATANO-KUN! IT'S ALL SORTED OUT NOW!

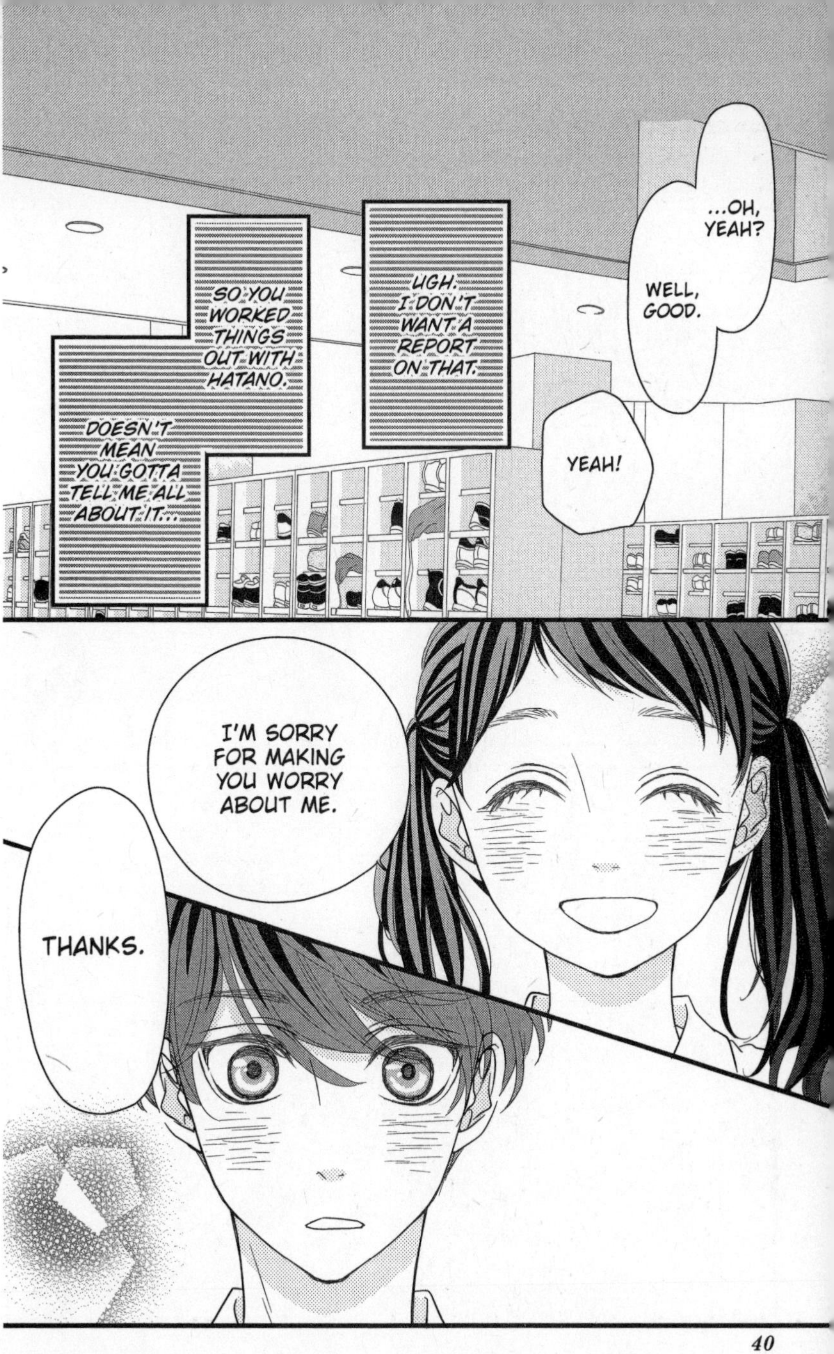
...OH, YEAH?
WELL, GOOD.
YEAH!
UGH. I DON'T WANT A REPORT ON THAT.
SO YOU WORKED THINGS OUT WITH HATANO.
DOESN'T MEAN YOU GOTTA TELL ME ALL ABOUT IT...
I'M SORRY FOR MAKING YOU WORRY ABOUT ME.
THANKS.

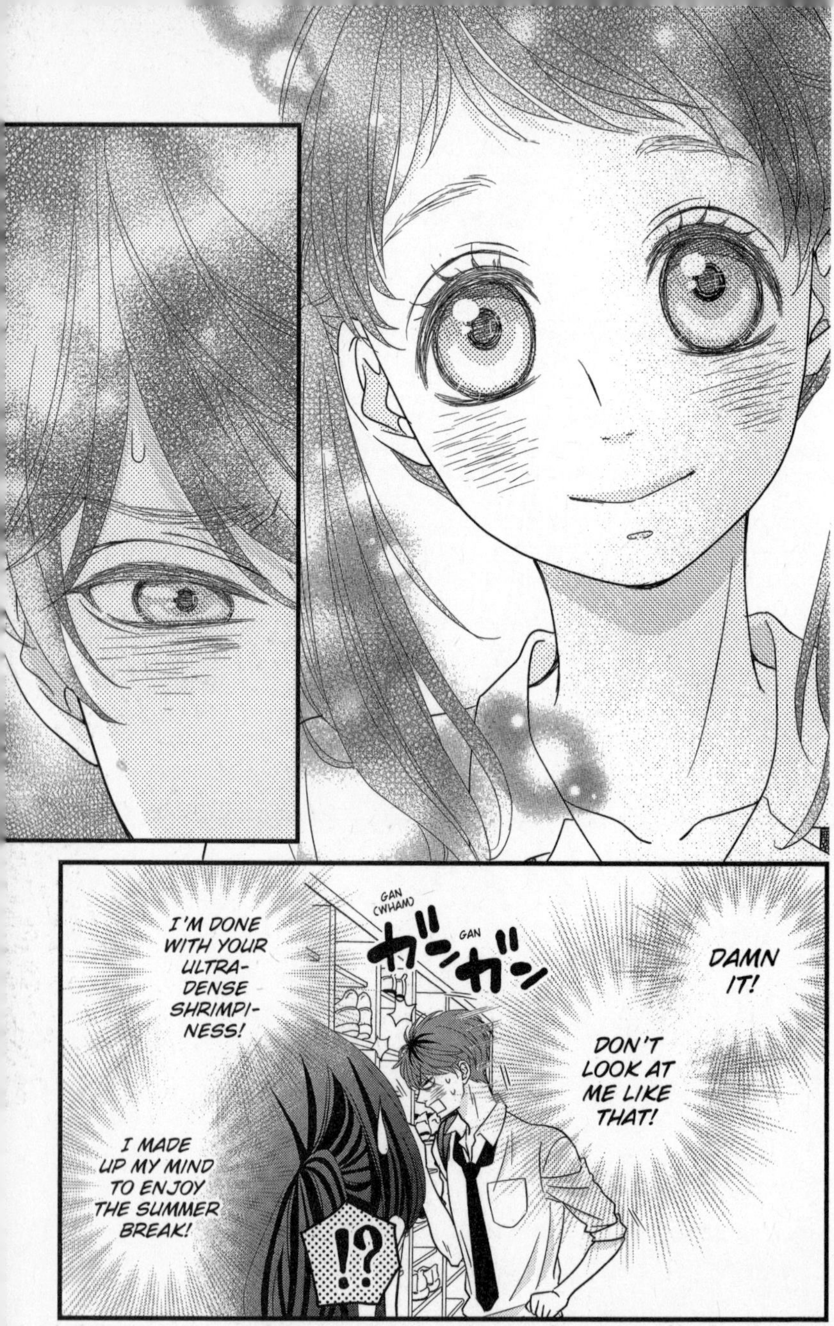
DAMN IT!
DON'T LOOK AT ME LIKE THAT!
GAN (WHAM)
GAN
I'M DONE WITH YOUR ULTRA-DENSE SHRIMPINESS!
I MADE UP MY MIND TO ENJOY THE SUMMER BREAK!
!?

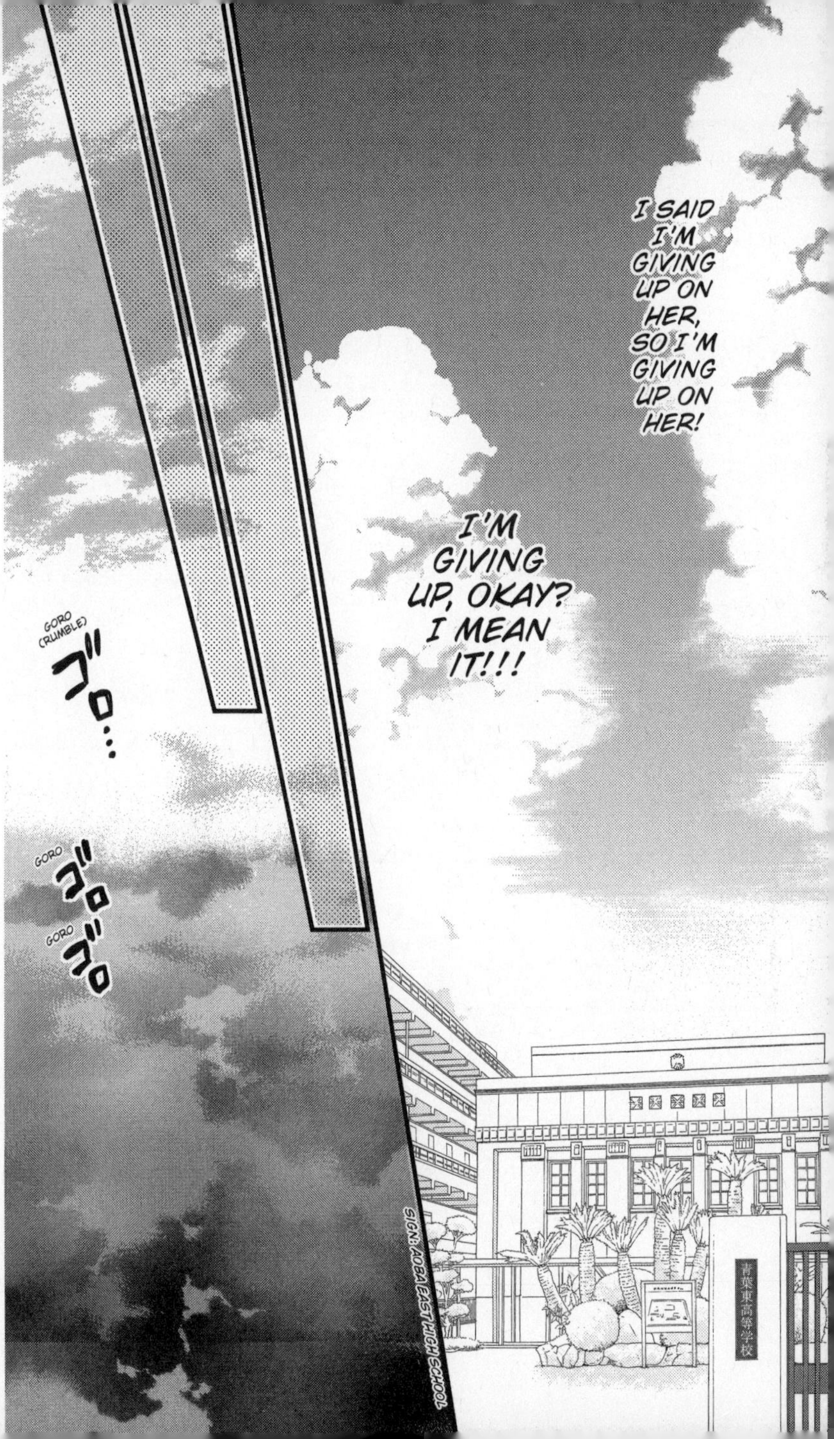
I SAID I'M GIVING UP ON HER, SO I'M GIVING UP ON HER!
I'M GIVING UP, OKAY? I MEAN IT!!!
GORO (RUMBLE)
ゴロ…
GORO
ゴロ
GORO
ゴロ
SIGN: AOBA EAST HIGH SCHOOL
青葉東高等学校

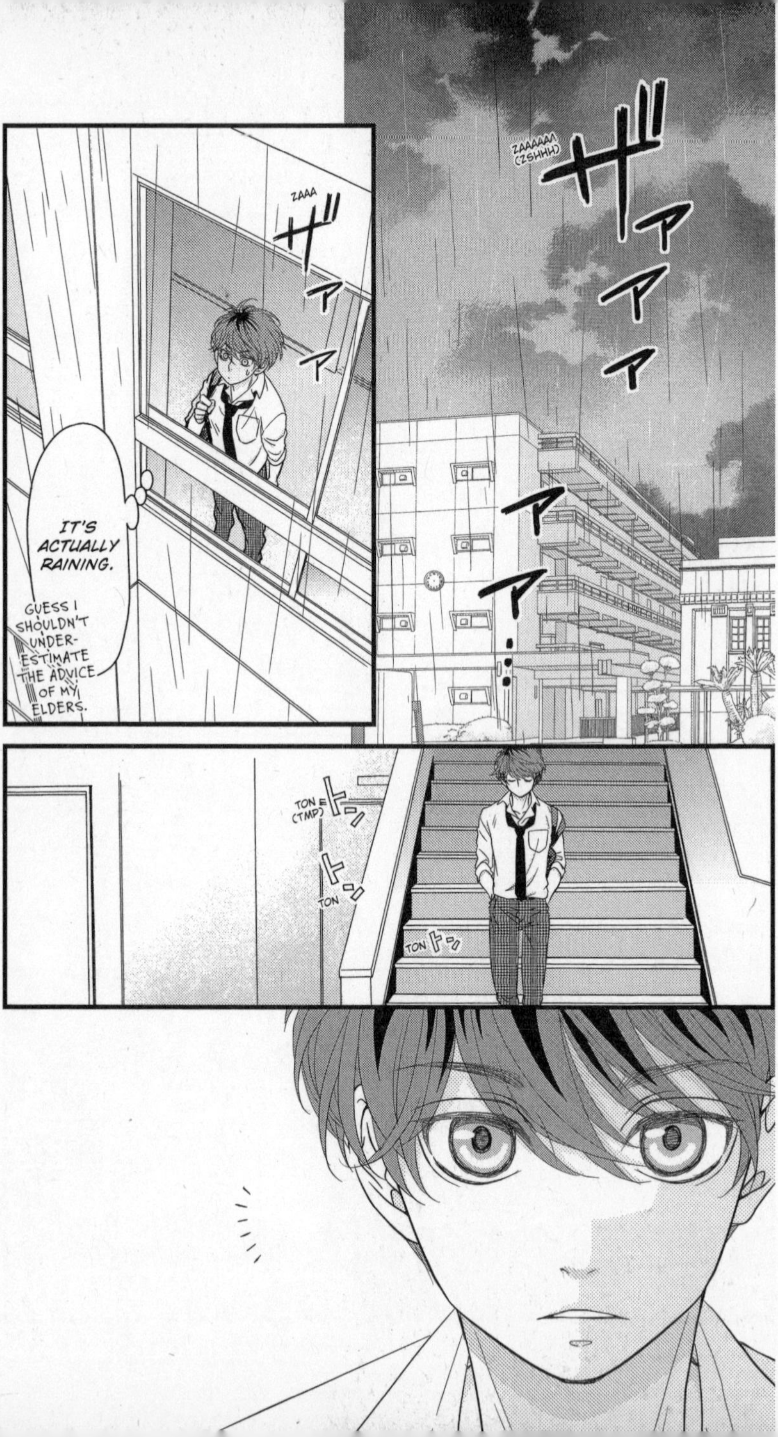
ZAAAAAA (ZSHHH)
ザァァァアア…
ZAAA
ザァァ
IT'S ACTUALLY RAINING.
GUESS I SHOULDN'T UNDER-ESTIMATE THE ADVICE OF MY ELDERS.
TON (TMP)
トッ
トッ
TON
TON
トッ

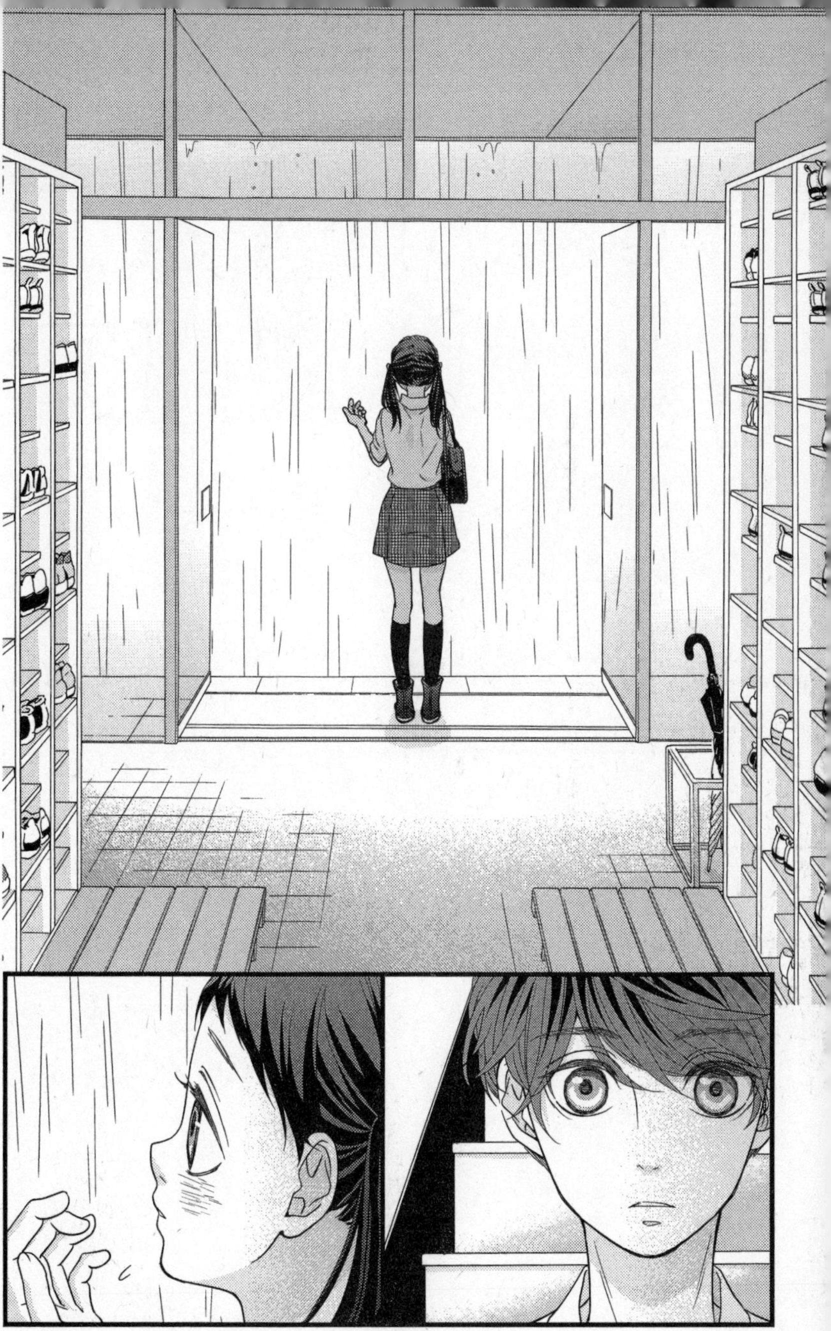

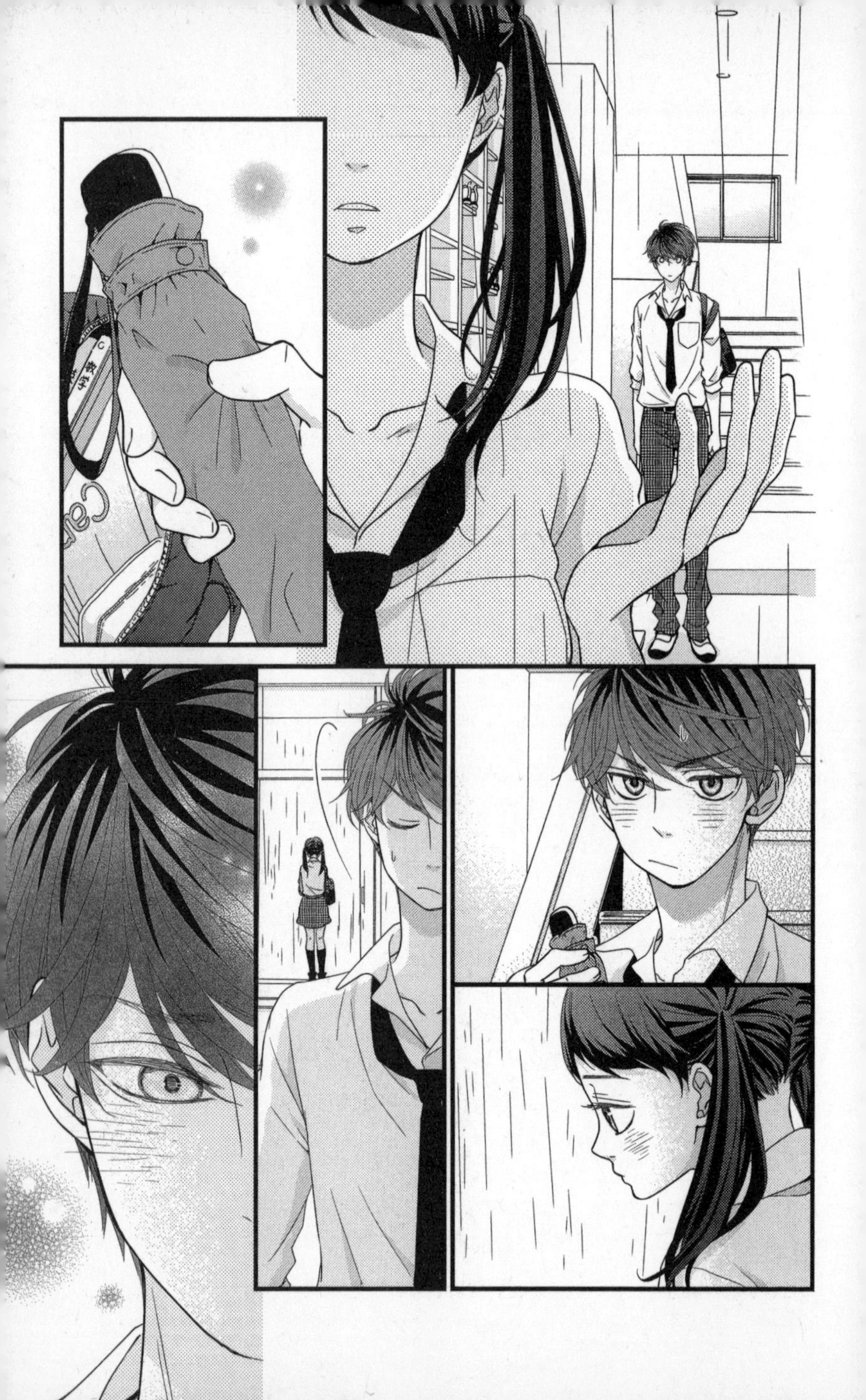

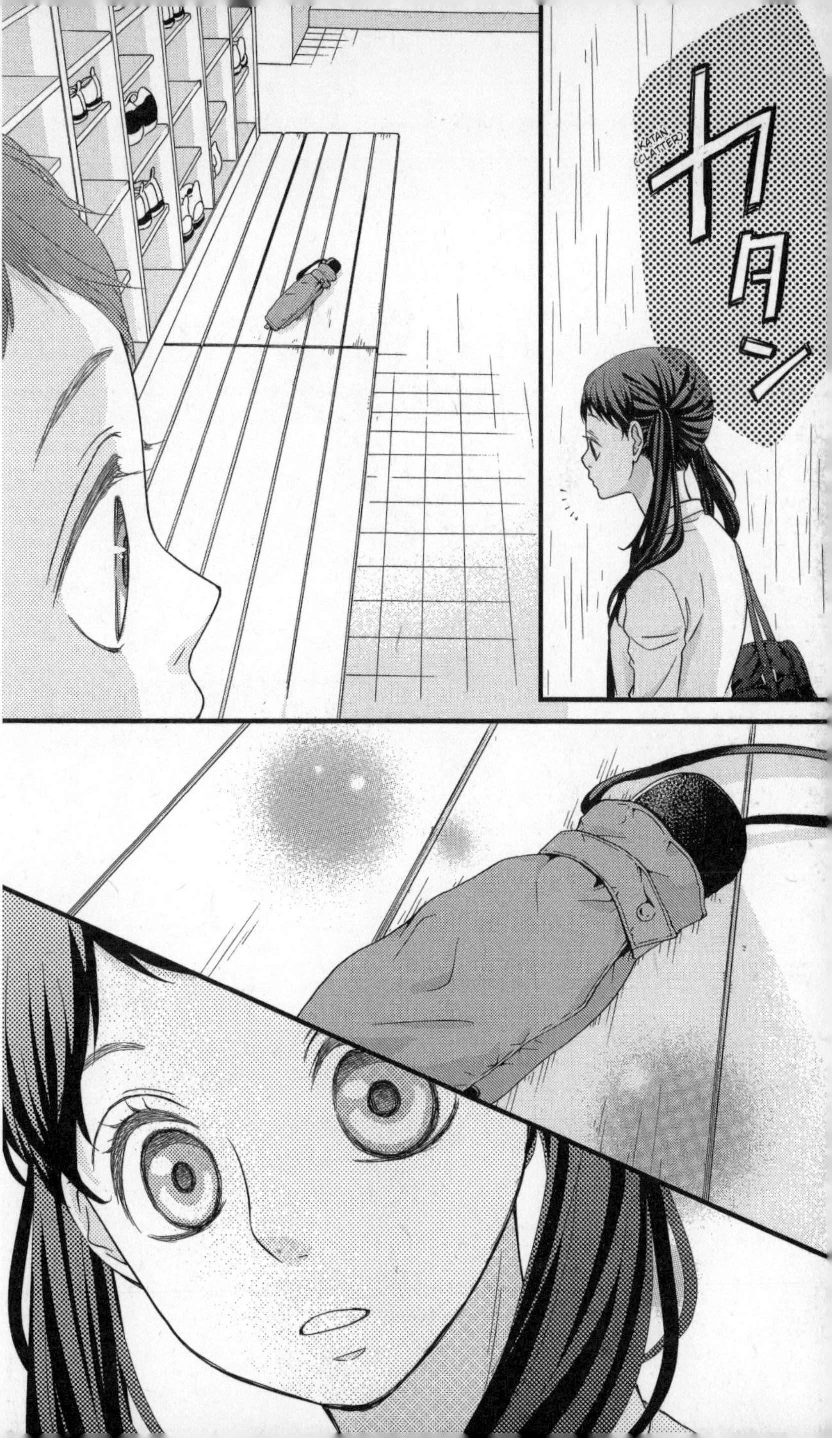
カタン
KATAN (CLATTER)

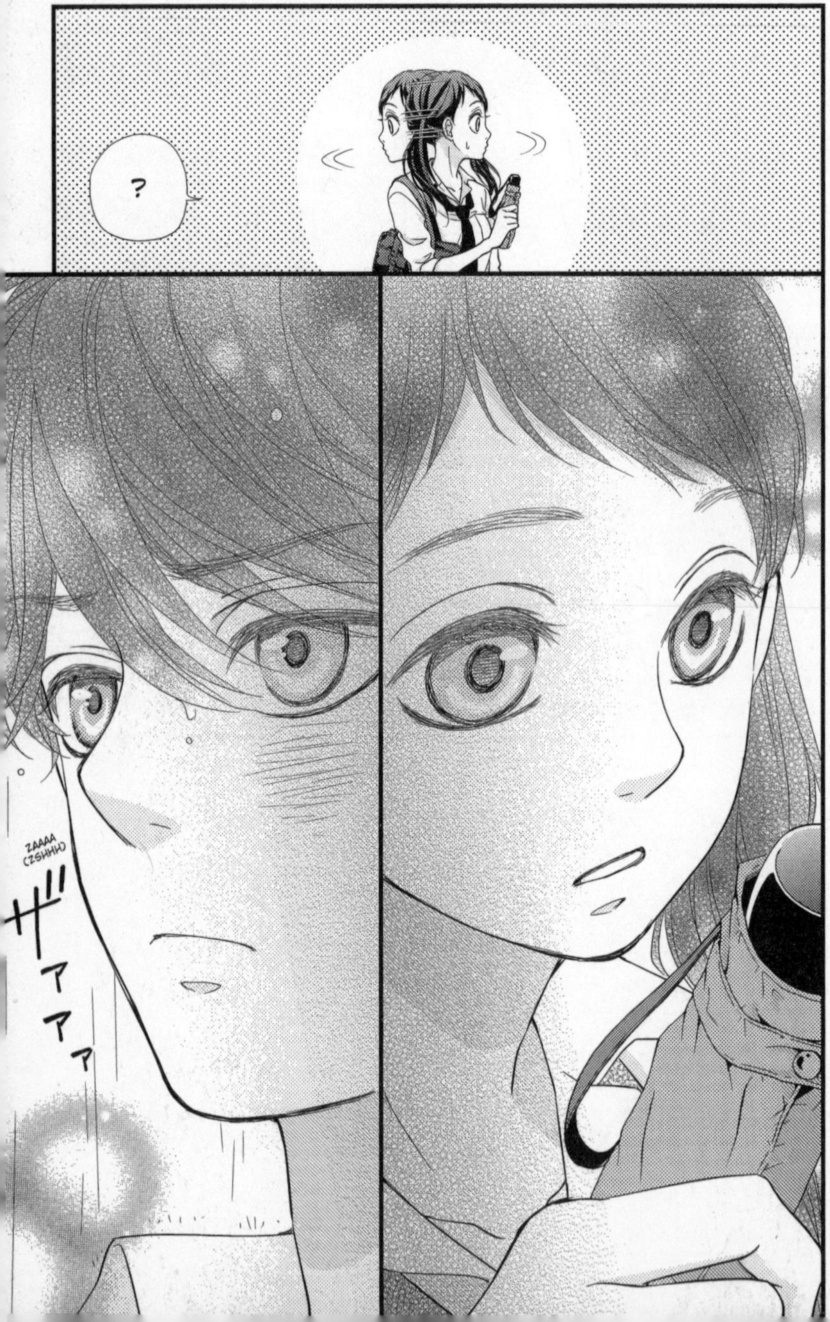
?
ZAAAA (ZSHHH)
ザァァァ

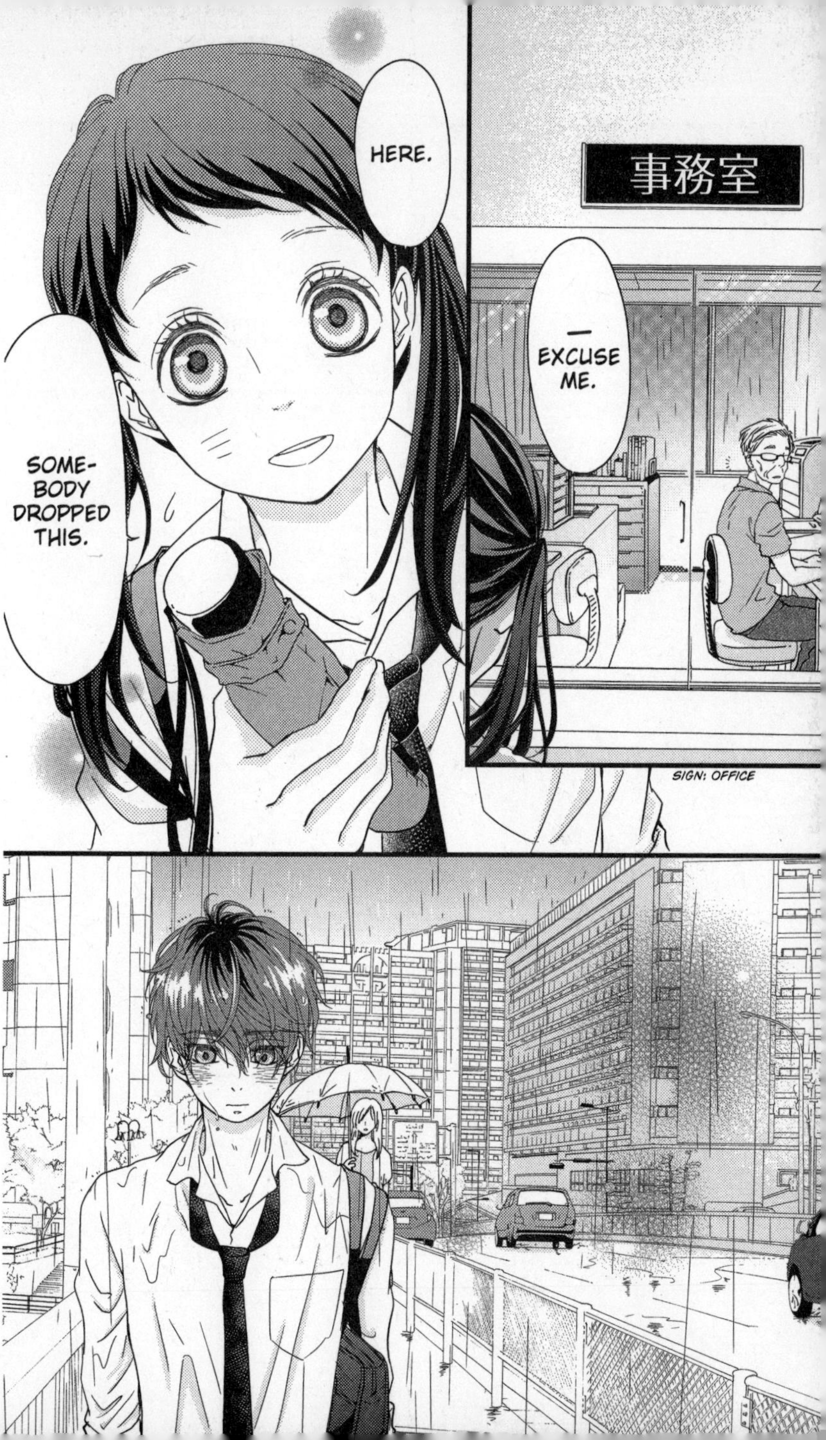
事務室
— EXCUSE ME.
SIGN: OFFICE
HERE.
SOME-BODY DROPPED THIS.

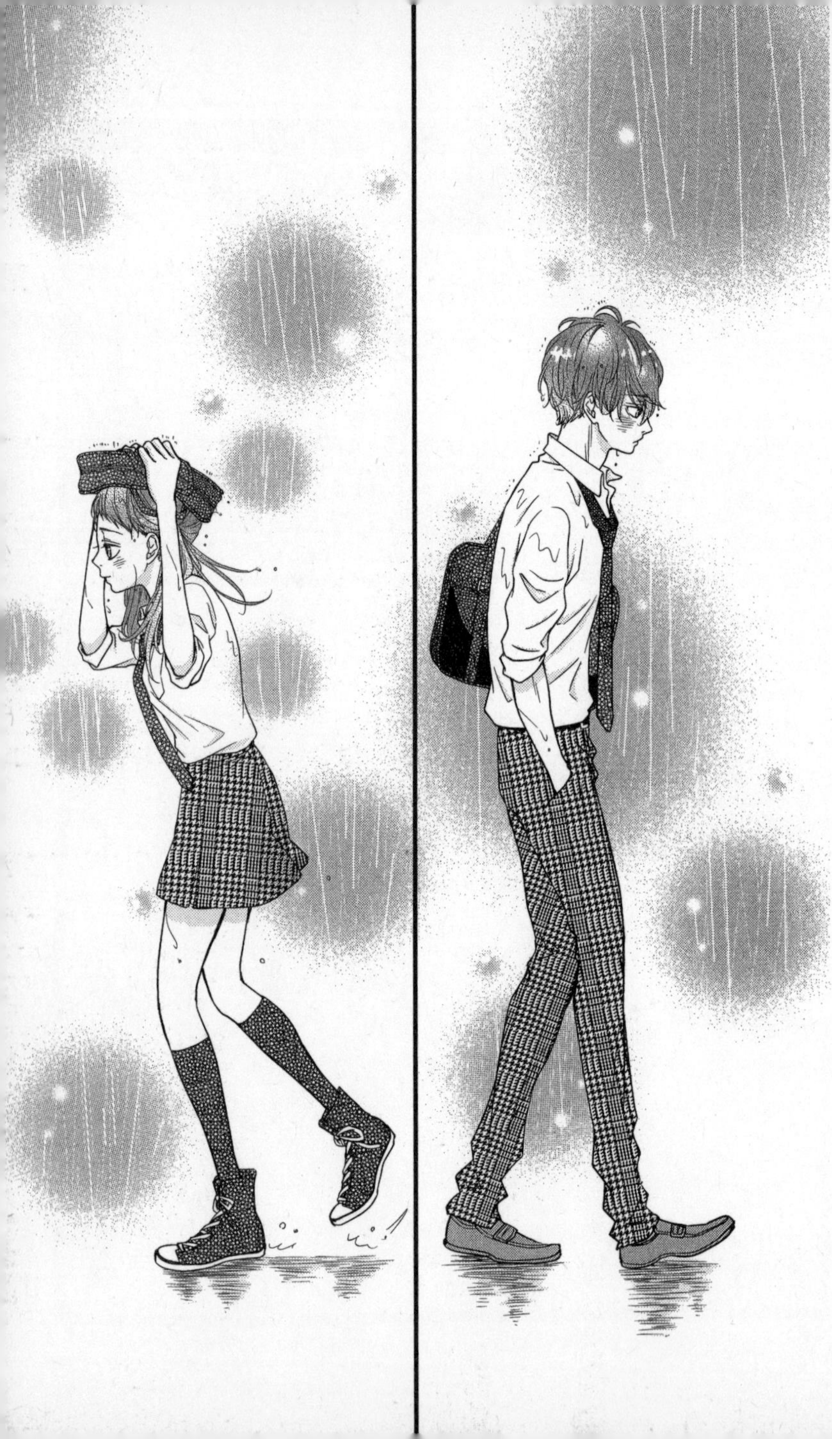

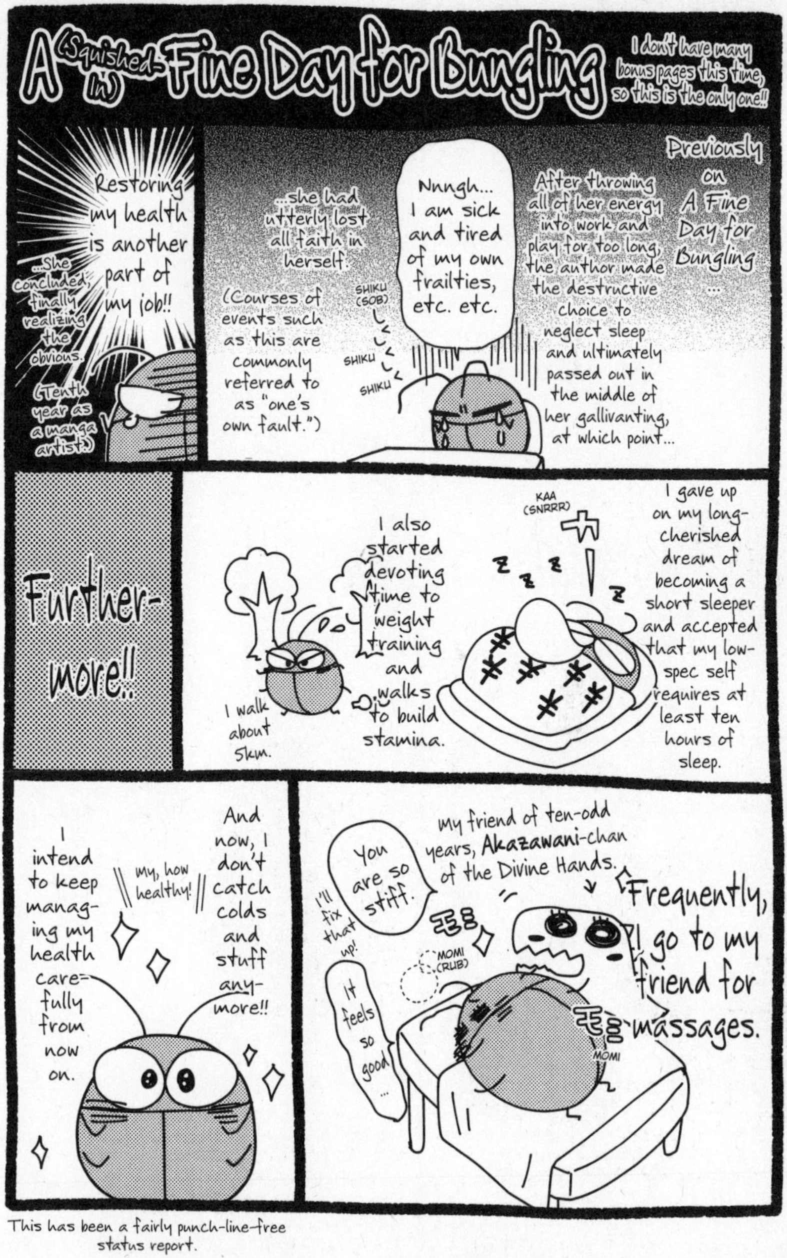
A (Squished-In) Fine Day for Bungling
I don't have many bonus pages this time, so this is the only one!!
Previously on A Fine Day for Bungling...
After throwing all of her energy into work and play for too long, the author made the destructive choice to neglect sleep and ultimately passed out in the middle of her gallivanting, at which point...
Nnngh... I am sick and tired of my own frailties, etc. etc.
SHIKU (SOB)
SHIKU
SHIKU
...she had utterly lost all faith in herself.
(Courses of events such as this are commonly referred to as "one's own fault.")
Restoring my health is another part of my job!!
...She concluded, finally realizing the obvious.
(Tenth year as a manga artist.)
I gave up on my long-cherished dream of becoming a short sleeper and accepted that my low-spec self requires at least ten hours of sleep.
KAA (SNRRR)
I also started devoting time to weight training and walks to build stamina.
I walk about 5km.
Furthermore!!
Frequently, I go to my friend for massages.
My friend of ten-odd years, Akazawani-chan of the Divine Hands.
You are so stiff.
I'll fix that up!
MOMI (RUB)
MOMI
It feels so good...
And now, I don't catch colds and stuff anymore!!
My, how healthy!
I intend to keep managing my health carefully from now on.

This has been a fairly punch-line-free status report.

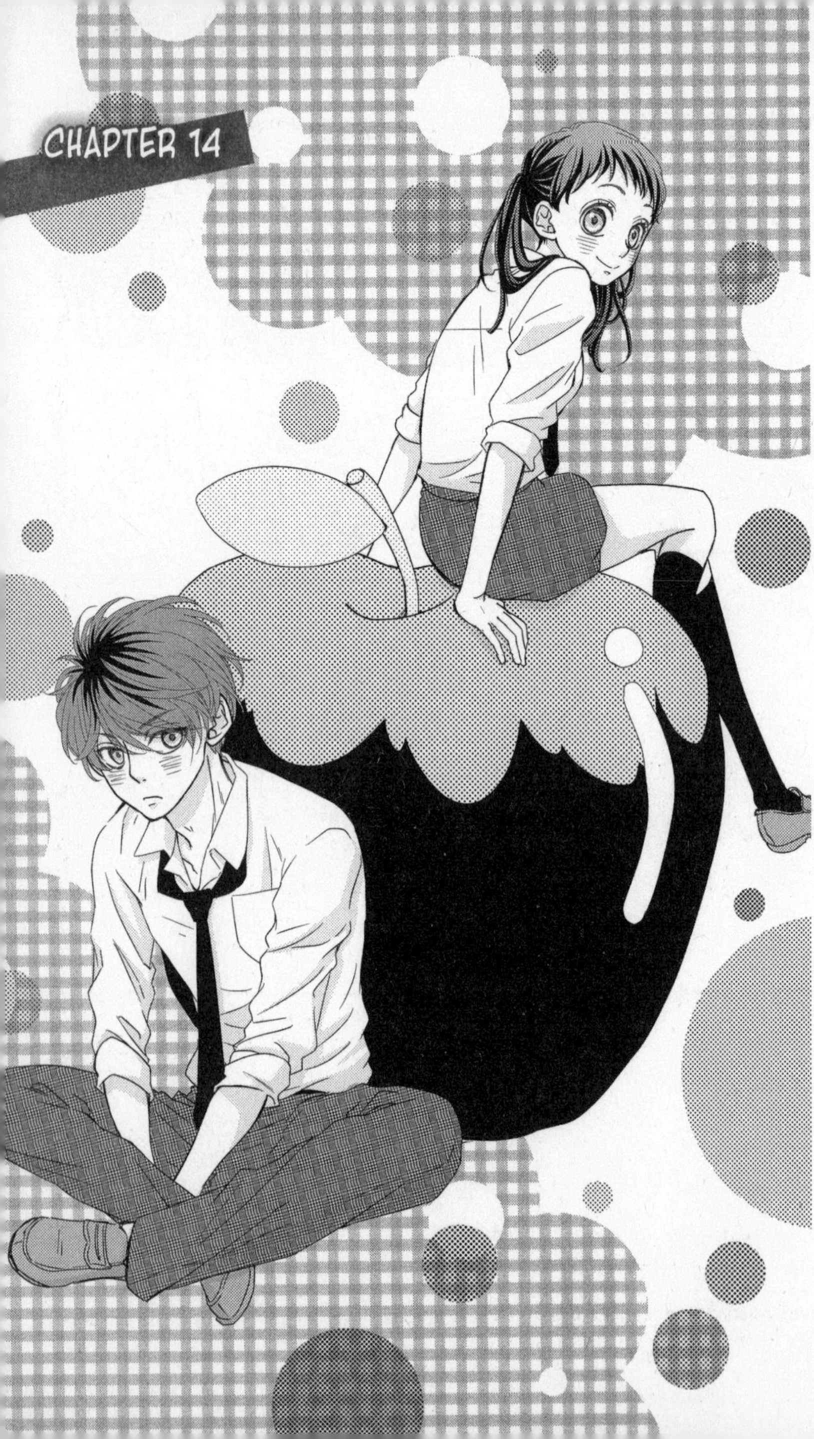
CHAPTER 14

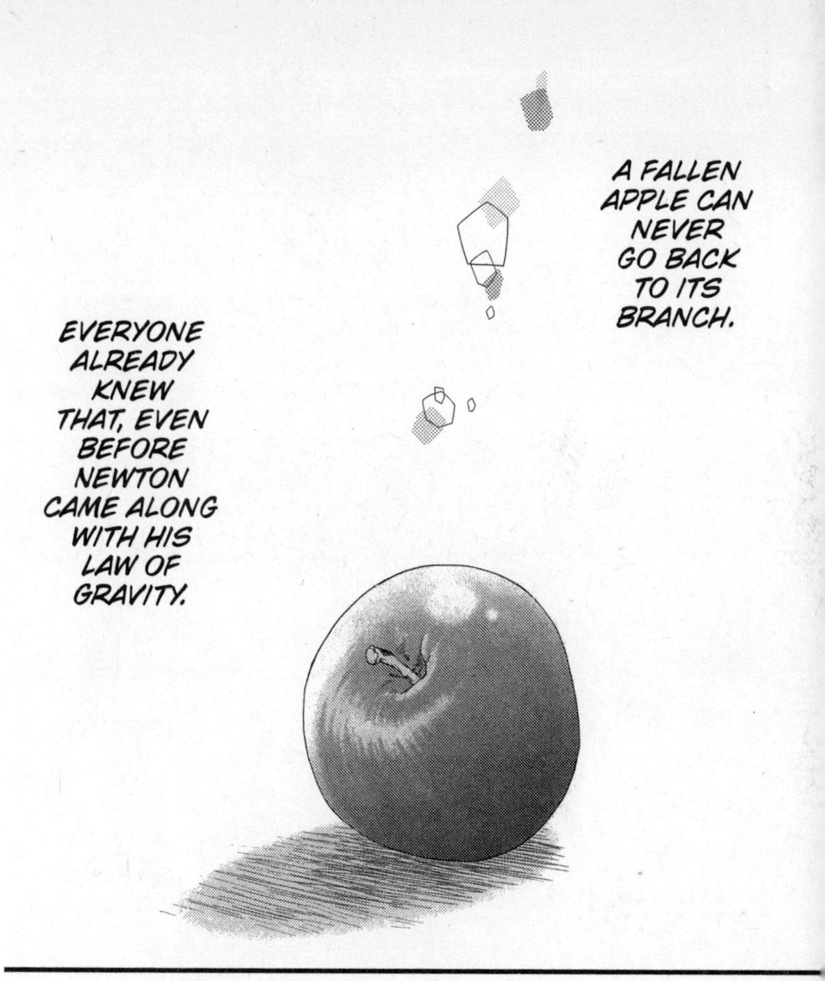
A FALLEN APPLE CAN NEVER GO BACK TO ITS BRANCH.
EVERYONE ALREADY KNEW THAT, EVEN BEFORE NEWTON CAME ALONG WITH HIS LAW OF GRAVITY.

hatsu haru

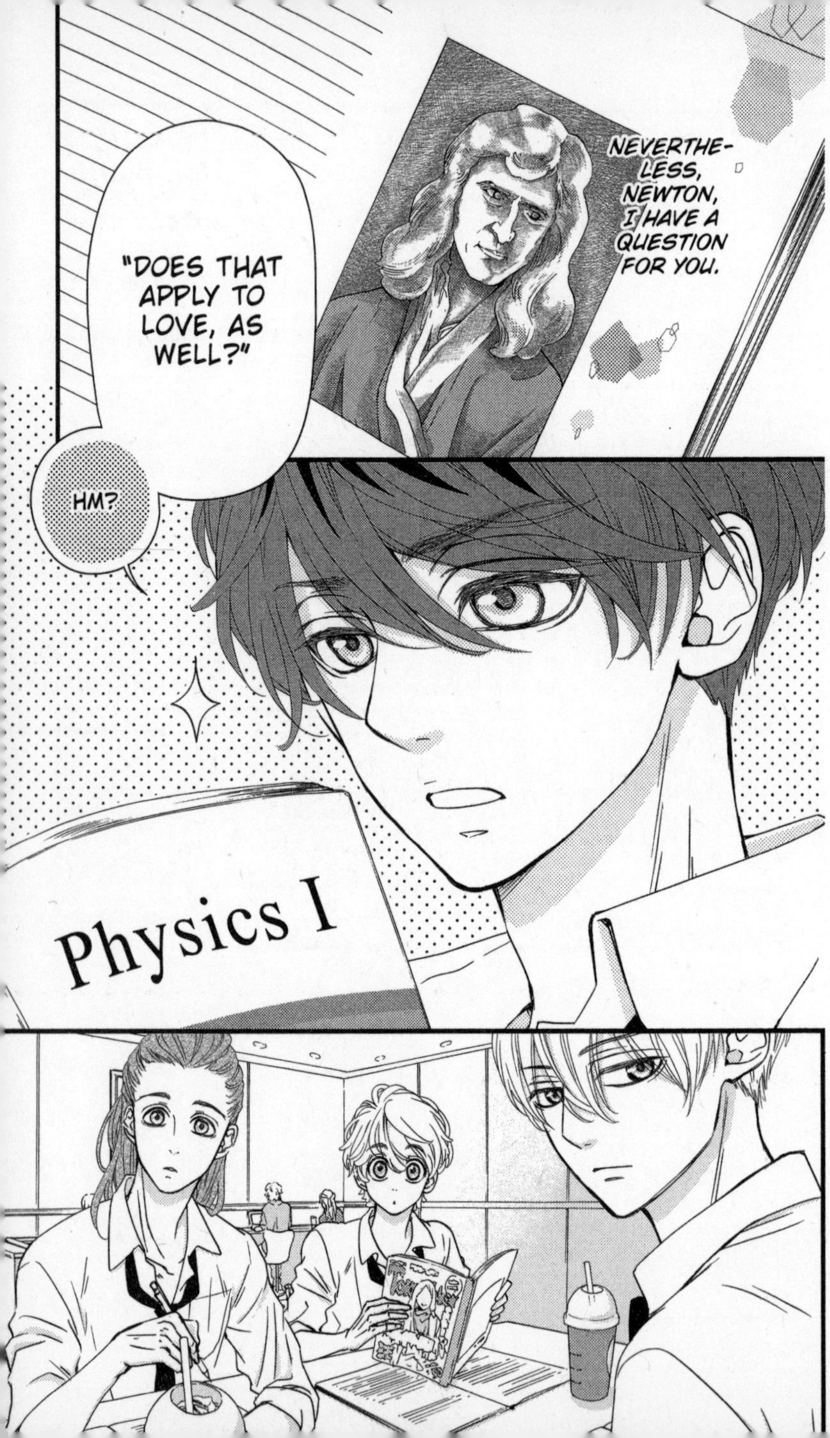
NEVERTHE-LESS, NEWTON, I HAVE A QUESTION FOR YOU.
"DOES THAT APPLY TO LOVE, AS WELL?"
HM?
Physics I

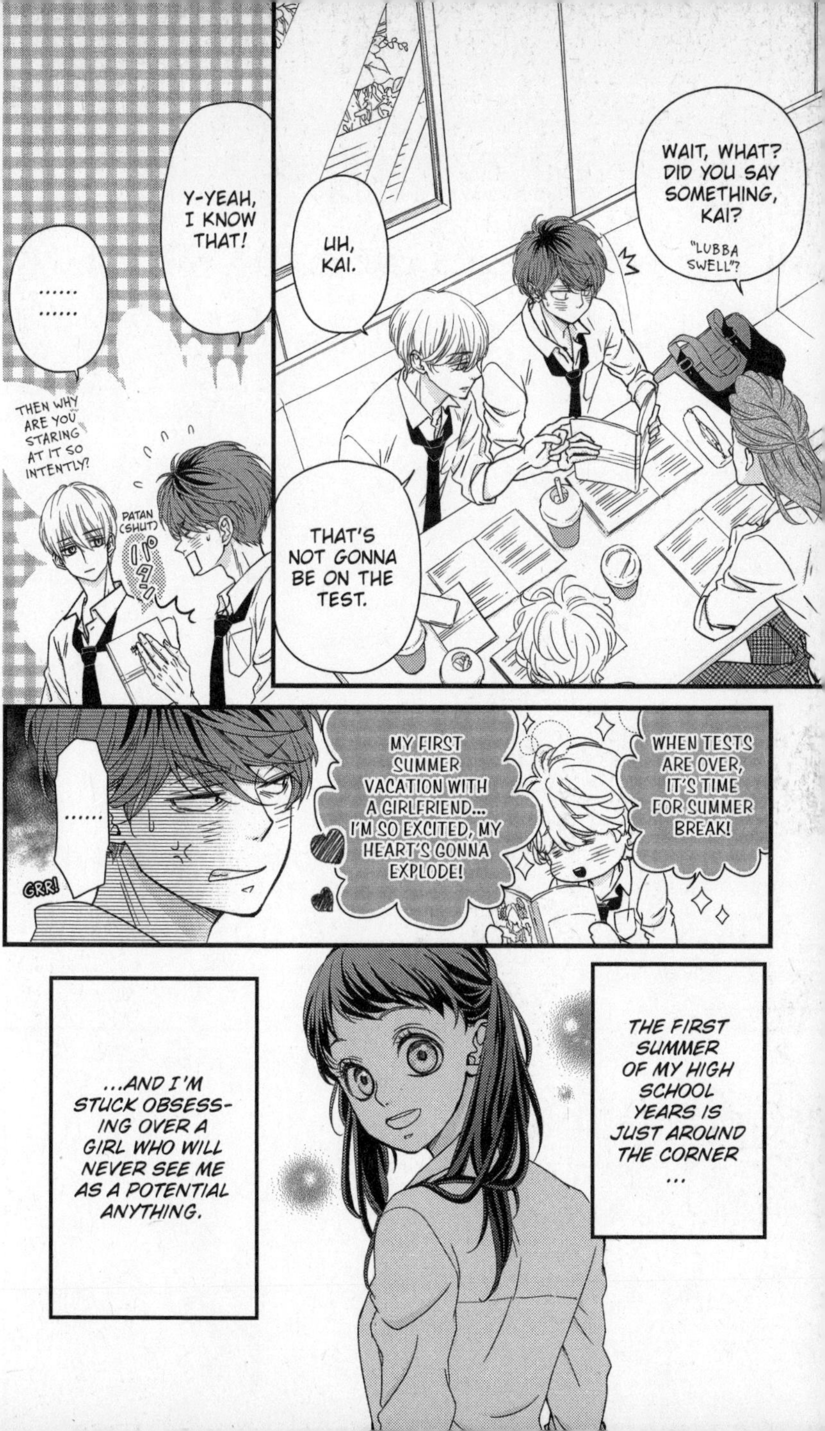
WAIT, WHAT? DID YOU SAY SOMETHING, KAI?
"LUBBA SWELL"?
UH, KAI.
THAT'S NOT GONNA BE ON THE TEST.
Y-YEAH, I KNOW THAT!
......
......
THEN WHY ARE YOU STARING AT IT SO INTENTLY?
PATAN (SHUT)
WHEN TESTS ARE OVER, IT'S TIME FOR SUMMER BREAK!
MY FIRST SUMMER VACATION WITH A GIRLFRIEND... I'M SO EXCITED, MY HEART'S GONNA EXPLODE!
......
GRR!
THE FIRST SUMMER OF MY HIGH SCHOOL YEARS IS JUST AROUND THE CORNER ...
...AND I'M STUCK OBSESSING OVER A GIRL WHO WILL NEVER SEE ME AS A POTENTIAL ANYTHING.

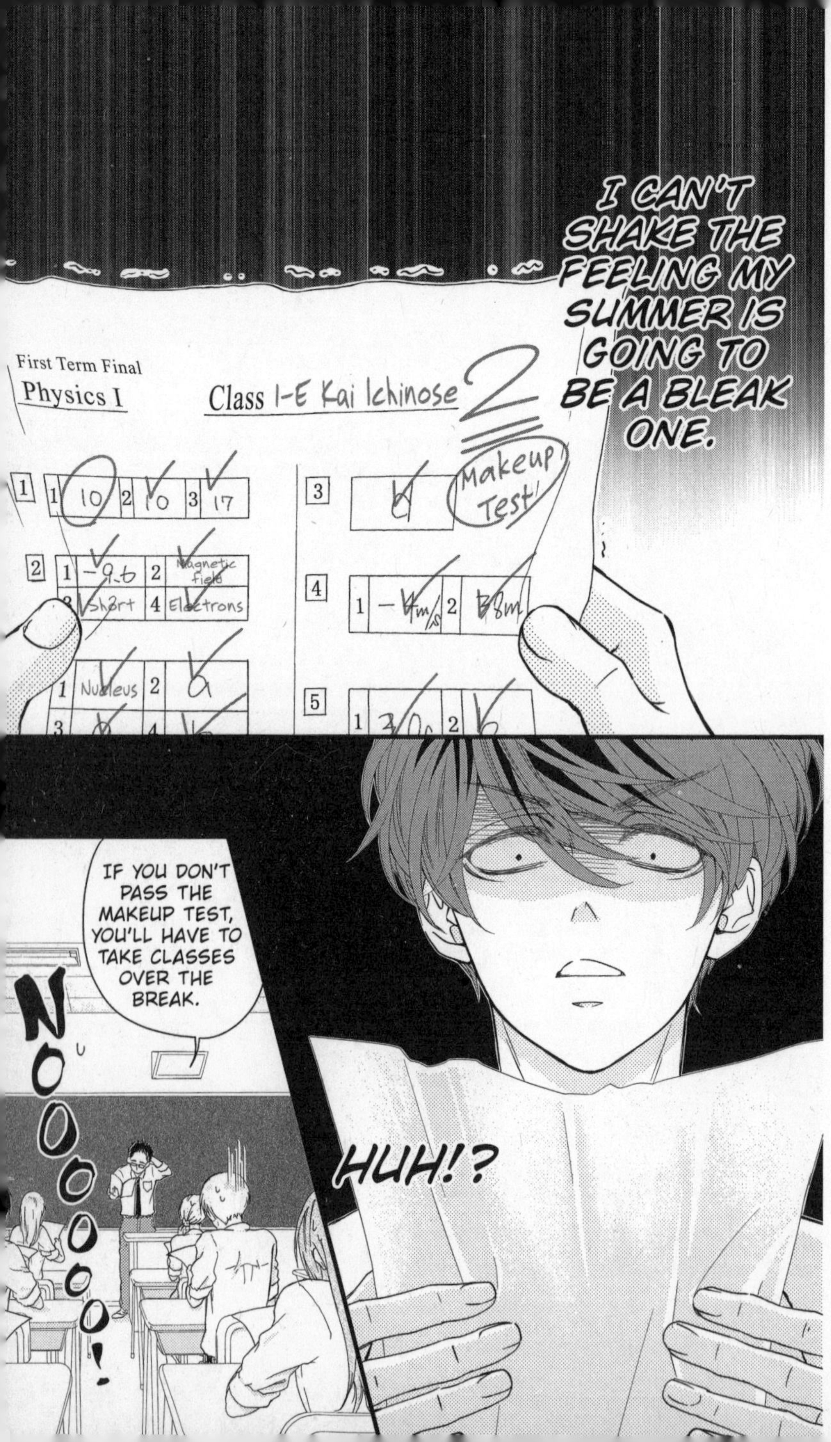
First Term Final
Physics I
Class 1-E Kai Ichinose
2
Makeup Test
Magnetic field
Short
Electrons
Nucleus
I CAN'T SHAKE THE FEELING MY SUMMER IS GOING TO BE A BLEAK ONE.
HUH!?
IF YOU DON'T PASS THE MAKEUP TEST, YOU'LL HAVE TO TAKE CLASSES OVER THE BREAK.
NOOOOO!

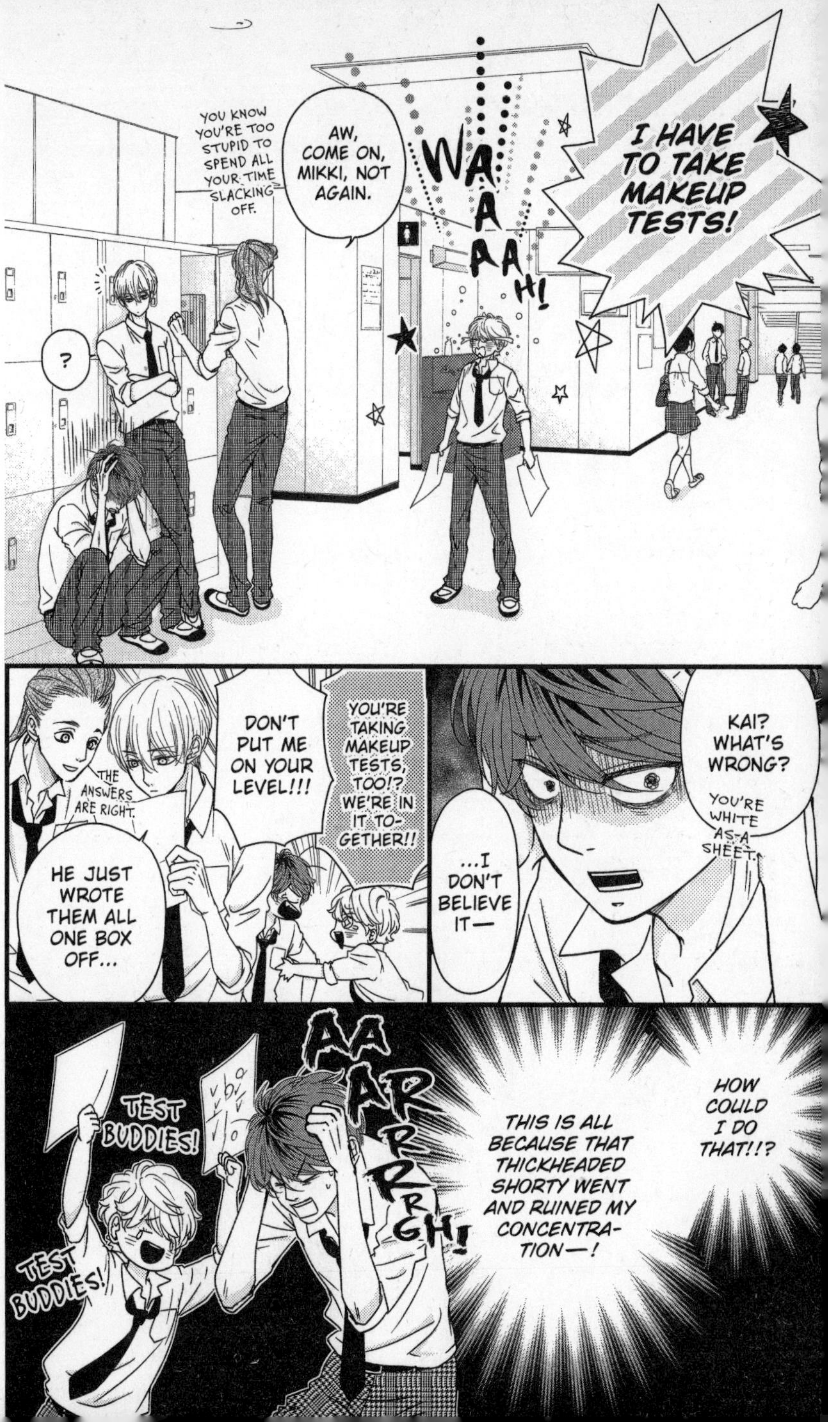
I HAVE TO TAKE MAKEUP TESTS!
WAAAAH!
AW, COME ON, MIKKI, NOT AGAIN.
YOU KNOW YOU'RE TOO STUPID TO SPEND ALL YOUR TIME SLACKING OFF.
?
KAI? WHAT'S WRONG?
YOU'RE WHITE AS A SHEET.
...I DON'T BELIEVE IT—
YOU'RE TAKING MAKEUP TESTS, TOO!? WE'RE IN IT TO-GETHER!!
DON'T PUT ME ON YOUR LEVEL!!!
THE ANSWERS ARE RIGHT.
HE JUST WROTE THEM ALL ONE BOX OFF...
HOW COULD I DO THAT!!?
THIS IS ALL BECAUSE THAT THICKHEADED SHORTY WENT AND RUINED MY CONCENTRA-TION—!
AAARRRGH!
TEST BUDDIES!
TEST BUDDIES!

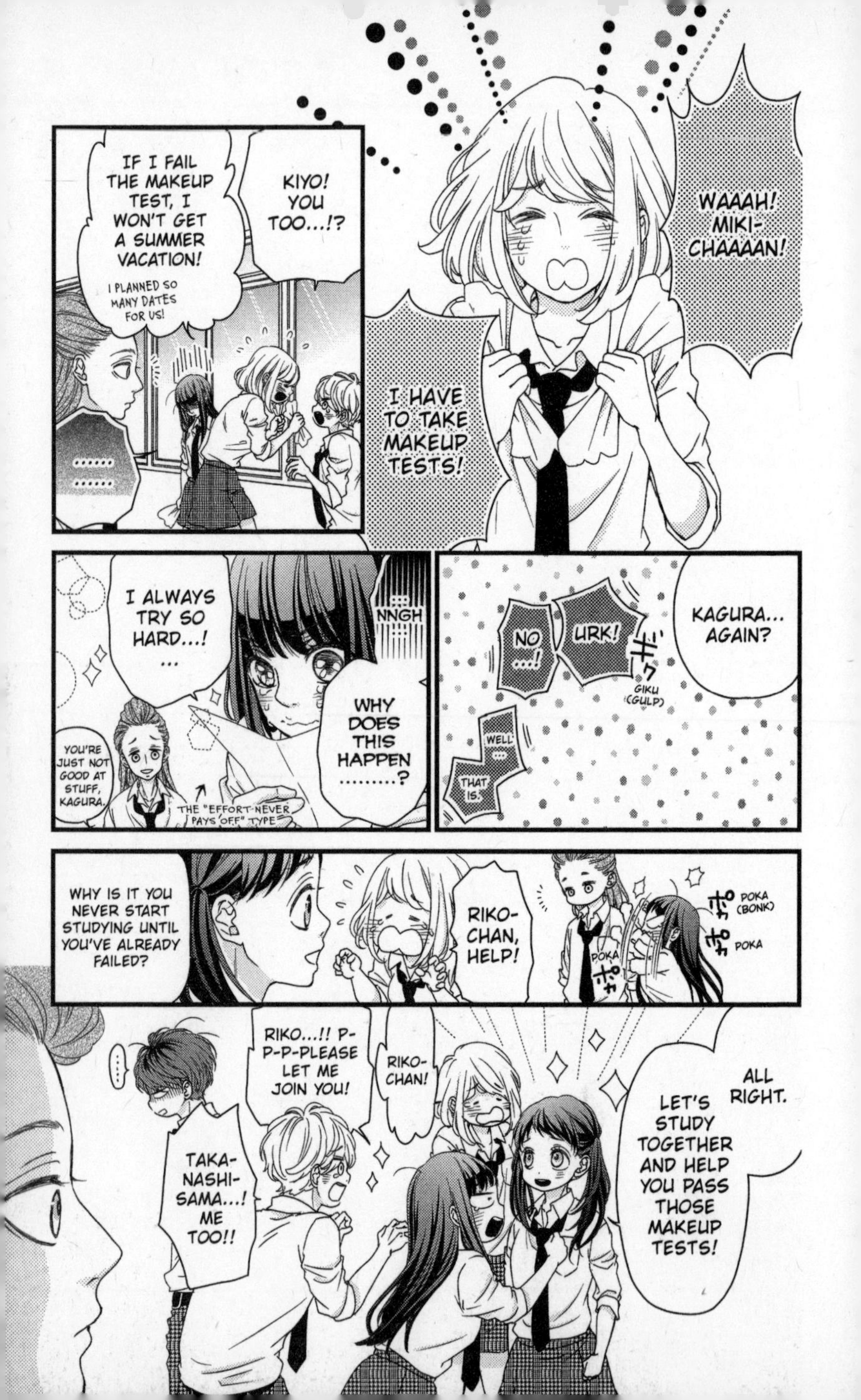
WAAAH! MIKI-CHAAAAN!
I HAVE TO TAKE MAKEUP TESTS!
KIYO! YOU TOO...!?
IF I FAIL THE MAKEUP TEST, I WON'T GET A SUMMER VACATION!
I PLANNED SO MANY DATES FOR US!
....
KAGURA... AGAIN?
URK!
NO ...!
ギク GIKU (GULP)
WELL ... THAT IS.
...NNGH...
WHY DOES THIS HAPPEN ....?
I ALWAYS TRY SO HARD...! ...
THE "EFFORT NEVER PAYS OFF" TYPE
YOU'RE JUST NOT GOOD AT STUFF, KAGURA.
ポカ POKA (BONK)
ポカ POKA
ポカ POKA
RIKO-CHAN, HELP!
WHY IS IT YOU NEVER START STUDYING UNTIL YOU'VE ALREADY FAILED?
ALL RIGHT.
LET'S STUDY TOGETHER AND HELP YOU PASS THOSE MAKEUP TESTS!
RIKO-CHAN!
RIKO...!! P-P-P-PLEASE LET ME JOIN YOU!
TAKA-NASHI-SAMA...! ME TOO!!
......

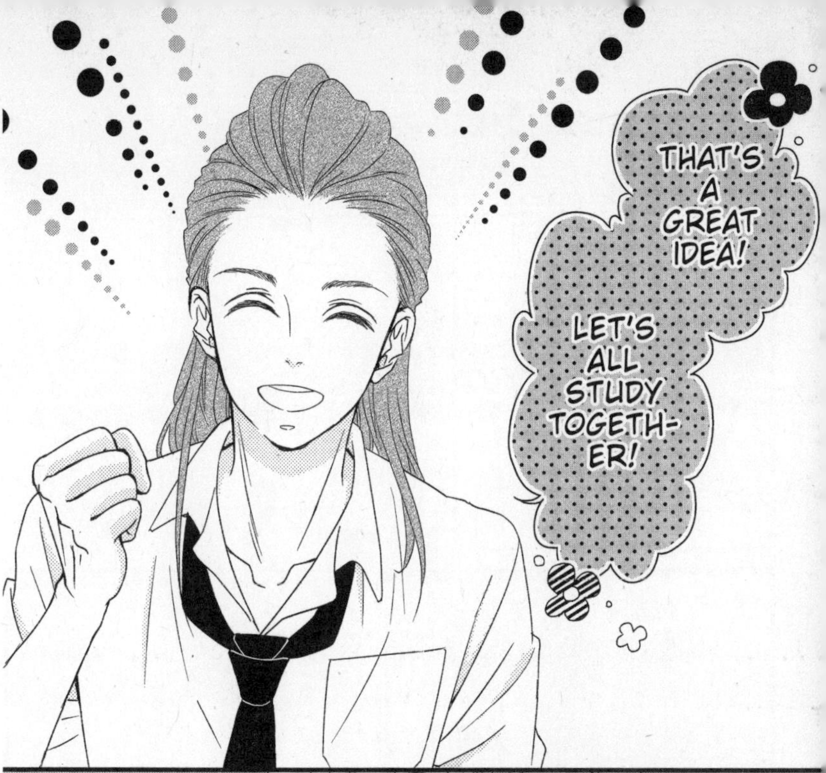
THAT'S A GREAT IDEA!
LET'S ALL STUDY TOGETHER!
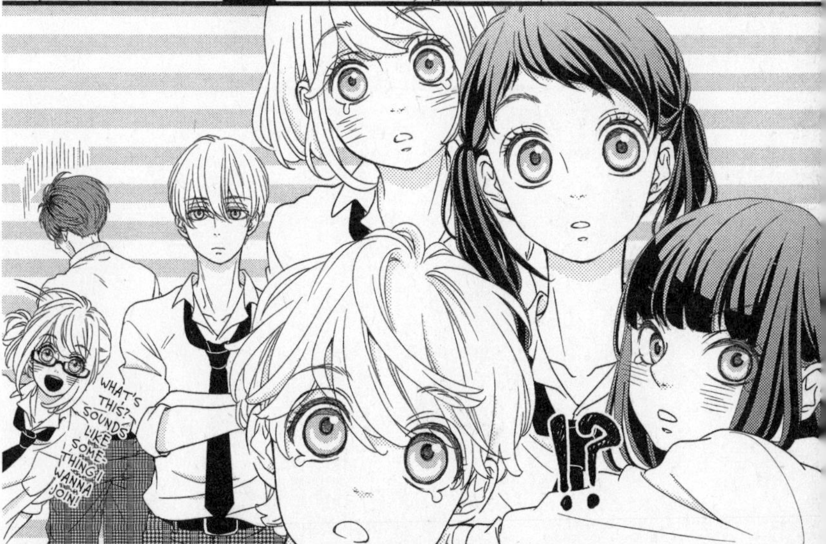
!!?
WHAT'S THIS? SOUNDS LIKE SOMETHING I WANNA JOIN!

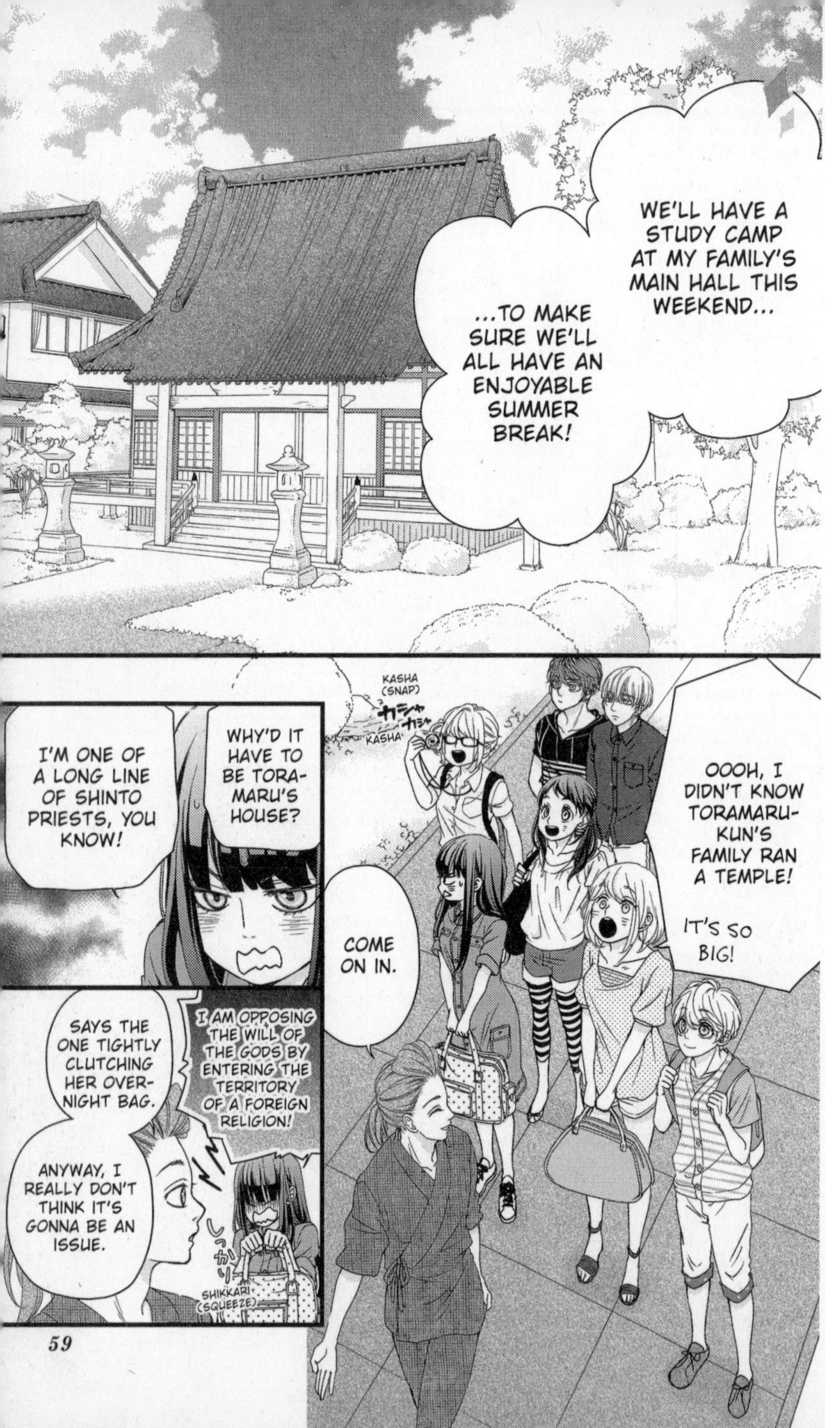
WE'LL HAVE A STUDY CAMP AT MY FAMILY'S MAIN HALL THIS WEEKEND...
...TO MAKE SURE WE'LL ALL HAVE AN ENJOYABLE SUMMER BREAK!
OOOH, I DIDN'T KNOW TORAMARU-KUN'S FAMILY RAN A TEMPLE!
IT'S SO BIG!
KASHA (SNAP)
カシャ
カシャ
KASHA
COME ON IN.
WHY'D IT HAVE TO BE TORA-MARU'S HOUSE?
I'M ONE OF A LONG LINE OF SHINTO PRIESTS, YOU KNOW!
I AM OPPOSING THE WILL OF THE GODS BY ENTERING THE TERRITORY OF A FOREIGN RELIGION!
SAYS THE ONE TIGHTLY CLUTCHING HER OVER-NIGHT BAG.
ANYWAY, I REALLY DON'T THINK IT'S GONNA BE AN ISSUE.
しっかり
SHIKKARI (SQUEEZE)

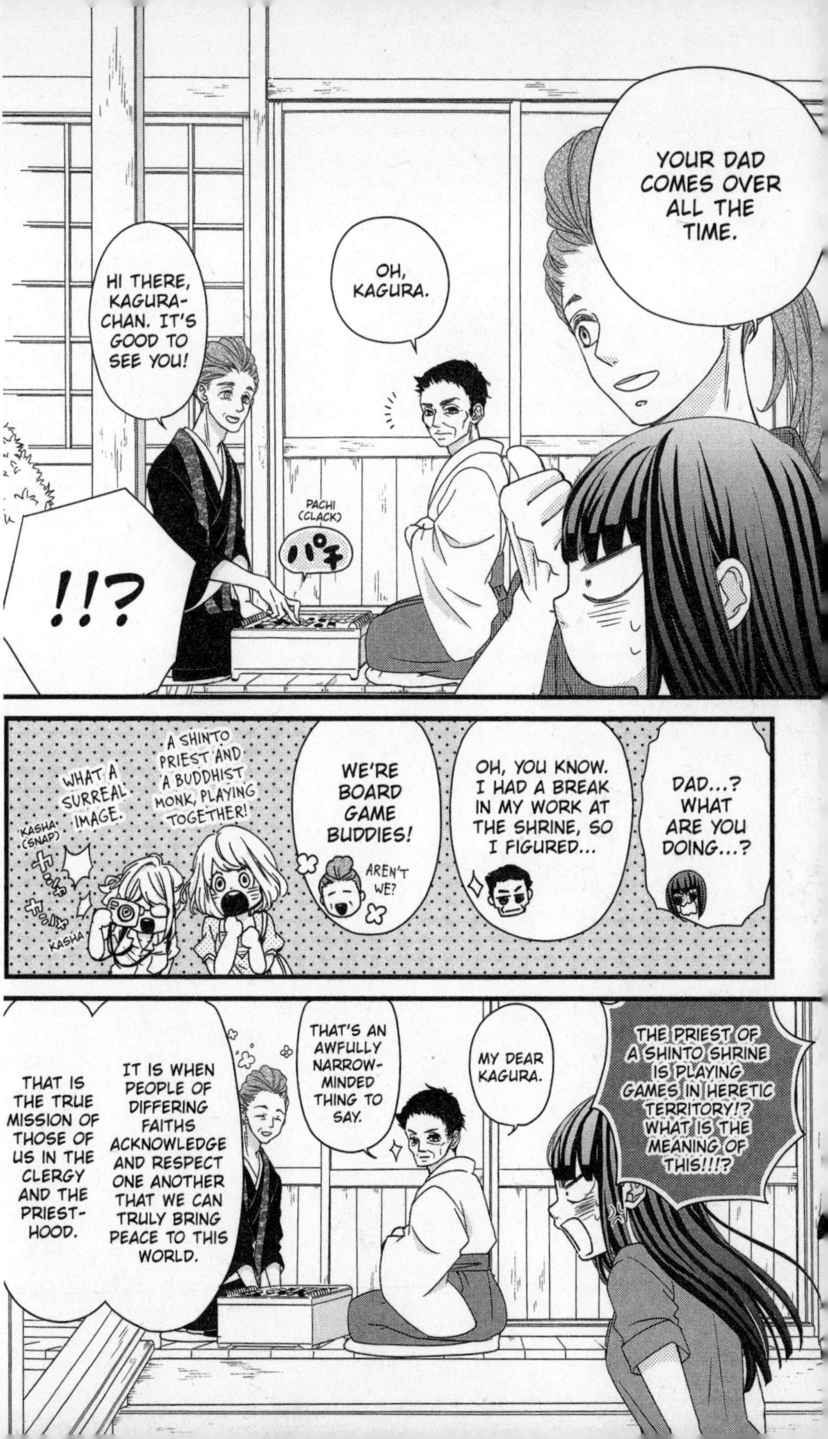
YOUR DAD COMES OVER ALL THE TIME.
OH, KAGURA.
HI THERE, KAGURA-CHAN. IT'S GOOD TO SEE YOU!
PACHI (CLACK)
パチ
!!?
DAD...? WHAT ARE YOU DOING...?
OH, YOU KNOW. I HAD A BREAK IN MY WORK AT THE SHRINE, SO I FIGURED...
WE'RE BOARD GAME BUDDIES!
AREN'T WE?
A SHINTO PRIEST AND A BUDDHIST MONK, PLAYING TOGETHER!
WHAT A SURREAL IMAGE.
KASHA (SNAP)
KASHA
THE PRIEST OF A SHINTO SHRINE IS PLAYING GAMES IN HERETIC TERRITORY!? WHAT IS THE MEANING OF THIS!!!?
MY DEAR KAGURA.
THAT'S AN AWFULLY NARROW-MINDED THING TO SAY.
IT IS WHEN PEOPLE OF DIFFERING FAITHS ACKNOWLEDGE AND RESPECT ONE ANOTHER THAT WE CAN TRULY BRING PEACE TO THIS WORLD.
THAT IS THE TRUE MISSION OF THOSE OF US IN THE CLERGY AND THE PRIESTHOOD.

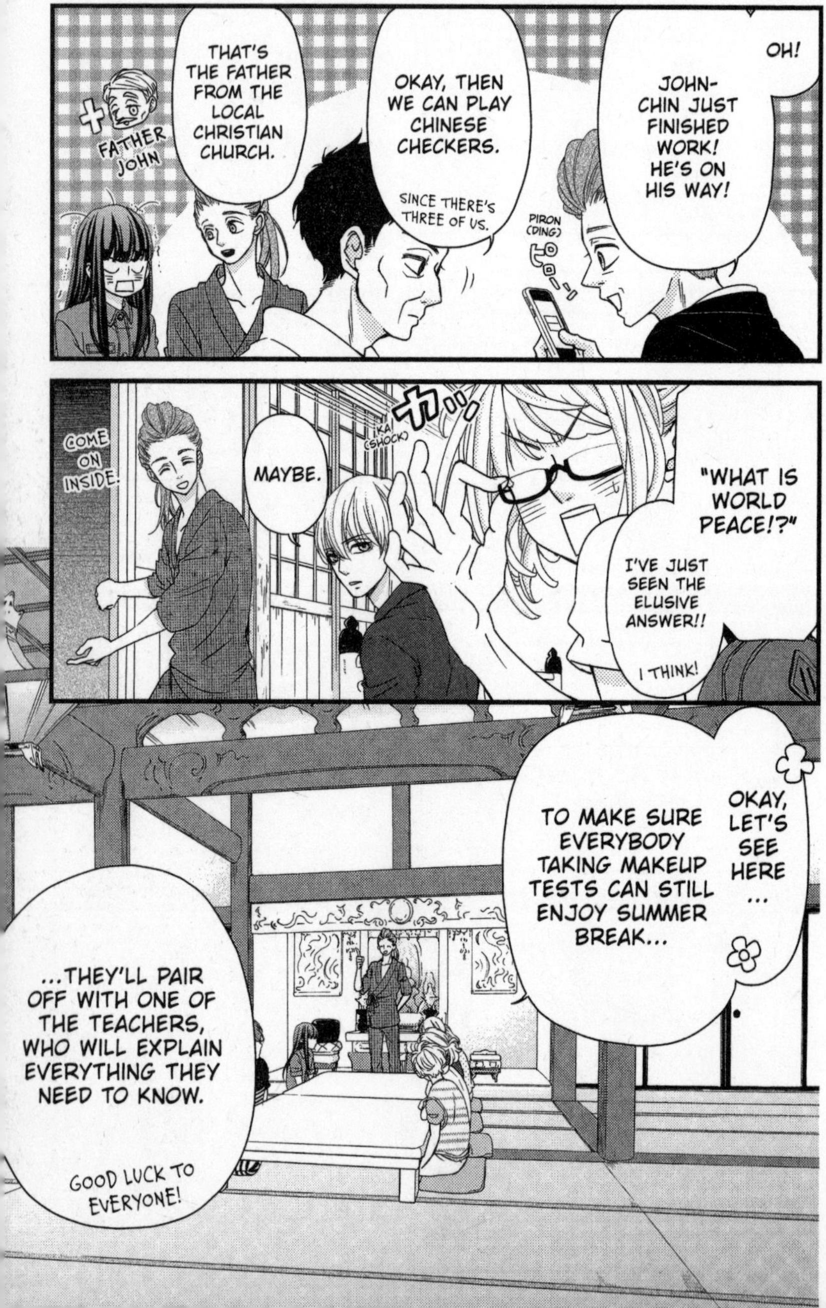
OH!
JOHN-CHIN JUST FINISHED WORK! HE'S ON HIS WAY!
PIRON (DING)
OKAY, THEN WE CAN PLAY CHINESE CHECKERS.
SINCE THERE'S THREE OF US.
THAT'S THE FATHER FROM THE LOCAL CHRISTIAN CHURCH.
FATHER JOHN
"WHAT IS WORLD PEACE!?"
I'VE JUST SEEN THE ELUSIVE ANSWER!!
I THINK!
KA! (SHOCK)
MAYBE.
COME ON INSIDE.
OKAY, LET'S SEE HERE ...
TO MAKE SURE EVERYBODY TAKING MAKEUP TESTS CAN STILL ENJOY SUMMER BREAK...
...THEY'LL PAIR OFF WITH ONE OF THE TEACHERS, WHO WILL EXPLAIN EVERYTHING THEY NEED TO KNOW.
GOOD LUCK TO EVERYONE!

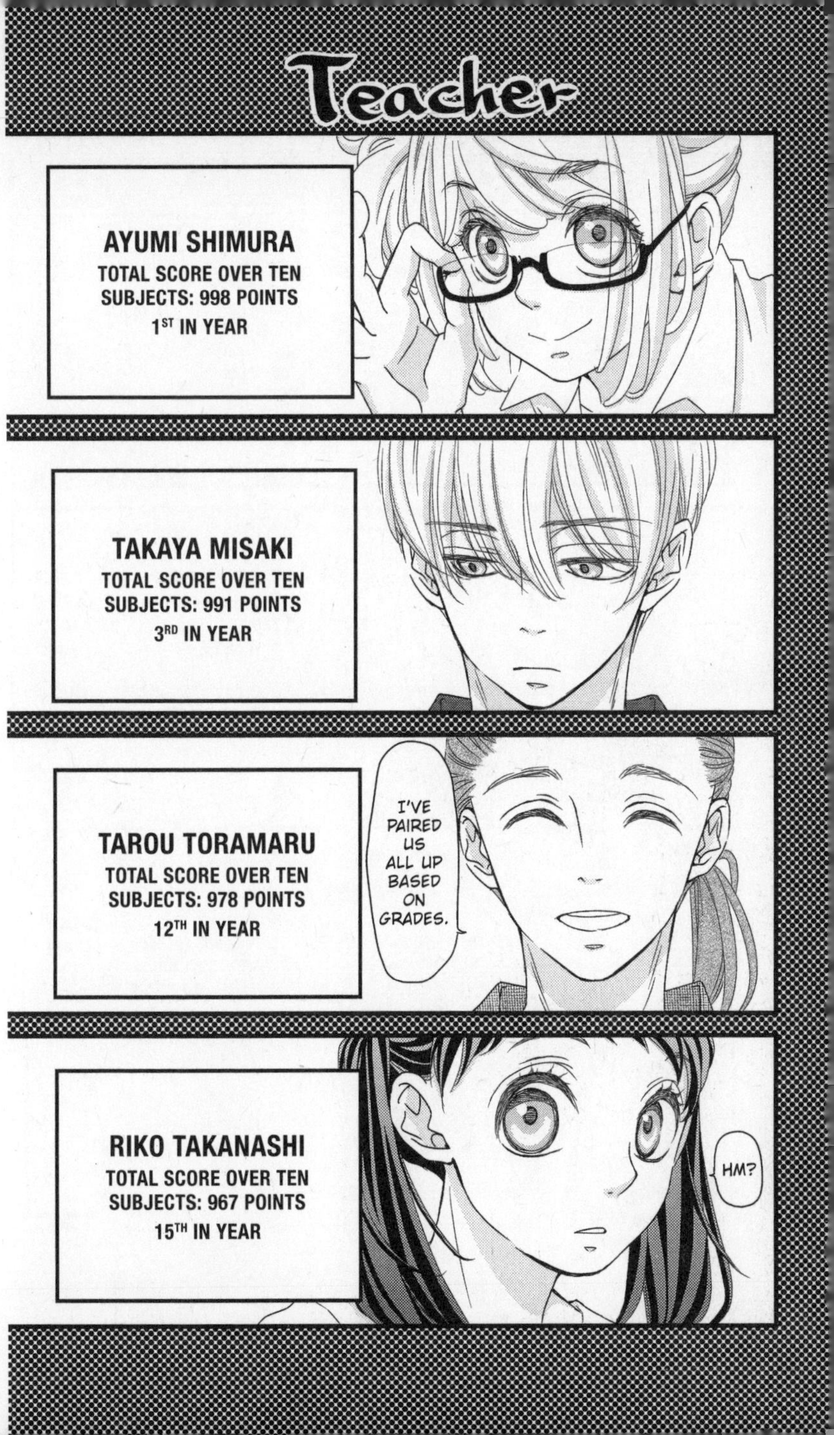
Teacher
AYUMI SHIMURA
TOTAL SCORE OVER TEN SUBJECTS: 998 POINTS
1ST IN YEAR
TAKAYA MISAKI
TOTAL SCORE OVER TEN SUBJECTS: 991 POINTS
3RD IN YEAR
I'VE PAIRED US ALL UP BASED ON GRADES.
TAROU TORAMARU
TOTAL SCORE OVER TEN SUBJECTS: 978 POINTS
12TH IN YEAR
HM?
RIKO TAKANASHI
TOTAL SCORE OVER TEN SUBJECTS: 967 POINTS
15TH IN YEAR

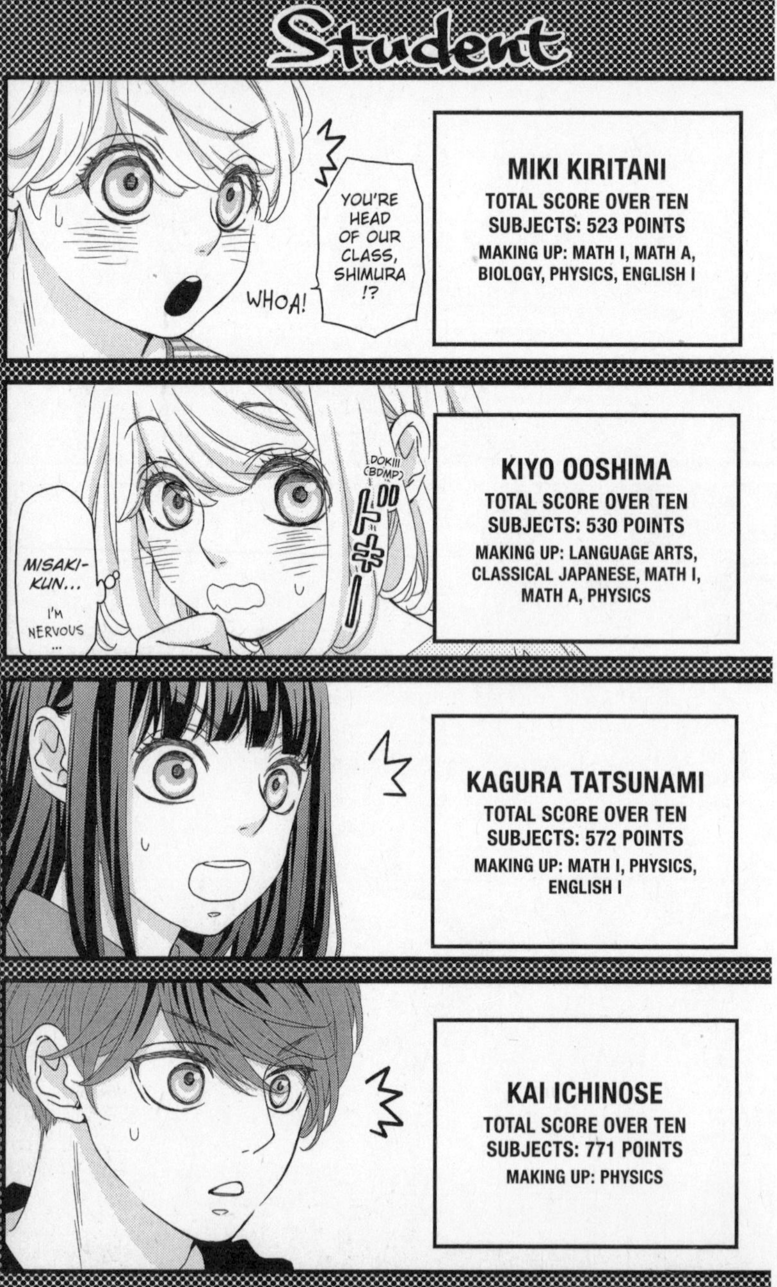
Student
MIKI KIRITANI
TOTAL SCORE OVER TEN SUBJECTS: 523 POINTS
MAKING UP: MATH I, MATH A, BIOLOGY, PHYSICS, ENGLISH I
YOU'RE HEAD OF OUR CLASS, SHIMURA !?
WHOA!
KIYO OOSHIMA
TOTAL SCORE OVER TEN SUBJECTS: 530 POINTS
MAKING UP: LANGUAGE ARTS, CLASSICAL JAPANESE, MATH I, MATH A, PHYSICS
DOKIII (BDMP)
MISAKI-KUN...
I'M NERVOUS ...
KAGURA TATSUNAMI
TOTAL SCORE OVER TEN SUBJECTS: 572 POINTS
MAKING UP: MATH I, PHYSICS, ENGLISH I
KAI ICHINOSE
TOTAL SCORE OVER TEN SUBJECTS: 771 POINTS
MAKING UP: PHYSICS

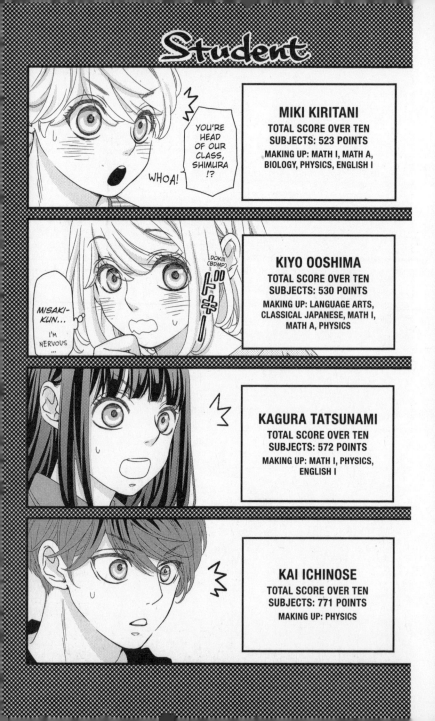

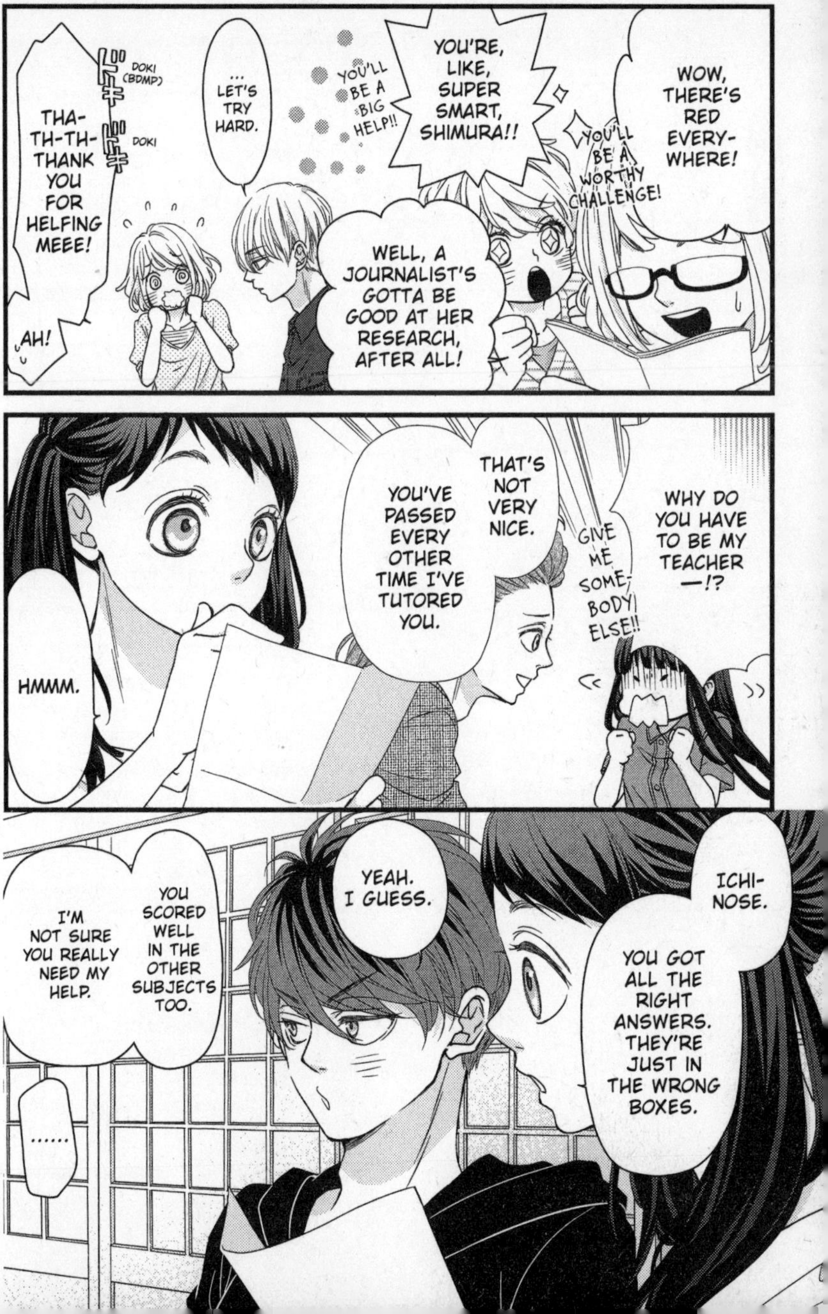
WOW, THERE'S RED EVERY-WHERE!
YOU'LL BE A WORTHY CHALLENGE!
YOU'RE, LIKE, SUPER SMART, SHIMURA!!
WELL, A JOURNALIST'S GOTTA BE GOOD AT HER RESEARCH, AFTER ALL!
YOU'LL BE A BIG HELP!!
... LET'S TRY HARD.
DOKI (BDMP)
DOKI
THA-TH-TH-THANK YOU FOR HELFING MEEE!
AH!
WHY DO YOU HAVE TO BE MY TEACHER—!?
GIVE ME SOMEBODY ELSE!!
THAT'S NOT VERY NICE.
YOU'VE PASSED EVERY OTHER TIME I'VE TUTORED YOU.
HMMM.
ICHI-NOSE.
YOU GOT ALL THE RIGHT ANSWERS. THEY'RE JUST IN THE WRONG BOXES.
YEAH. I GUESS.
YOU SCORED WELL IN THE OTHER SUBJECTS TOO.
I'M NOT SURE YOU REALLY NEED MY HELP.
......

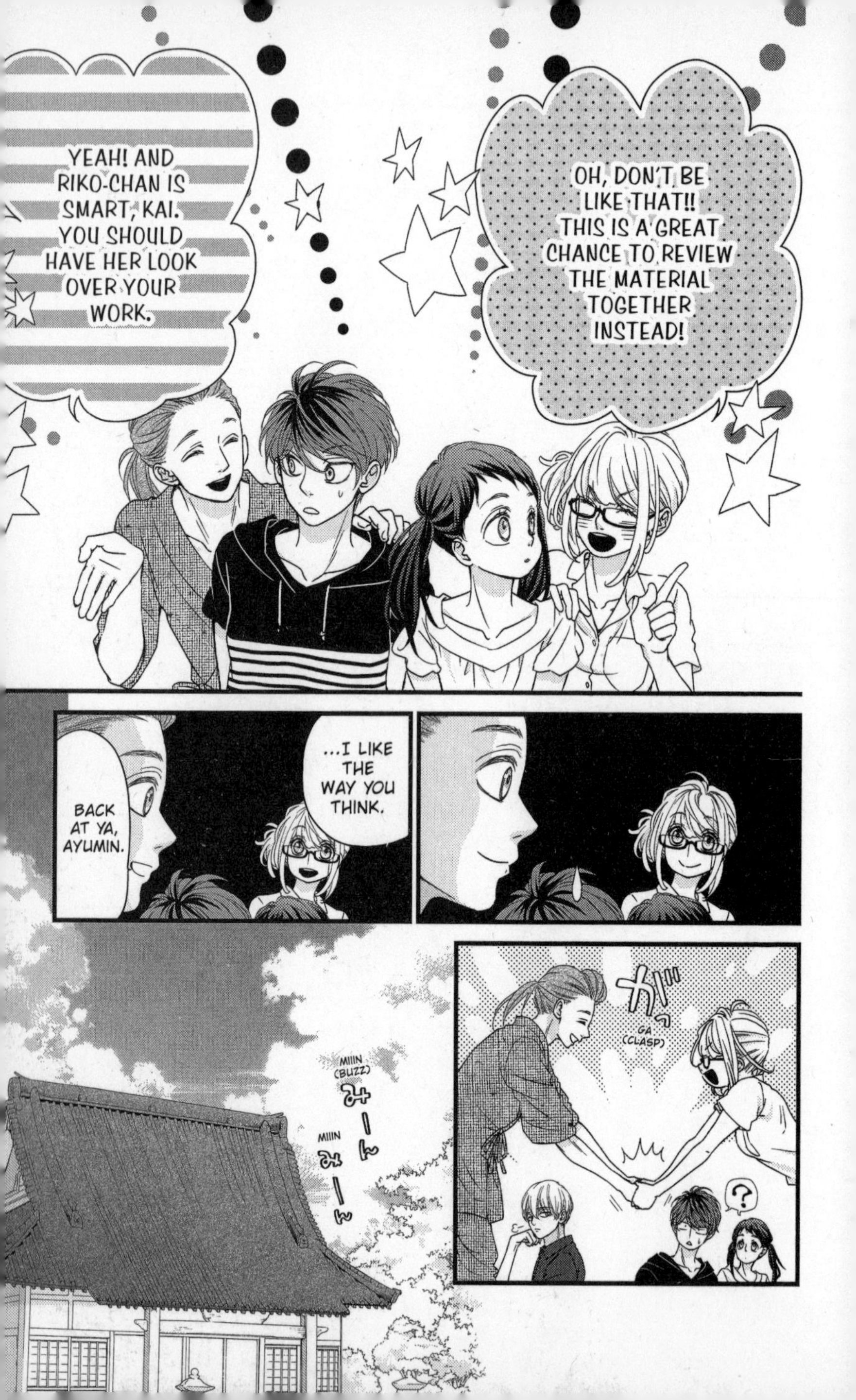
OH, DON'T BE LIKE THAT!! THIS IS A GREAT CHANCE TO REVIEW THE MATERIAL TOGETHER INSTEAD!
YEAH! AND RIKO-CHAN IS SMART, KAI. YOU SHOULD HAVE HER LOOK OVER YOUR WORK.
...I LIKE THE WAY YOU THINK.
BACK AT YA, AYUMIN.
ガッ
GA (CLASP)
?
みーん
MIIIN (BUZZ)
みーん
MIIIN

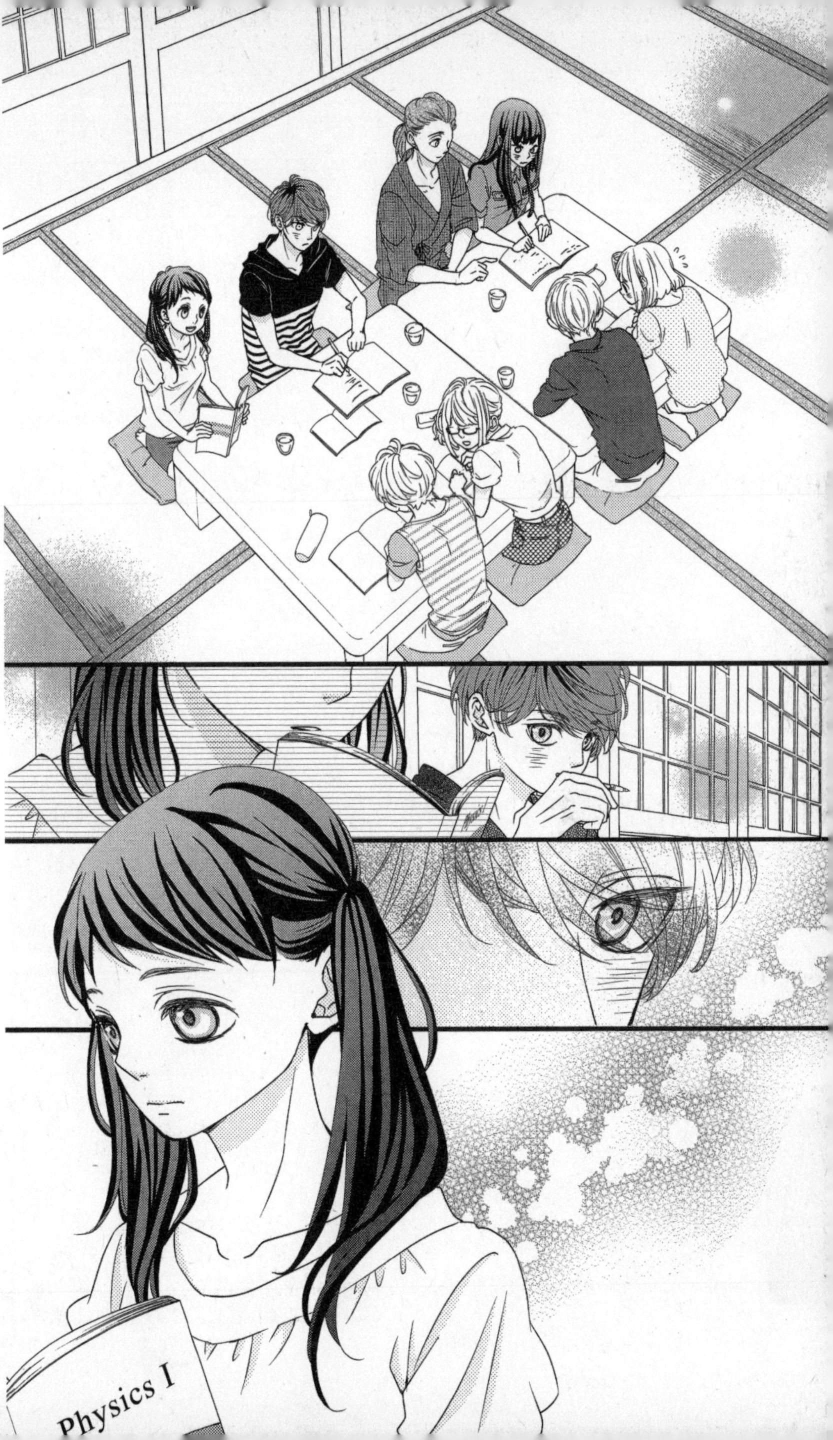
Physics I

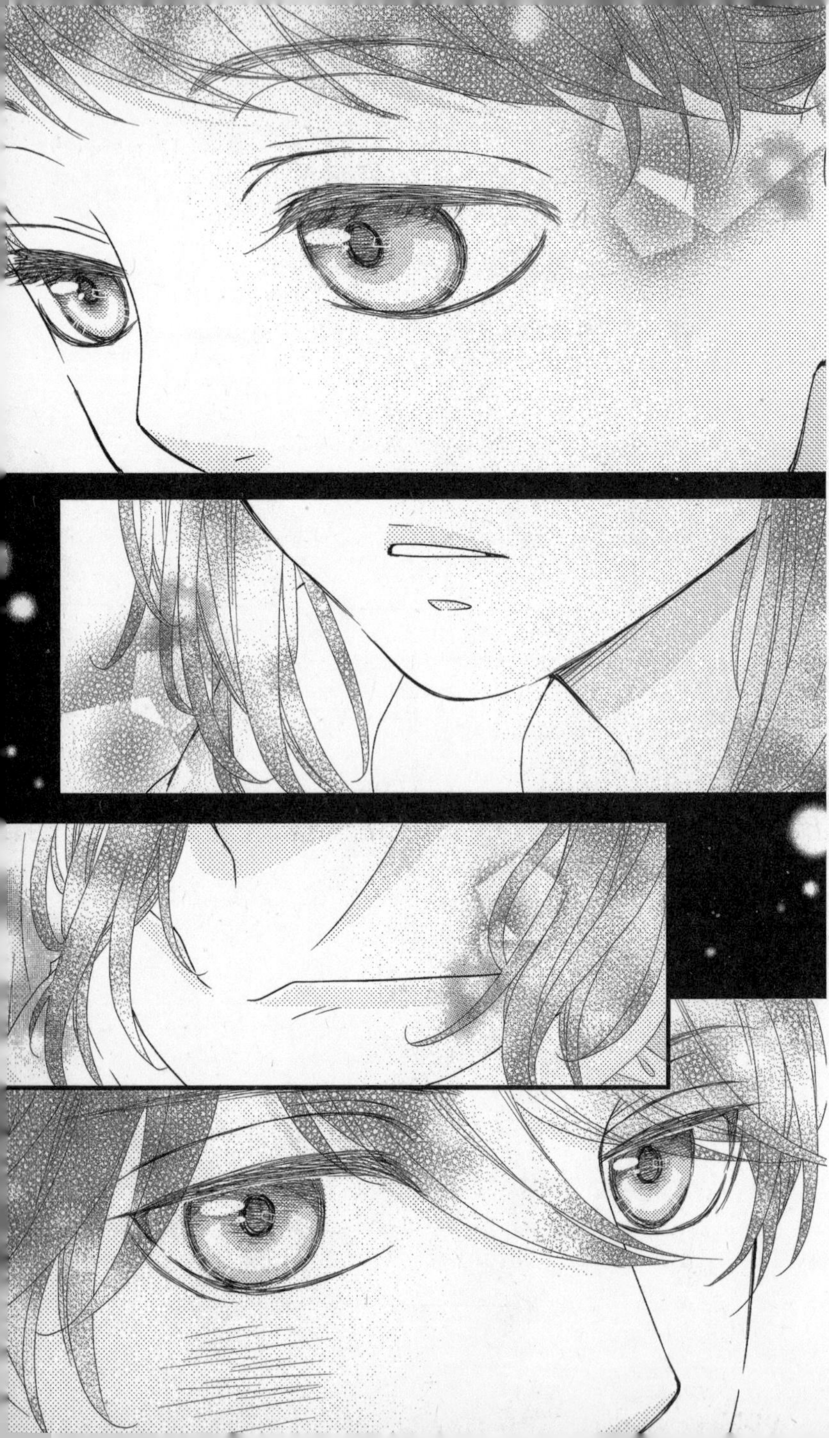

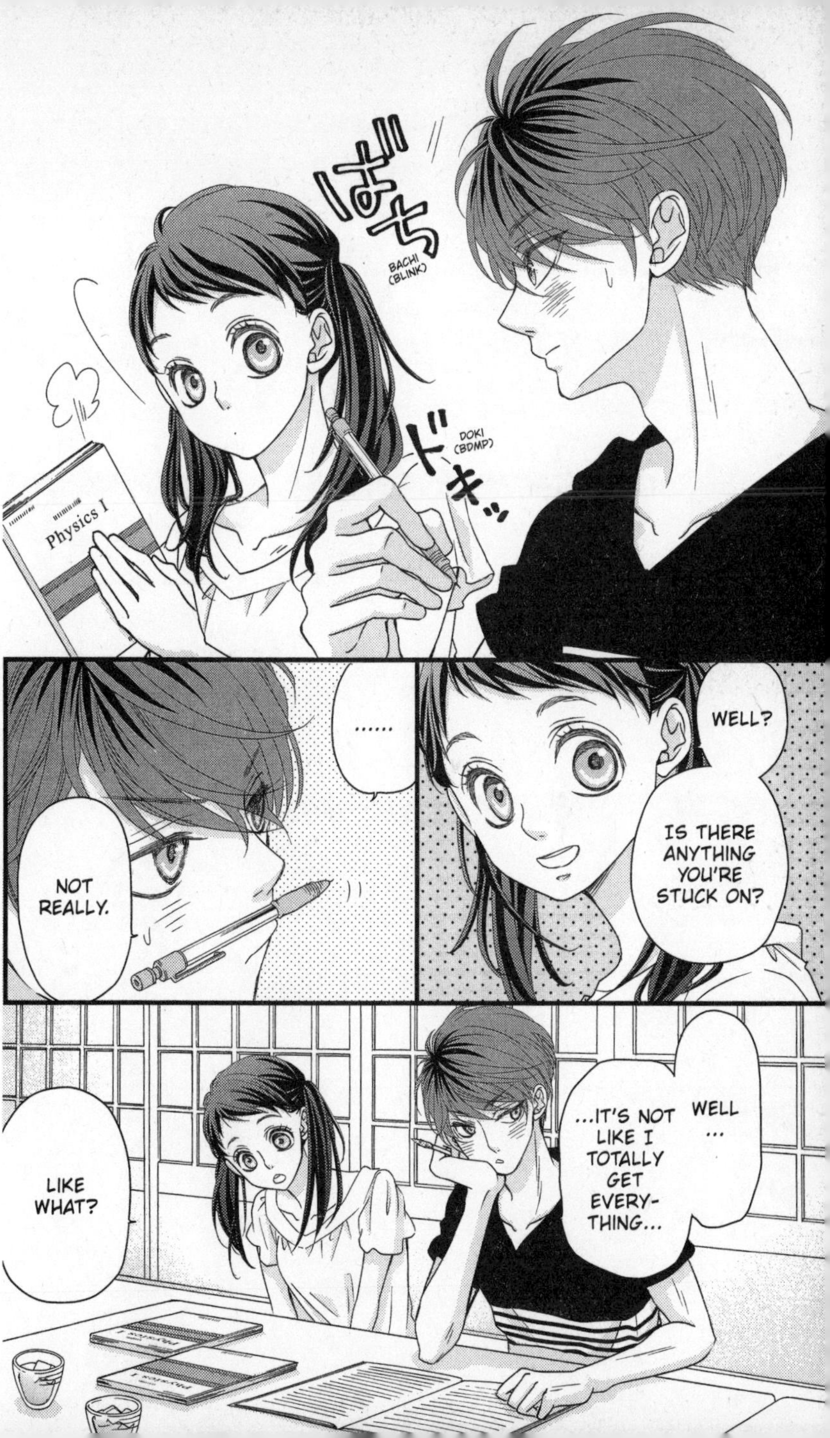
ばち
BACHI (BLINK)
ドキッ
DOKI (BDMP)
Physics I
WELL?
IS THERE ANYTHING YOU'RE STUCK ON?
......
NOT REALLY.
WELL ...
...IT'S NOT LIKE I TOTALLY GET EVERY-THING...
LIKE WHAT?

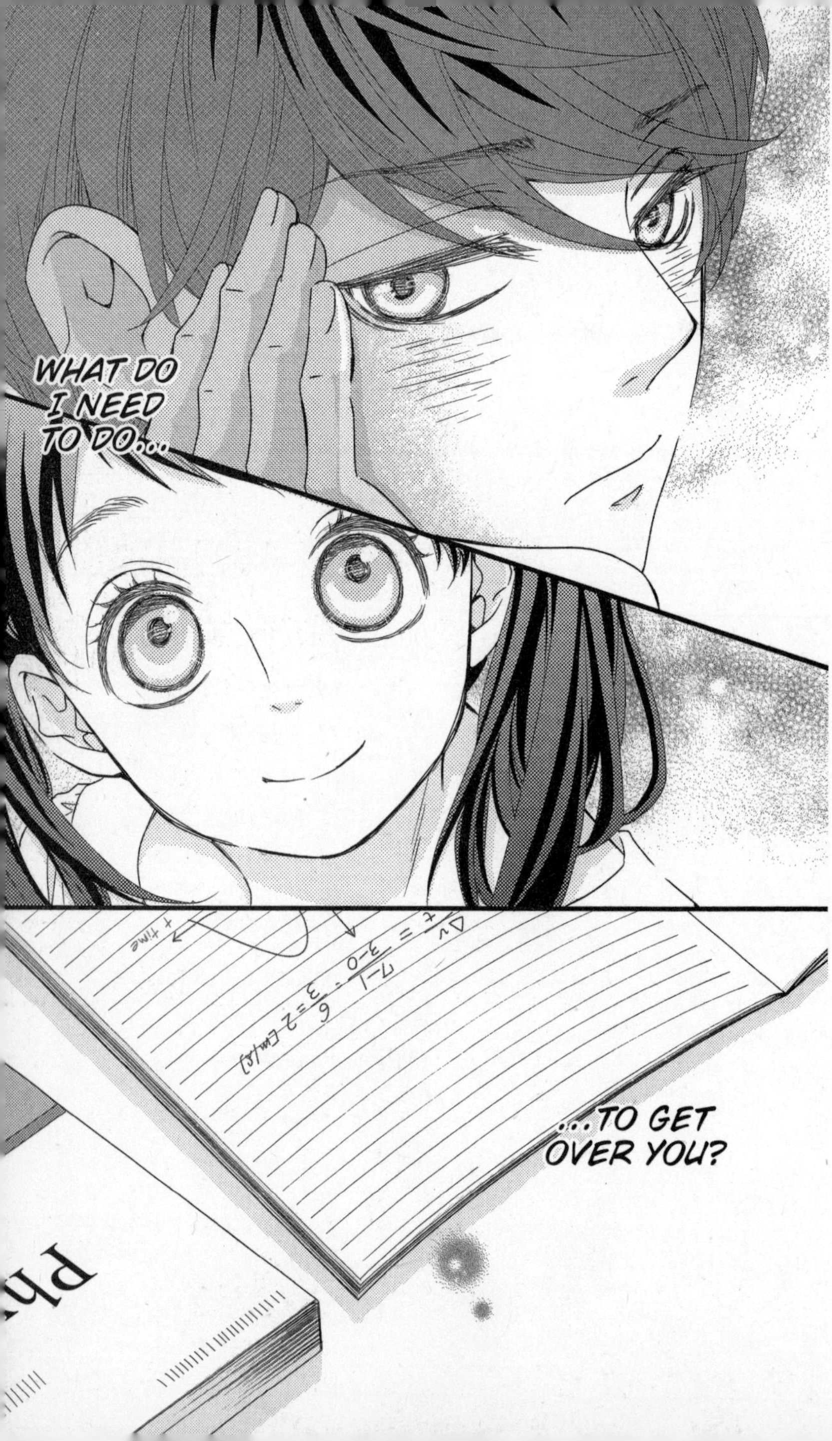
WHAT DO I NEED TO DO...
...TO GET OVER YOU?

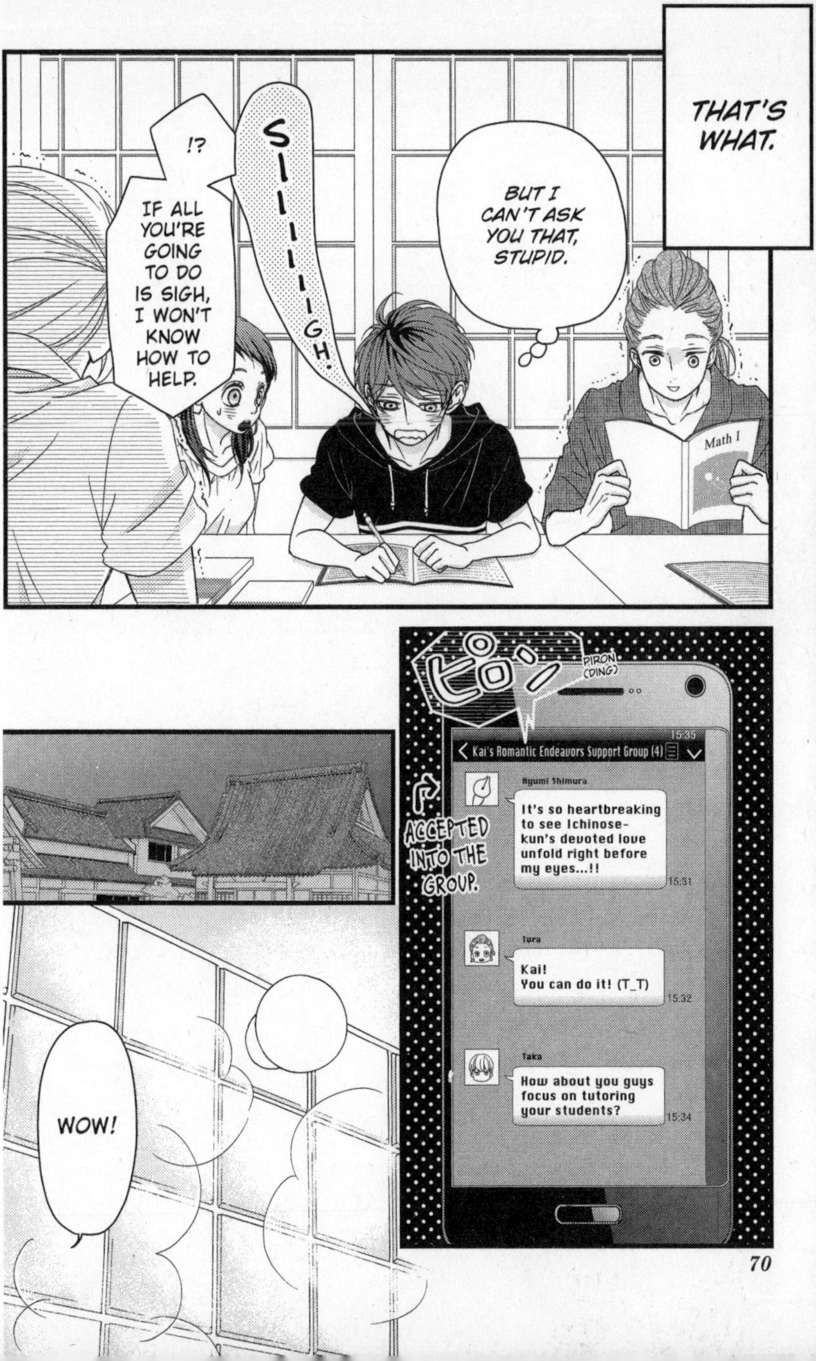
THAT'S WHAT.
BUT I CAN'T ASK YOU THAT, STUPID.
SIIIIGH.
!?
IF ALL YOU'RE GOING TO DO IS SIGH, I WON'T KNOW HOW TO HELP.
PIRON (DING)
15:35
Kai's Romantic Endeavors Support Group (4)
ACCEPTED INTO THE GROUP.
Ayumi Shimura
It's so heartbreaking to see Ichinose-kun's devoted love unfold right before my eyes...!!
15:31
Tora
Kai!
You can do it! (T_T)
15:32
Taka
How about you guys focus on tutoring your students?
15:34
WOW!

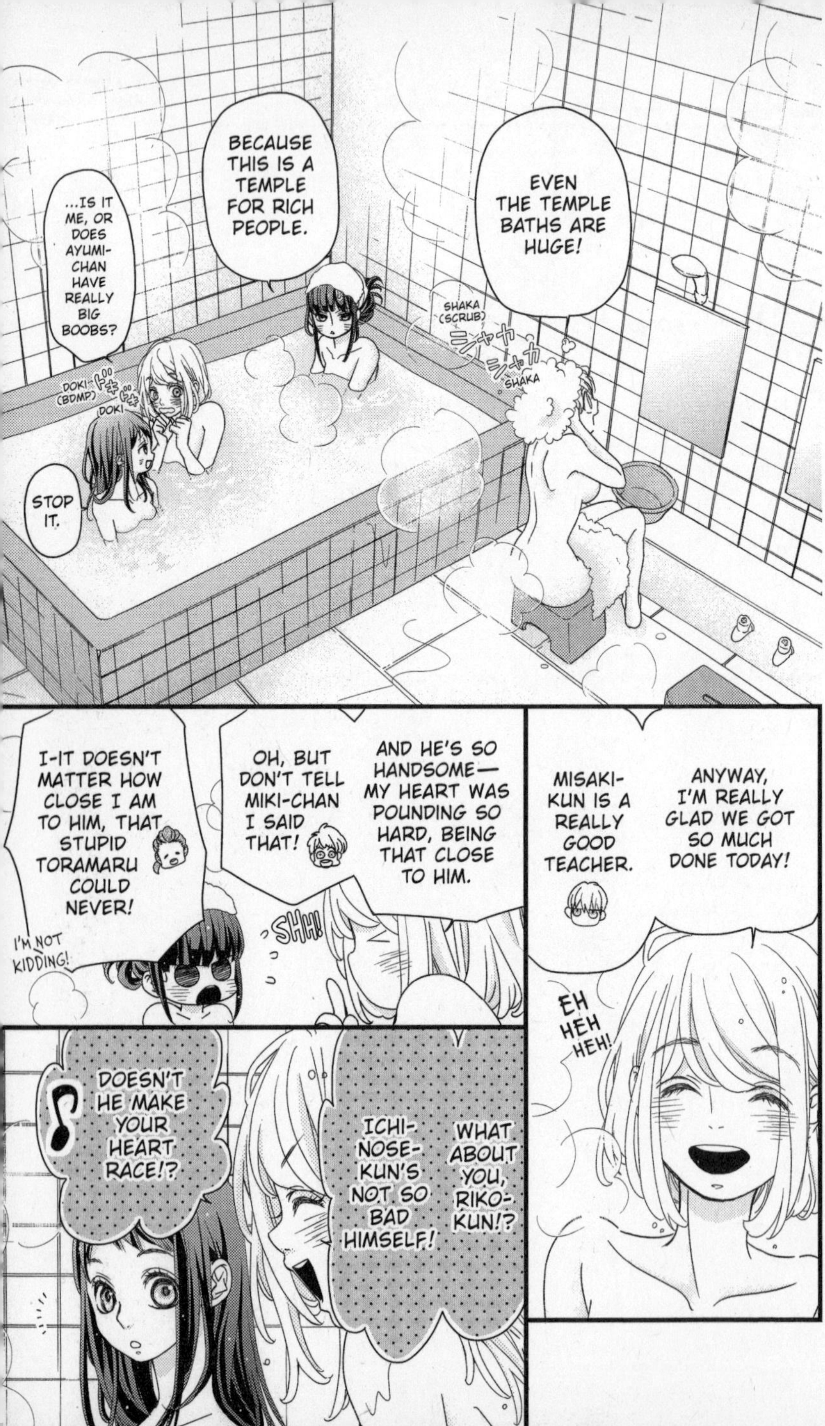
EVEN THE TEMPLE BATHS ARE HUGE!
SHAKA (SCRUB)
SHAKA
BECAUSE THIS IS A TEMPLE FOR RICH PEOPLE.
...IS IT ME, OR DOES AYUMI-CHAN HAVE REALLY BIG BOOBS?
DOKI (BDMP)
DOKI
STOP IT.
ANYWAY, I'M REALLY GLAD WE GOT SO MUCH DONE TODAY!
MISAKI-KUN IS A REALLY GOOD TEACHER.
EH HEH HEH!
AND HE'S SO HANDSOME—MY HEART WAS POUNDING SO HARD, BEING THAT CLOSE TO HIM.
OH, BUT DON'T TELL MIKI-CHAN I SAID THAT!
SHH!
I-IT DOESN'T MATTER HOW CLOSE I AM TO HIM, THAT STUPID TORAMARU COULD NEVER!
I'M NOT KIDDING!
WHAT ABOUT YOU, RIKO-KUN!?
ICHINOSE-KUN'S NOT SO BAD HIMSELF!
DOESN'T HE MAKE YOUR HEART RACE!?

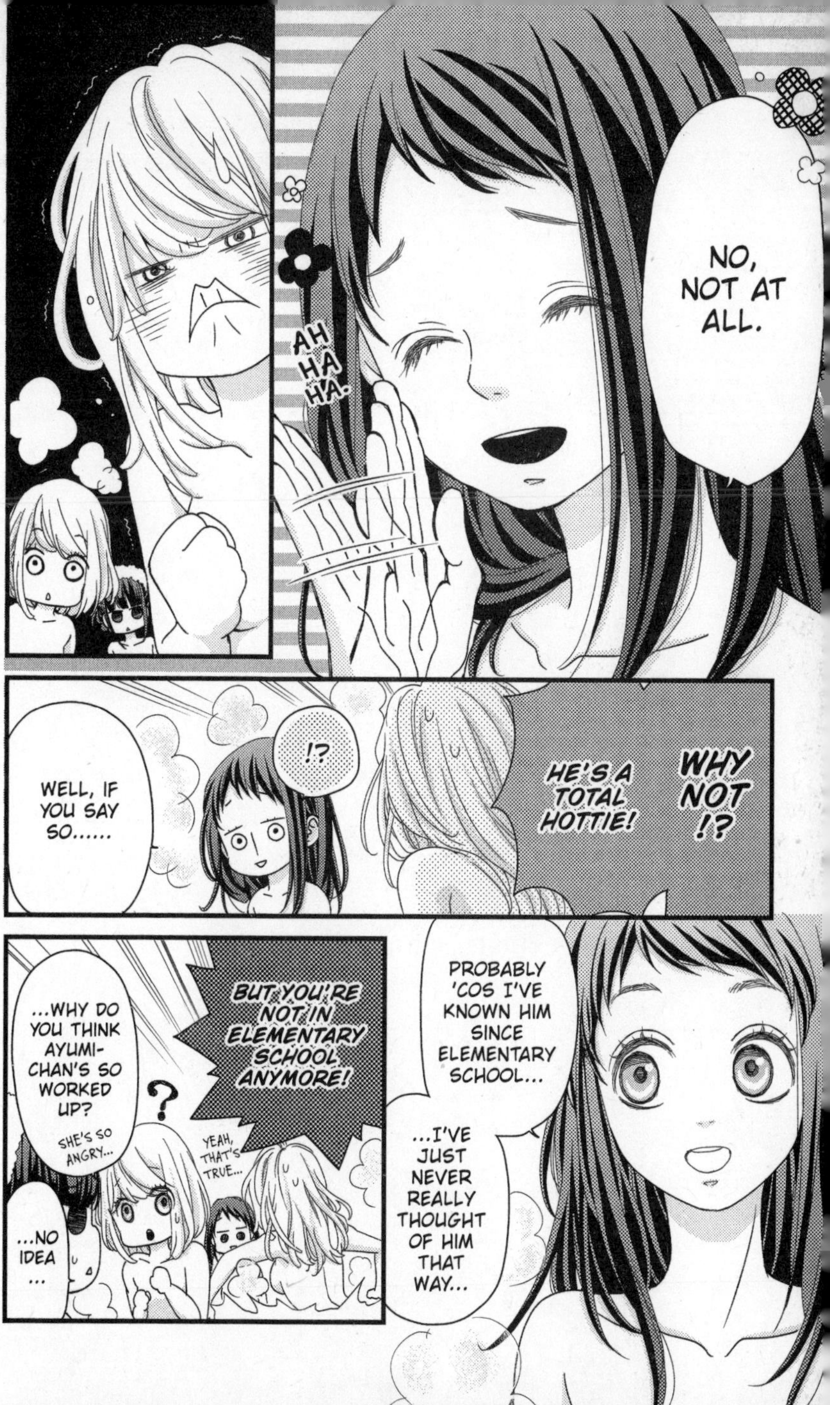
NO, NOT AT ALL.
AH HA HA.
WHY NOT!?
HE'S A TOTAL HOTTIE!
!?
WELL, IF YOU SAY SO......
PROBABLY 'COS I'VE KNOWN HIM SINCE ELEMENTARY SCHOOL...
...I'VE JUST NEVER REALLY THOUGHT OF HIM THAT WAY...
BUT YOU'RE NOT IN ELEMENTARY SCHOOL ANYMORE!
YEAH, THAT'S TRUE...
...WHY DO YOU THINK AYUMI-CHAN'S SO WORKED UP?
SHE'S SO ANGRY...
?
...NO IDEA...

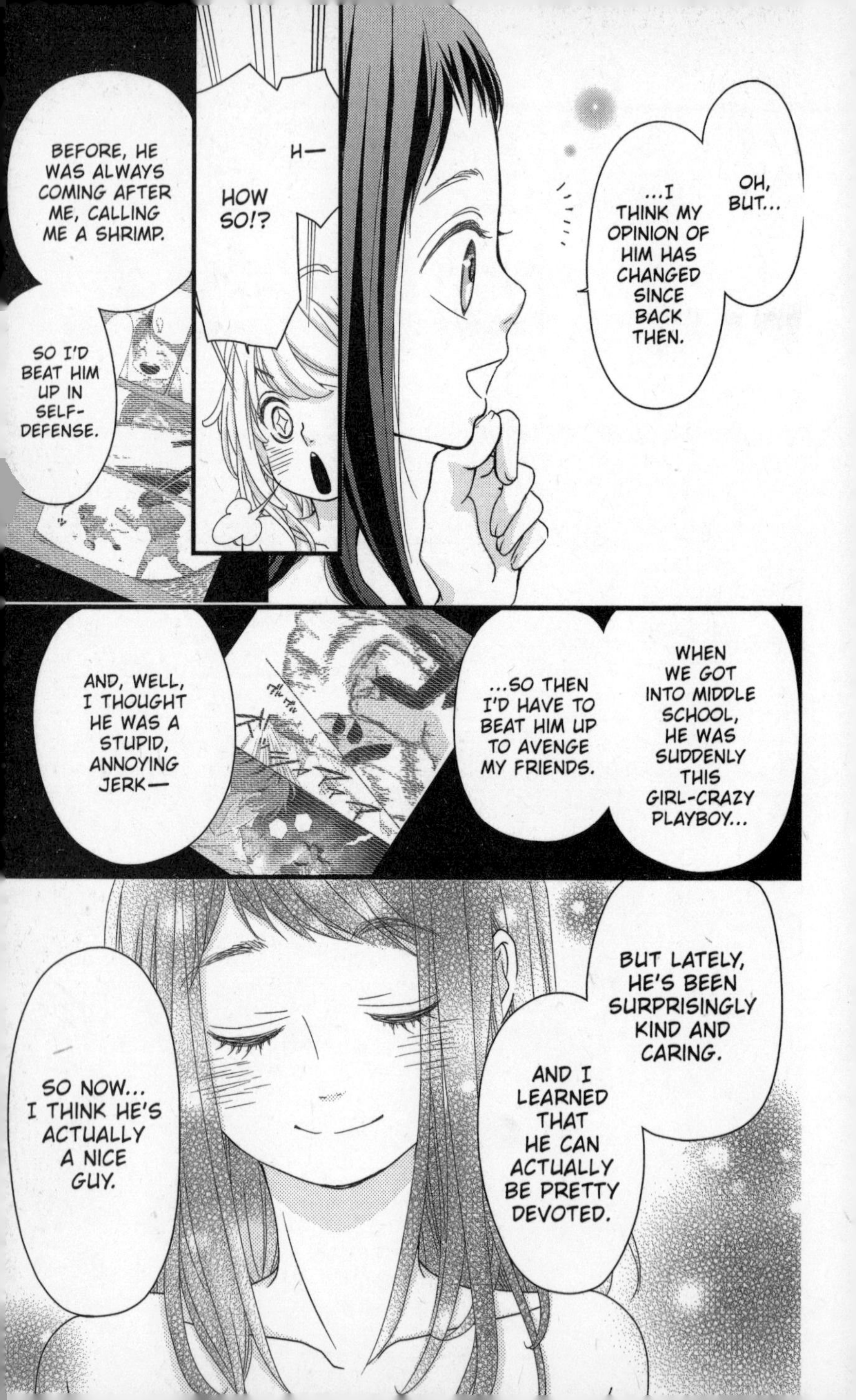
OH, BUT...
...I THINK MY OPINION OF HIM HAS CHANGED SINCE BACK THEN.
H—
HOW SO!?
BEFORE, HE WAS ALWAYS COMING AFTER ME, CALLING ME A SHRIMP.
SO I'D BEAT HIM UP IN SELF-DEFENSE.
WHEN WE GOT INTO MIDDLE SCHOOL, HE WAS SUDDENLY THIS GIRL-CRAZY PLAYBOY...
...SO THEN I'D HAVE TO BEAT HIM UP TO AVENGE MY FRIENDS.
AND, WELL, I THOUGHT HE WAS A STUPID, ANNOYING JERK—
BUT LATELY, HE'S BEEN SURPRISINGLY KIND AND CARING.
AND I LEARNED THAT HE CAN ACTUALLY BE PRETTY DEVOTED.
SO NOW... I THINK HE'S ACTUALLY A NICE GUY.

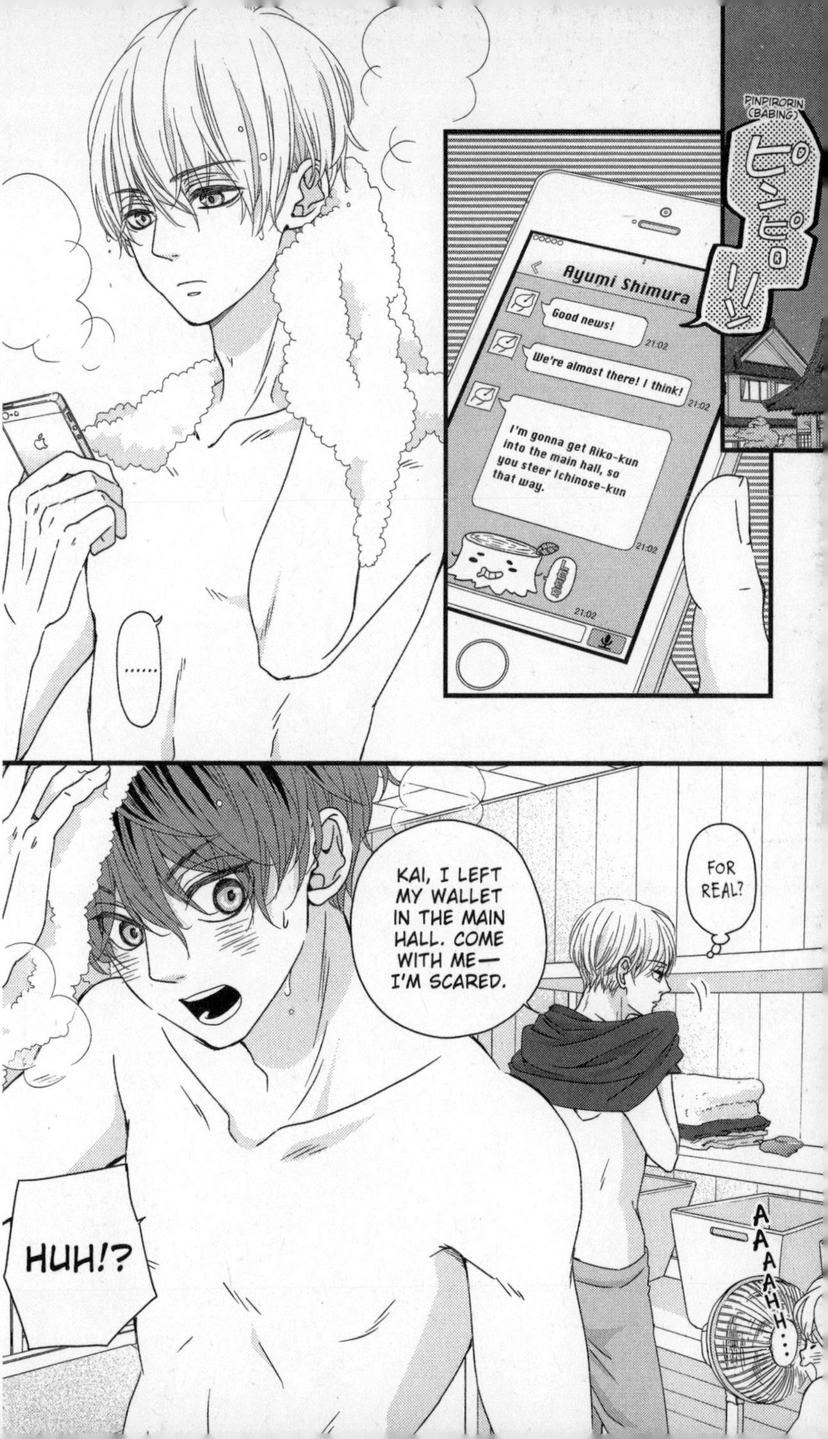
PINPIRORIN (BABING)
Ayumi Shimura
Good news!
21:02
We're almost there! I think!
21:02
I'm gonna get Riko-kun into the main hall, so you steer Ichinose-kun that way.
21:02
21:02
......
FOR REAL?
KAI, I LEFT MY WALLET IN THE MAIN HALL. COME WITH ME— I'M SCARED.
HUH!?
AAAAHH...

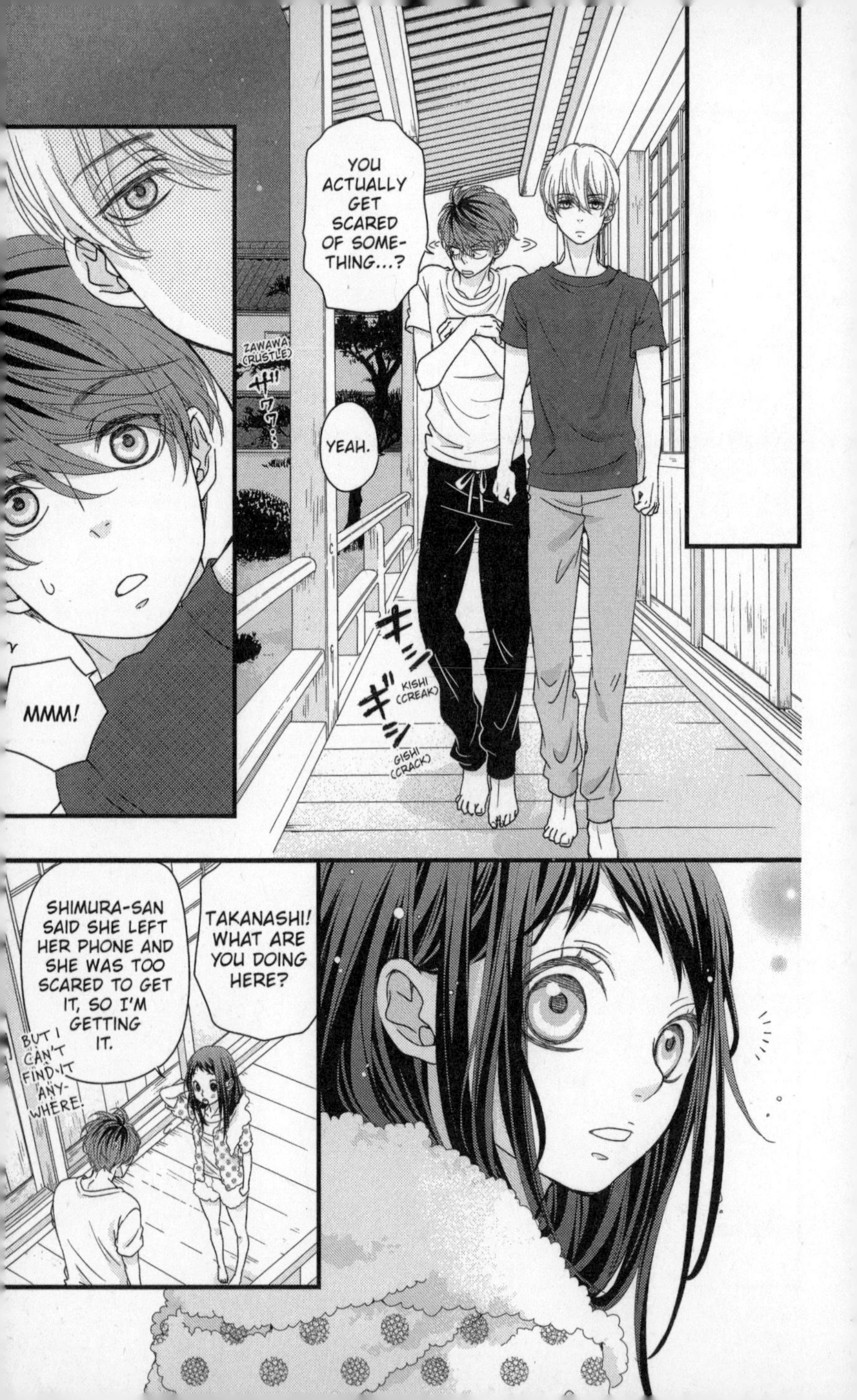

YOU ACTUALLY GET SCARED OF SOME-THING...?
ZAWAWA (RUSTLE)
YEAH.
KISHI (CREAK)
GISHI (CRACK)
MMM!
TAKANASHI! WHAT ARE YOU DOING HERE?
SHIMURA-SAN SAID SHE LEFT HER PHONE AND SHE WAS TOO SCARED TO GET IT, SO I'M GETTING IT.
BUT I CAN'T FIND IT ANY-WHERE.

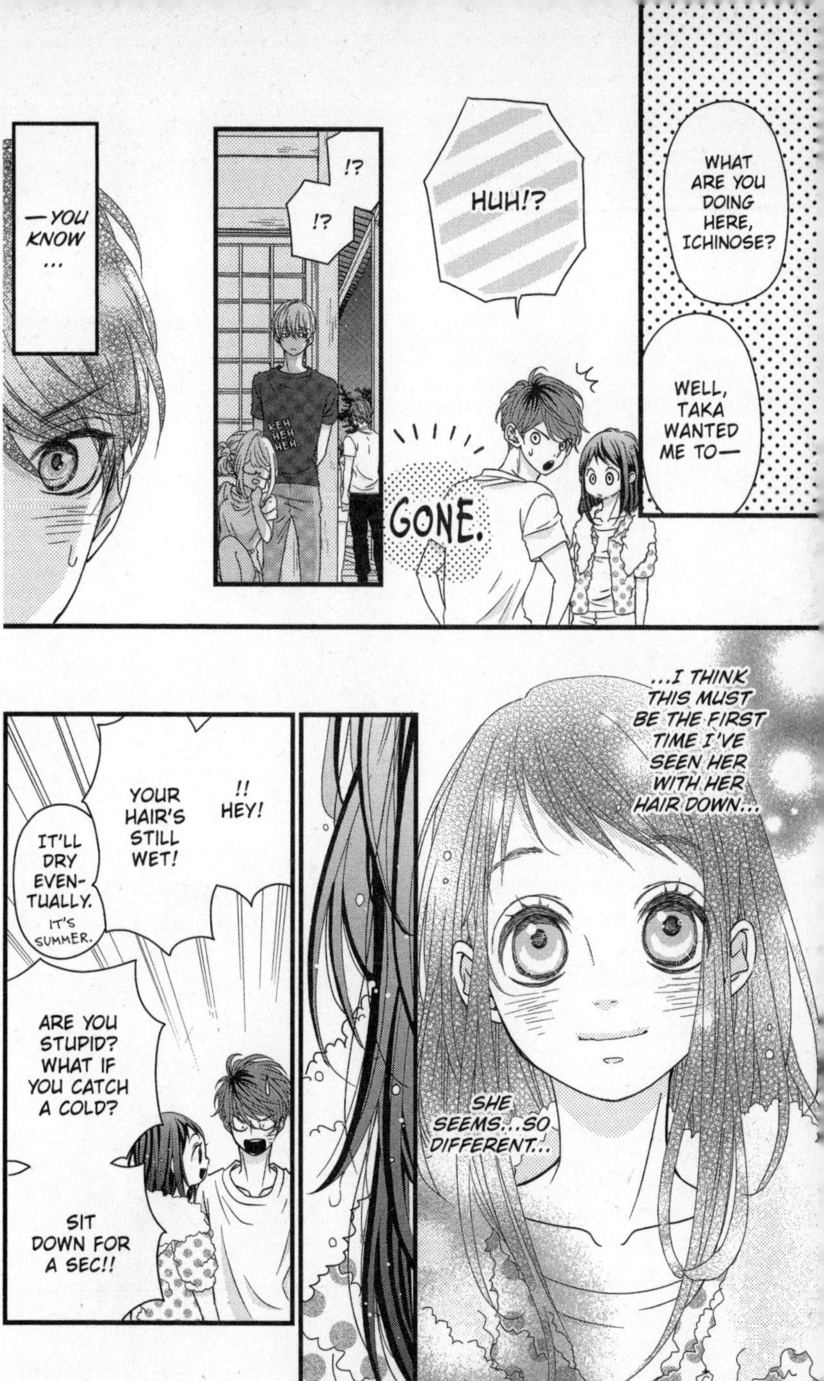
WHAT ARE YOU DOING HERE, ICHINOSE?
WELL, TAKA WANTED ME TO—
HUH!?
GONE.
!?
!?
KEH HEH HEH.
—YOU KNOW...
...I THINK THIS MUST BE THE FIRST TIME I'VE SEEN HER WITH HER HAIR DOWN...
SHE SEEMS...SO DIFFERENT...
!! HEY!
YOUR HAIR'S STILL WET!
IT'LL DRY EVENTUALLY.
IT'S SUMMER.
ARE YOU STUPID? WHAT IF YOU CATCH A COLD?
SIT DOWN FOR A SEC!!

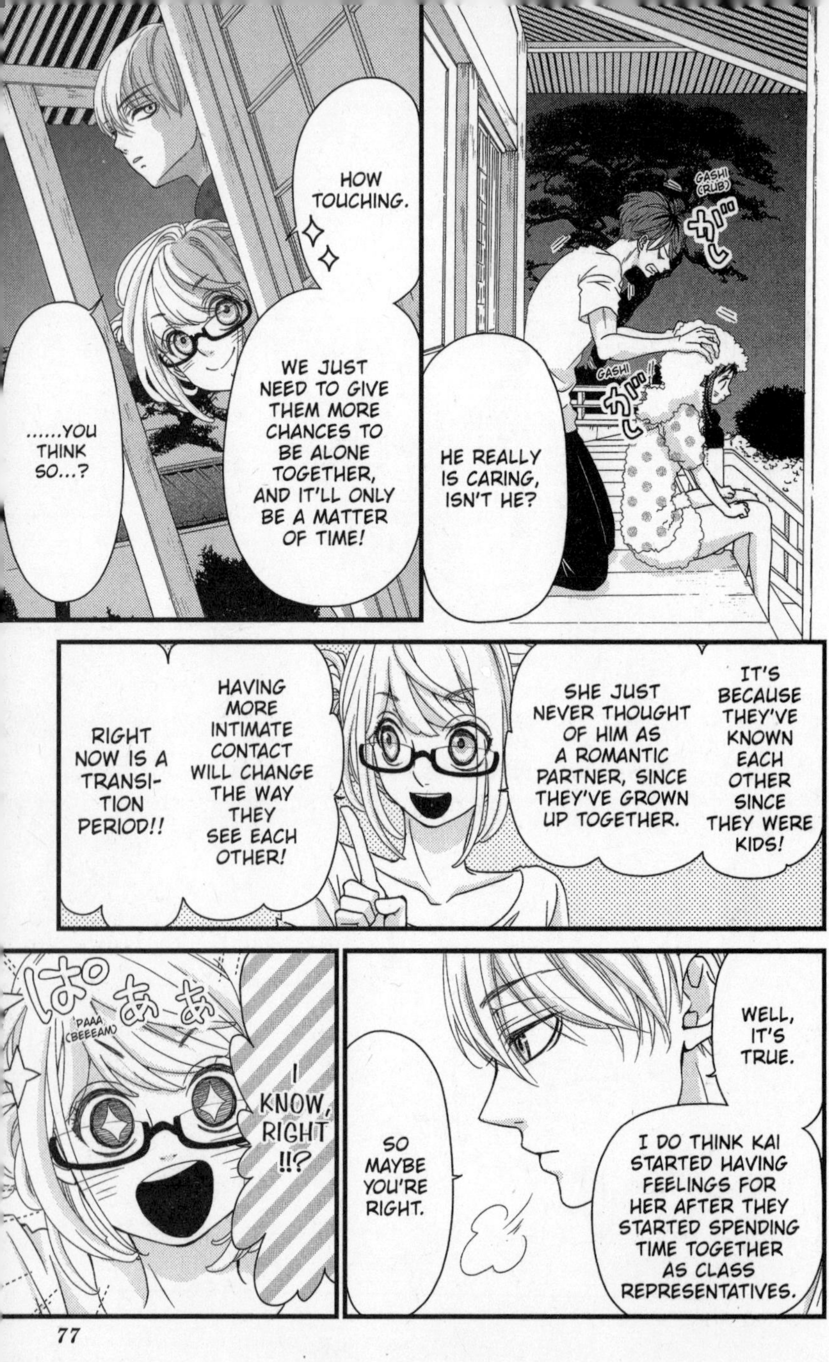
GASHI (RUB)
GASHI
HE REALLY IS CARING, ISN'T HE?
HOW TOUCHING.
WE JUST NEED TO GIVE THEM MORE CHANCES TO BE ALONE TOGETHER, AND IT'LL ONLY BE A MATTER OF TIME!
......YOU THINK SO...?
IT'S BECAUSE THEY'VE KNOWN EACH OTHER SINCE THEY WERE KIDS!
SHE JUST NEVER THOUGHT OF HIM AS A ROMANTIC PARTNER, SINCE THEY'VE GROWN UP TOGETHER.
HAVING MORE INTIMATE CONTACT WILL CHANGE THE WAY THEY SEE EACH OTHER!
RIGHT NOW IS A TRANSI-TION PERIOD!!
WELL, IT'S TRUE.
I DO THINK KAI STARTED HAVING FEELINGS FOR HER AFTER THEY STARTED SPENDING TIME TOGETHER AS CLASS REPRESENTATIVES.
SO MAYBE YOU'RE RIGHT.
PAAA (BEEEAM)
I KNOW, RIGHT!!?

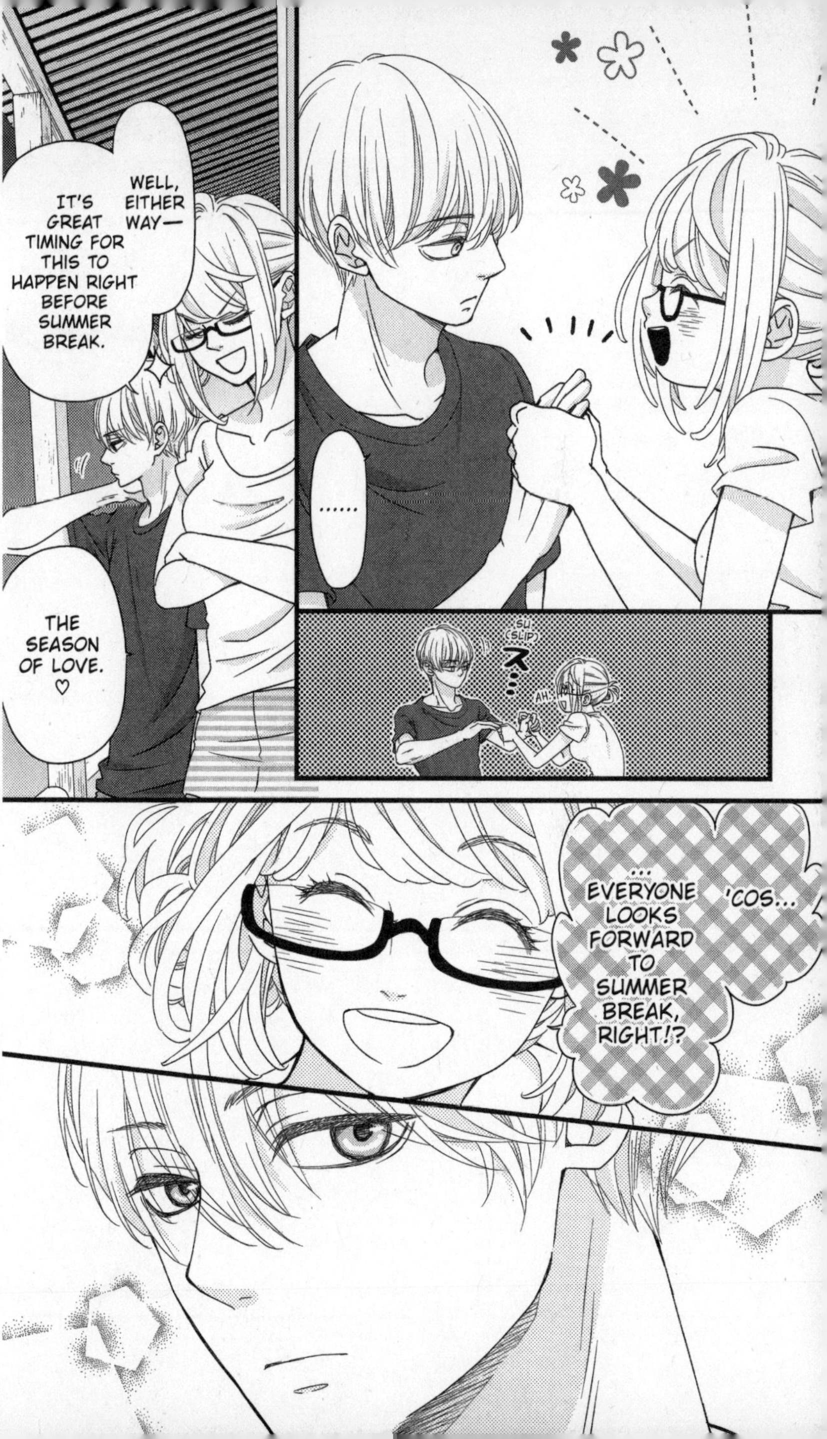
......
SU (SLIP)
ス...
AH.
WELL, EITHER WAY— IT'S GREAT TIMING FOR THIS TO HAPPEN RIGHT BEFORE SUMMER BREAK.
THE SEASON OF LOVE. ♡
'COS...
...EVERYONE LOOKS FORWARD TO SUMMER BREAK, RIGHT!?

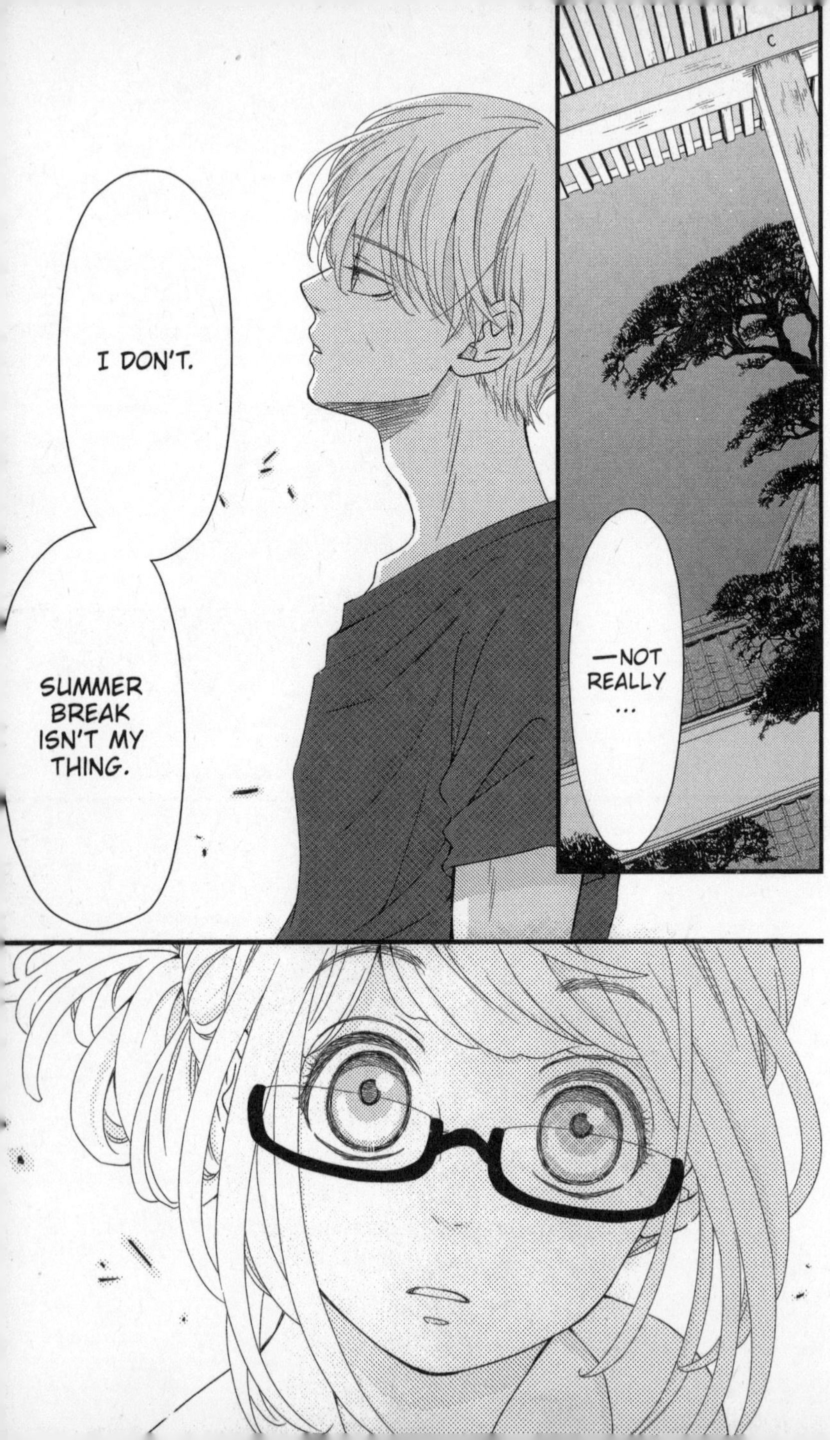
—NOT REALLY ...
I DON'T.
SUMMER BREAK ISN'T MY THING.

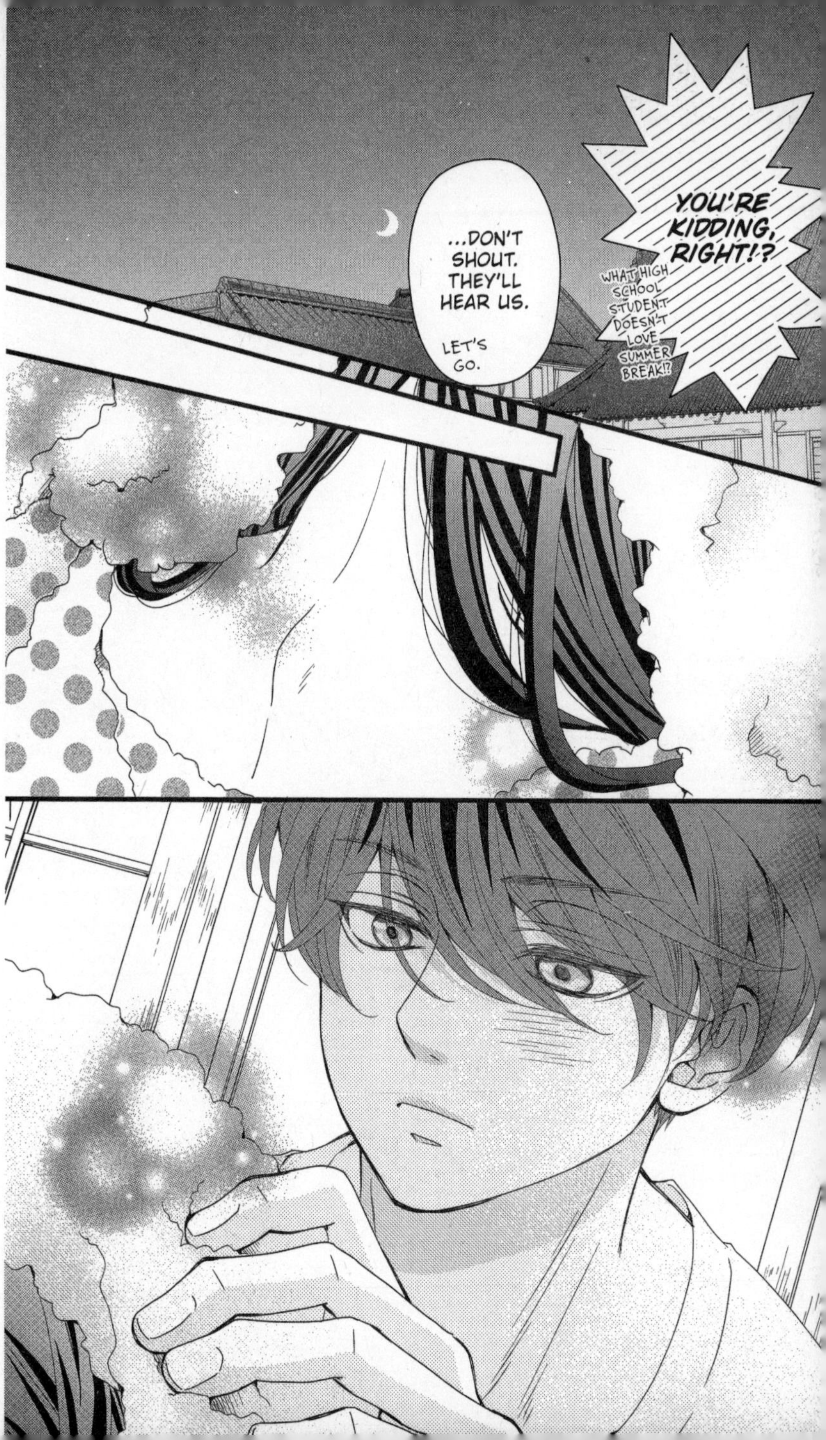
YOU'RE KIDDING, RIGHT!?
WHAT HIGH SCHOOL STUDENT DOESN'T LOVE SUMMER BREAK!?
...DON'T SHOUT. THEY'LL HEAR US.
LET'S GO.

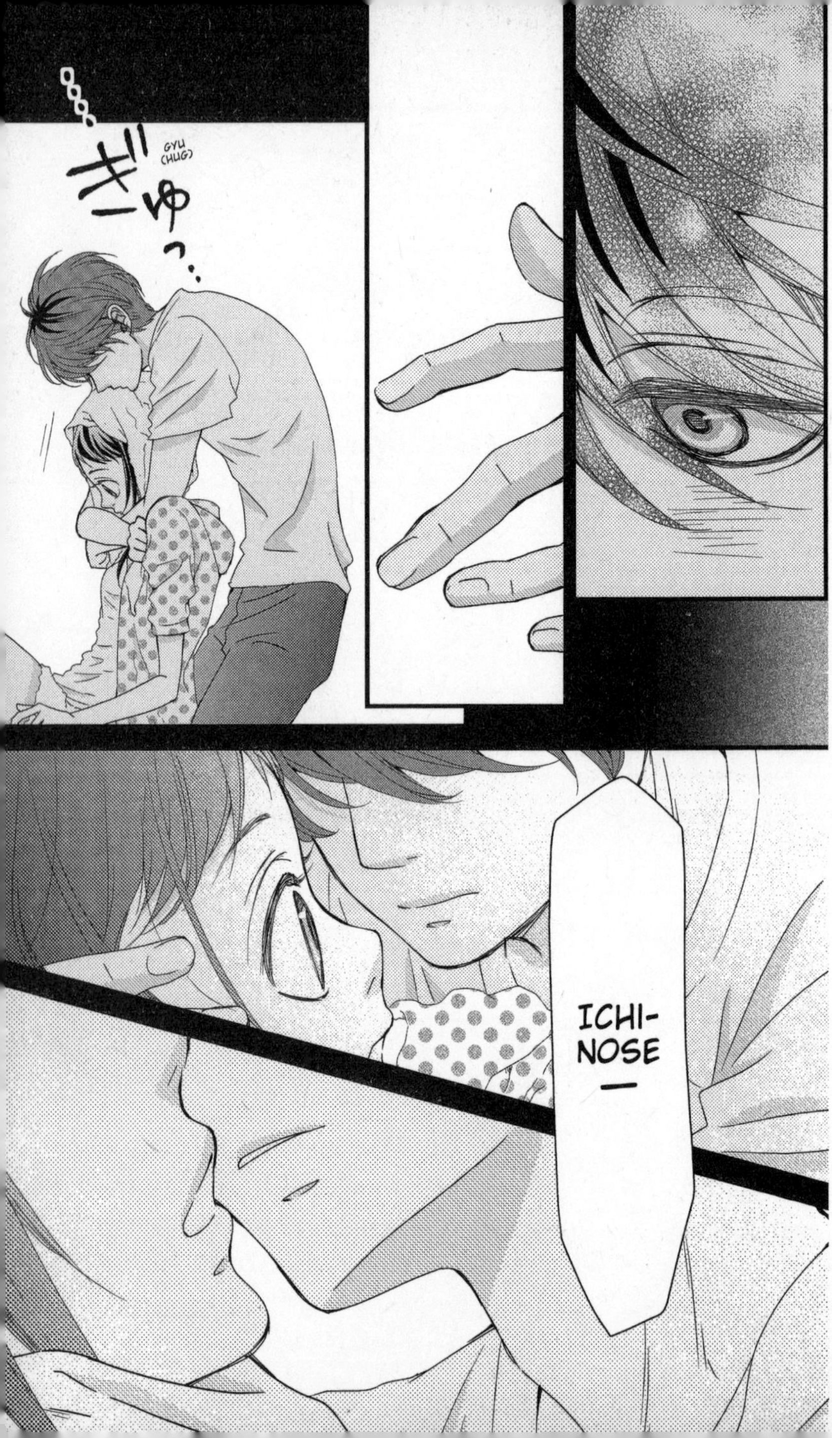
ぎゅっ…
GYU (HUG)
ICHI-
NOSE
—

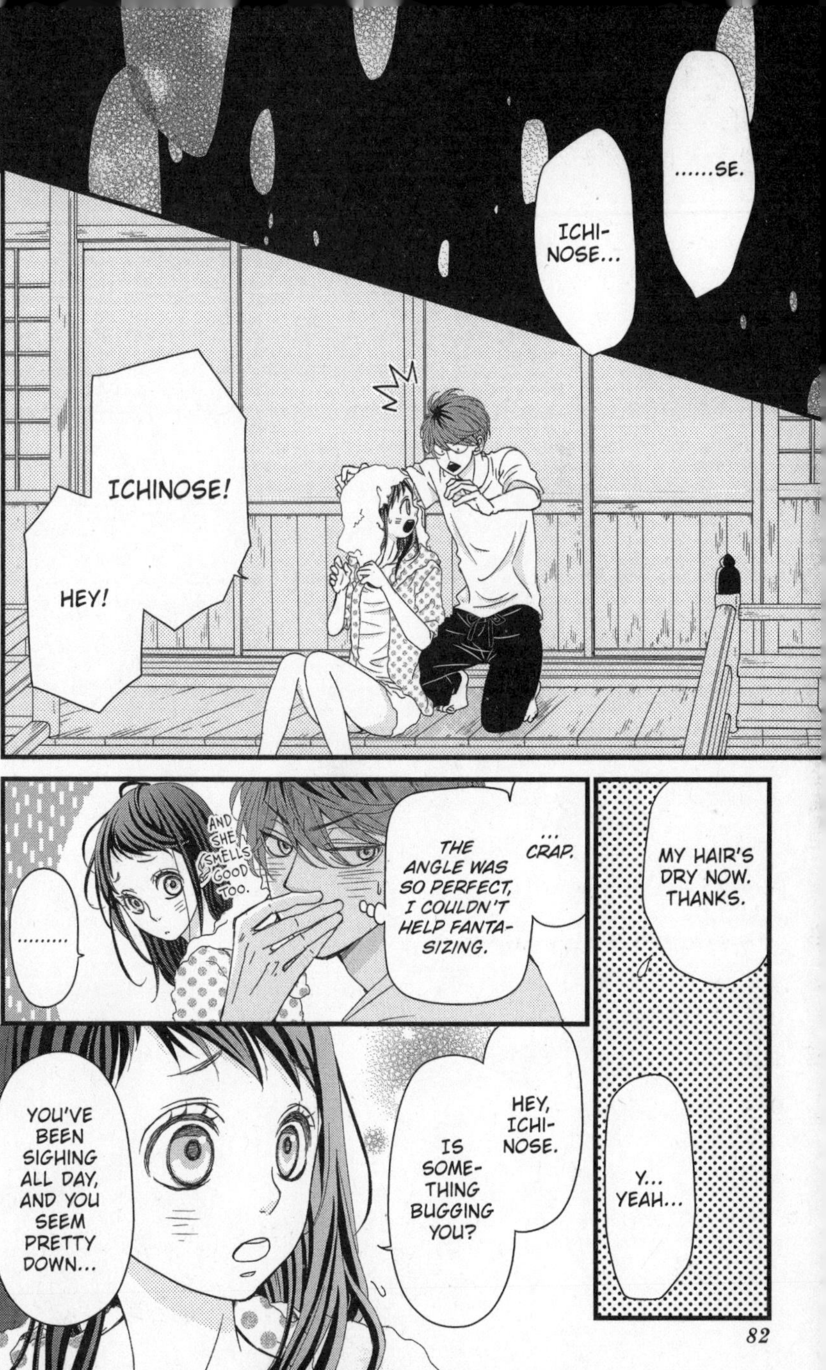
......SE.
ICHI-NOSE...
ICHINOSE!
HEY!
MY HAIR'S DRY NOW. THANKS.
Y... YEAH...
... CRAP.
THE ANGLE WAS SO PERFECT, I COULDN'T HELP FANTA-SIZING.
AND SHE SMELLS GOOD TOO.
....
HEY, ICHI-NOSE.
IS SOME-THING BUGGING YOU?
YOU'VE BEEN SIGHING ALL DAY, AND YOU SEEM PRETTY DOWN...

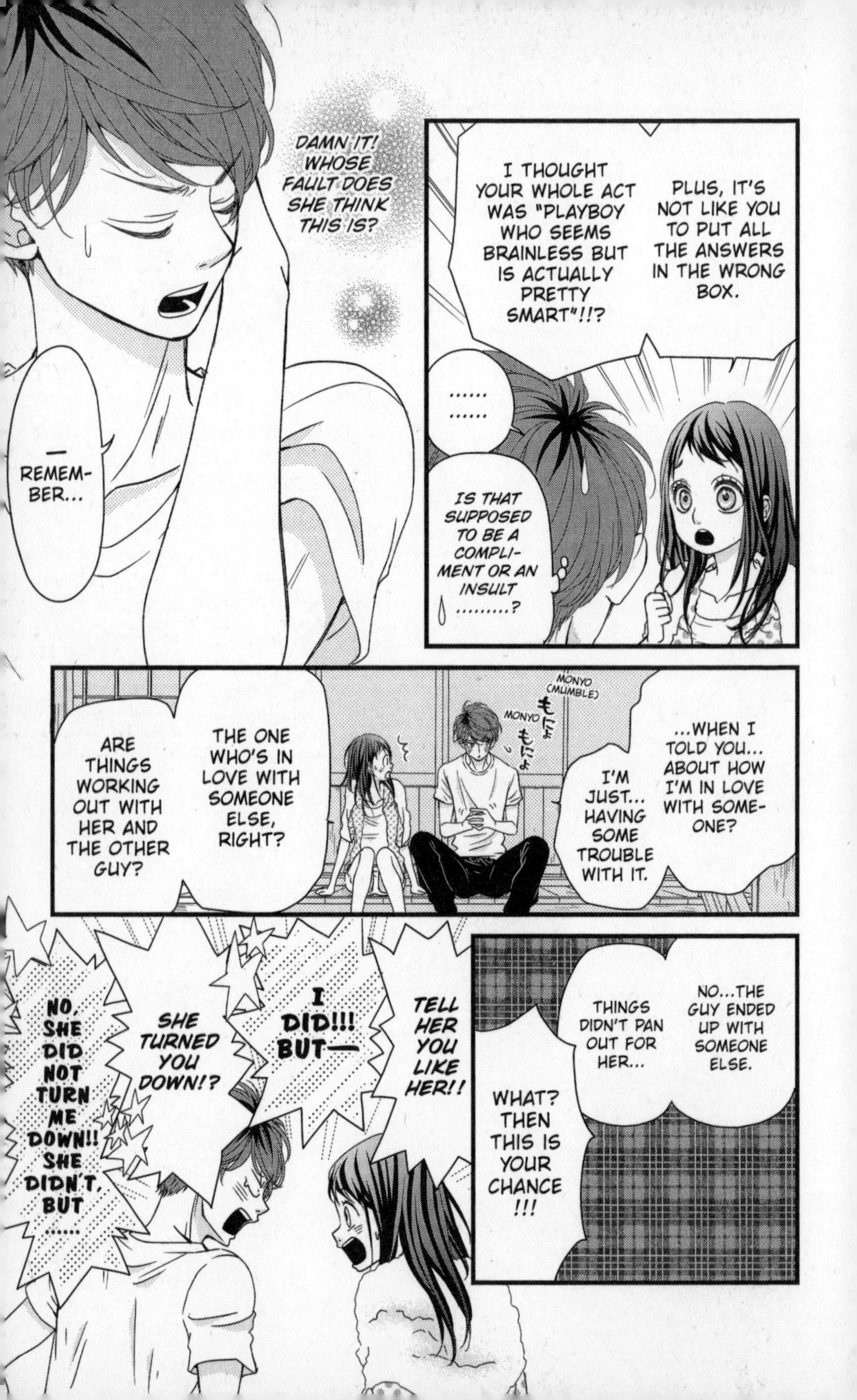

I THOUGHT YOUR WHOLE ACT WAS "PLAYBOY WHO SEEMS BRAINLESS BUT IS ACTUALLY PRETTY SMART"!!?
PLUS, IT'S NOT LIKE YOU TO PUT ALL THE ANSWERS IN THE WRONG BOX.
......
......
IS THAT SUPPOSED TO BE A COMPLIMENT OR AN INSULT ....?
DAMN IT! WHOSE FAULT DOES SHE THINK THIS IS?
—REMEMBER...
...WHEN I TOLD YOU... ABOUT HOW I'M IN LOVE WITH SOMEONE?
I'M JUST... HAVING SOME TROUBLE WITH IT.
MONYO (MUMBLE)
もにょ
MONYO
もにょ
THE ONE WHO'S IN LOVE WITH SOMEONE ELSE, RIGHT?
ARE THINGS WORKING OUT WITH HER AND THE OTHER GUY?
NO...THE GUY ENDED UP WITH SOMEONE ELSE.
THINGS DIDN'T PAN OUT FOR HER...
WHAT? THEN THIS IS YOUR CHANCE!!!
TELL HER YOU LIKE HER!!
I DID!!! BUT—
SHE TURNED YOU DOWN!?
NO, SHE DID NOT TURN ME DOWN!! SHE DIDN'T, BUT ......

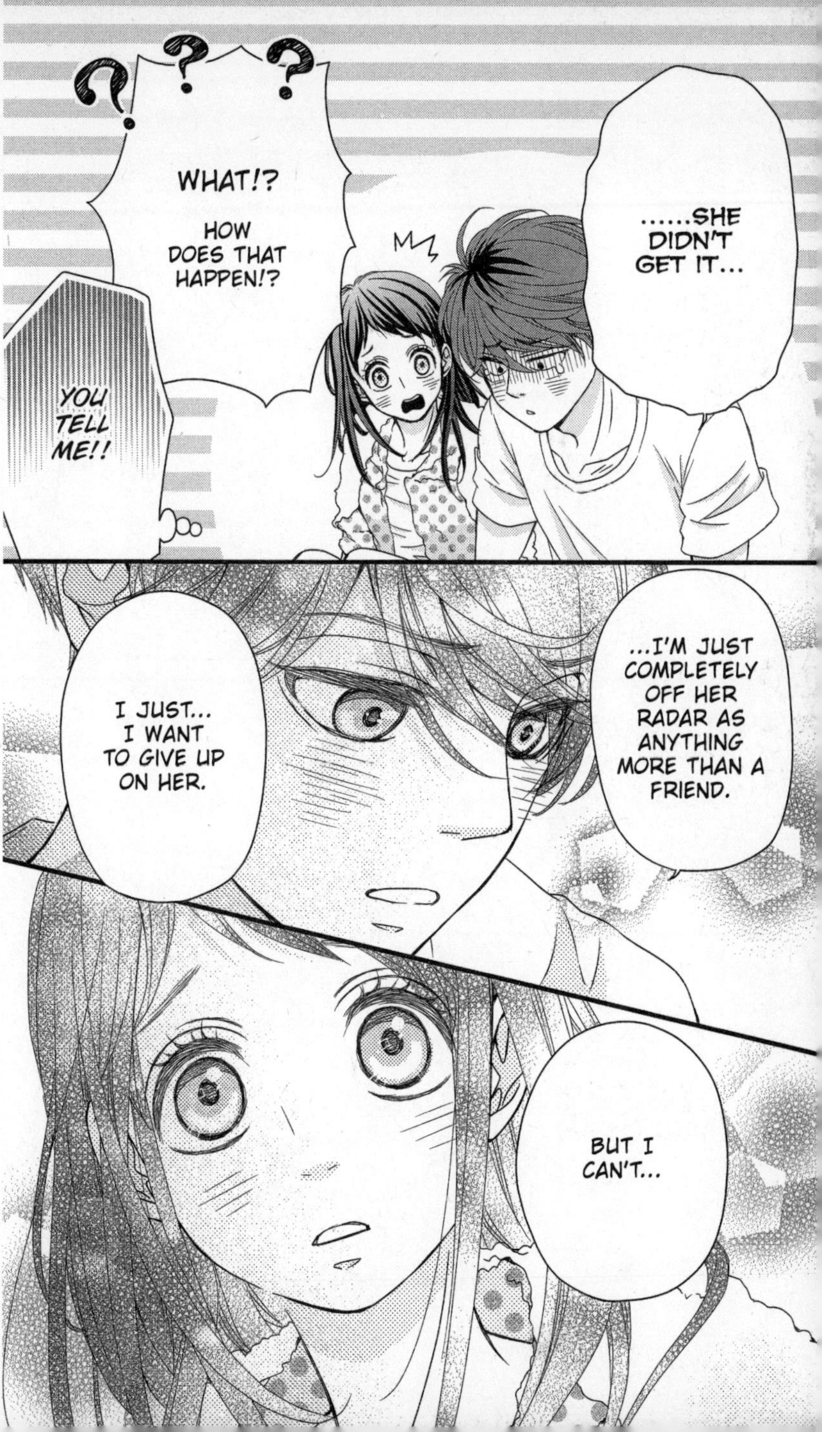
......SHE DIDN'T GET IT...
WHAT!? HOW DOES THAT HAPPEN!?
YOU TELL ME!!
...I'M JUST COMPLETELY OFF HER RADAR AS ANYTHING MORE THAN A FRIEND.
I JUST... I WANT TO GIVE UP ON HER.
BUT I CAN'T...

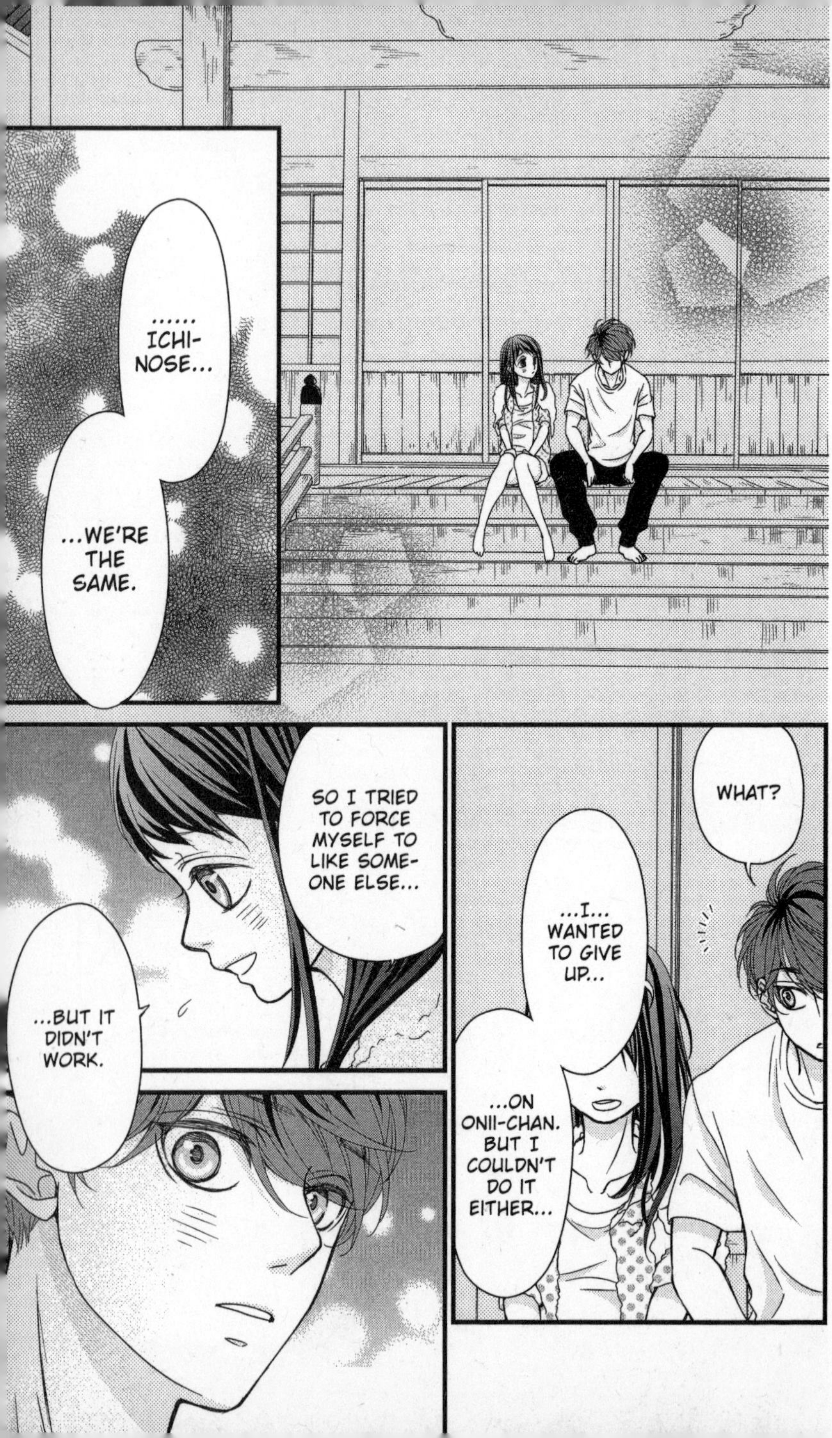

...... ICHINOSE...
...WE'RE THE SAME.
WHAT?
...I... WANTED TO GIVE UP...
...ON ONII-CHAN. BUT I COULDN'T DO IT EITHER...
SO I TRIED TO FORCE MYSELF TO LIKE SOMEONE ELSE...
...BUT IT DIDN'T WORK.

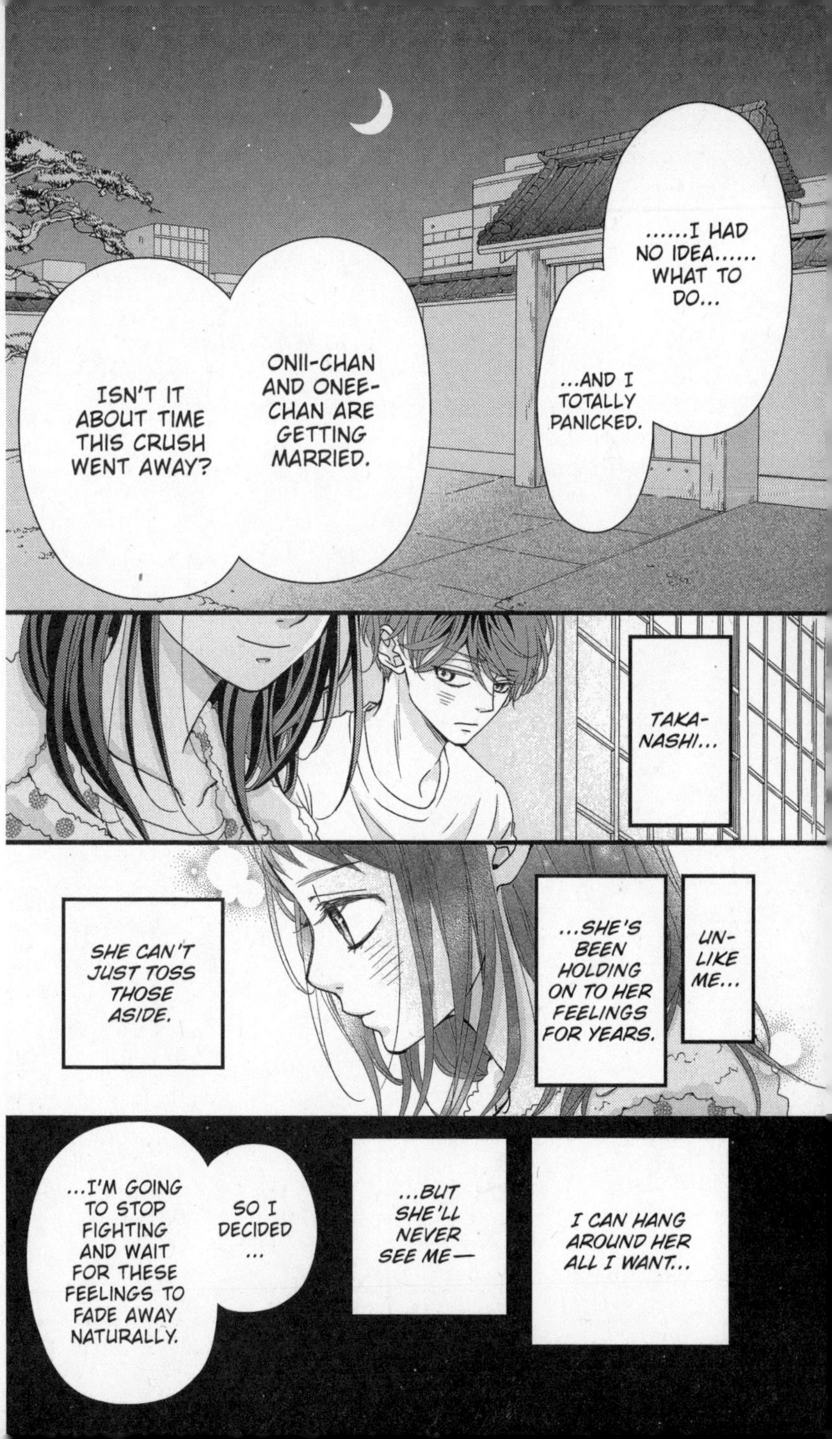
......I HAD NO IDEA...... WHAT TO DO...
...AND I TOTALLY PANICKED.
ONII-CHAN AND ONEE-CHAN ARE GETTING MARRIED.
ISN'T IT ABOUT TIME THIS CRUSH WENT AWAY?
TAKA-NASHI...
UN-LIKE ME...
...SHE'S BEEN HOLDING ON TO HER FEELINGS FOR YEARS.
SHE CAN'T JUST TOSS THOSE ASIDE.
I CAN HANG AROUND HER ALL I WANT...
...BUT SHE'LL NEVER SEE ME—
SO I DECIDED ...
...I'M GOING TO STOP FIGHTING AND WAIT FOR THESE FEELINGS TO FADE AWAY NATURALLY.

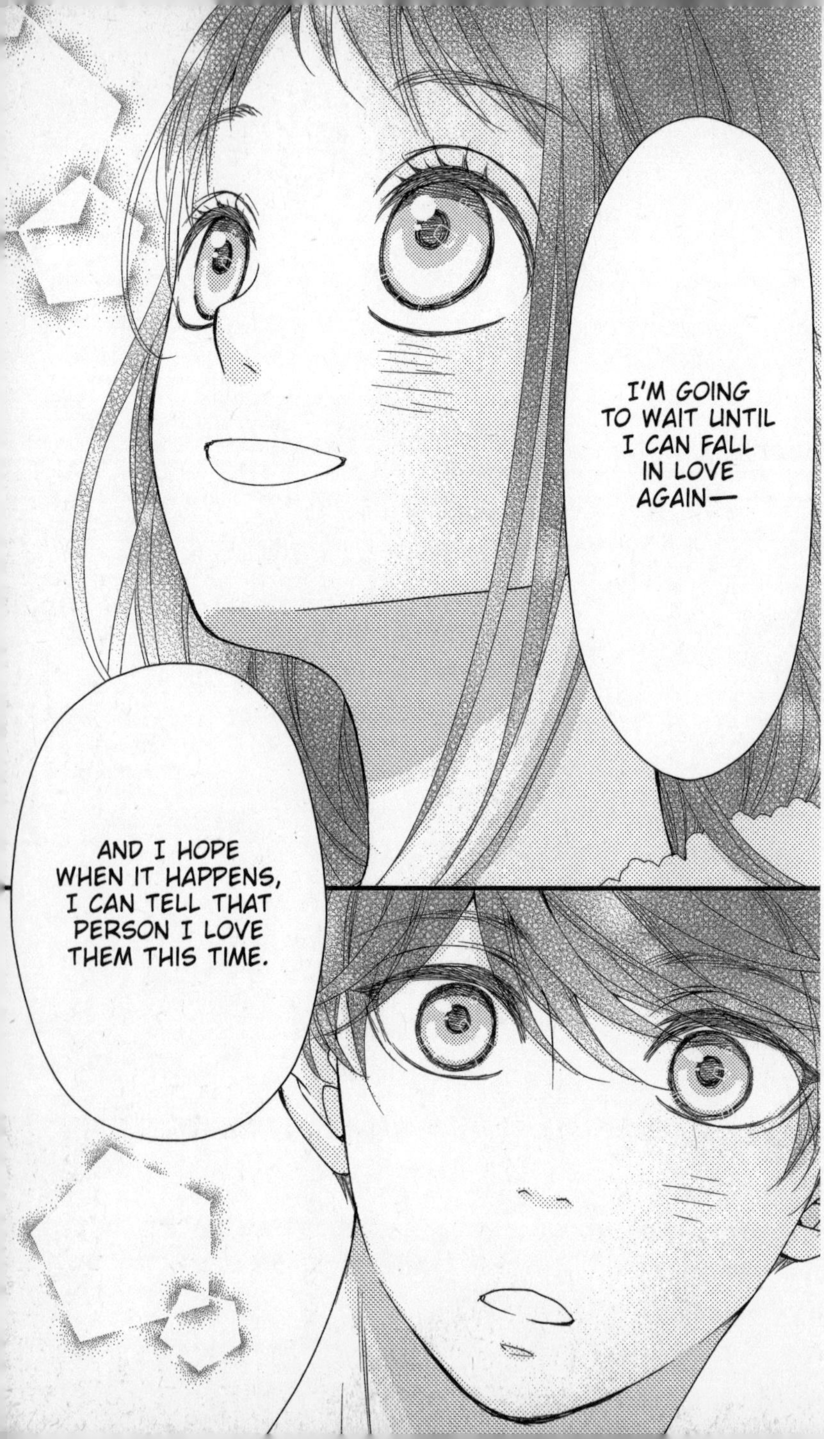
I'M GOING TO WAIT UNTIL I CAN FALL IN LOVE AGAIN—
AND I HOPE WHEN IT HAPPENS, I CAN TELL THAT PERSON I LOVE THEM THIS TIME.

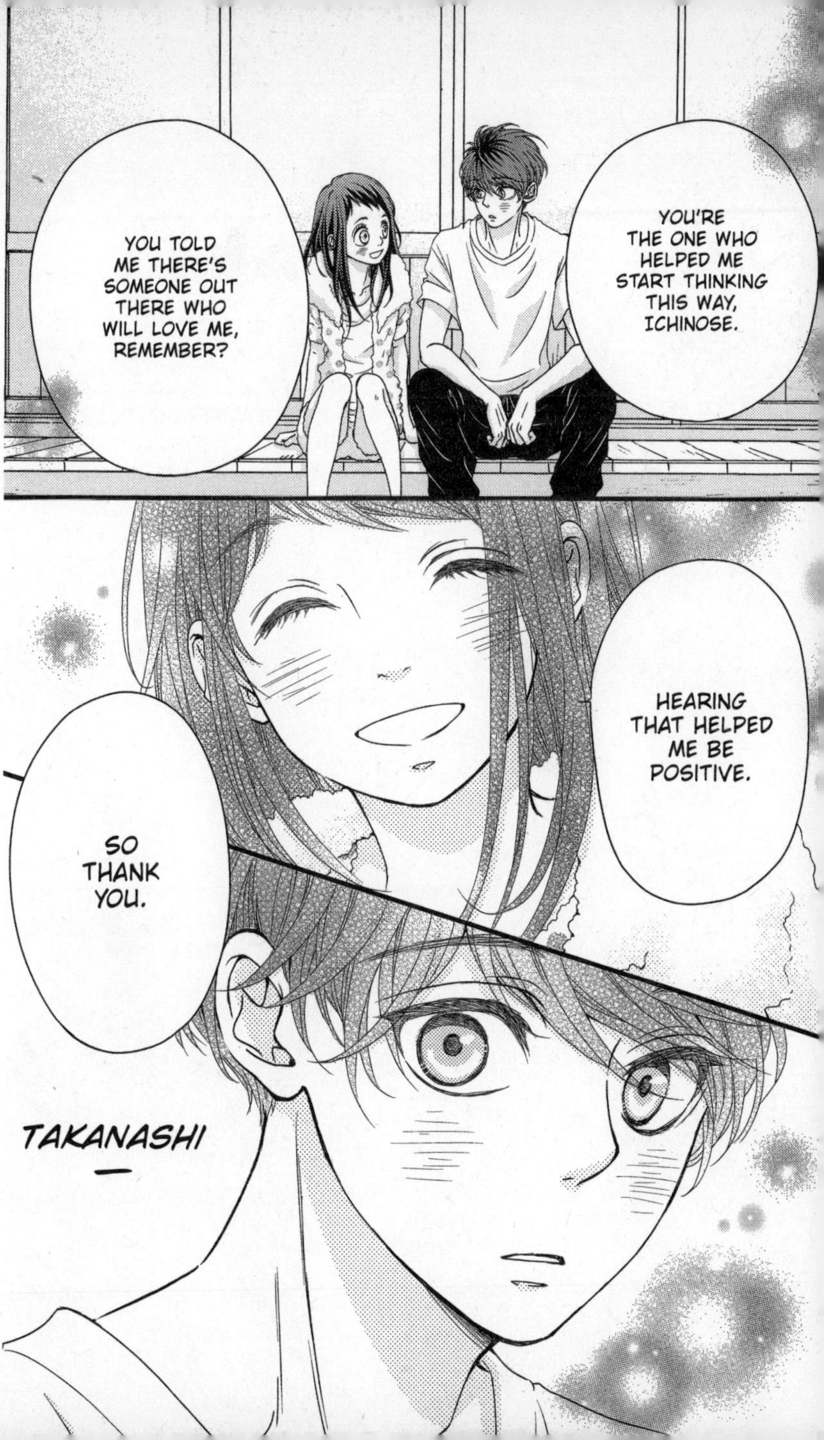
YOU'RE THE ONE WHO HELPED ME START THINKING THIS WAY, ICHINOSE.
YOU TOLD ME THERE'S SOMEONE OUT THERE WHO WILL LOVE ME, REMEMBER?
HEARING THAT HELPED ME BE POSITIVE.
SO THANK YOU.
TAKANASHI —

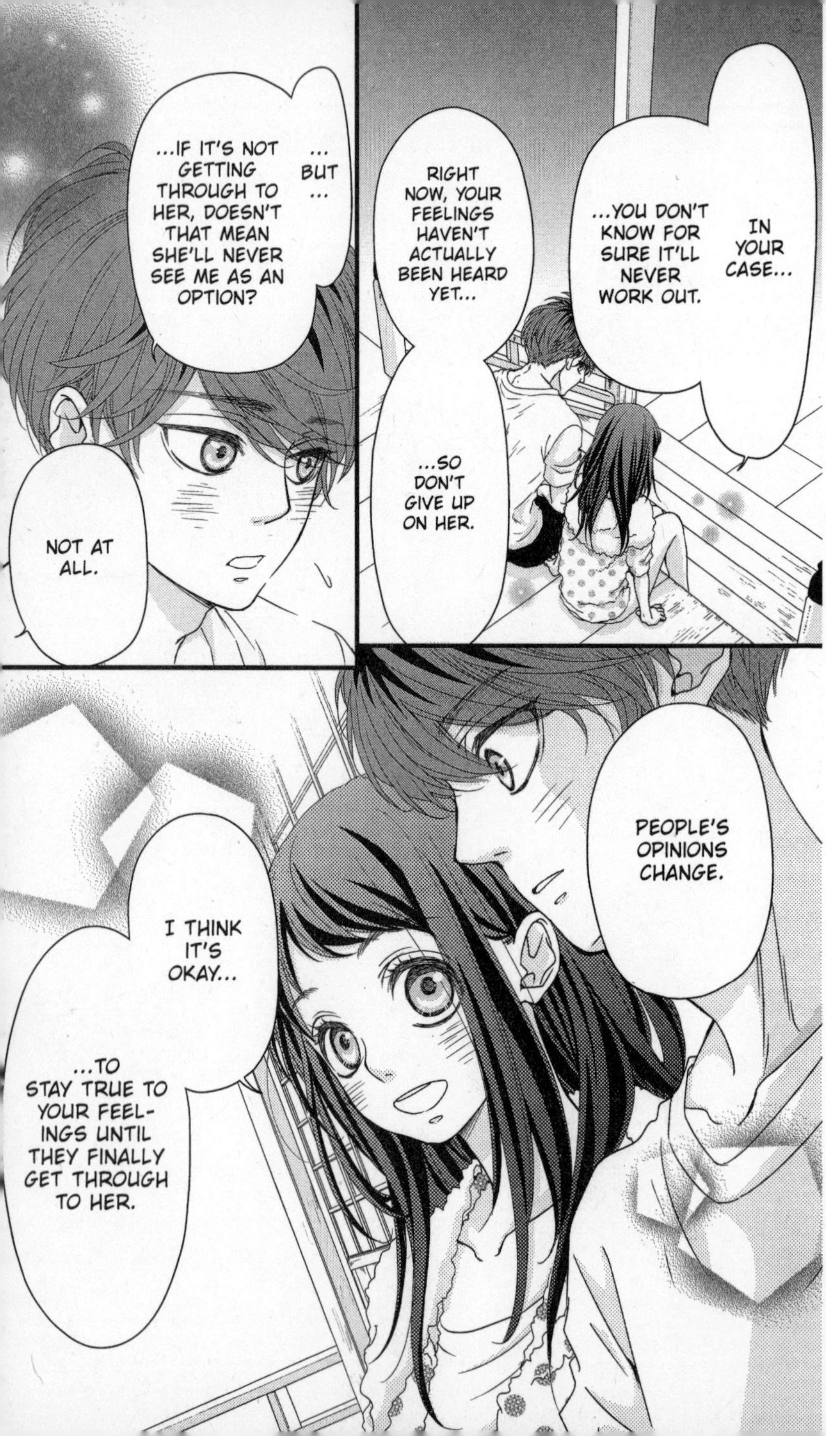
IN YOUR CASE...
...YOU DON'T KNOW FOR SURE IT'LL NEVER WORK OUT.
RIGHT NOW, YOUR FEELINGS HAVEN'T ACTUALLY BEEN HEARD YET...
...SO DON'T GIVE UP ON HER.
... BUT ...
...IF IT'S NOT GETTING THROUGH TO HER, DOESN'T THAT MEAN SHE'LL NEVER SEE ME AS AN OPTION?
NOT AT ALL.
PEOPLE'S OPINIONS CHANGE.
I THINK IT'S OKAY...
...TO STAY TRUE TO YOUR FEEL-INGS UNTIL THEY FINALLY GET THROUGH TO HER.

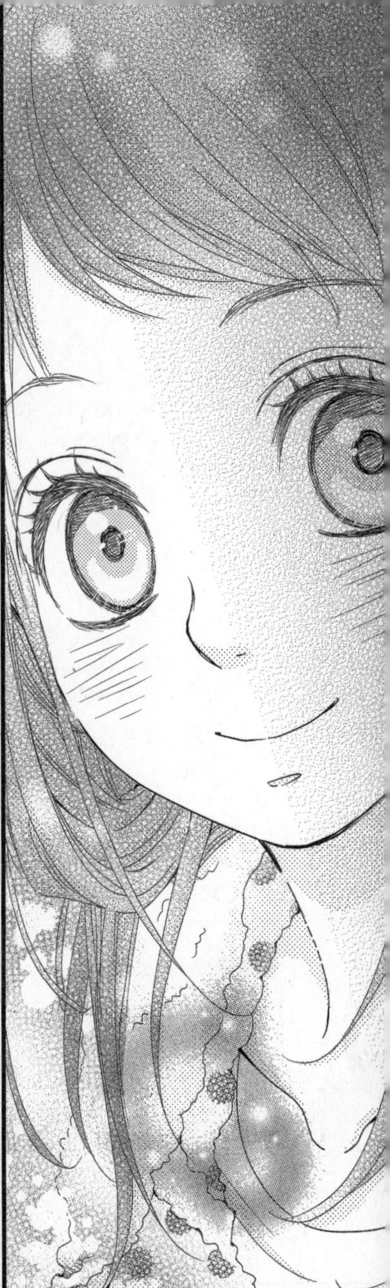

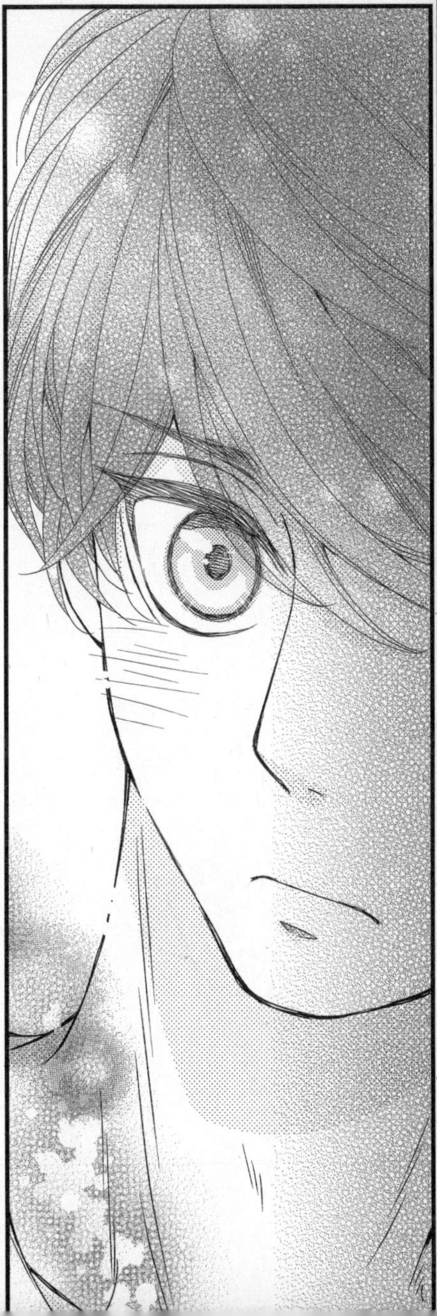

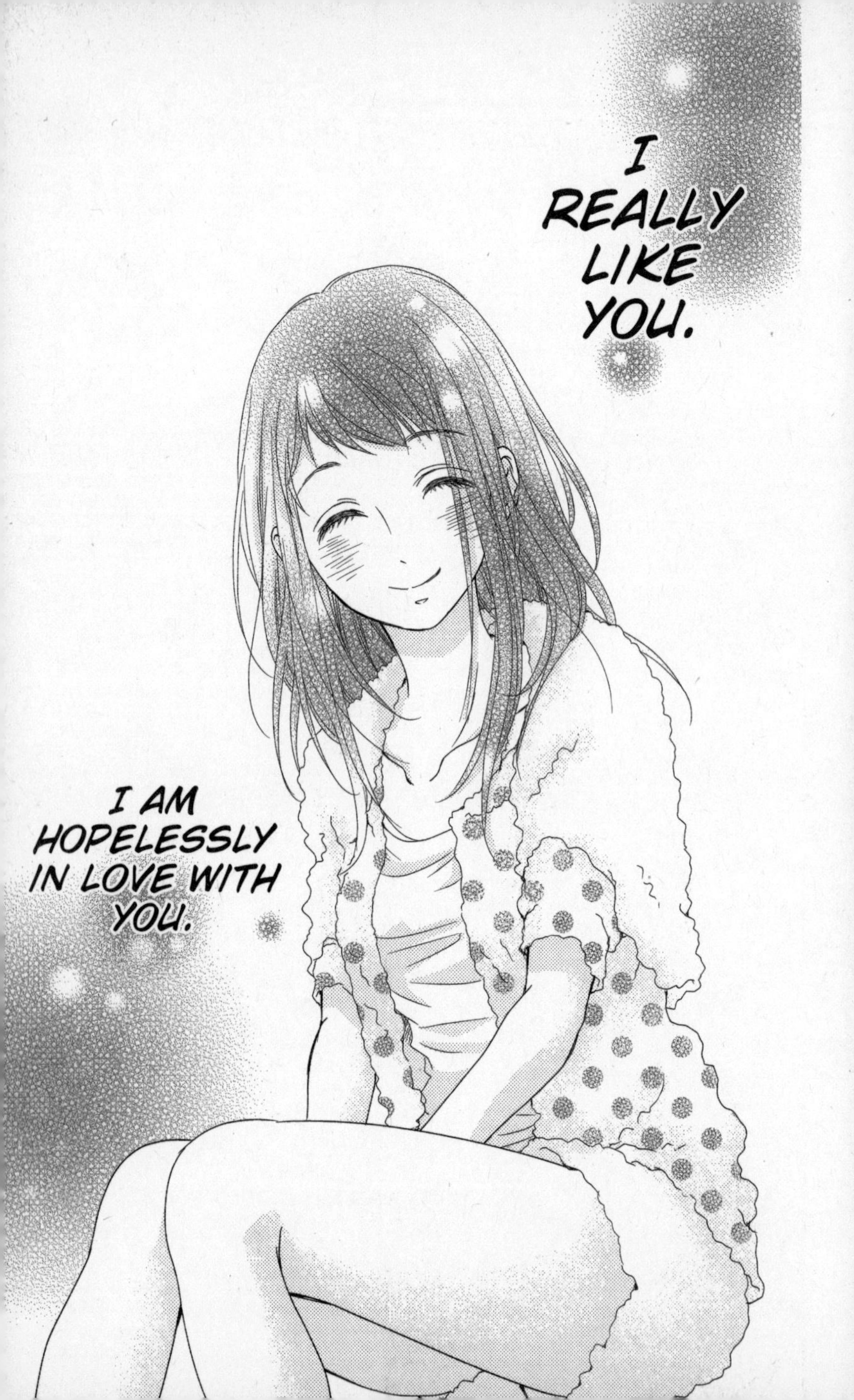
I REALLY LIKE YOU.
I AM HOPELESSLY IN LOVE WITH YOU.

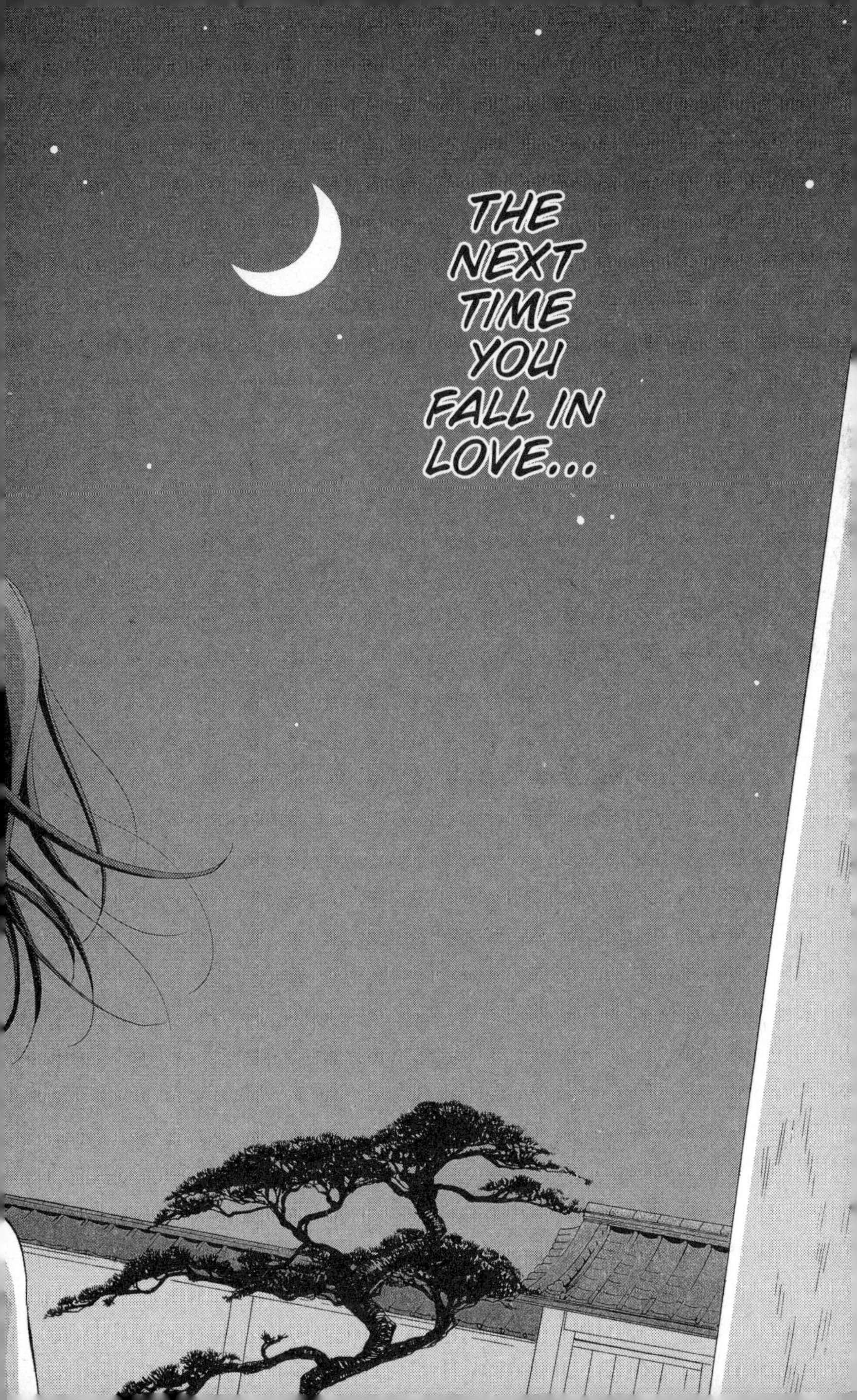
THE NEXT TIME YOU FALL IN LOVE...

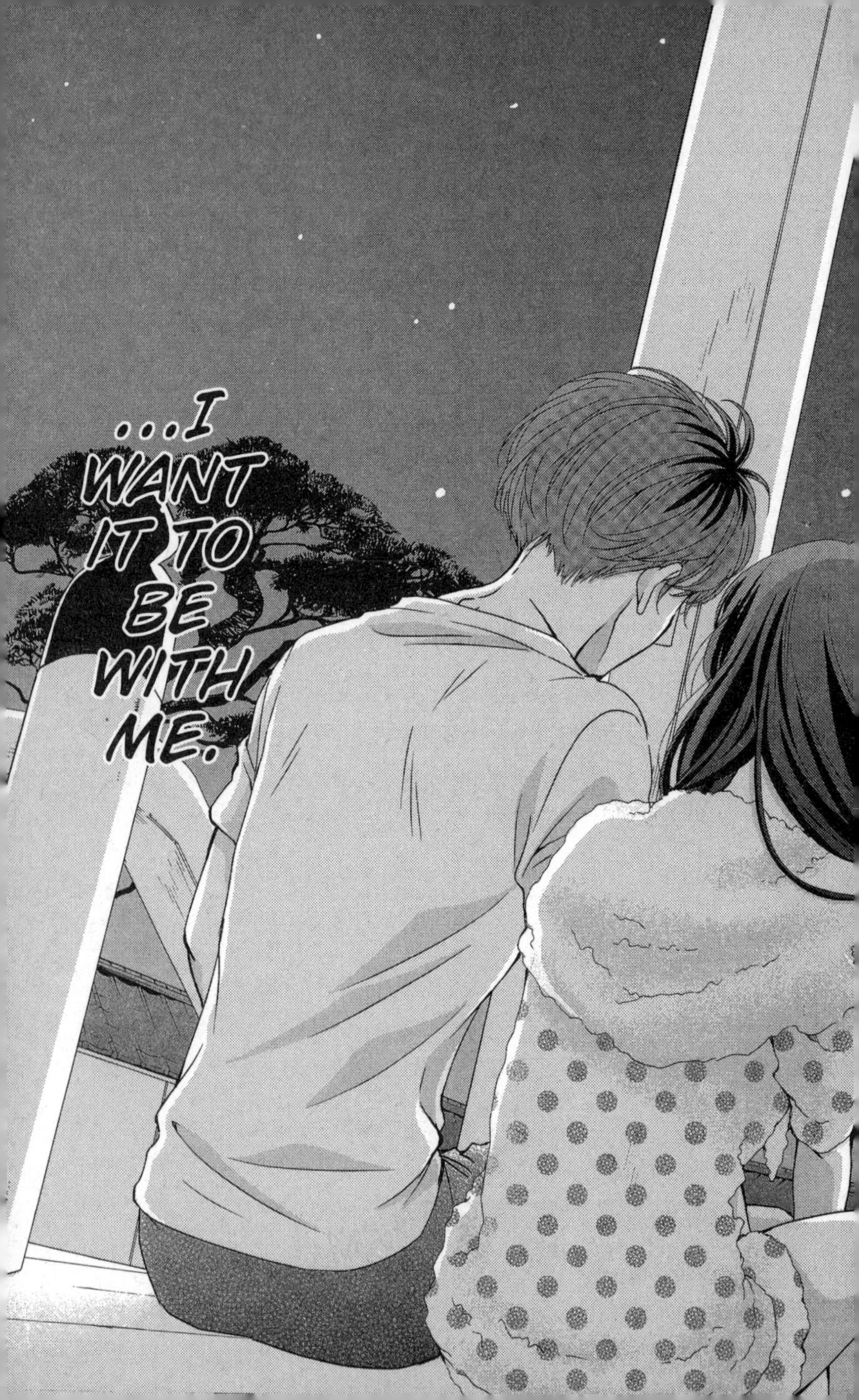
...I WANT IT TO BE WITH ME.

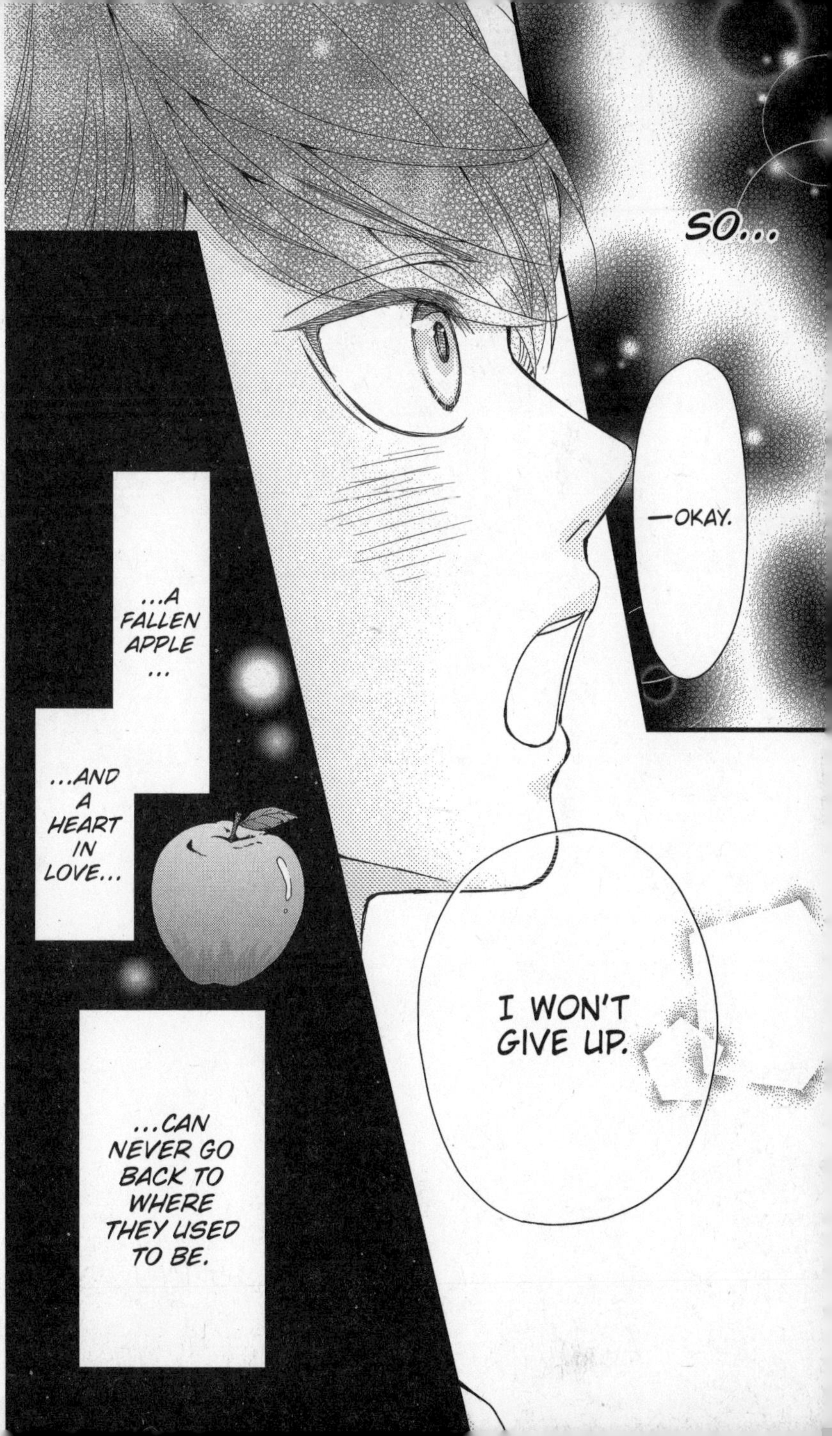
SO...
—OKAY.
I WON'T GIVE UP.
...A FALLEN APPLE ...
...AND A HEART IN LOVE...
...CAN NEVER GO BACK TO WHERE THEY USED TO BE.

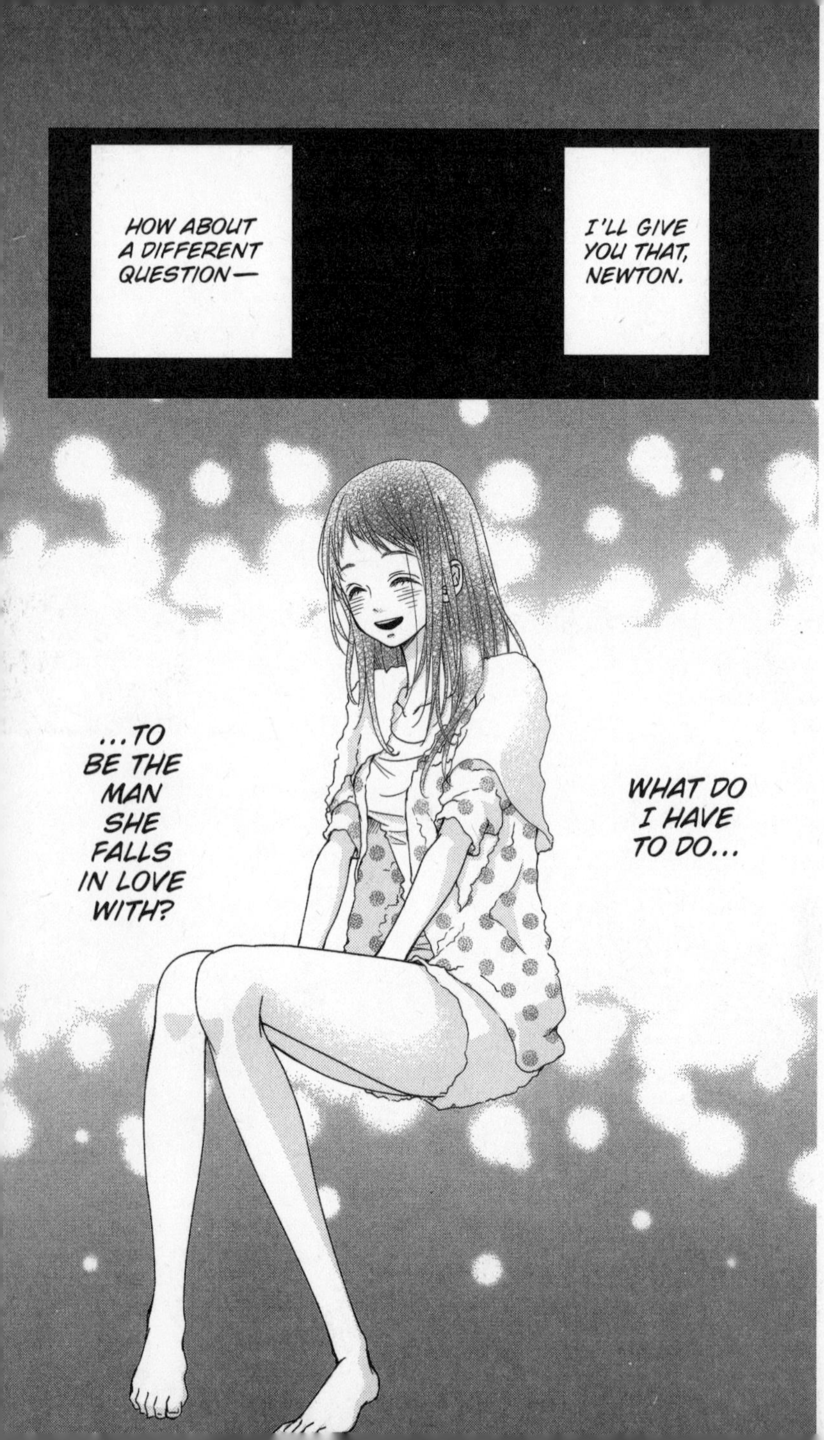
I'LL GIVE YOU THAT, NEWTON.
HOW ABOUT A DIFFERENT QUESTION—
WHAT DO I HAVE TO DO...
...TO BE THE MAN SHE FALLS IN LOVE WITH?

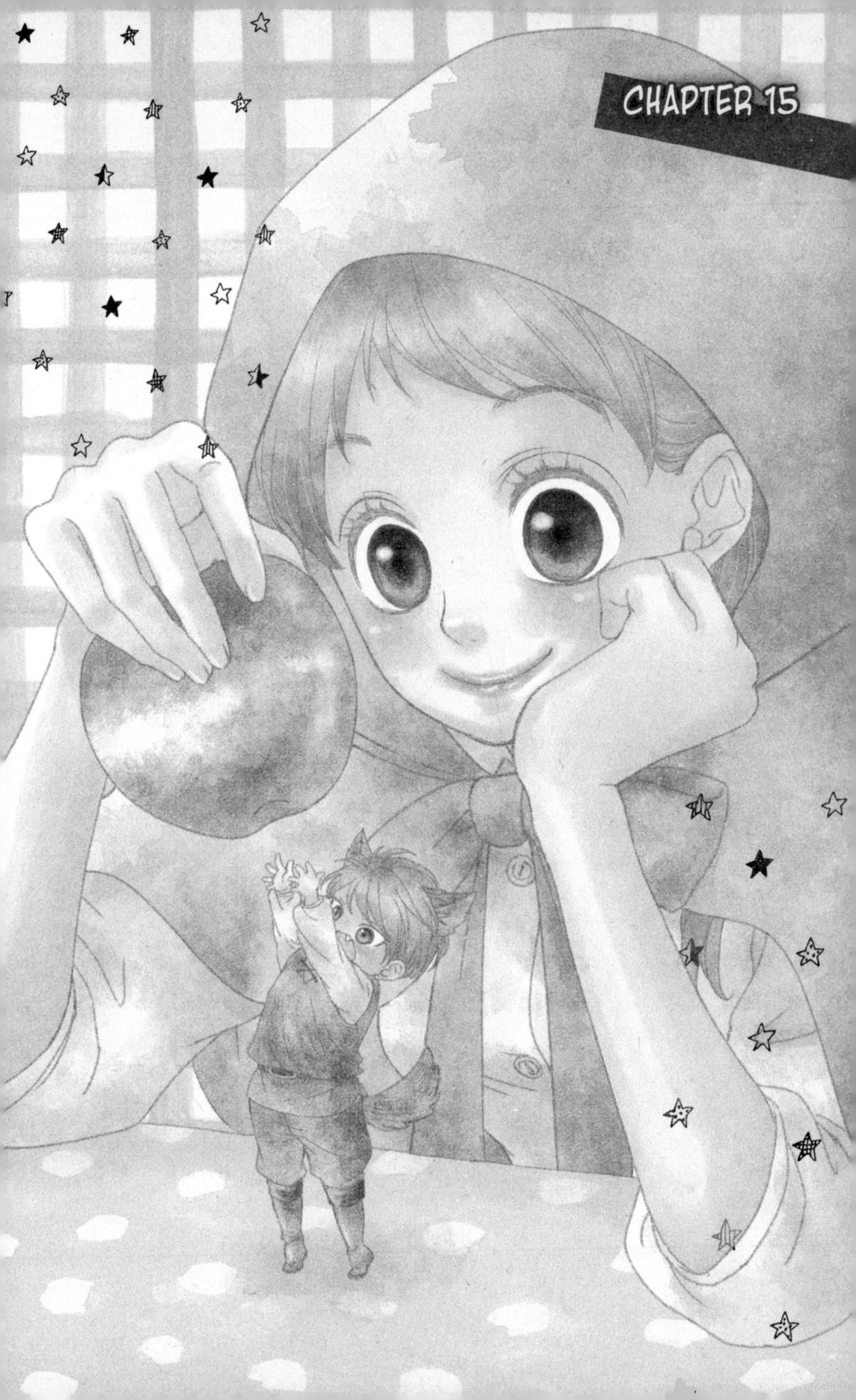
CHAPTER 15

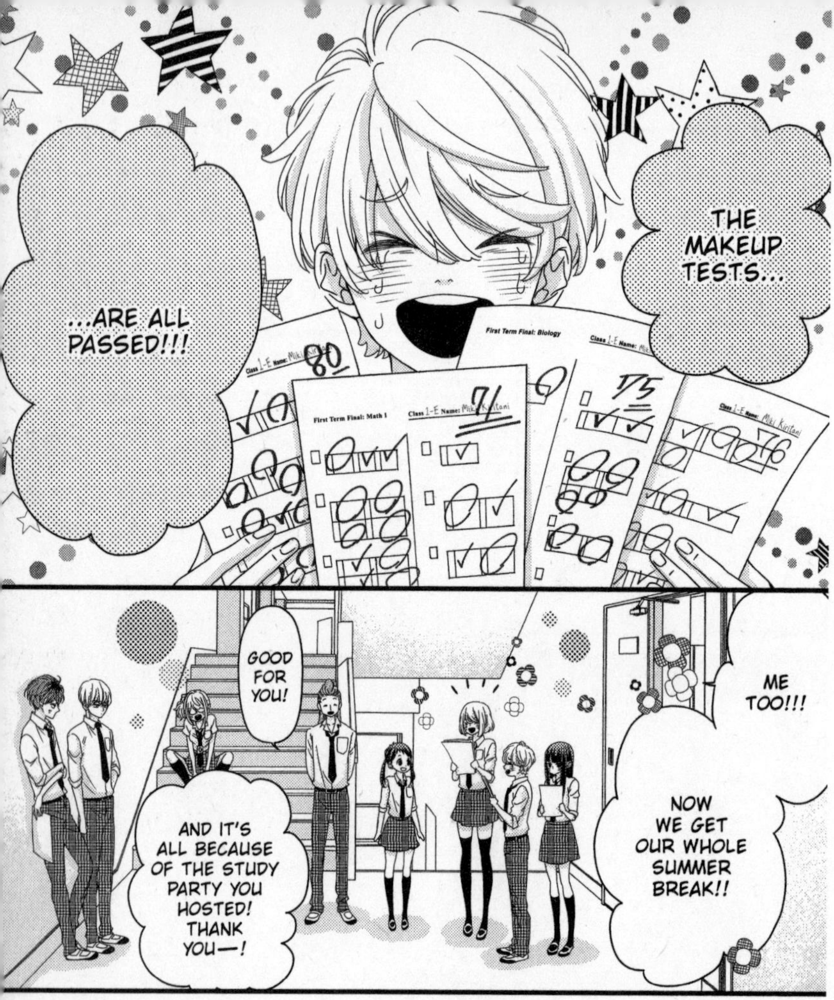
THE MAKEUP TESTS...
...ARE ALL PASSED!!!
First Term Final: Biology
Class 1-E Name: Miki Kiritani
First Term Final: Math 1
ME TOO!!!
NOW WE GET OUR WHOLE SUMMER BREAK!!
GOOD FOR YOU!
AND IT'S ALL BECAUSE OF THE STUDY PARTY YOU HOSTED! THANK YOU—!

hatsu haru

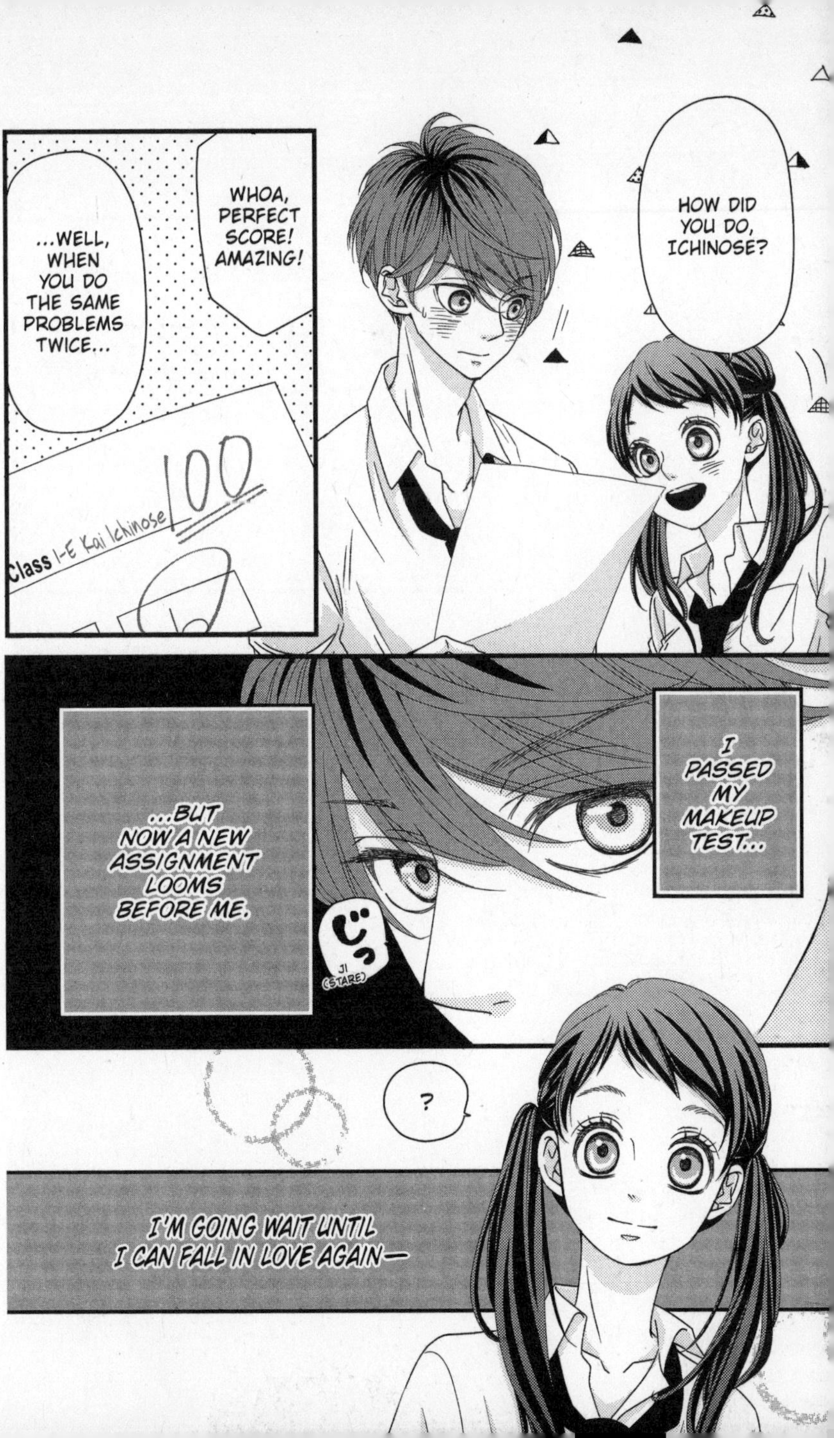
HOW DID YOU DO, ICHINOSE?
WHOA, PERFECT SCORE! AMAZING!
...WELL, WHEN YOU DO THE SAME PROBLEMS TWICE...
Class 1-E Kai Ichinose
100
I PASSED MY MAKEUP TEST...
...BUT NOW A NEW ASSIGNMENT LOOMS BEFORE ME.
じっ
JI (STARE)
?
I'M GOING WAIT UNTIL I CAN FALL IN LOVE AGAIN—

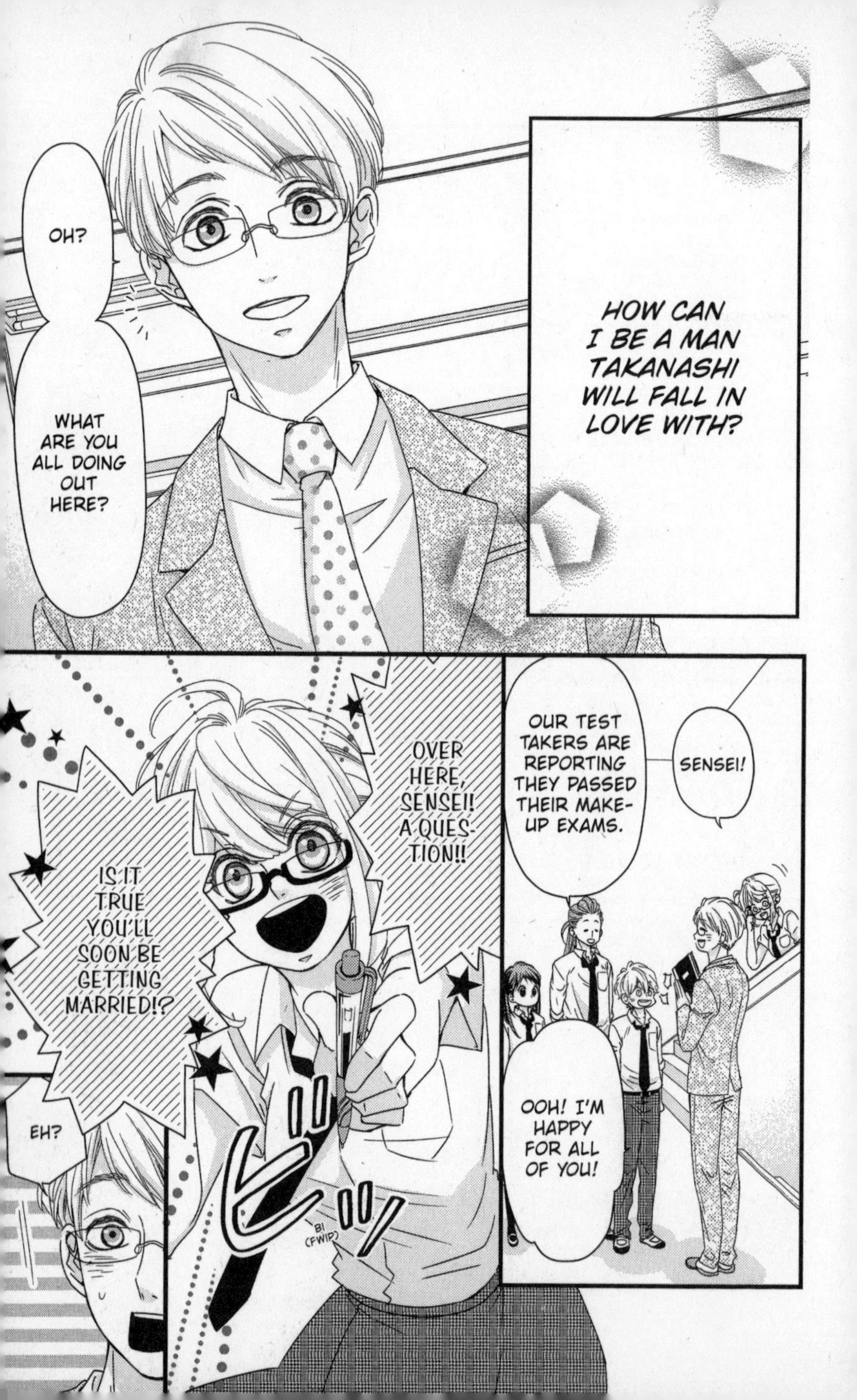
HOW CAN I BE A MAN TAKANASHI WILL FALL IN LOVE WITH?
OH?
WHAT ARE YOU ALL DOING OUT HERE?
SENSEI!
OUR TEST TAKERS ARE REPORTING THEY PASSED THEIR MAKE-UP EXAMS.
OOH! I'M HAPPY FOR ALL OF YOU!
OVER HERE, SENSEI!! A QUESTION!!
IS IT TRUE YOU'LL SOON BE GETTING MARRIED!?
BI (FWIP)
EH?

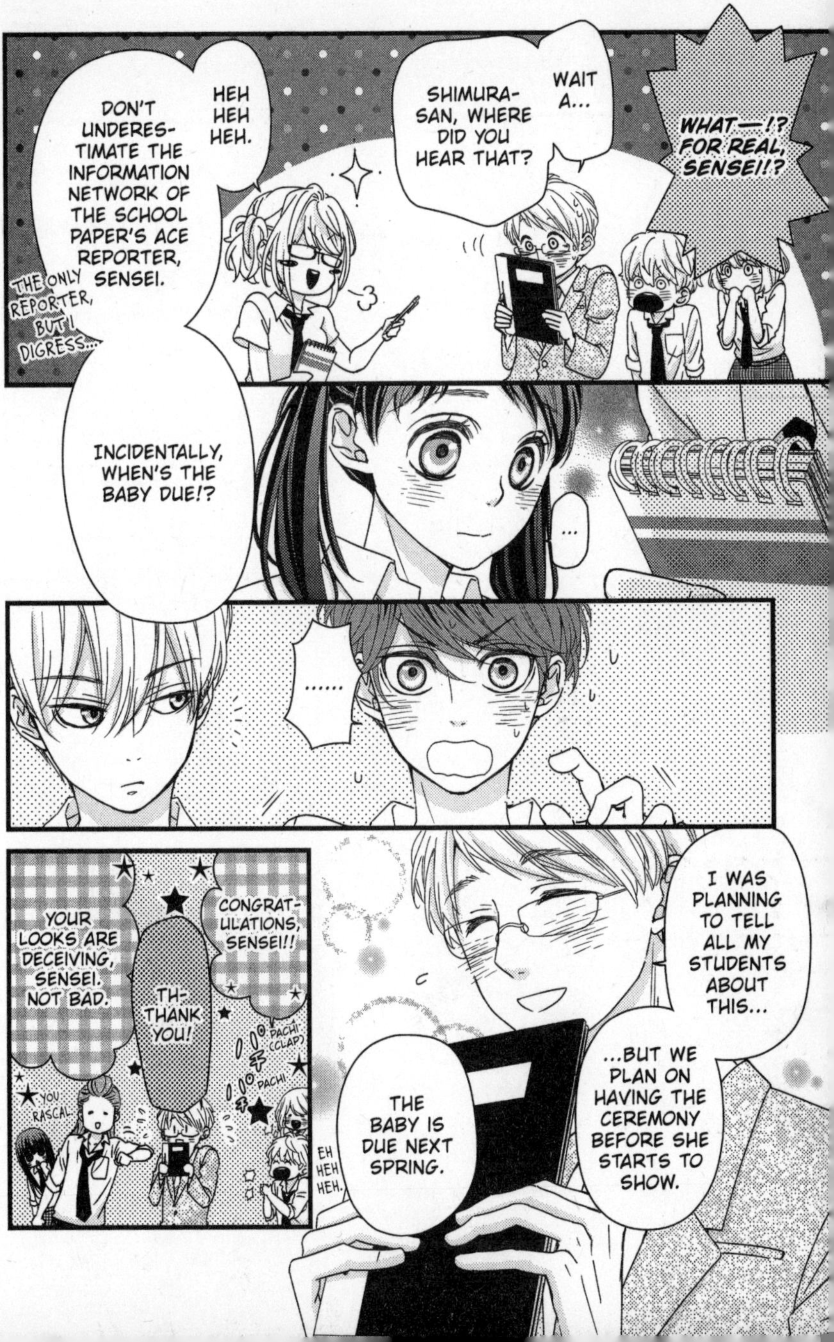
WHAT—!? FOR REAL, SENSEI!?
WAIT A...
SHIMURA-SAN, WHERE DID YOU HEAR THAT?
HEH HEH HEH.
DON'T UNDERESTIMATE THE INFORMATION NETWORK OF THE SCHOOL PAPER'S ACE REPORTER, SENSEI.
THE ONLY REPORTER, BUT I DIGRESS...
...
INCIDENTALLY, WHEN'S THE BABY DUE!?
......
I WAS PLANNING TO TELL ALL MY STUDENTS ABOUT THIS...
...BUT WE PLAN ON HAVING THE CEREMONY BEFORE SHE STARTS TO SHOW.
THE BABY IS DUE NEXT SPRING.
EH HEH HEH.
CONGRATULATIONS, SENSEI!!
TH-THANK YOU!
YOUR LOOKS ARE DECEIVING, SENSEI. NOT BAD.
PACHI (CLAP)
PACHI
YOU RASCAL.

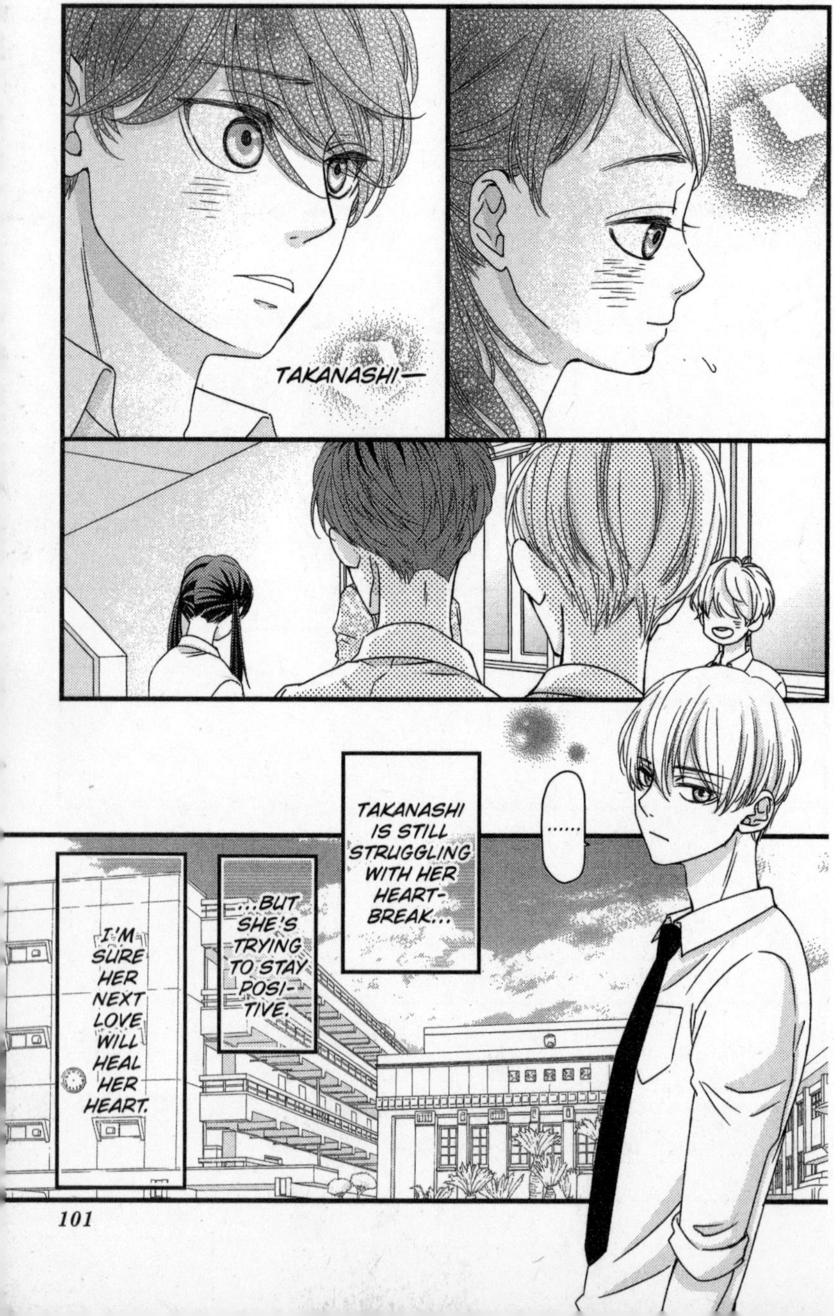
TAKANASHI—
......
TAKANASHI IS STILL STRUGGLING WITH HER HEART-BREAK...
...BUT SHE'S TRYING TO STAY POSI-TIVE.
I'M SURE HER NEXT LOVE WILL HEAL HER HEART.

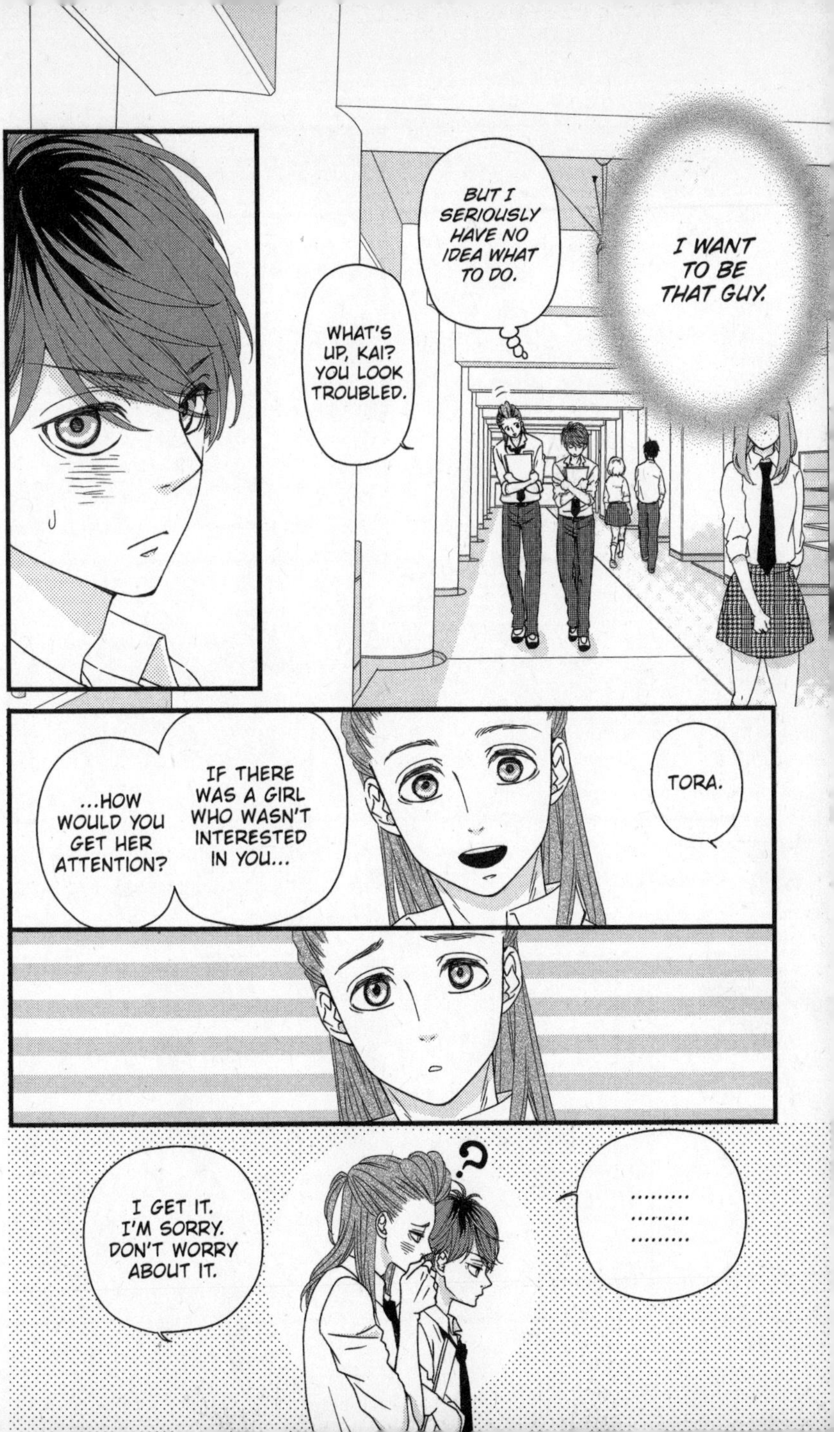
I WANT TO BE THAT GUY.
BUT I SERIOUSLY HAVE NO IDEA WHAT TO DO.
WHAT'S UP, KAI? YOU LOOK TROUBLED.
TORA.
IF THERE WAS A GIRL WHO WASN'T INTERESTED IN YOU...
...HOW WOULD YOU GET HER ATTENTION?
?
....
....
....
I GET IT. I'M SORRY. DON'T WORRY ABOUT IT.

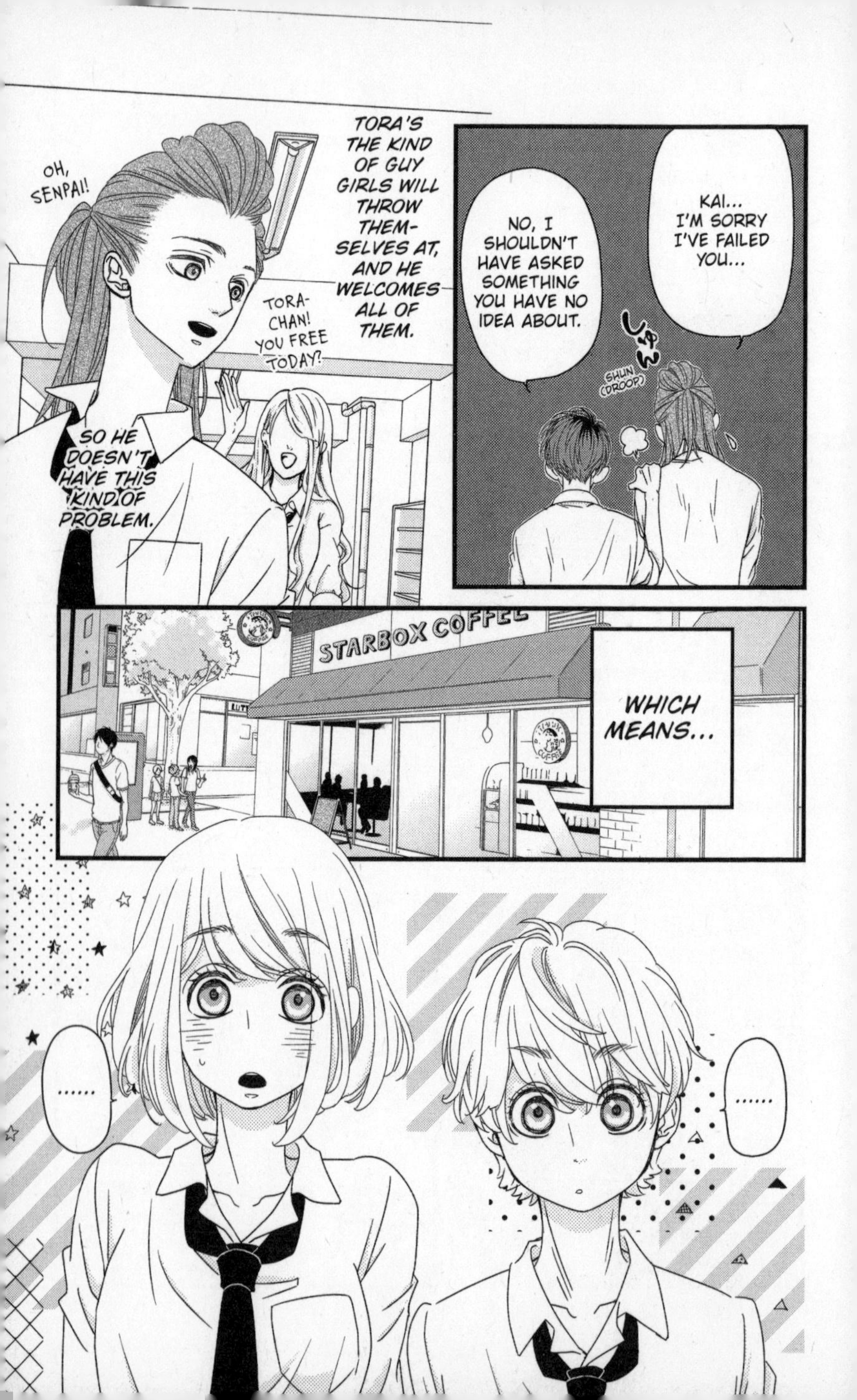
KAI... I'M SORRY I'VE FAILED YOU...
NO, I SHOULDN'T HAVE ASKED SOMETHING YOU HAVE NO IDEA ABOUT.
しゅん
SHUN (DROOP)
TORA'S THE KIND OF GUY GIRLS WILL THROW THEM-SELVES AT, AND HE WELCOMES ALL OF THEM.
TORA-CHAN! YOU FREE TODAY?
OH, SENPAI!
SO HE DOESN'T HAVE THIS KIND OF PROBLEM.
STARBOX COFFEE
WHICH MEANS...
......
......

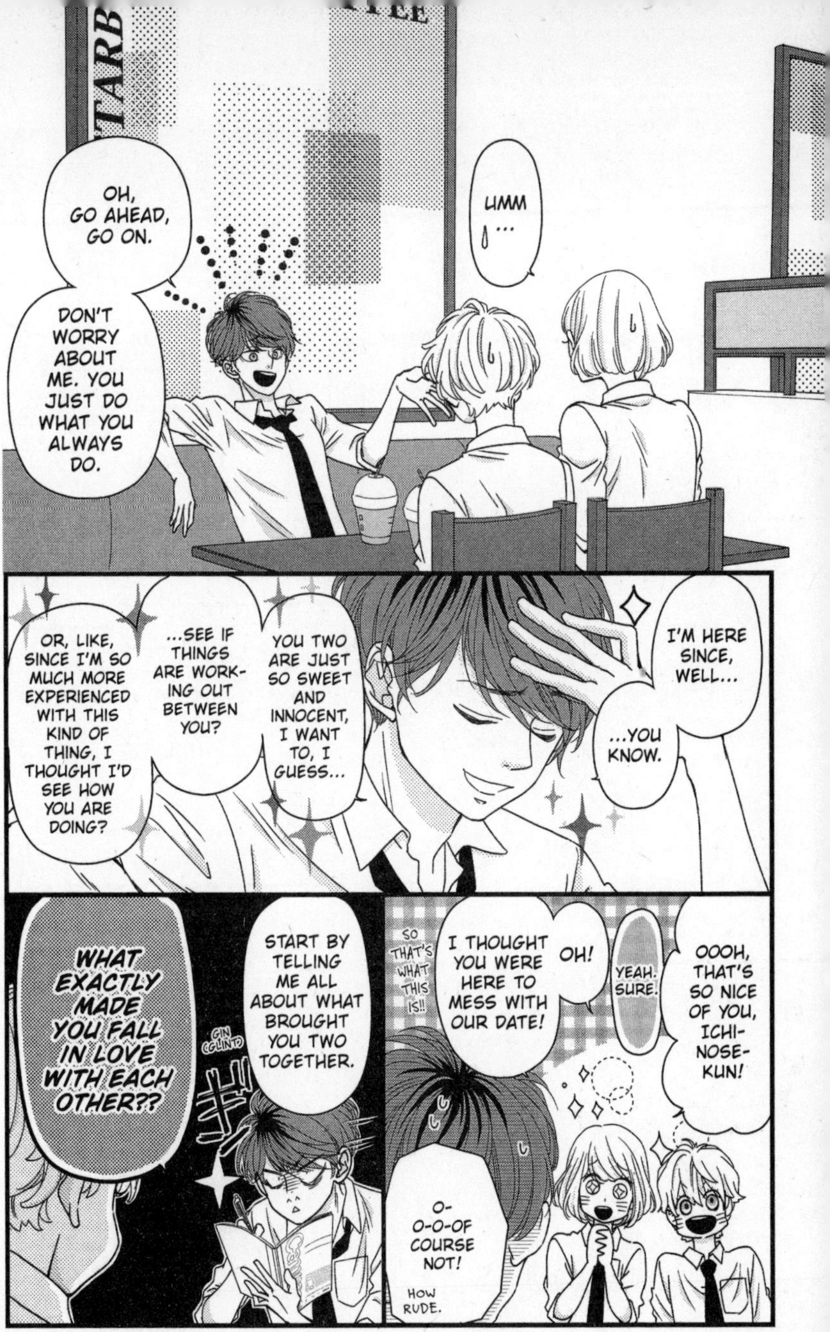
UMM...
OH, GO AHEAD, GO ON.
DON'T WORRY ABOUT ME. YOU JUST DO WHAT YOU ALWAYS DO.
I'M HERE SINCE, WELL...
...YOU KNOW.
YOU TWO ARE JUST SO SWEET AND INNOCENT, I WANT TO, I GUESS...
...SEE IF THINGS ARE WORKING OUT BETWEEN YOU?
OR, LIKE, SINCE I'M SO MUCH MORE EXPERIENCED WITH THIS KIND OF THING, I THOUGHT I'D SEE HOW YOU ARE DOING?
OOOH, THAT'S SO NICE OF YOU, ICHINOSE-KUN!
YEAH. SURE.
OH!
I THOUGHT YOU WERE HERE TO MESS WITH OUR DATE!
SO THAT'S WHAT THIS IS!!
O-O-O-O-OF COURSE NOT!
HOW RUDE.
START BY TELLING ME ALL ABOUT WHAT BROUGHT YOU TWO TOGETHER.
GIN (GLINT)
WHAT EXACTLY MADE YOU FALL IN LOVE WITH EACH OTHER??

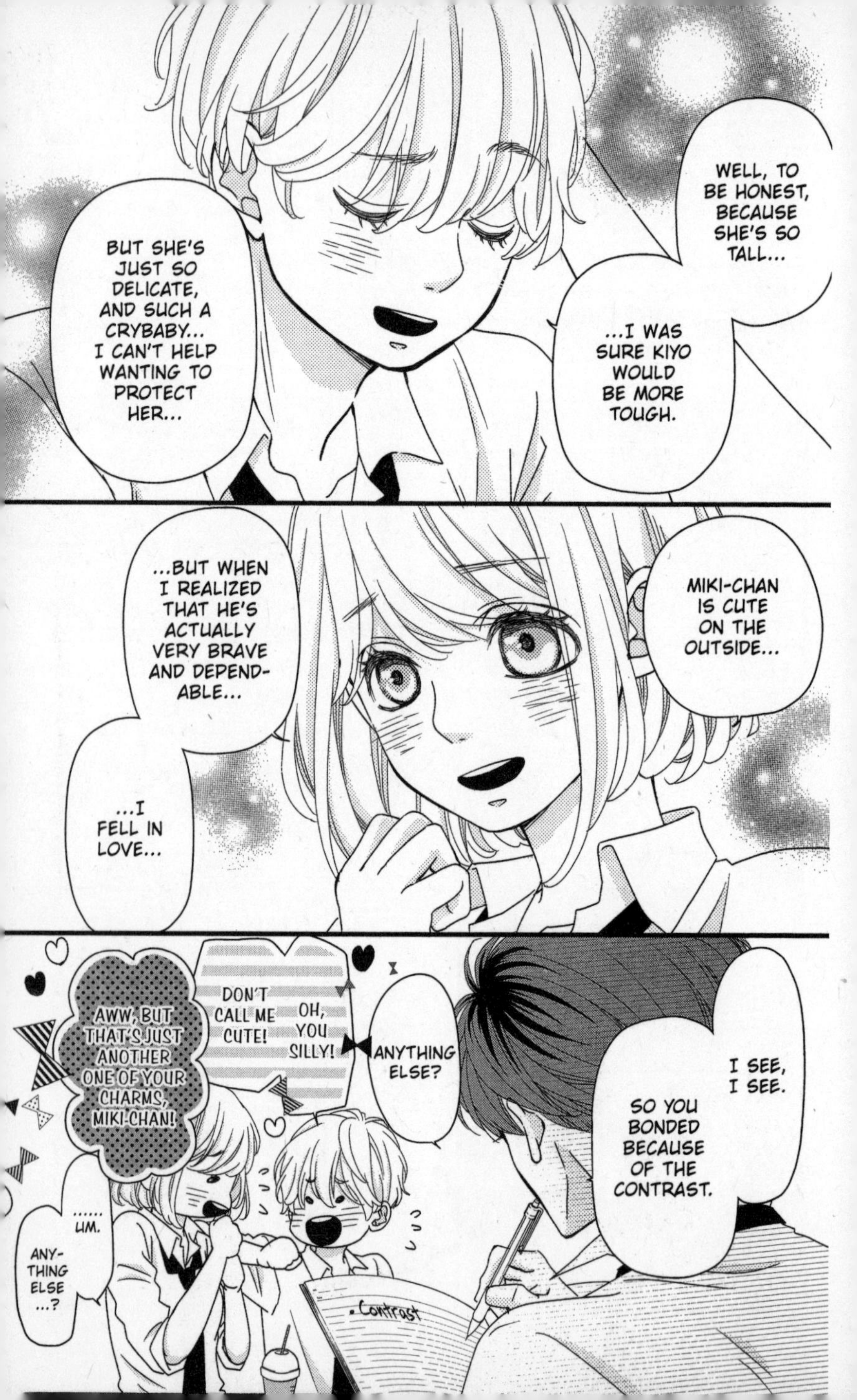
WELL, TO BE HONEST, BECAUSE SHE'S SO TALL...
...I WAS SURE KIYO WOULD BE MORE TOUGH.
BUT SHE'S JUST SO DELICATE, AND SUCH A CRYBABY... I CAN'T HELP WANTING TO PROTECT HER...
MIKI-CHAN IS CUTE ON THE OUTSIDE...
...BUT WHEN I REALIZED THAT HE'S ACTUALLY VERY BRAVE AND DEPEND-ABLE...
...I FELL IN LOVE...
I SEE, I SEE.
SO YOU BONDED BECAUSE OF THE CONTRAST.
ANYTHING ELSE?
OH, YOU SILLY!
DON'T CALL ME CUTE!
AWW, BUT THAT'S JUST ANOTHER ONE OF YOUR CHARMS, MIKI-CHAN!
......UM.
ANY-THING ELSE ...?
• Contrast

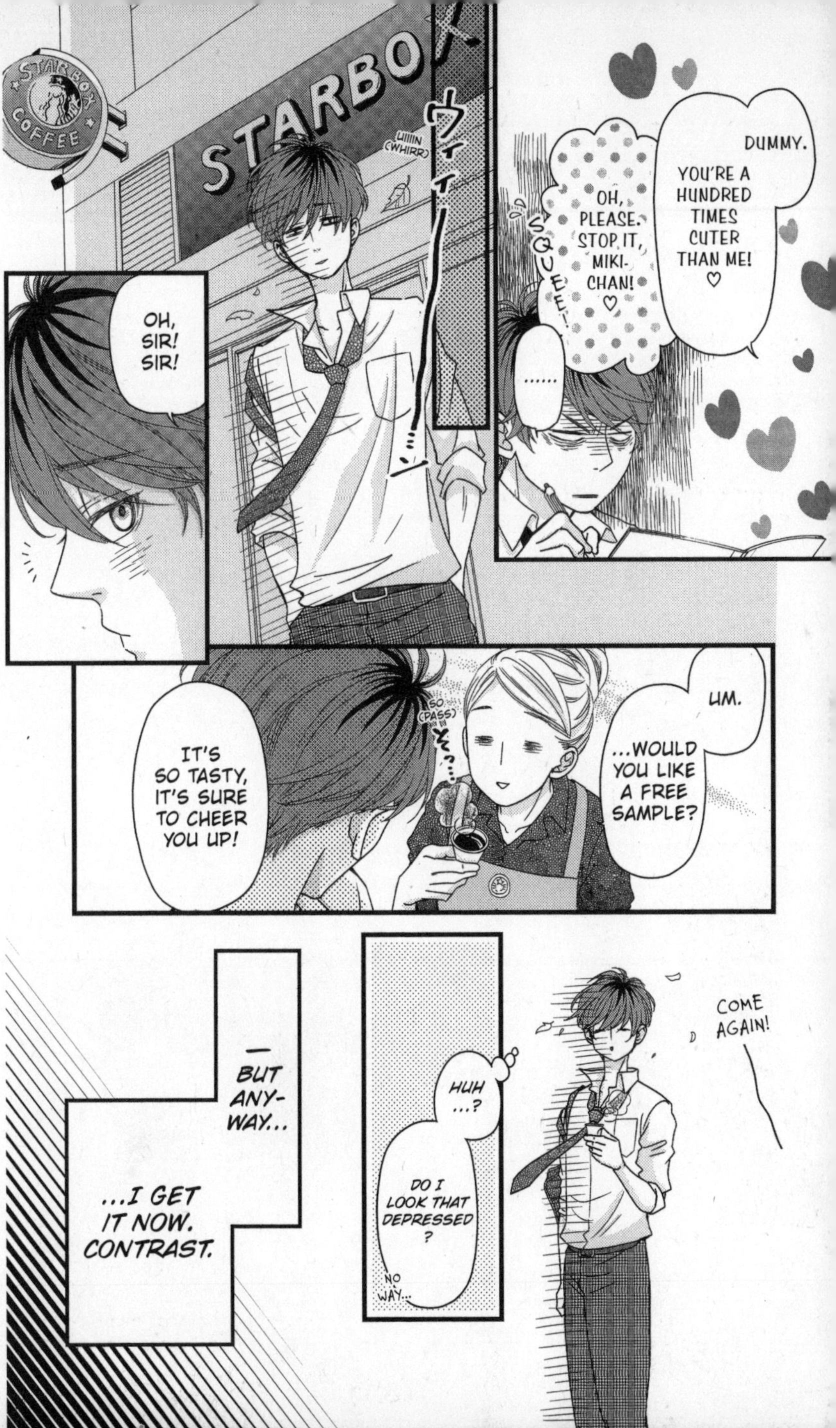
DUMMY.
YOU'RE A HUNDRED TIMES CUTER THAN ME! ♡
OH, PLEASE. STOP IT, MIKI-CHAN! ♡
SQUEE!
......
STARBOX COFFEE
STARBO
UIIIN (WHIRR)
OH, SIR! SIR!
UM.
...WOULD YOU LIKE A FREE SAMPLE?
SO (PASS)
IT'S SO TASTY, IT'S SURE TO CHEER YOU UP!
COME AGAIN!
HUH ...?
DO I LOOK THAT DEPRESSED ?
NO WAY...
—BUT ANYWAY...
...I GET IT NOW. CONTRAST.

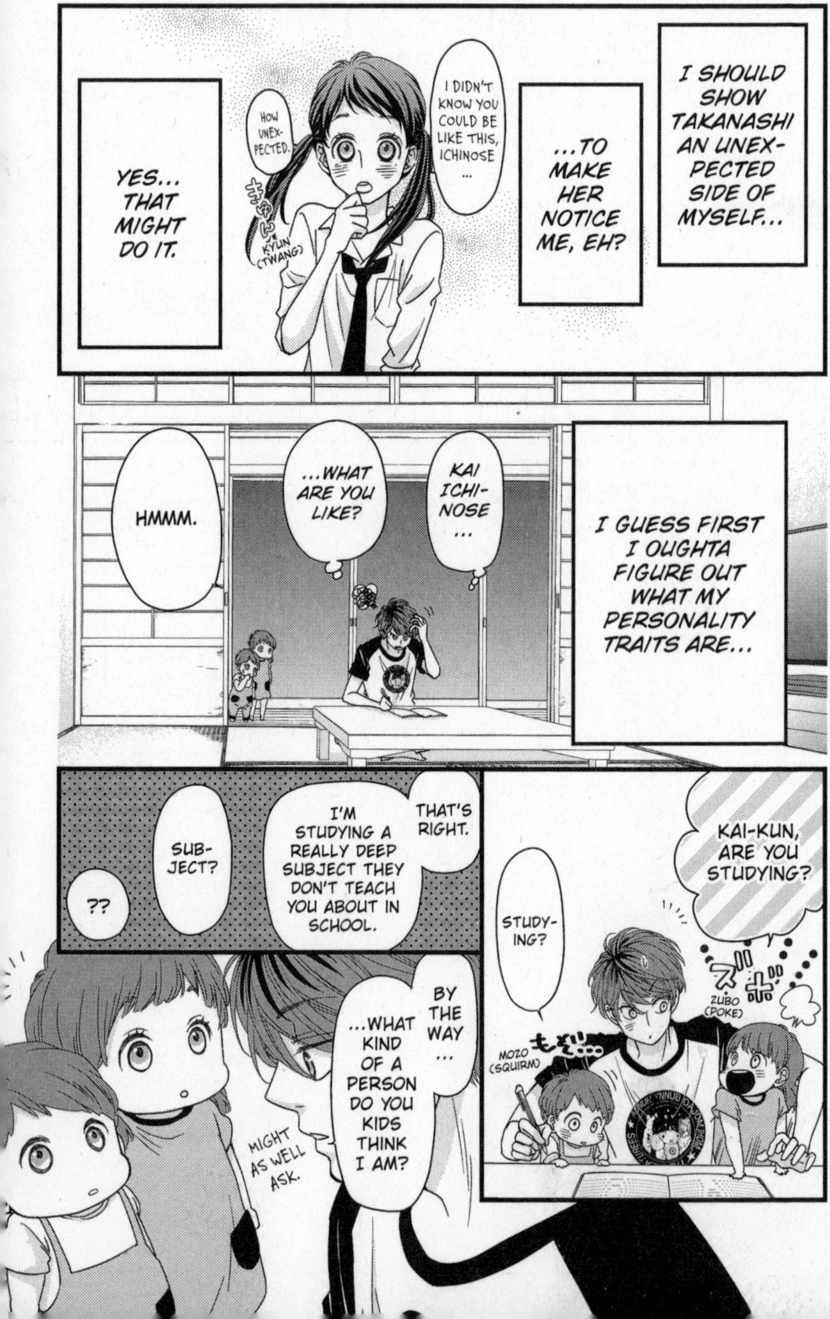
I SHOULD SHOW TAKANASHI AN UNEX-PECTED SIDE OF MYSELF...
...TO MAKE HER NOTICE ME, EH?
I DIDN'T KNOW YOU COULD BE LIKE THIS, ICHINOSE...
HOW UNEX-PECTED.
KYUN (TWANG)
YES... THAT MIGHT DO IT.
I GUESS FIRST I OUGHTA FIGURE OUT WHAT MY PERSONALITY TRAITS ARE...
KAI ICHI-NOSE...
...WHAT ARE YOU LIKE?
HMMM.
KAI-KUN, ARE YOU STUDYING?
ZUBO (POKE)
STUDY-ING?
MOZO (SQUIRM)
THAT'S RIGHT.
I'M STUDYING A REALLY DEEP SUBJECT THEY DON'T TEACH YOU ABOUT IN SCHOOL.
SUB-JECT?
??
BY THE WAY...
...WHAT KIND OF A PERSON DO YOU KIDS THINK I AM?
MIGHT AS WELL ASK.

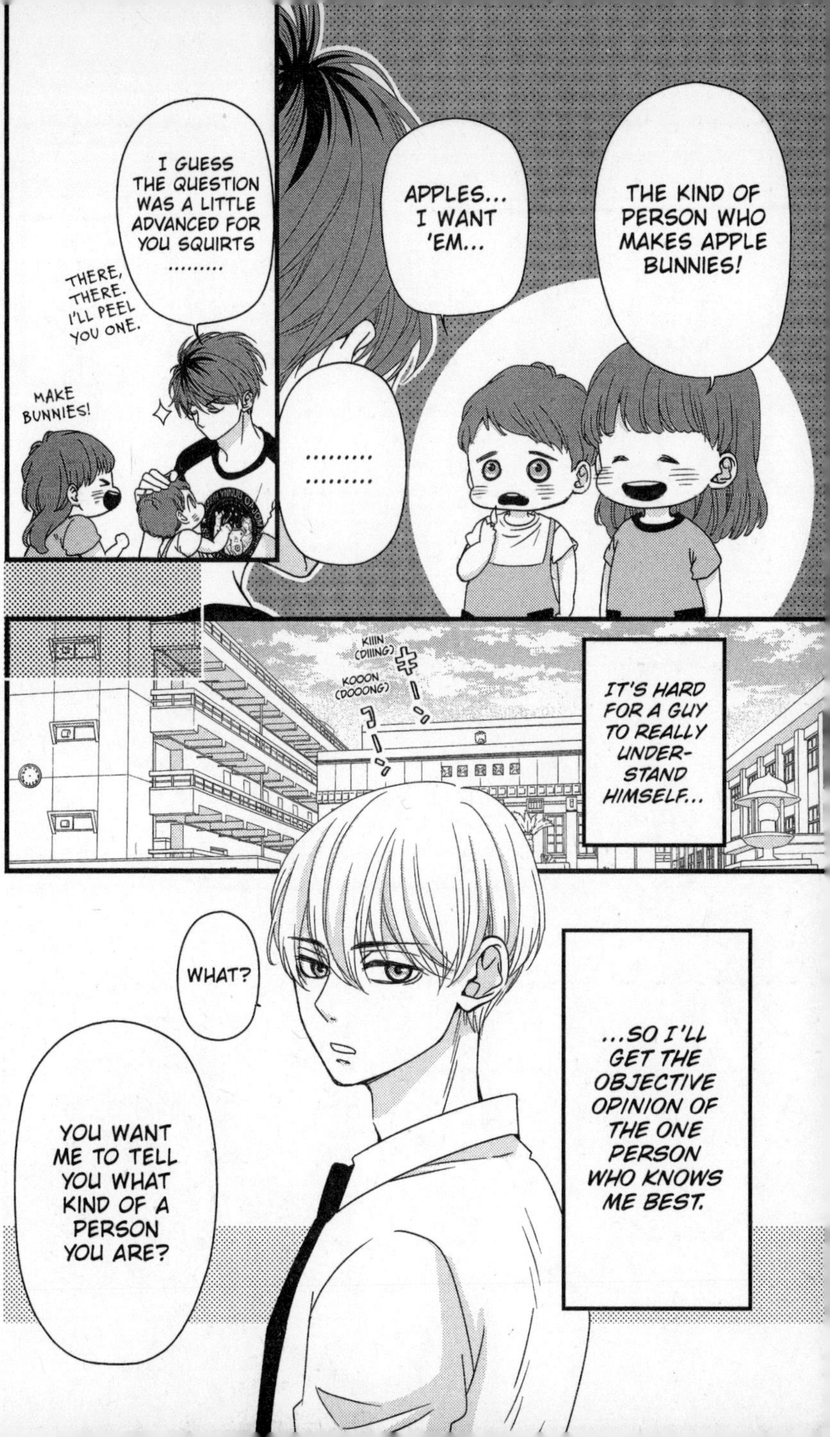
THE KIND OF PERSON WHO MAKES APPLE BUNNIES!
APPLES... I WANT 'EM...
....
I GUESS THE QUESTION WAS A LITTLE ADVANCED FOR YOU SQUIRTS ....
THERE, THERE. I'LL PEEL YOU ONE.
MAKE BUNNIES!
IT'S HARD FOR A GUY TO REALLY UNDER-STAND HIMSELF...
KIIIN (DIIING)
KOOON (DOOONG)
...SO I'LL GET THE OBJECTIVE OPINION OF THE ONE PERSON WHO KNOWS ME BEST.
WHAT?
YOU WANT ME TO TELL YOU WHAT KIND OF A PERSON YOU ARE?

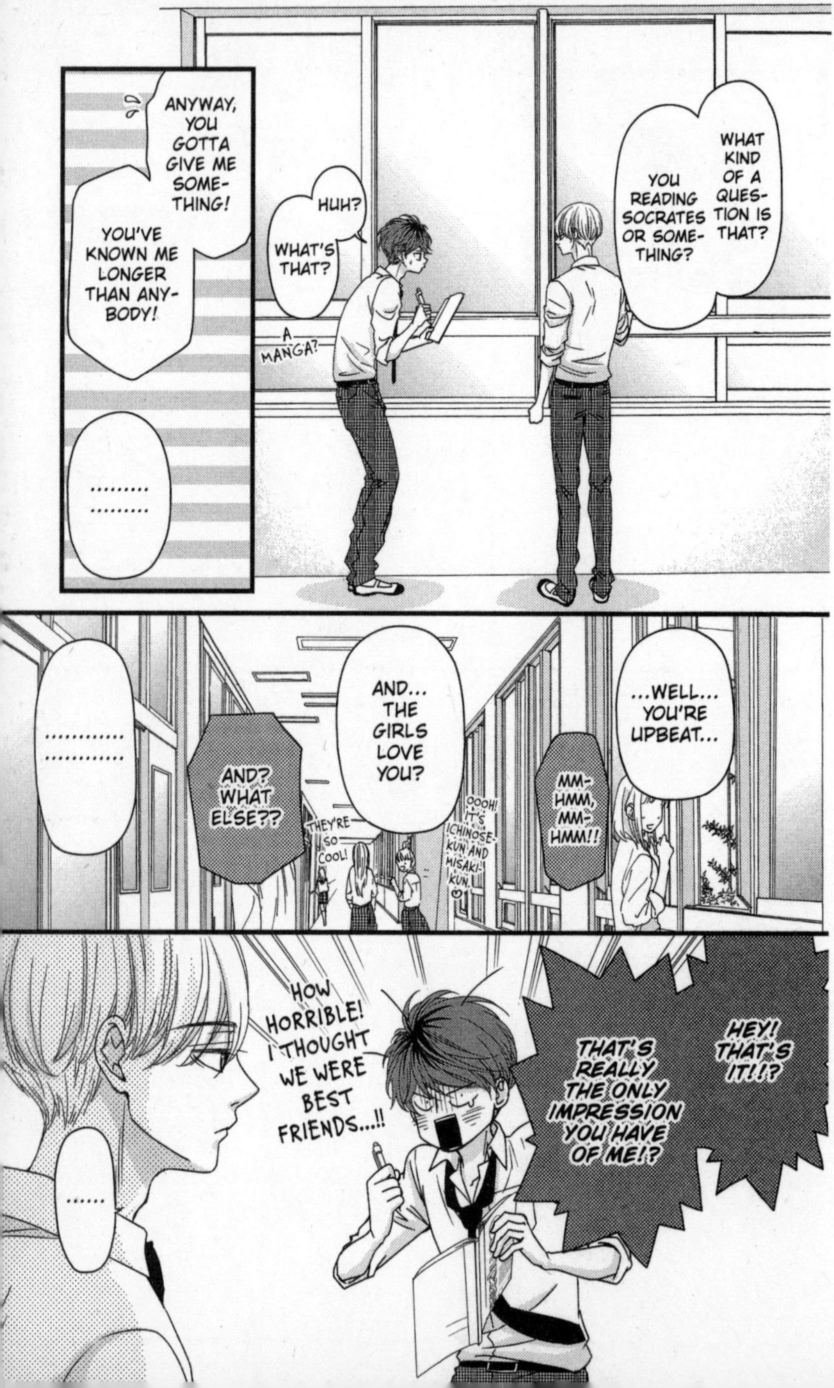
WHAT KIND OF A QUES-TION IS THAT?
YOU READING SOCRATES OR SOME-THING?
HUH?
WHAT'S THAT?
A MANGA?
ANYWAY, YOU GOTTA GIVE ME SOME-THING!
YOU'VE KNOWN ME LONGER THAN ANY-BODY!
....
...WELL... YOU'RE UPBEAT...
MM-HMM, MM-HMM!!
OOOH! IT'S ICHINOSE-KUN AND MISAKI-KUN.
AND... THE GIRLS LOVE YOU?
THEY'RE SO COOL!
AND? WHAT ELSE??
....
HEY! THAT'S IT!!?
THAT'S REALLY THE ONLY IMPRESSION YOU HAVE OF ME!?
HOW HORRIBLE! I THOUGHT WE WERE BEST FRIENDS...!!
......

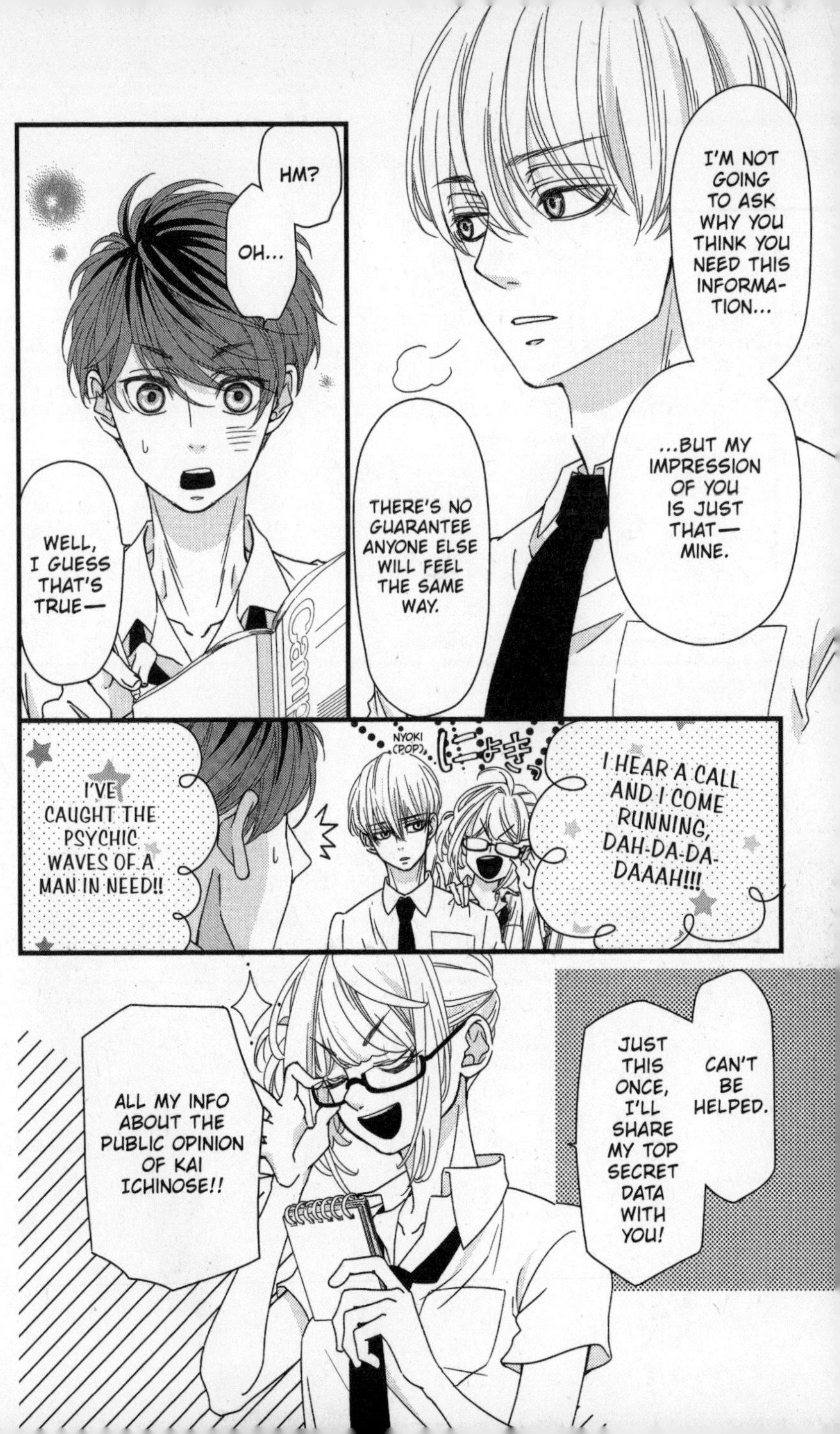
I'M NOT GOING TO ASK WHY YOU THINK YOU NEED THIS INFORMATION...
...BUT MY IMPRESSION OF YOU IS JUST THAT—MINE.
THERE'S NO GUARANTEE ANYONE ELSE WILL FEEL THE SAME WAY.
HM?
OH...
WELL, I GUESS THAT'S TRUE—
I HEAR A CALL AND I COME RUNNING, DAH-DA-DA-DAAAH!!!
NYOKI (POP)
I'VE CAUGHT THE PSYCHIC WAVES OF A MAN IN NEED!!
CAN'T BE HELPED.
JUST THIS ONCE, I'LL SHARE MY TOP SECRET DATA WITH YOU!
ALL MY INFO ABOUT THE PUBLIC OPINION OF KAI ICHINOSE!!

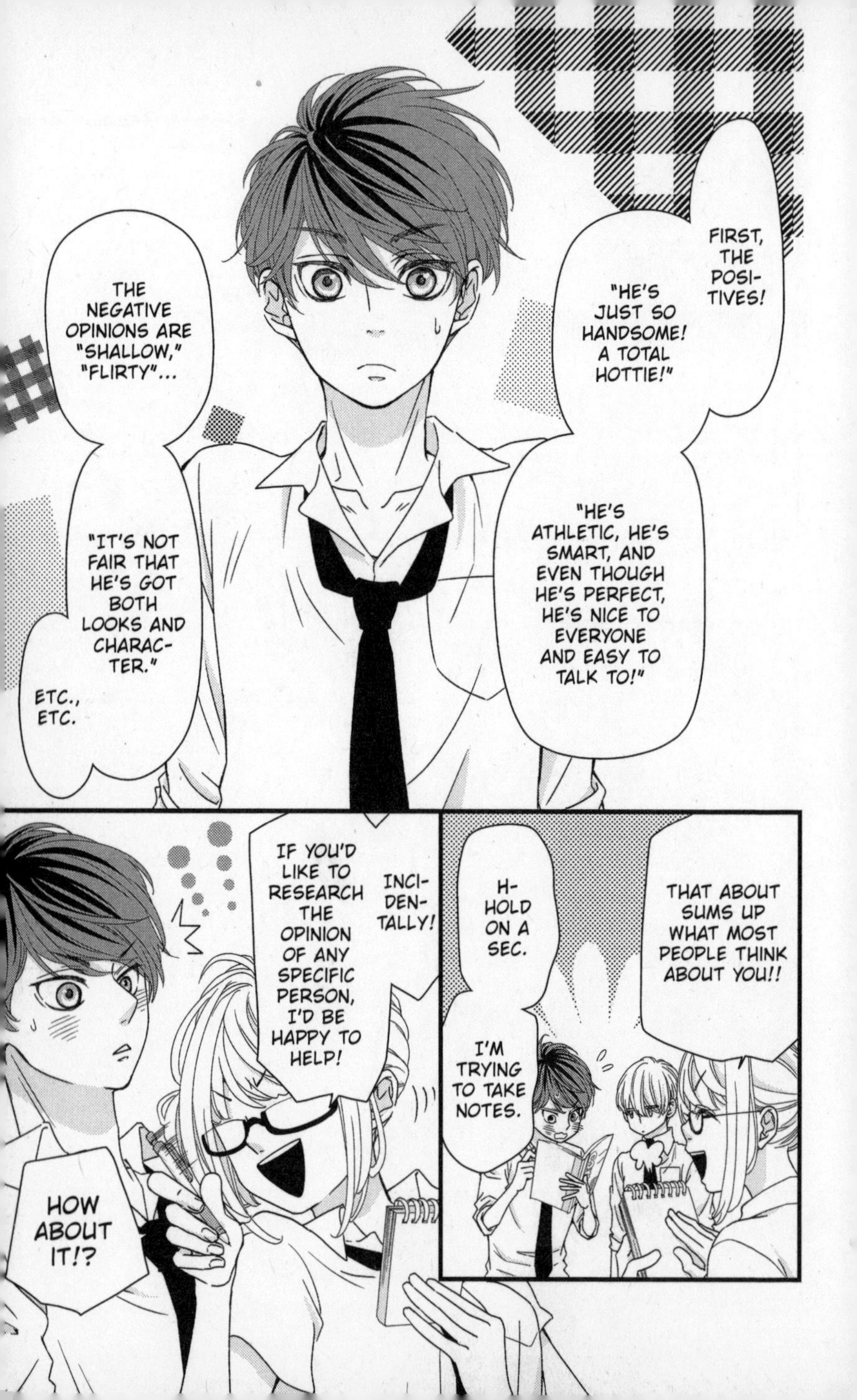
FIRST, THE POSI-TIVES!
"HE'S JUST SO HANDSOME! A TOTAL HOTTIE!"
"HE'S ATHLETIC, HE'S SMART, AND EVEN THOUGH HE'S PERFECT, HE'S NICE TO EVERYONE AND EASY TO TALK TO!"
THE NEGATIVE OPINIONS ARE "SHALLOW," "FLIRTY"...
"IT'S NOT FAIR THAT HE'S GOT BOTH LOOKS AND CHARAC-TER."
ETC., ETC.
THAT ABOUT SUMS UP WHAT MOST PEOPLE THINK ABOUT YOU!!
H-HOLD ON A SEC.
I'M TRYING TO TAKE NOTES.
INCI-DEN-TALLY!
IF YOU'D LIKE TO RESEARCH THE OPINION OF ANY SPECIFIC PERSON, I'D BE HAPPY TO HELP!
HOW ABOUT IT!?

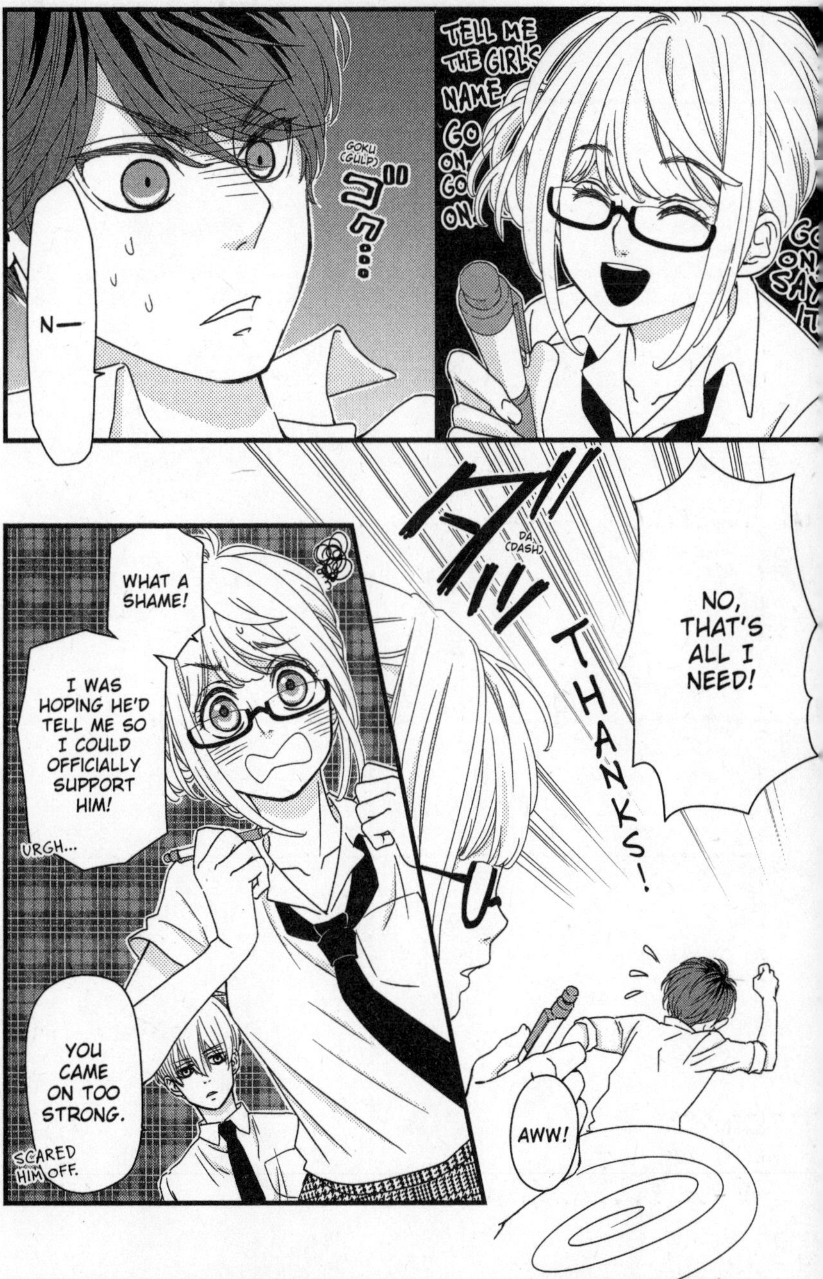
TELL ME THE GIRL'S NAME
GO ON, GO ON.
GO ON SAY IT
GOKU (GULP)
N—
NO, THAT'S ALL I NEED!
DA (DASH)
THANKS!
AWW!
WHAT A SHAME!
I WAS HOPING HE'D TELL ME SO I COULD OFFICIALLY SUPPORT HIM!
URGH...
YOU CAME ON TOO STRONG.
SCARED HIM OFF.

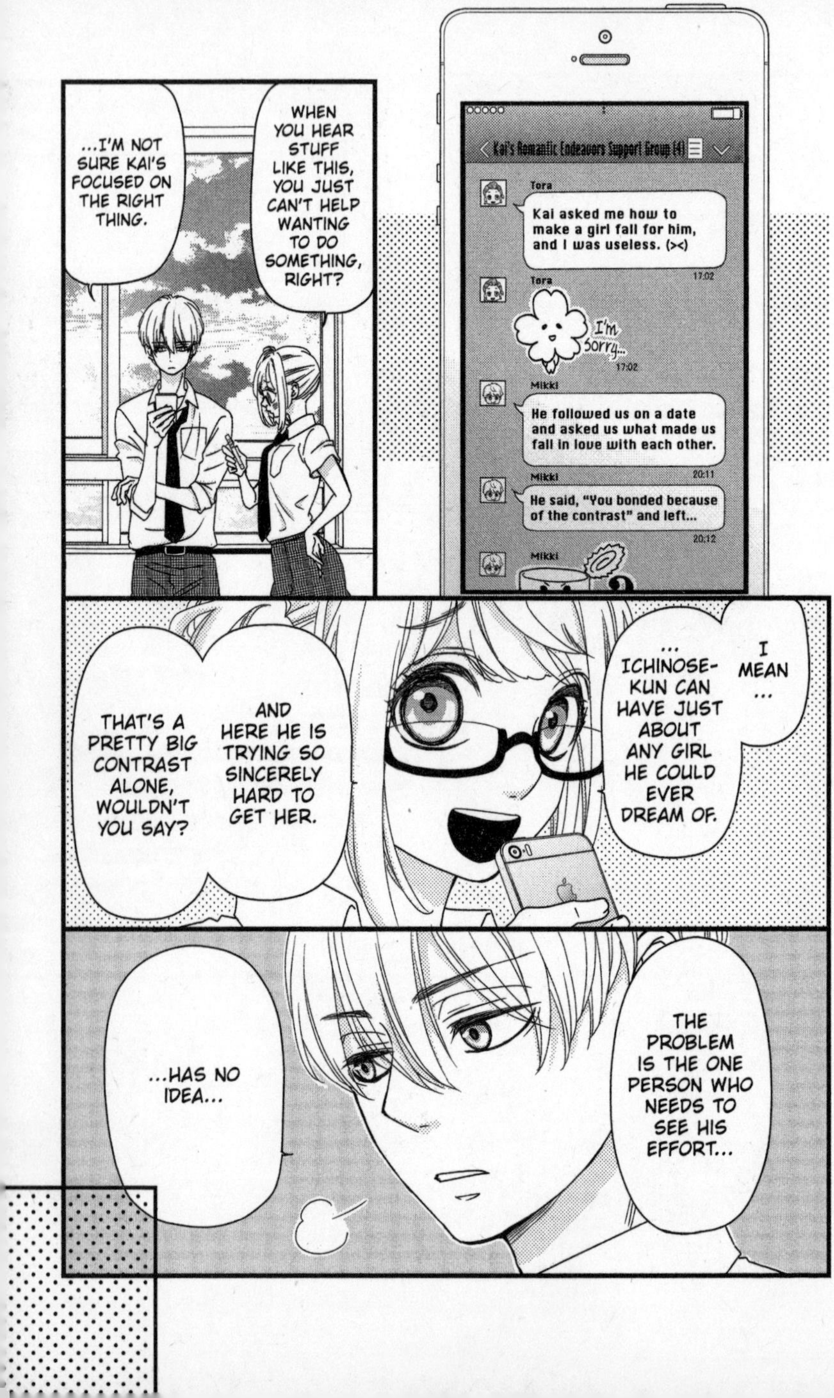
Kai's Romantic Endeavors Support Group (4)
Tora
Kai asked me how to make a girl fall for him, and I was useless. (><)
17:02
Tora
I'm Sorry...
17:02
Mikki
He followed us on a date and asked us what made us fall in love with each other.
20:11
Mikki
He said, "You bonded because of the contrast" and left...
20:12
Mikki
WHEN YOU HEAR STUFF LIKE THIS, YOU JUST CAN'T HELP WANTING TO DO SOMETHING, RIGHT?
...I'M NOT SURE KAI'S FOCUSED ON THE RIGHT THING.
I MEAN...
...ICHINOSE-KUN CAN HAVE JUST ABOUT ANY GIRL HE COULD EVER DREAM OF.
AND HERE HE IS TRYING SO SINCERELY HARD TO GET HER.
THAT'S A PRETTY BIG CONTRAST ALONE, WOULDN'T YOU SAY?
THE PROBLEM IS THE ONE PERSON WHO NEEDS TO SEE HIS EFFORT...
...HAS NO IDEA...

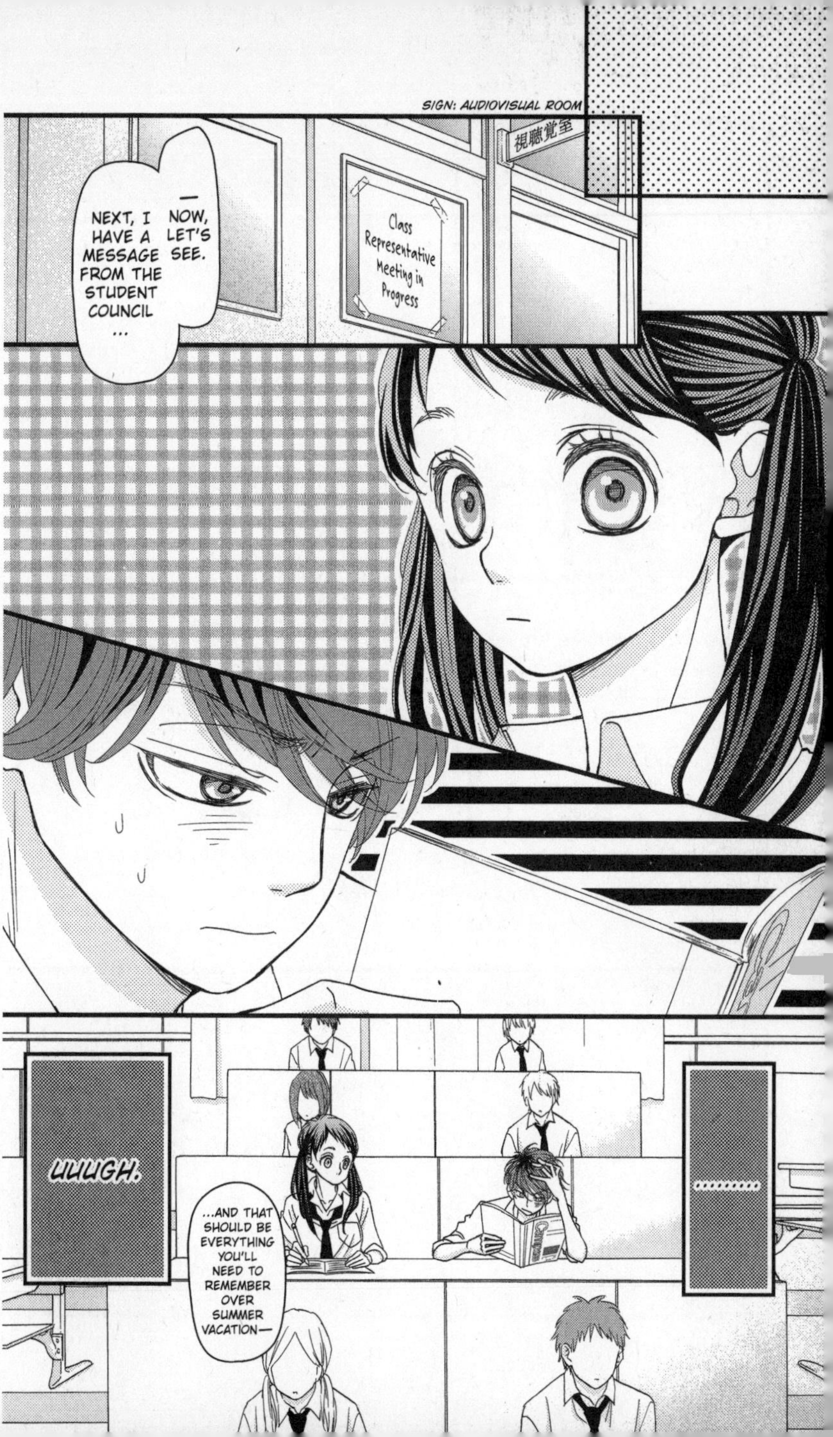
SIGN: AUDIOVISUAL ROOM
視聴覚室
Class Representative Meeting in Progress
—NOW, LET'S SEE.
NEXT, I HAVE A MESSAGE FROM THE STUDENT COUNCIL ...
....
...AND THAT SHOULD BE EVERYTHING YOU'LL NEED TO REMEMBER OVER SUMMER VACATION—
UUUGH.

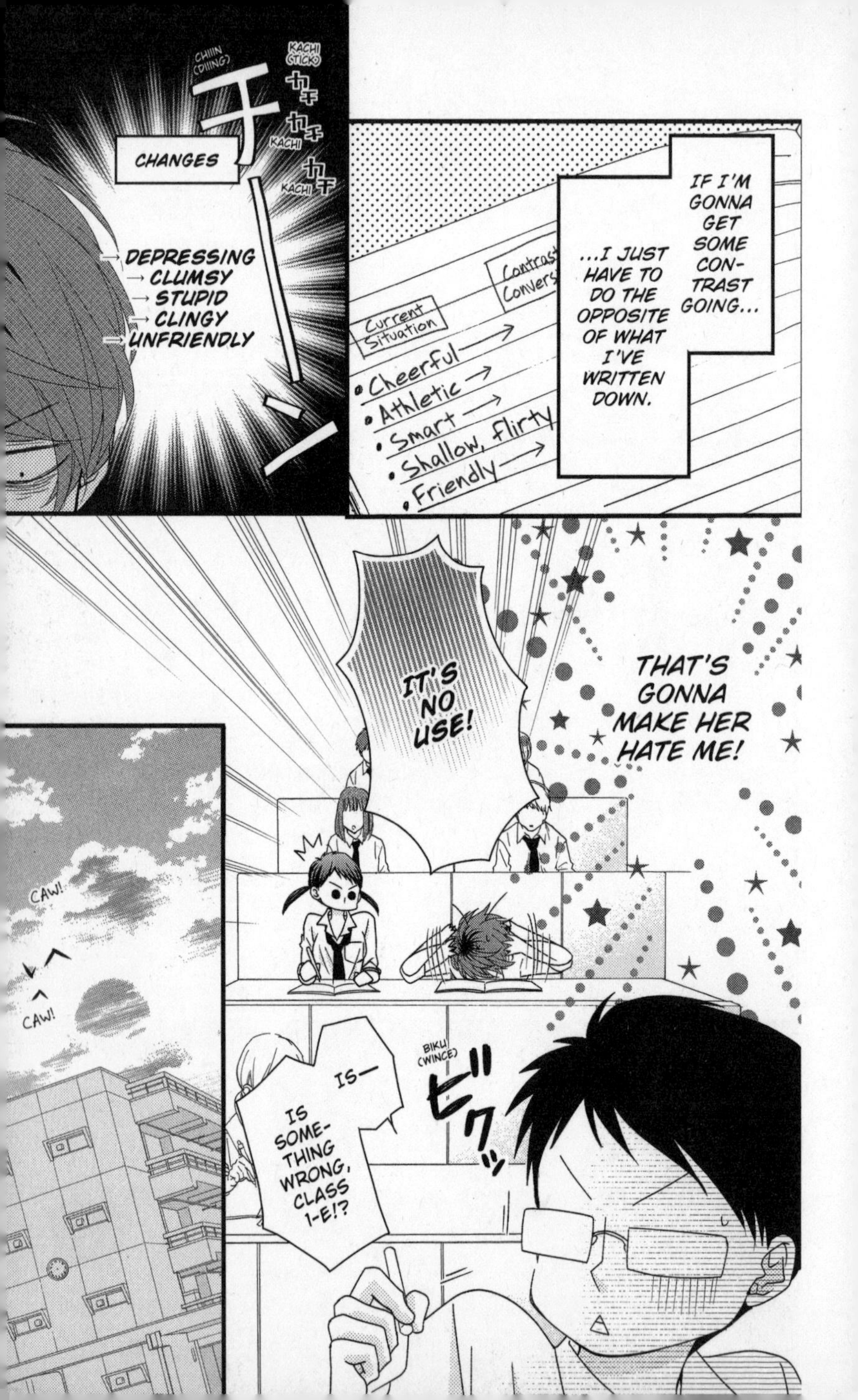
IF I'M GONNA GET SOME CONTRAST GOING...
...I JUST HAVE TO DO THE OPPOSITE OF WHAT I'VE WRITTEN DOWN.
Contrast
Current Situation
Cheerful
Athletic
Smart
Shallow, flirty
Friendly
KACHI (TICK)
KACHI
KACHI
CHIIIN (DIIING)
CHANGES
→DEPRESSING
→CLUMSY
→STUPID
→CLINGY
→UNFRIENDLY
THAT'S GONNA MAKE HER HATE ME!
IT'S NO USE!
BIKU (WINCE)
IS—
IS SOMETHING WRONG, CLASS 1-E!?
CAW!
CAW!

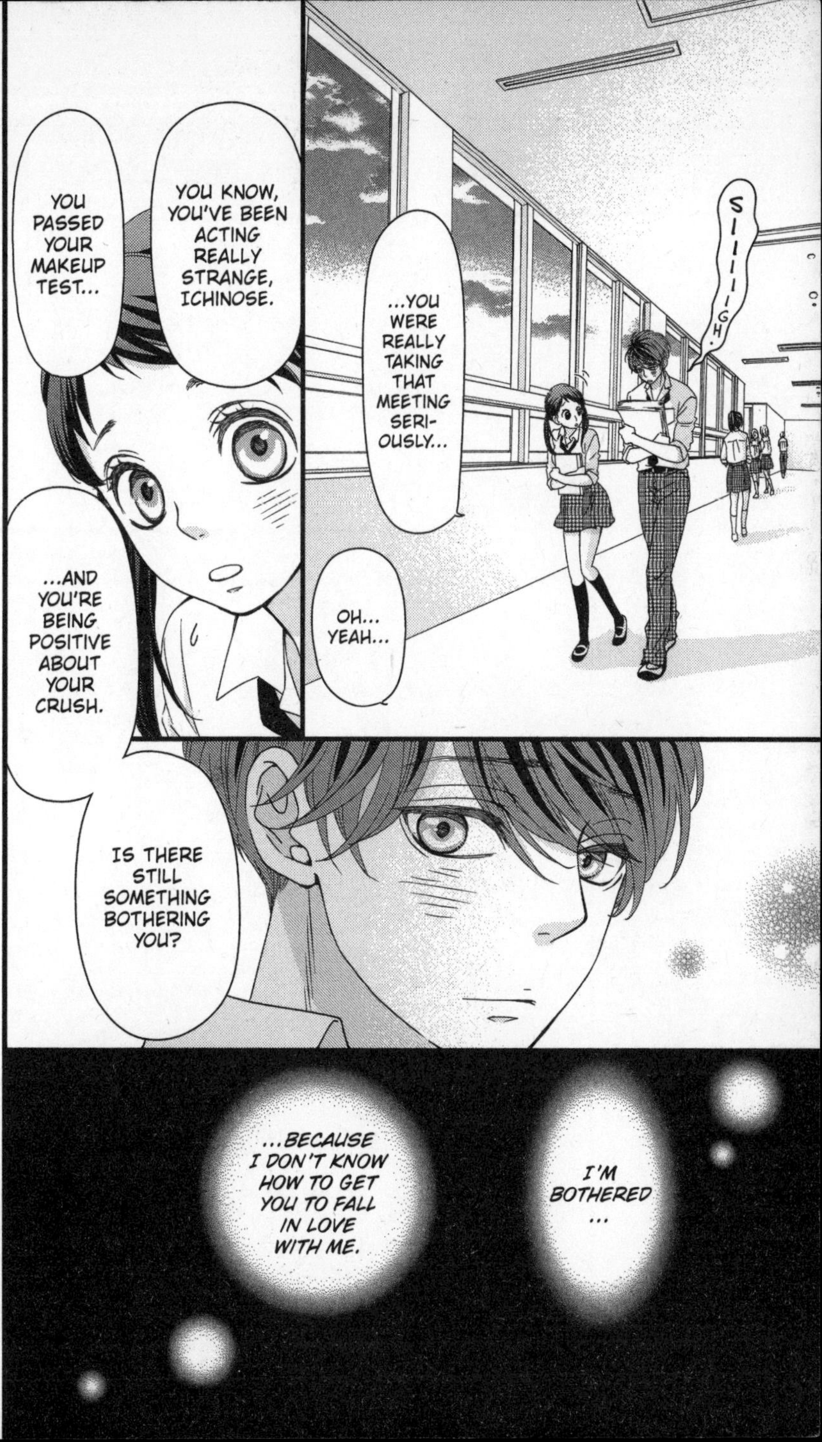
SIIIIIGH.
...YOU WERE REALLY TAKING THAT MEETING SERIOUSLY...
OH... YEAH...
YOU KNOW, YOU'VE BEEN ACTING REALLY STRANGE, ICHINOSE.
YOU PASSED YOUR MAKEUP TEST...
...AND YOU'RE BEING POSITIVE ABOUT YOUR CRUSH.
IS THERE STILL SOMETHING BOTHERING YOU?
I'M BOTHERED...
...BECAUSE I DON'T KNOW HOW TO GET YOU TO FALL IN LOVE WITH ME.

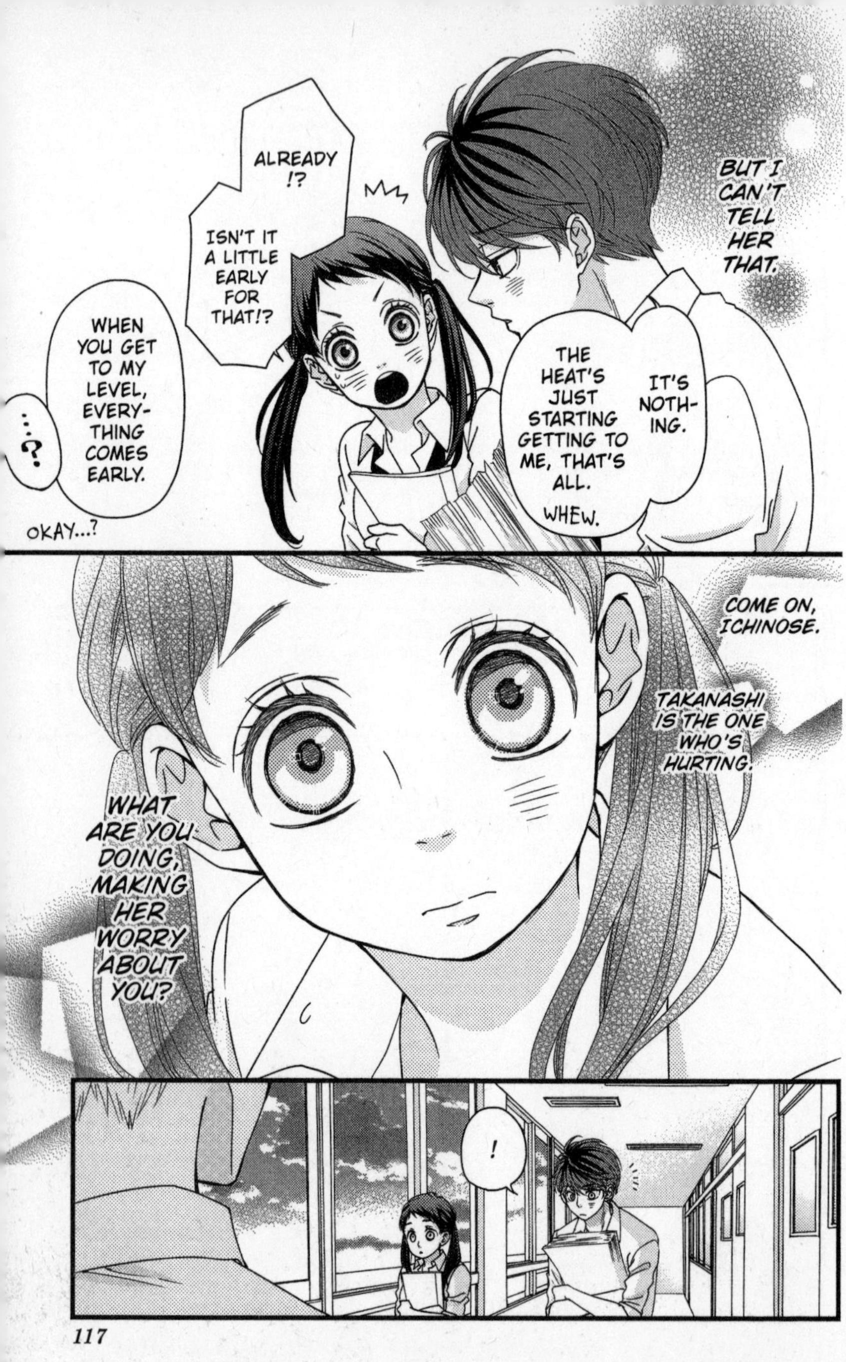
BUT I CAN'T TELL HER THAT.
IT'S NOTHING.
THE HEAT'S JUST STARTING GETTING TO ME, THAT'S ALL.
WHEW.
ALREADY!?
ISN'T IT A LITTLE EARLY FOR THAT!?
WHEN YOU GET TO MY LEVEL, EVERYTHING COMES EARLY.
...?
OKAY...?
COME ON, ICHINOSE.
TAKANASHI IS THE ONE WHO'S HURTING.
WHAT ARE YOU DOING, MAKING HER WORRY ABOUT YOU?
!

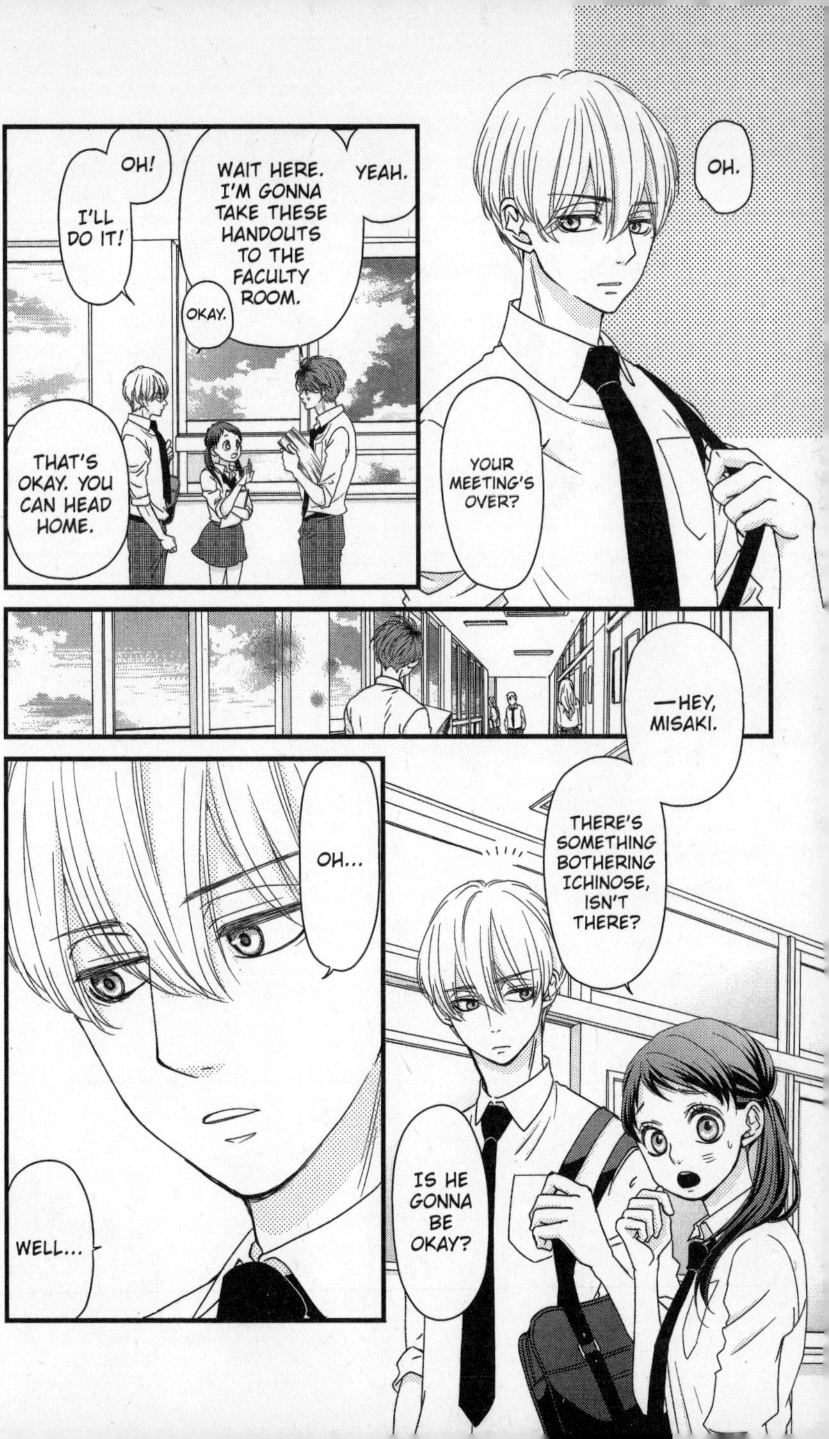
OH.
YOUR MEETING'S OVER?
YEAH.
WAIT HERE. I'M GONNA TAKE THESE HANDOUTS TO THE FACULTY ROOM.
OKAY.
OH! I'LL DO IT!
THAT'S OKAY. YOU CAN HEAD HOME.
—HEY, MISAKI.
THERE'S SOMETHING BOTHERING ICHINOSE, ISN'T THERE?
IS HE GONNA BE OKAY?
OH...
WELL...

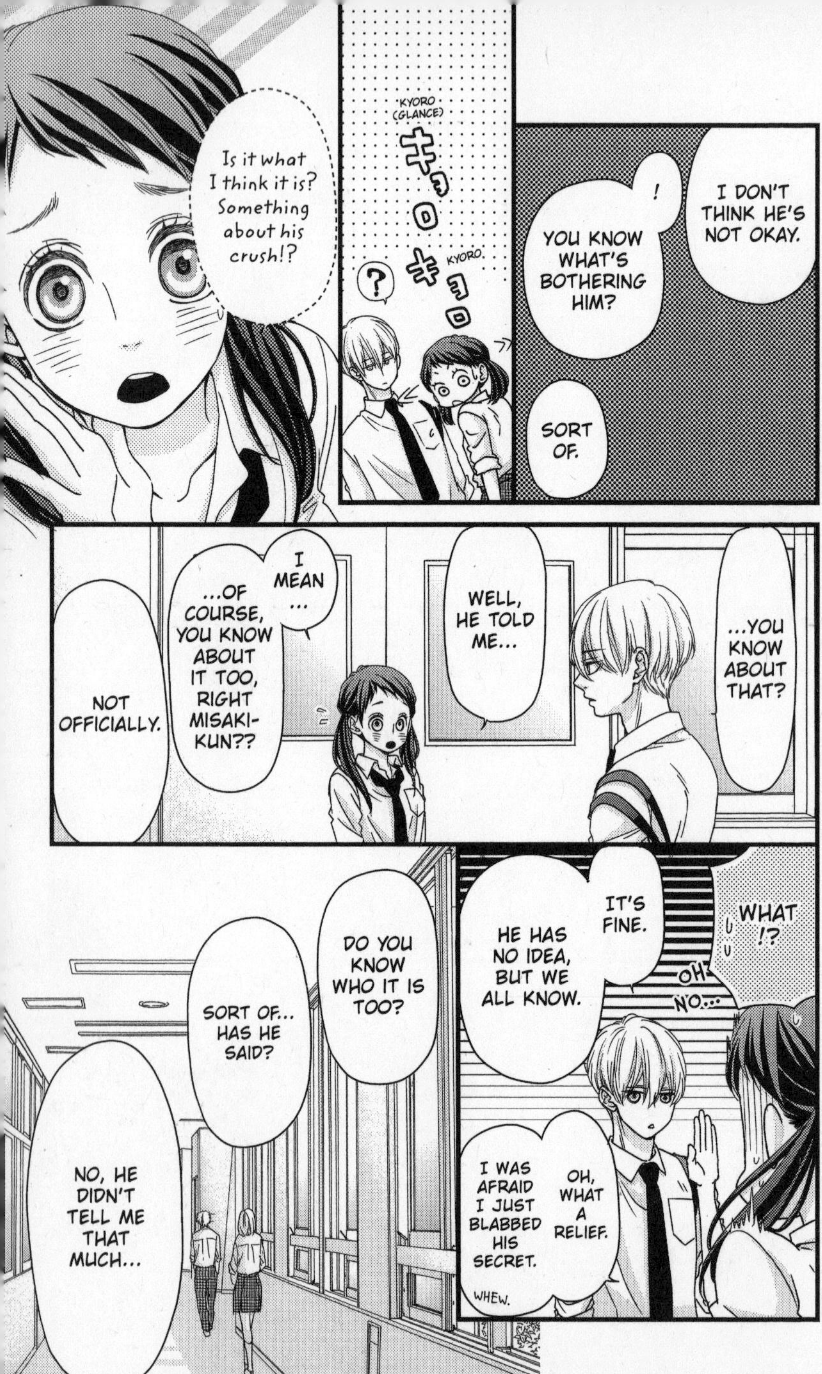
I DON'T THINK HE'S NOT OKAY.
!
YOU KNOW WHAT'S BOTHERING HIM?
SORT OF.
KYORO (GLANCE)
キョロ
KYORO.
キョロ
?
Is it what I think it is? Something about his crush!?
...YOU KNOW ABOUT THAT?
WELL, HE TOLD ME...
I MEAN...
...OF COURSE, YOU KNOW ABOUT IT TOO, RIGHT MISAKI-KUN??
NOT OFFICIALLY.
WHAT!?
OH NO...
IT'S FINE.
HE HAS NO IDEA, BUT WE ALL KNOW.
OH, WHAT A RELIEF.
I WAS AFRAID I JUST BLABBED HIS SECRET.
WHEW.
DO YOU KNOW WHO IT IS TOO?
SORT OF... HAS HE SAID?
NO, HE DIDN'T TELL ME THAT MUCH...

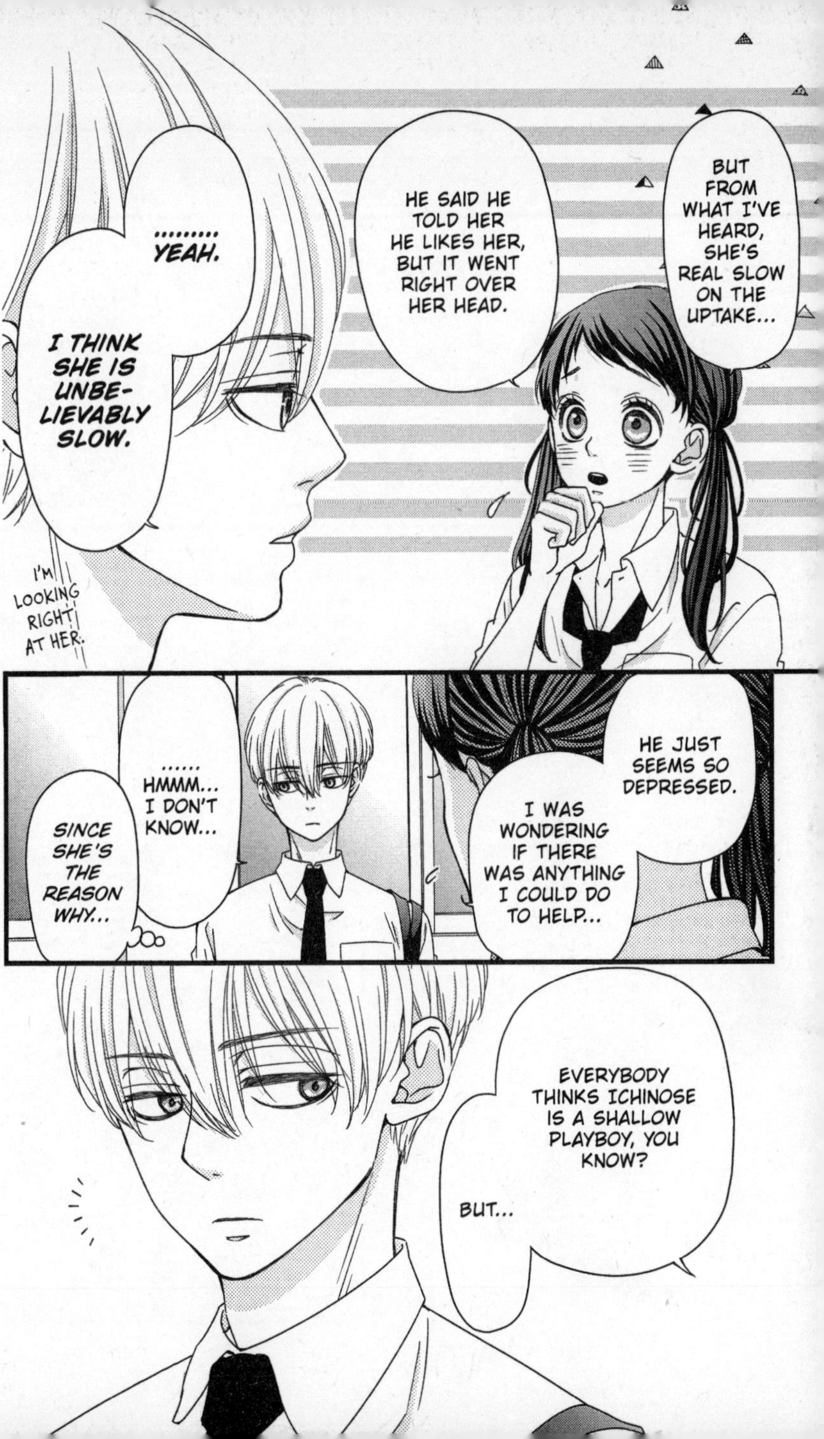
BUT FROM WHAT I'VE HEARD, SHE'S REAL SLOW ON THE UPTAKE...
HE SAID HE TOLD HER HE LIKES HER, BUT IT WENT RIGHT OVER HER HEAD.
.... YEAH.
I THINK SHE IS UNBE-LIEVABLY SLOW.
I'M LOOKING RIGHT AT HER.
HE JUST SEEMS SO DEPRESSED.
I WAS WONDERING IF THERE WAS ANYTHING I COULD DO TO HELP...
...... HMMM... I DON'T KNOW...
SINCE SHE'S THE REASON WHY...
EVERYBODY THINKS ICHINOSE IS A SHALLOW PLAYBOY, YOU KNOW?
BUT...

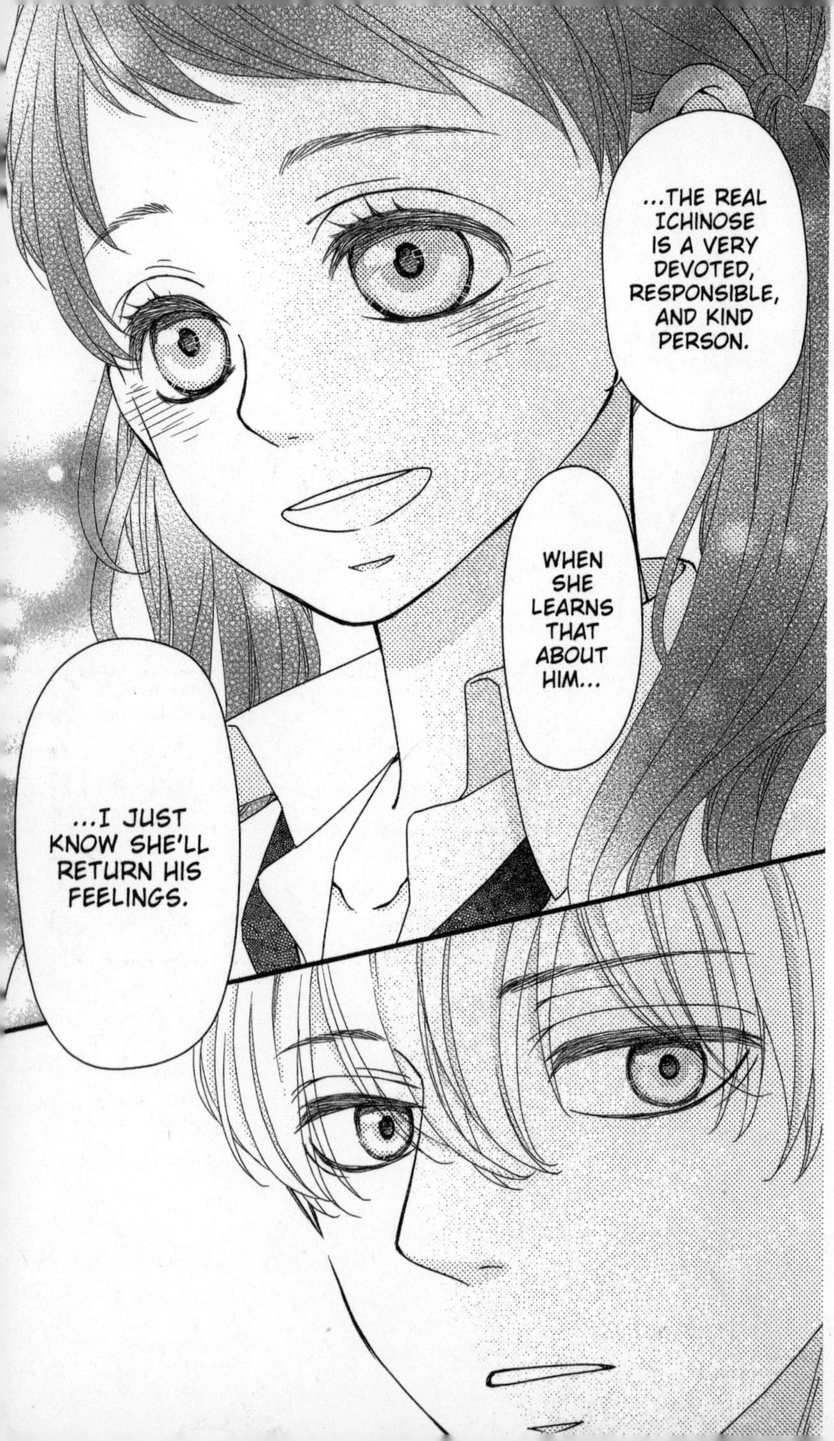
...THE REAL ICHINOSE IS A VERY DEVOTED, RESPONSIBLE, AND KIND PERSON.
WHEN SHE LEARNS THAT ABOUT HIM...
...I JUST KNOW SHE'LL RETURN HIS FEELINGS.

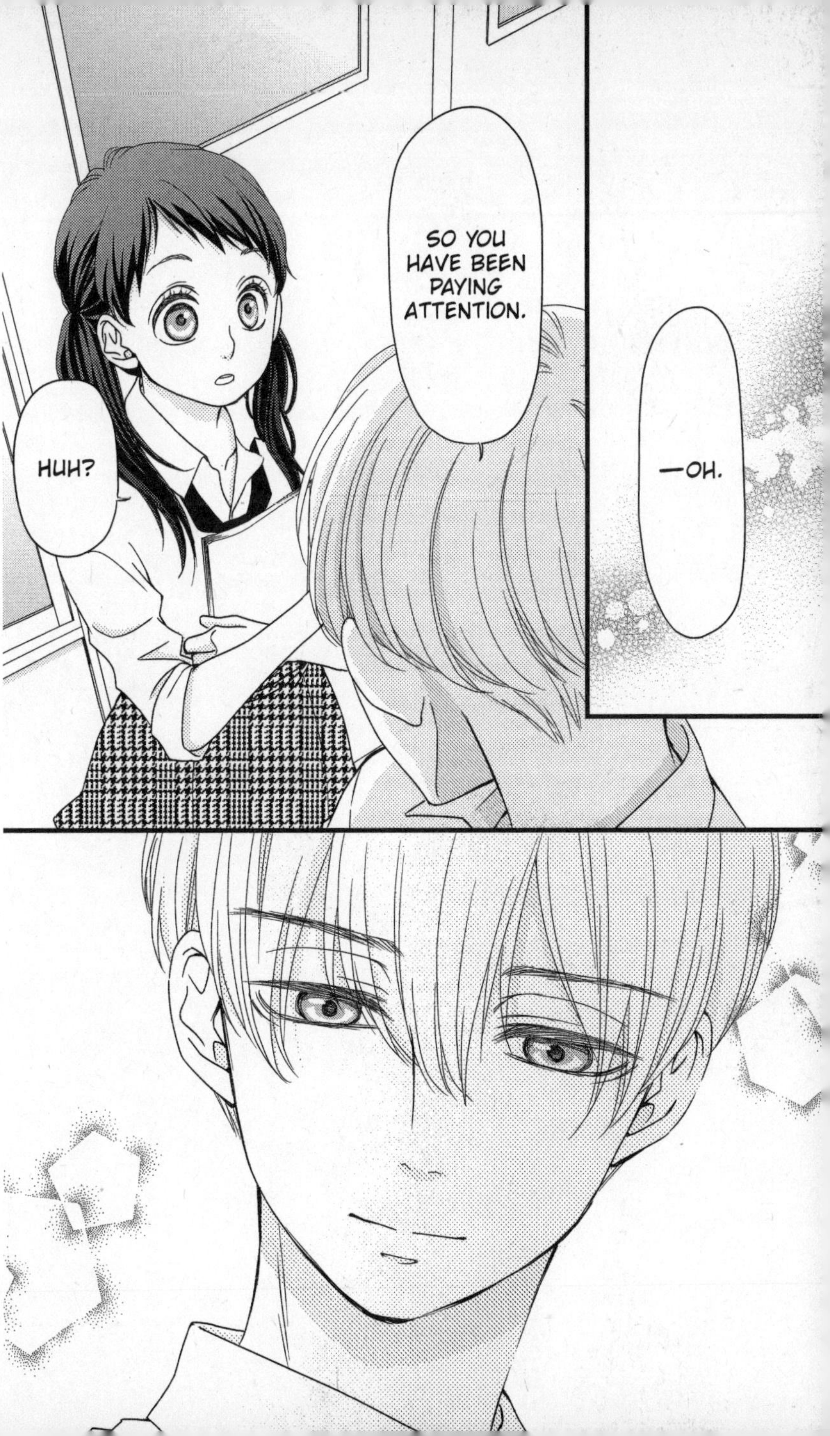
—OH.
SO YOU HAVE BEEN PAYING ATTENTION.
HUH?

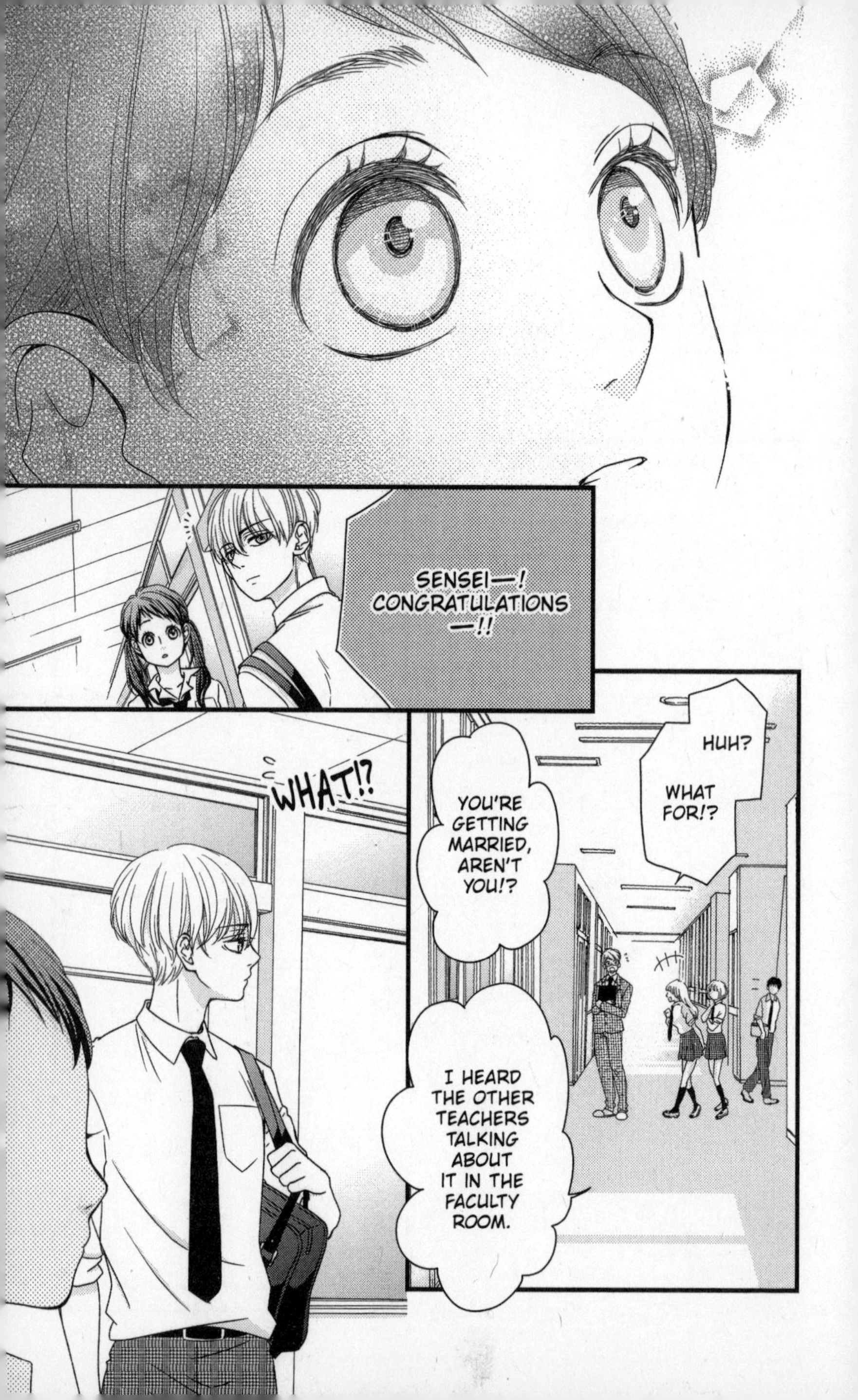
SENSEI—! CONGRATULATIONS—!!
HUH?
WHAT FOR!?
YOU'RE GETTING MARRIED, AREN'T YOU!?
I HEARD THE OTHER TEACHERS TALKING ABOUT IT IN THE FACULTY ROOM.
WHAT!?

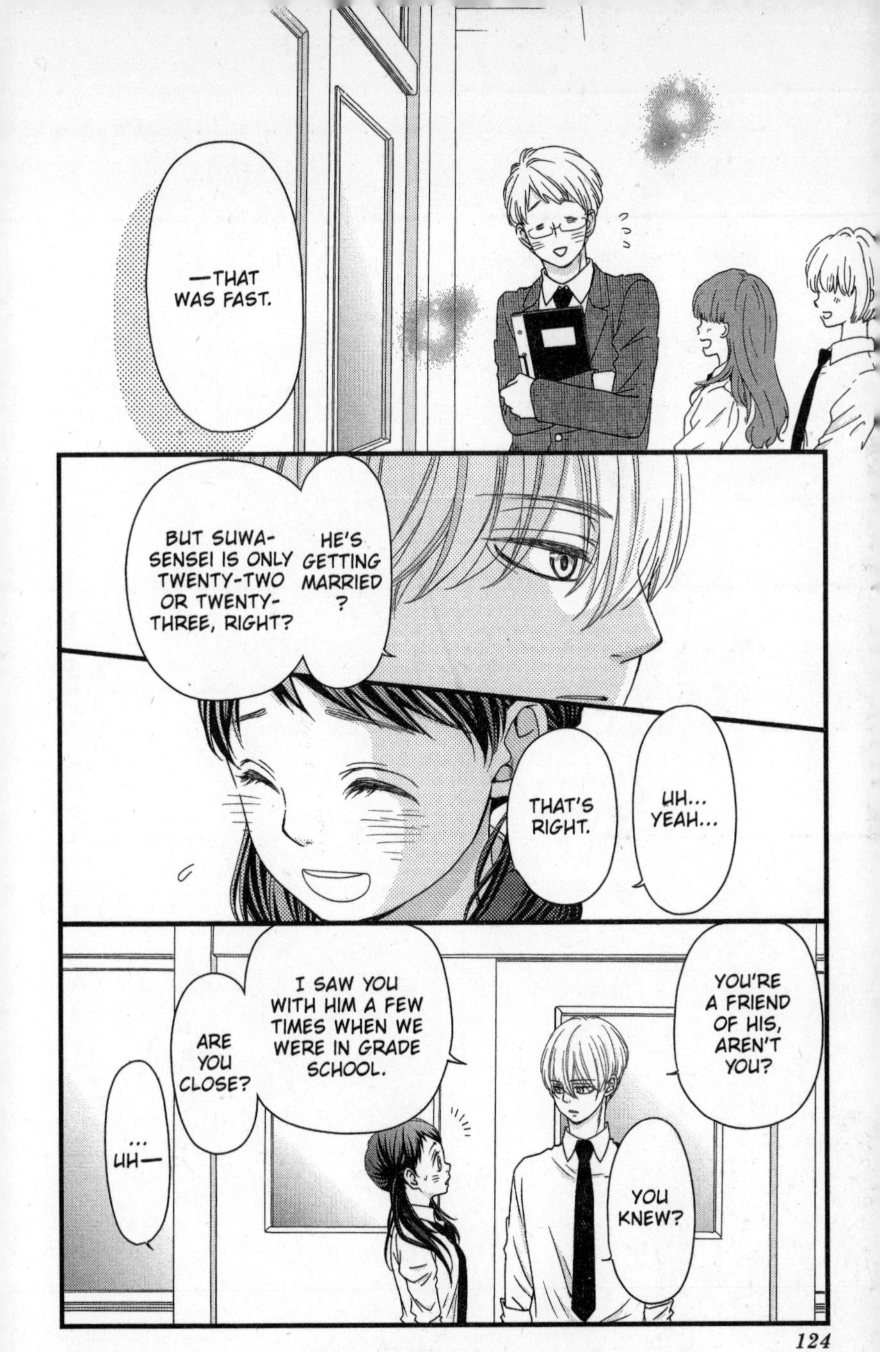
—THAT WAS FAST.
HE'S GETTING MARRIED?
BUT SUWA-SENSEI IS ONLY TWENTY-TWO OR TWENTY-THREE, RIGHT?
UH... YEAH...
THAT'S RIGHT.
YOU'RE A FRIEND OF HIS, AREN'T YOU?
YOU KNEW?
I SAW YOU WITH HIM A FEW TIMES WHEN WE WERE IN GRADE SCHOOL.
ARE YOU CLOSE?
... UH—

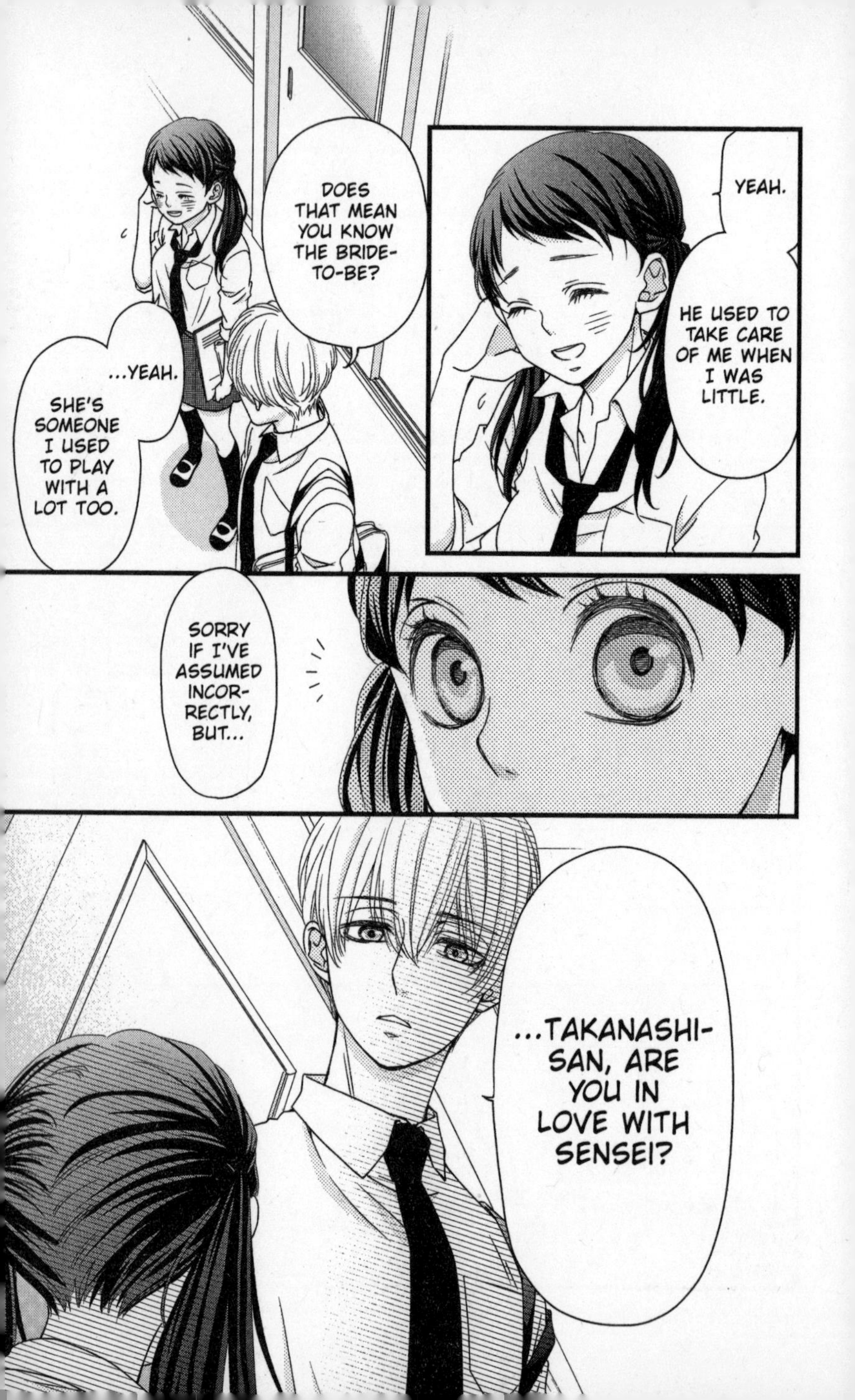
YEAH.
HE USED TO TAKE CARE OF ME WHEN I WAS LITTLE.
DOES THAT MEAN YOU KNOW THE BRIDE-TO-BE?
...YEAH.
SHE'S SOMEONE I USED TO PLAY WITH A LOT TOO.
SORRY IF I'VE ASSUMED INCOR-RECTLY, BUT...
...TAKANASHI-SAN, ARE YOU IN LOVE WITH SENSEI?

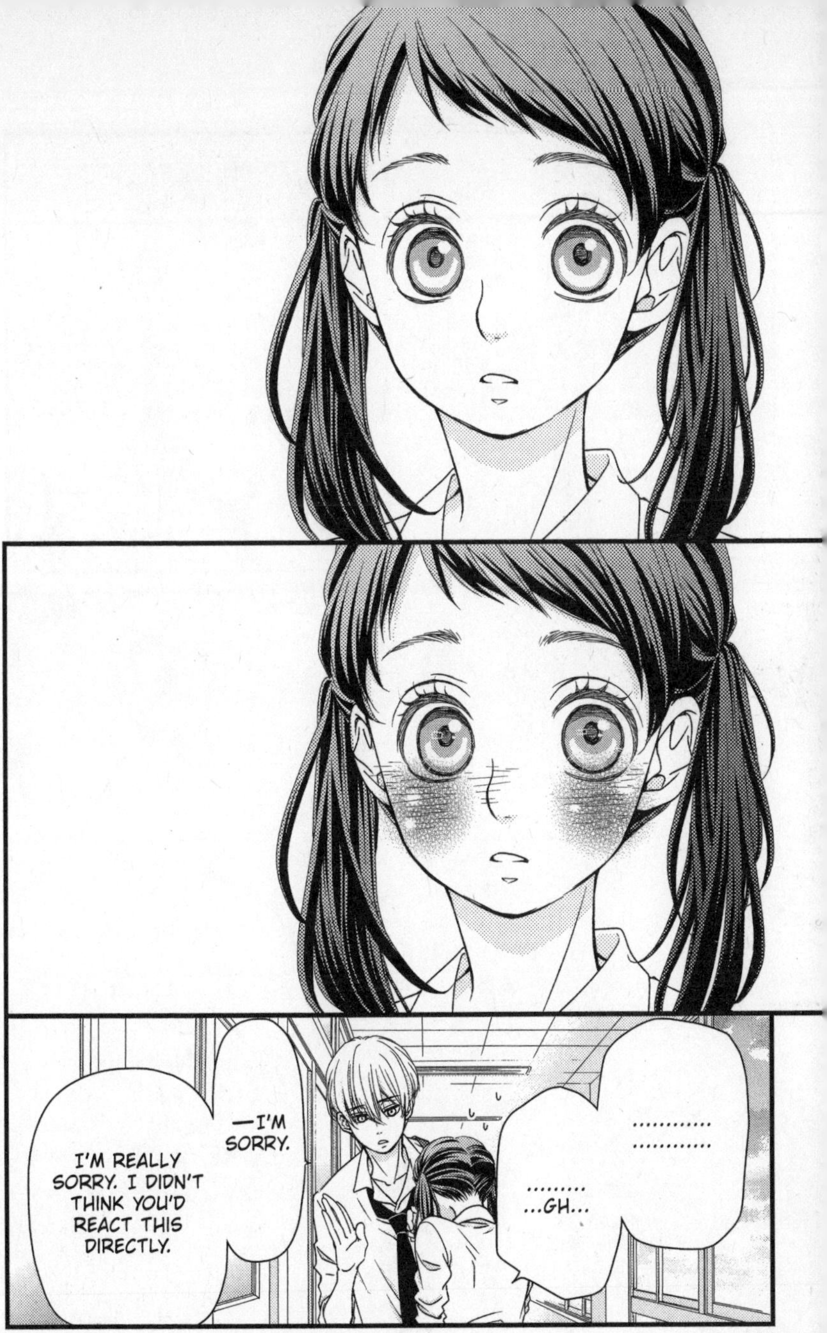
....GH...
—I'M SORRY.
I'M REALLY SORRY. I DIDN'T THINK YOU'D REACT THIS DIRECTLY.

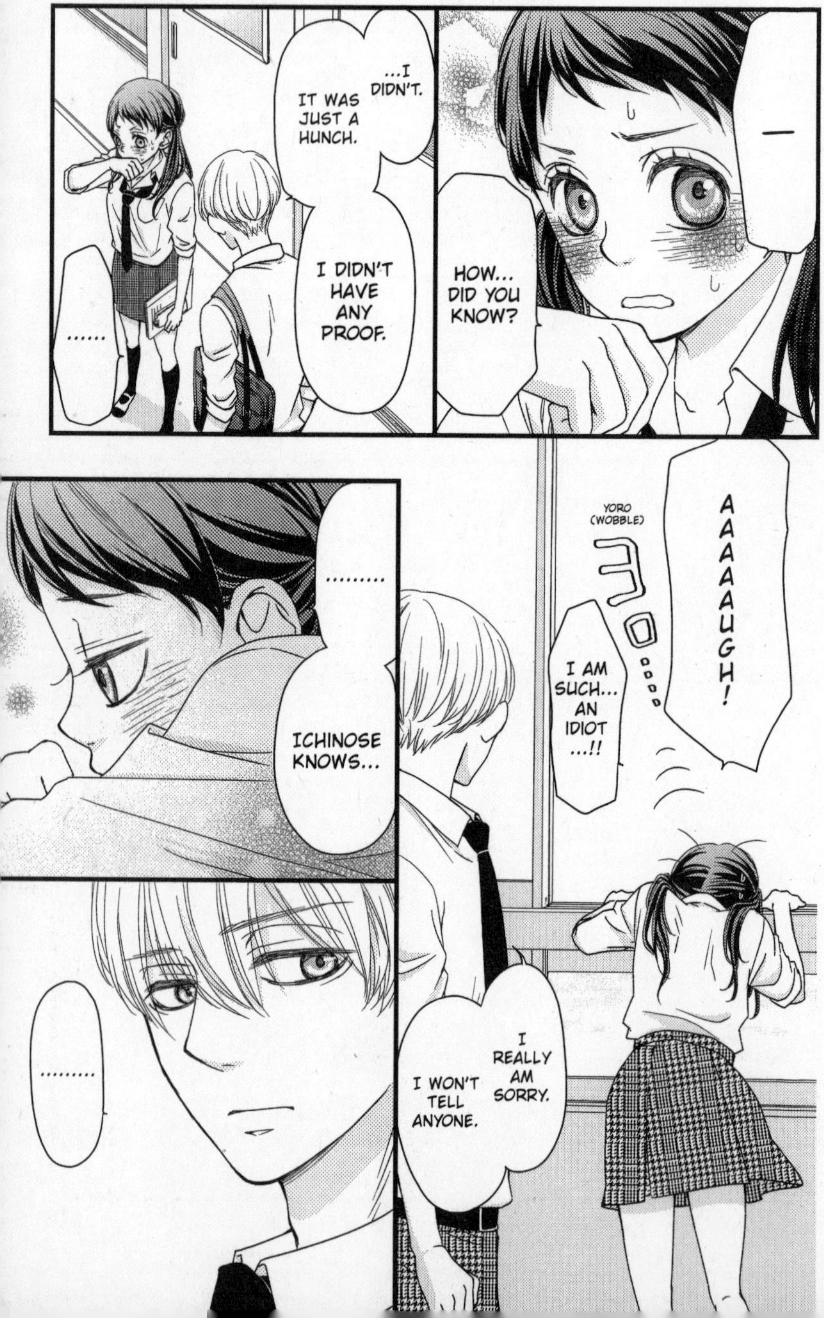
—
HOW... DID YOU KNOW?
...I DIDN'T.
IT WAS JUST A HUNCH.
I DIDN'T HAVE ANY PROOF.
......
AAAAAAUGH!
YORO (WOBBLE)
I AM SUCH... AN IDIOT ...!!
I REALLY AM SORRY.
I WON'T TELL ANYONE.
....
ICHINOSE KNOWS...
....

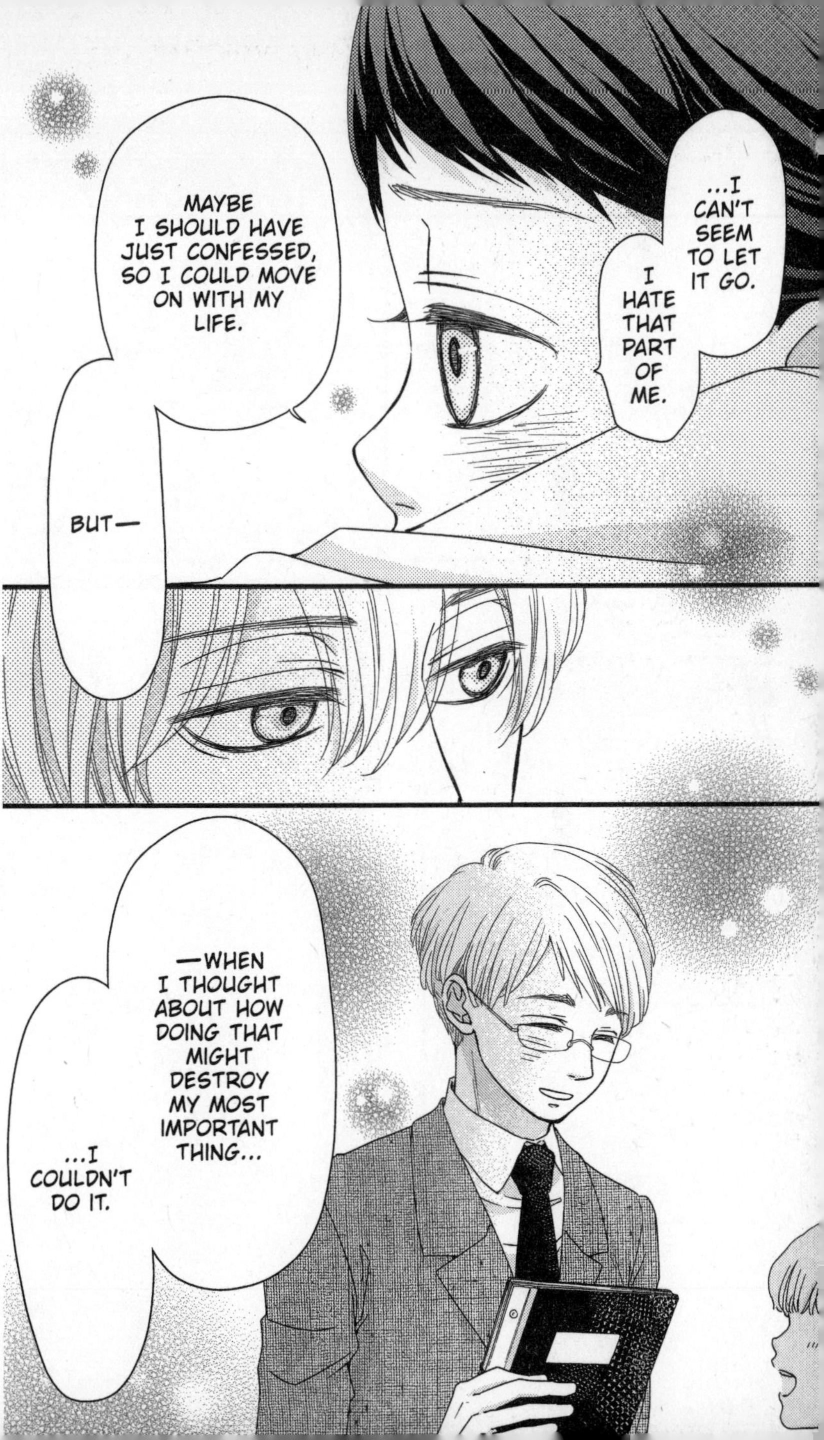
...I CAN'T SEEM TO LET IT GO.
I HATE THAT PART OF ME.
MAYBE I SHOULD HAVE JUST CONFESSED, SO I COULD MOVE ON WITH MY LIFE.
BUT—
—WHEN I THOUGHT ABOUT HOW DOING THAT MIGHT DESTROY MY MOST IMPORTANT THING...
...I COULDN'T DO IT.

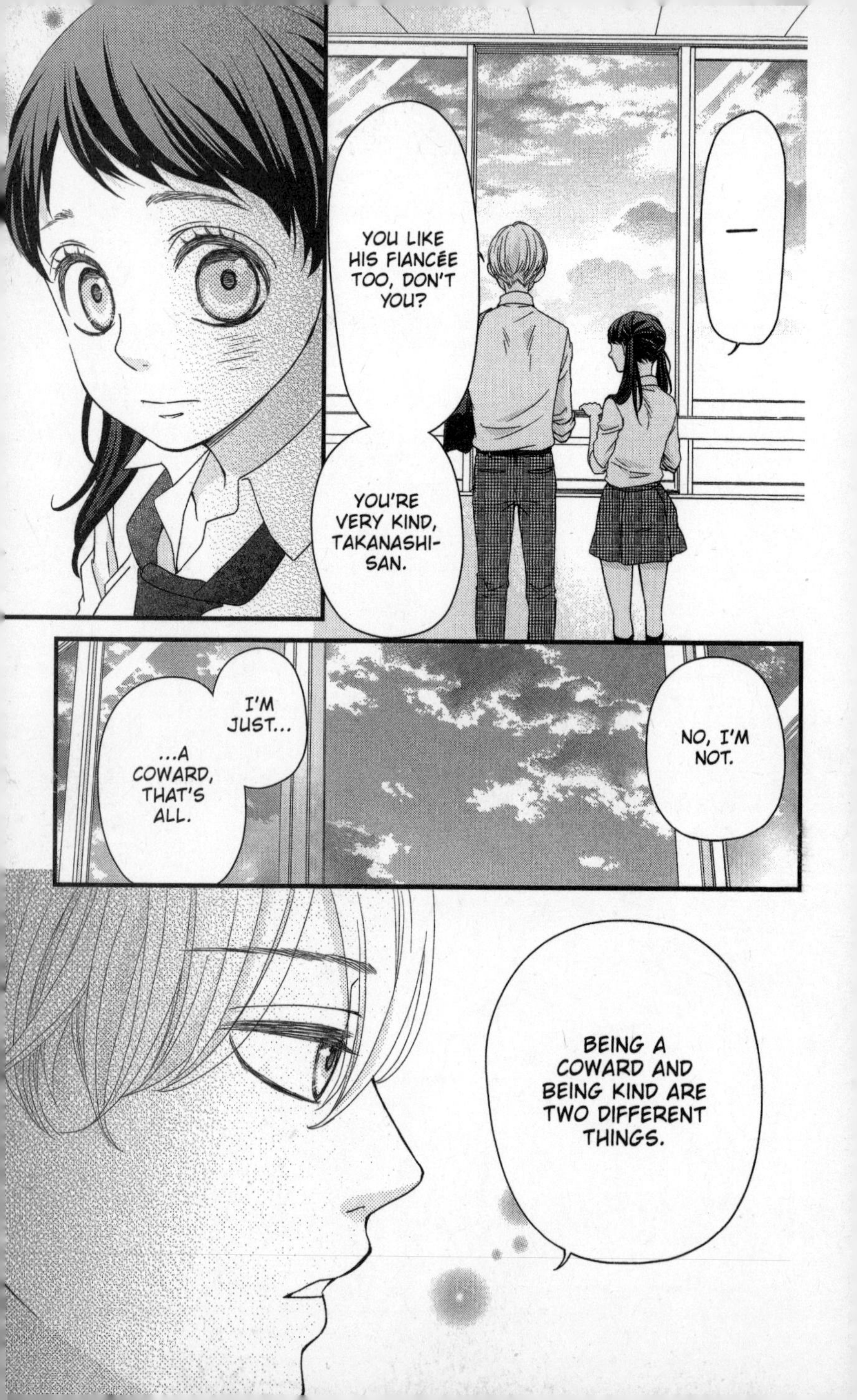
—
YOU LIKE HIS FIANCÉE TOO, DON'T YOU?
YOU'RE VERY KIND, TAKANASHI-SAN.
NO, I'M NOT.
I'M JUST...
...A COWARD, THAT'S ALL.
BEING A COWARD AND BEING KIND ARE TWO DIFFERENT THINGS.

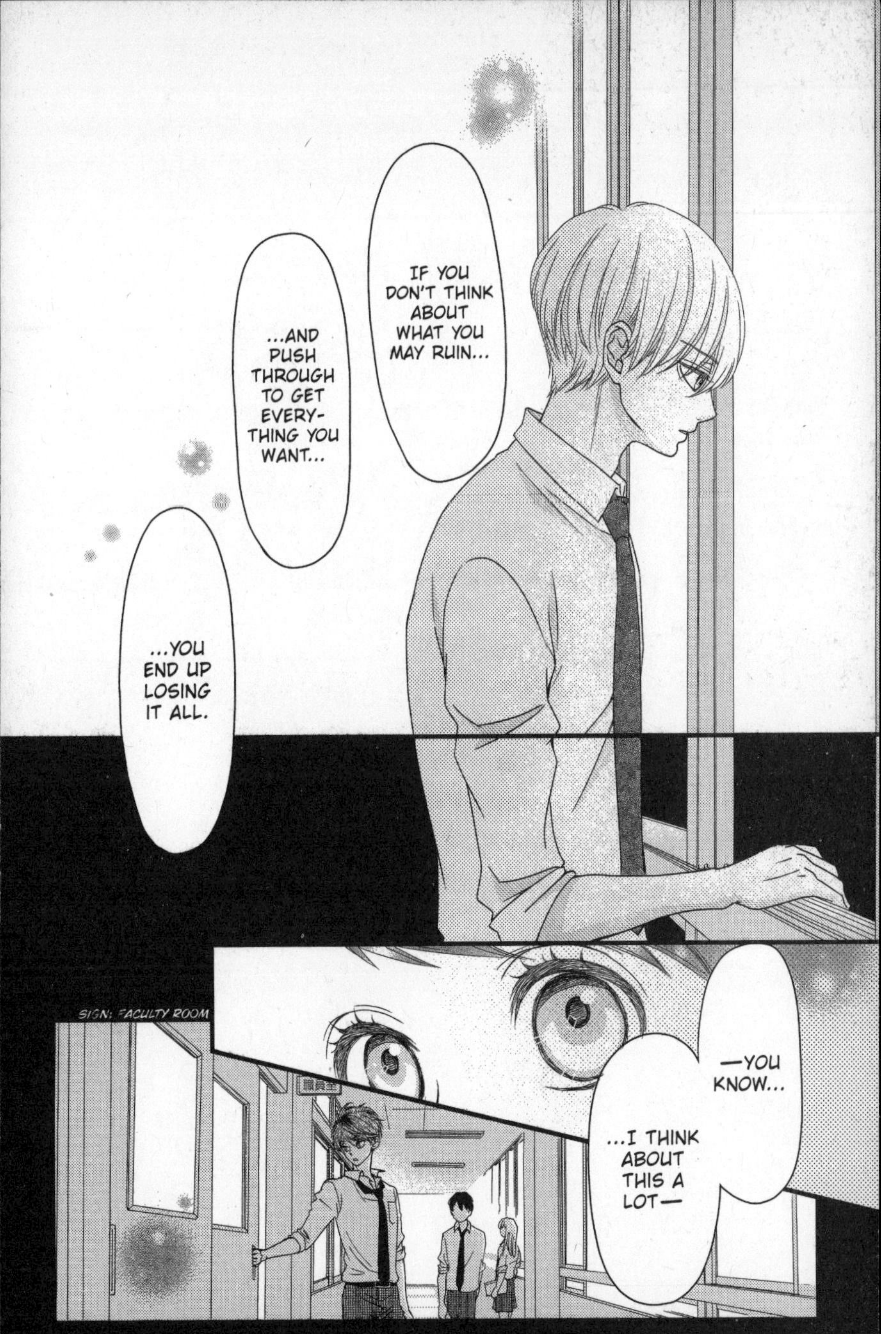
IF YOU DON'T THINK ABOUT WHAT YOU MAY RUIN...
...AND PUSH THROUGH TO GET EVERY-THING YOU WANT...
...YOU END UP LOSING IT ALL.
—YOU KNOW...
...I THINK ABOUT THIS A LOT—
SIGN: FACULTY ROOM

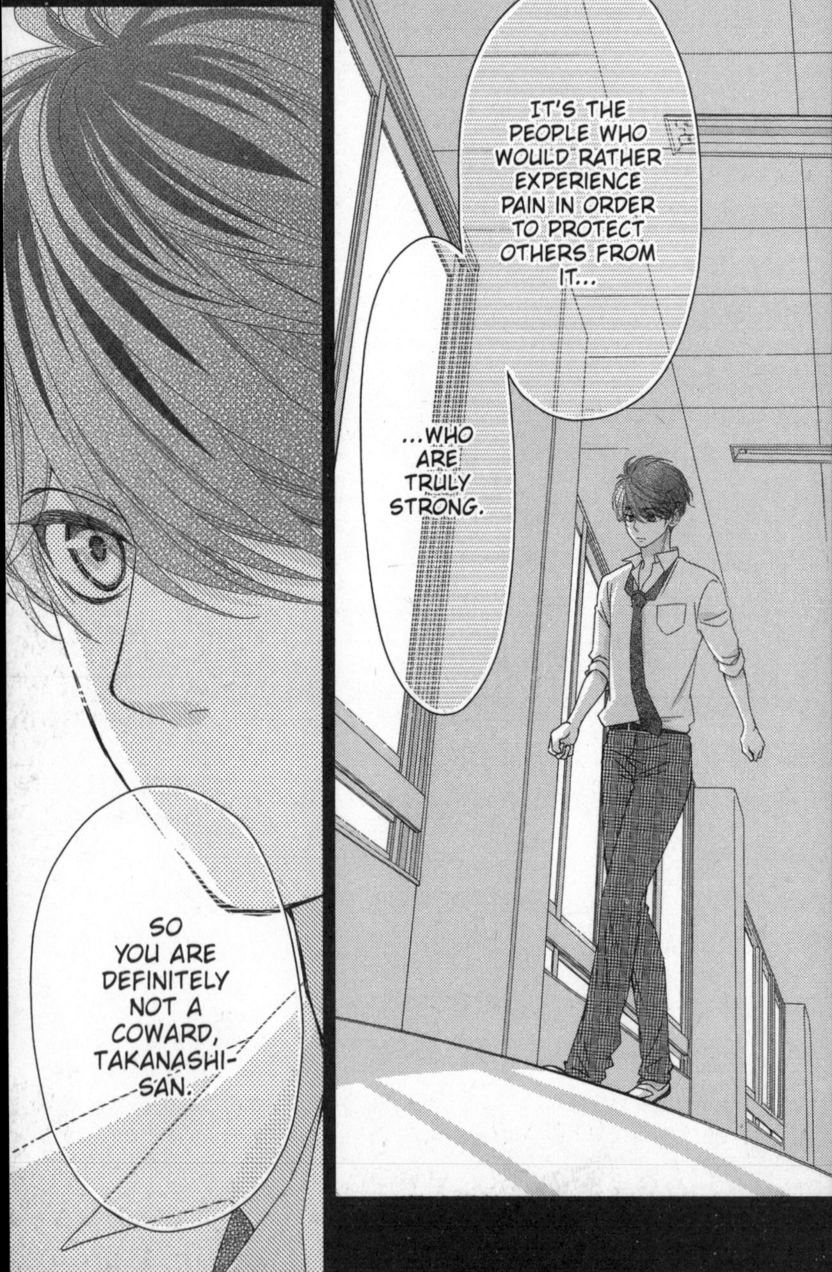
IT'S THE PEOPLE WHO WOULD RATHER EXPERIENCE PAIN IN ORDER TO PROTECT OTHERS FROM IT...
...WHO ARE TRULY STRONG.
SO YOU ARE DEFINITELY NOT A COWARD, TAKANASHI-SAN.

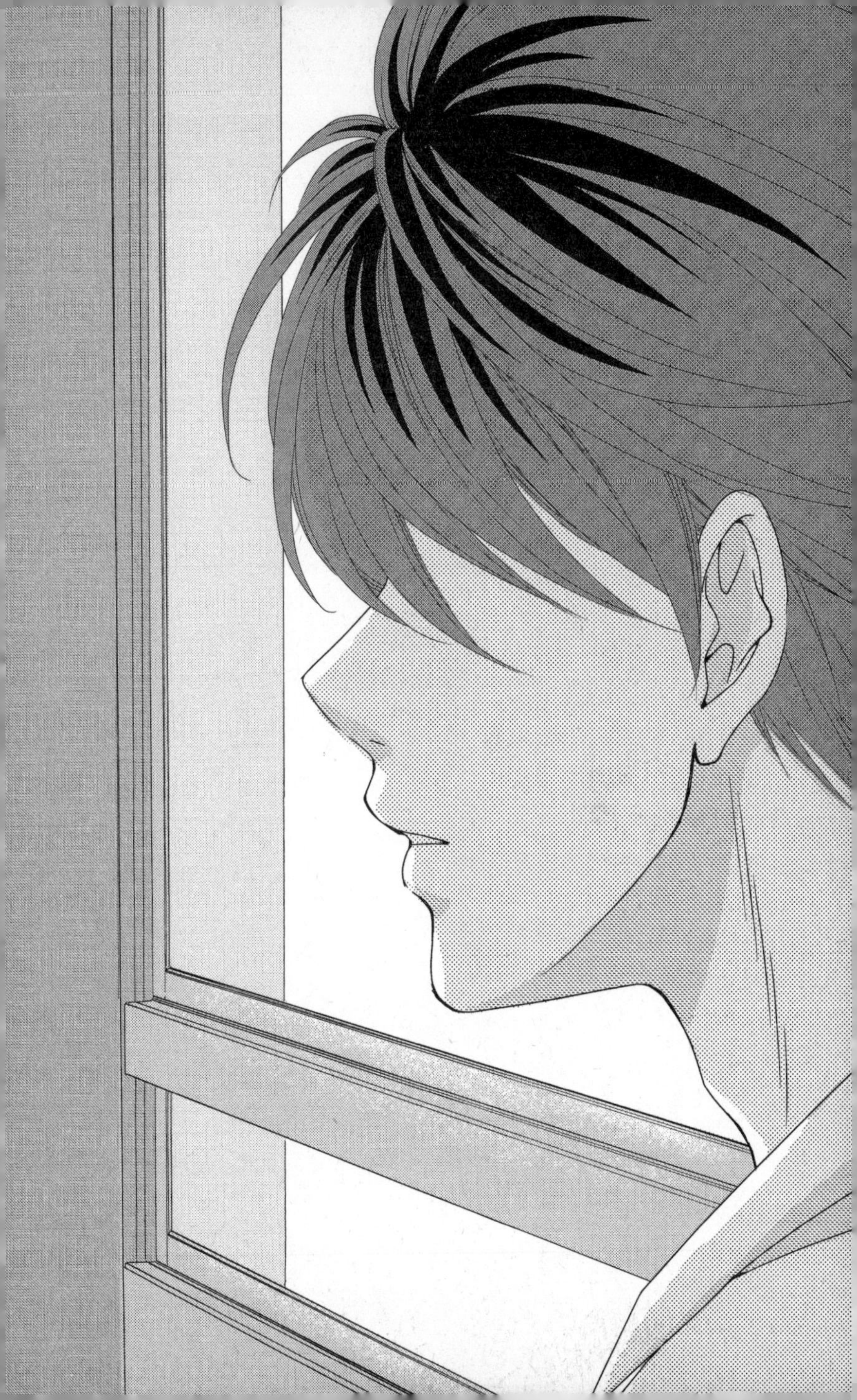

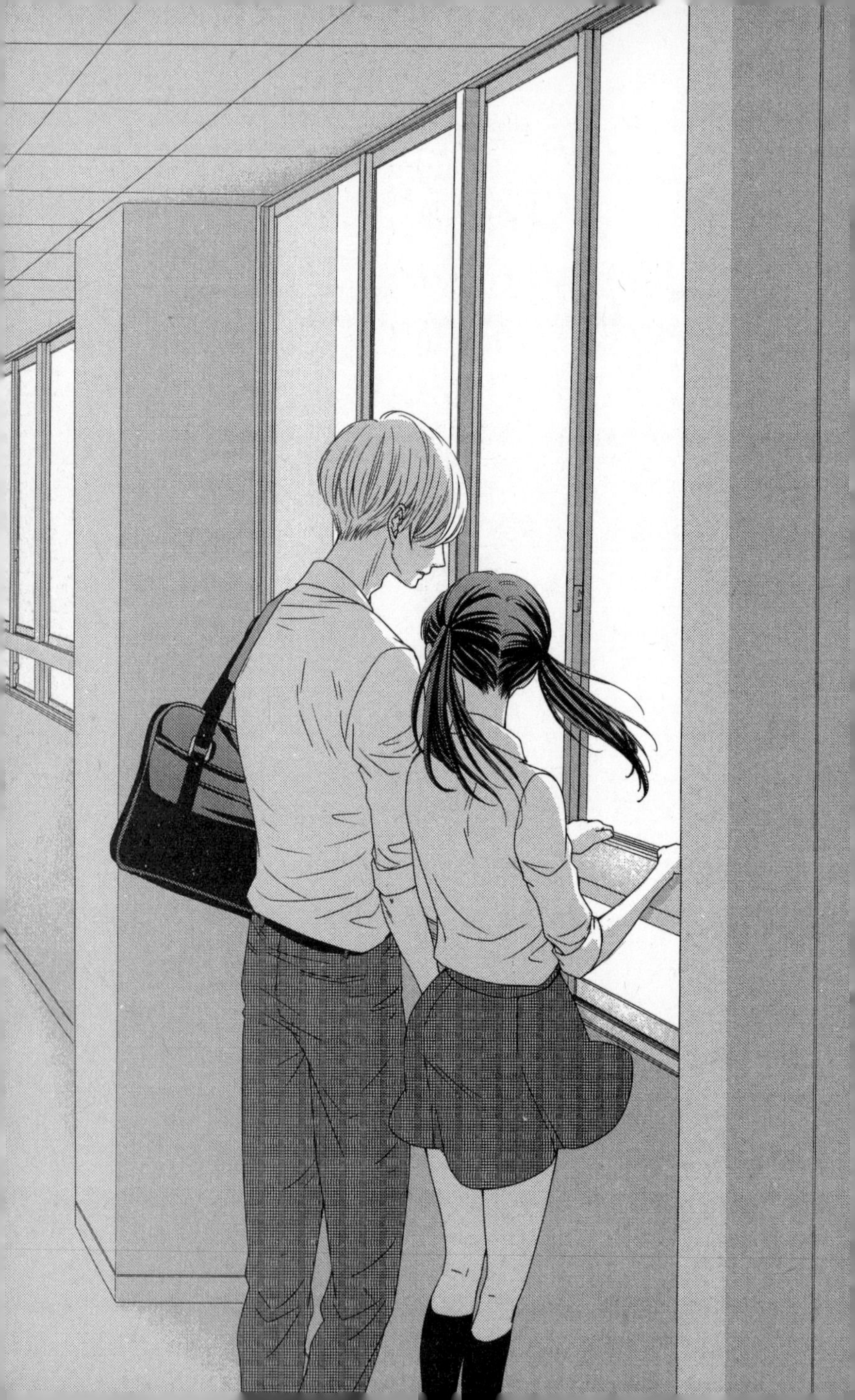

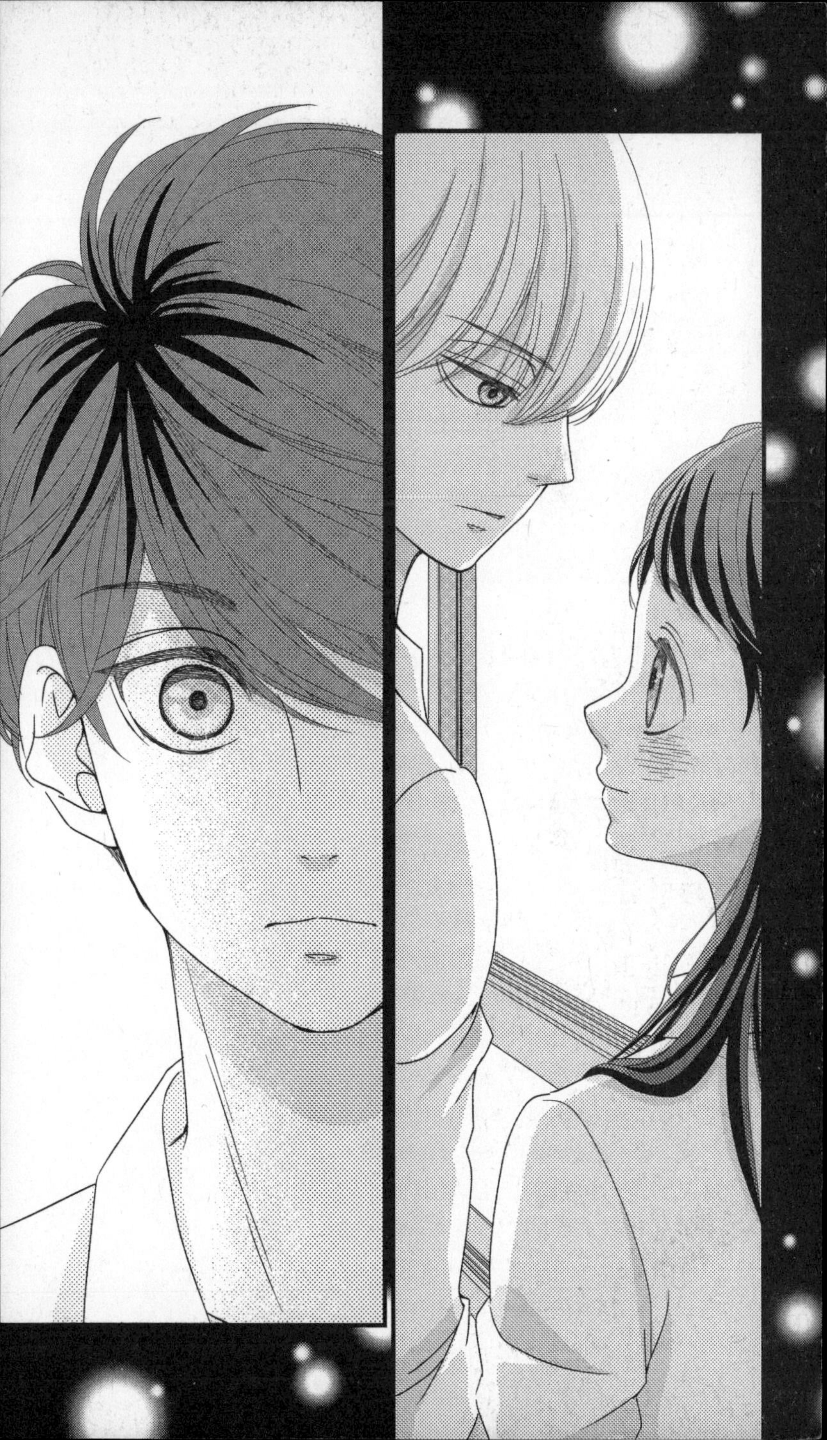

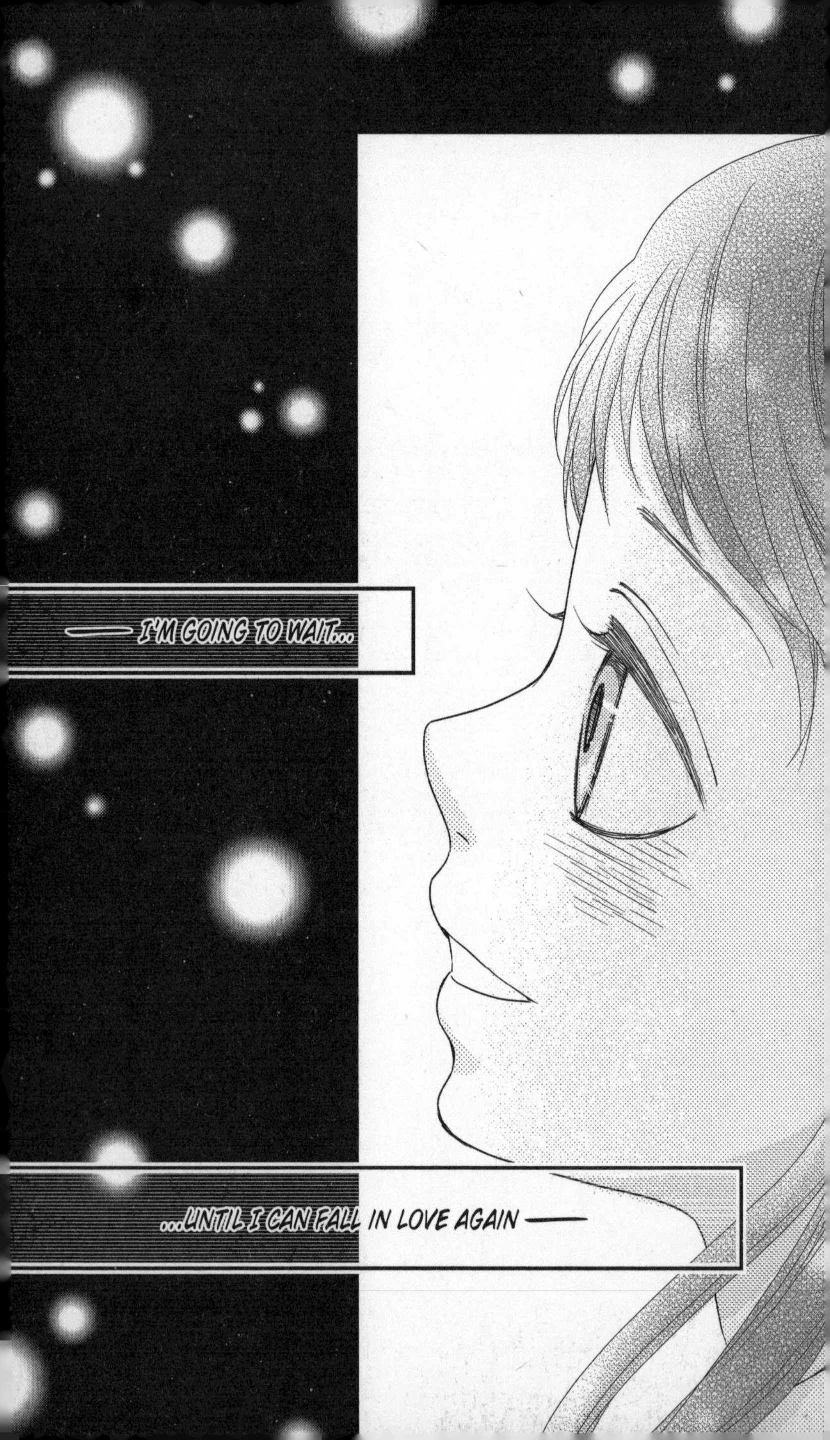
——I'M GOING TO WAIT...
...UNTIL I CAN FALL IN LOVE AGAIN——

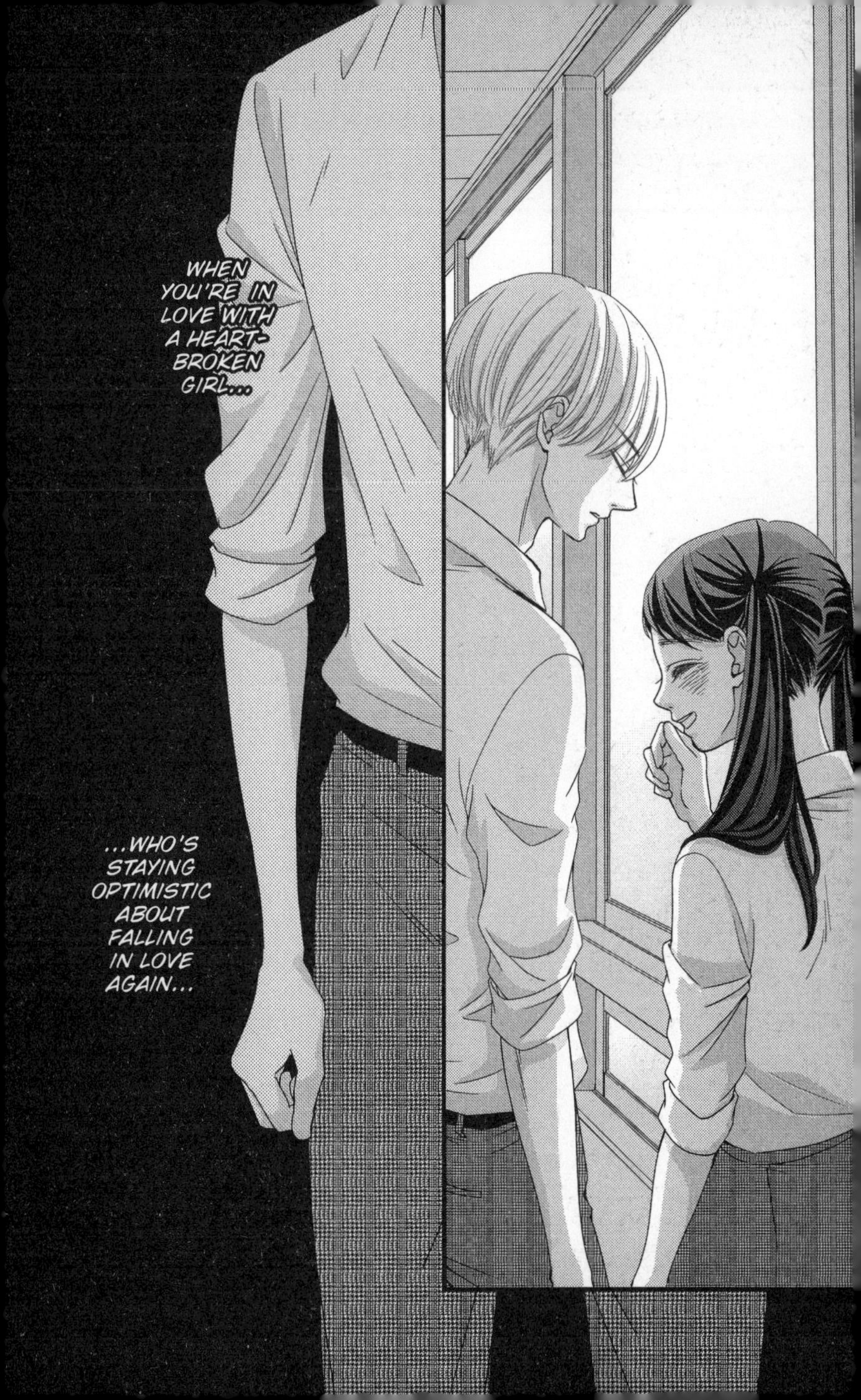
WHEN YOU'RE IN LOVE WITH A HEART-BROKEN GIRL...
...WHO'S STAYING OPTIMISTIC ABOUT FALLING IN LOVE AGAIN...

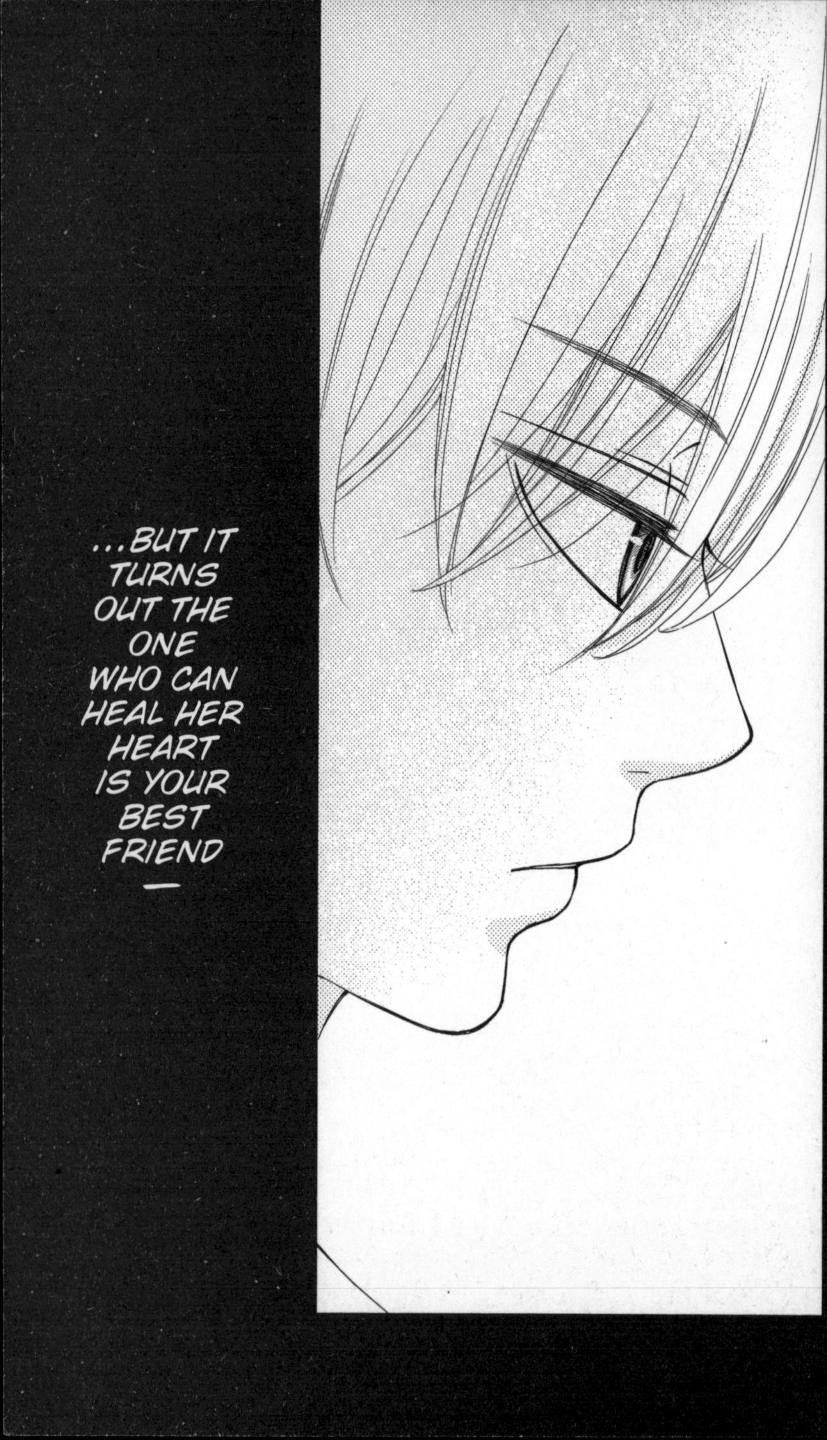
...BUT IT TURNS OUT THE ONE WHO CAN HEAL HER HEART IS YOUR BEST FRIEND —

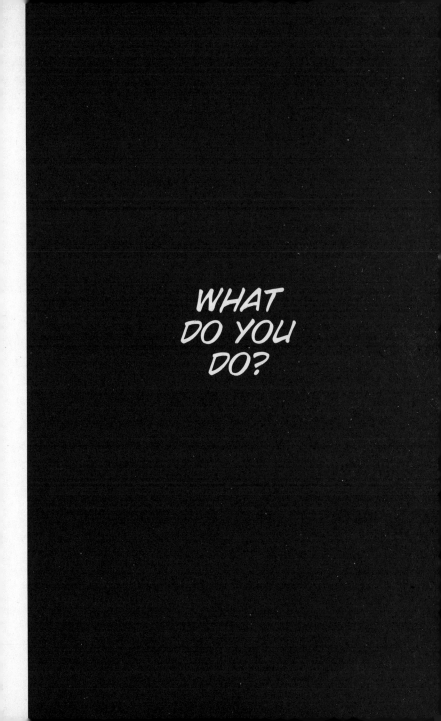

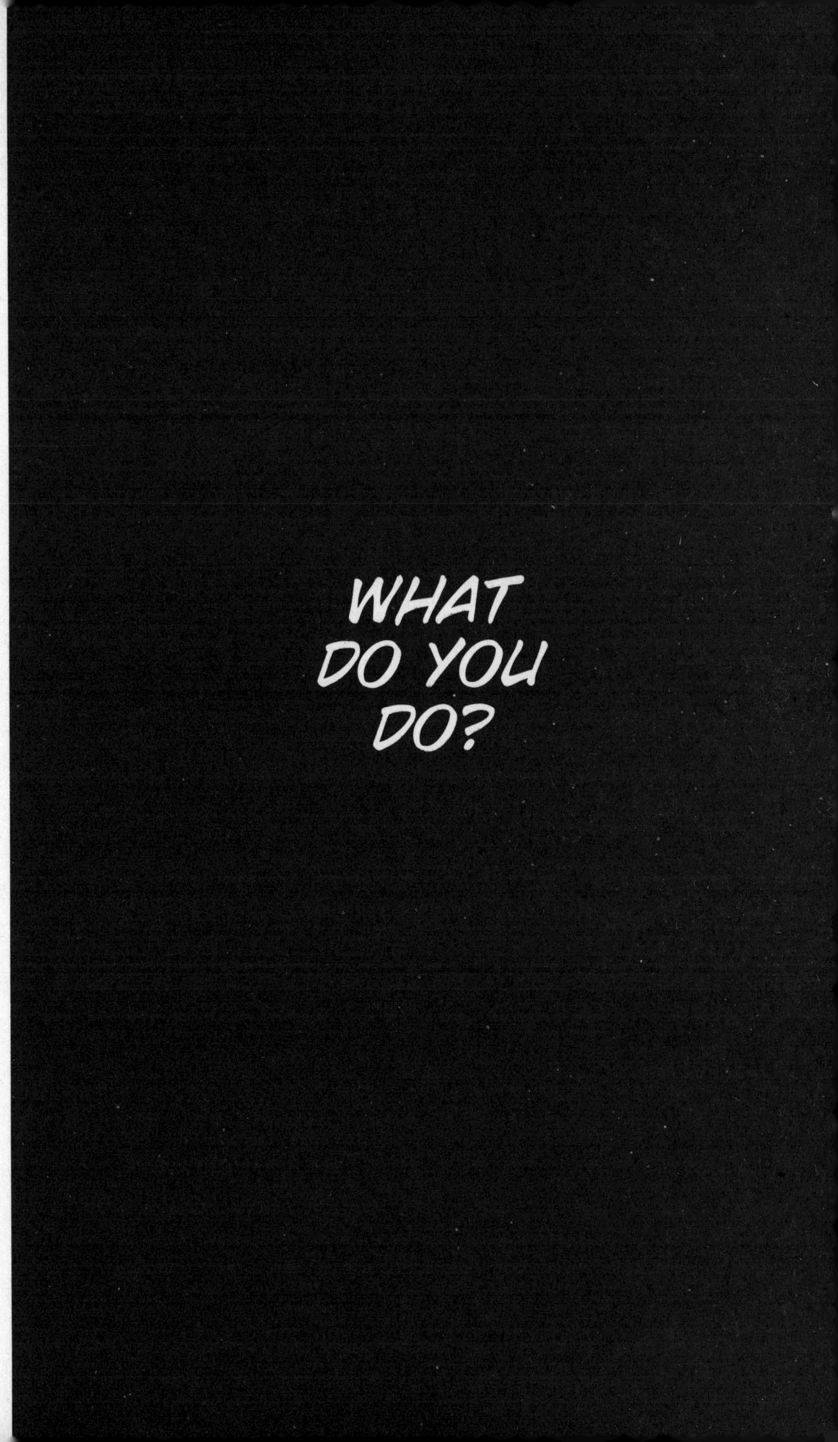
WHAT DO YOU DO?

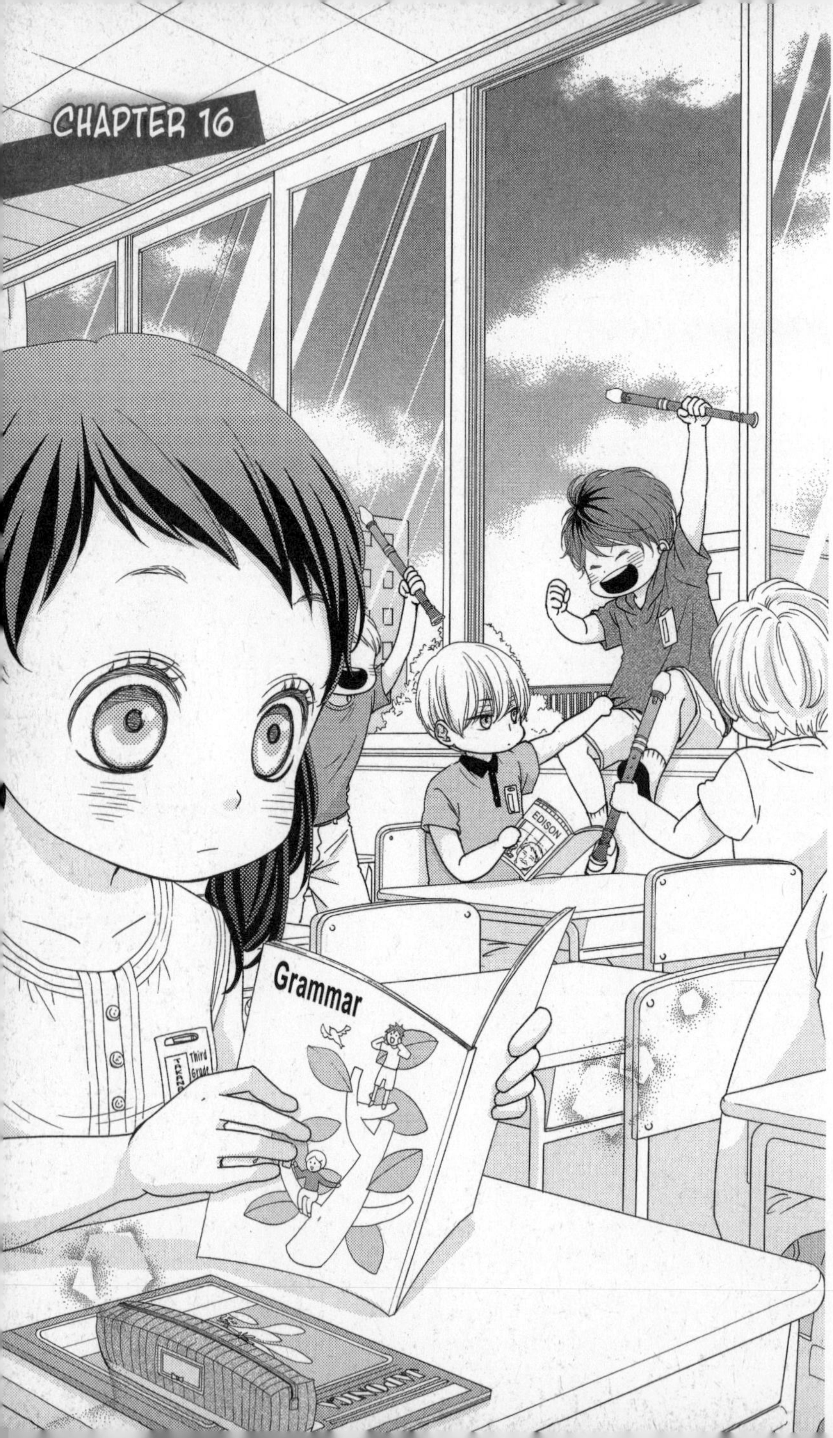
CHAPTER 16
EDISON
Third Grade
Grammar

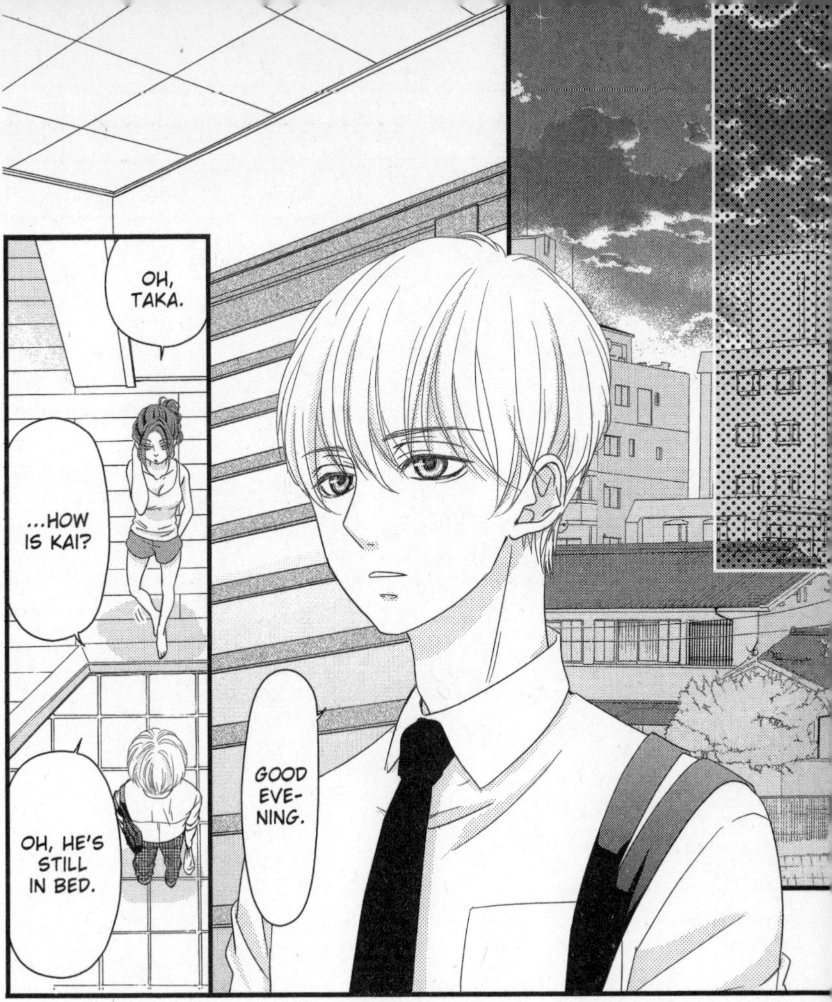
GOOD EVE-NING.
OH, TAKA.
...HOW IS KAI?
OH, HE'S STILL IN BED.

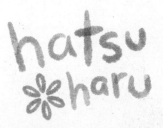

hatsu haru

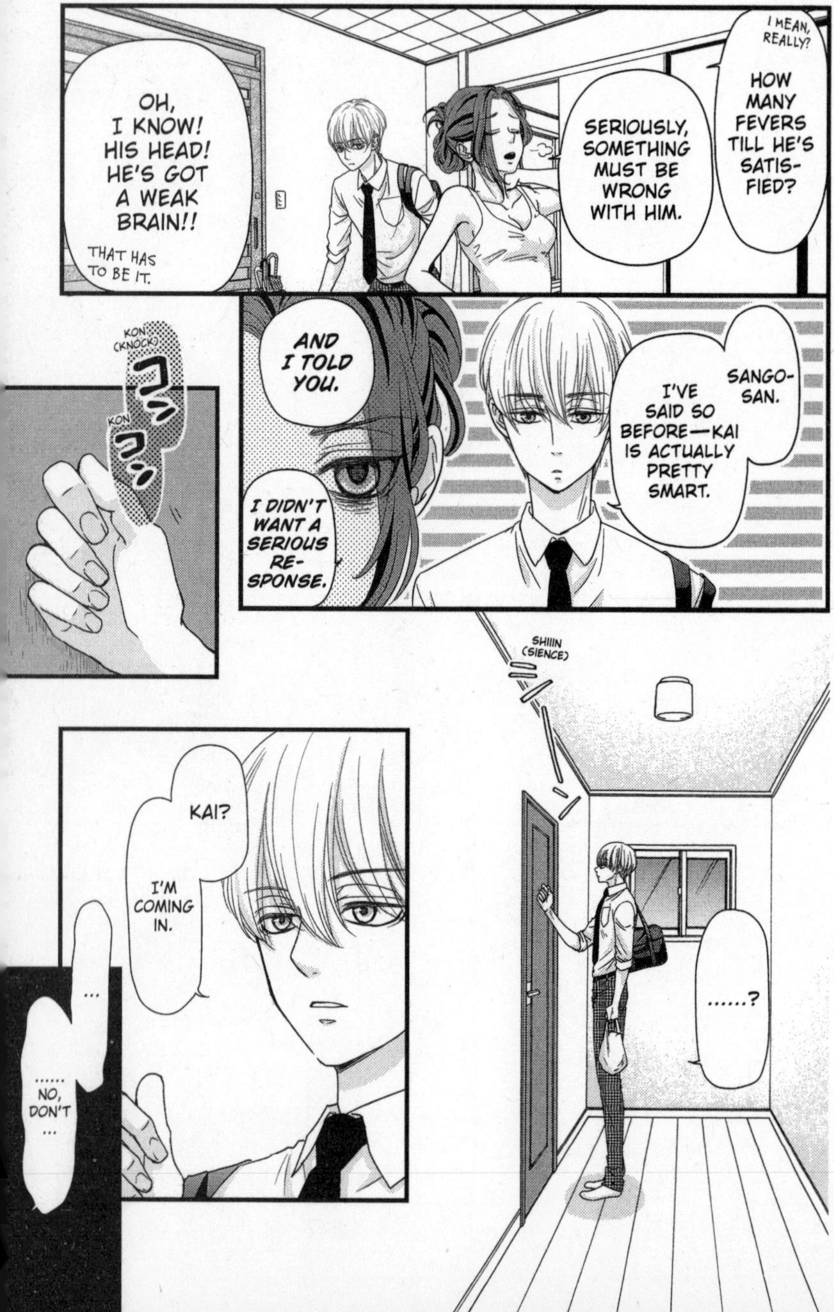
I MEAN, REALLY?
HOW MANY FEVERS TILL HE'S SATIS-FIED?
SERIOUSLY, SOMETHING MUST BE WRONG WITH HIM.
OH, I KNOW! HIS HEAD! HE'S GOT A WEAK BRAIN!!
THAT HAS TO BE IT.
SANGO-SAN.
I'VE SAID SO BEFORE—KAI IS ACTUALLY PRETTY SMART.
AND I TOLD YOU.
I DIDN'T WANT A SERIOUS RE-SPONSE.
KON (KNOCK)
KON
SHIIIN (SIENCE)
......?
KAI?
I'M COMING IN.
...
...... NO, DON'T ...

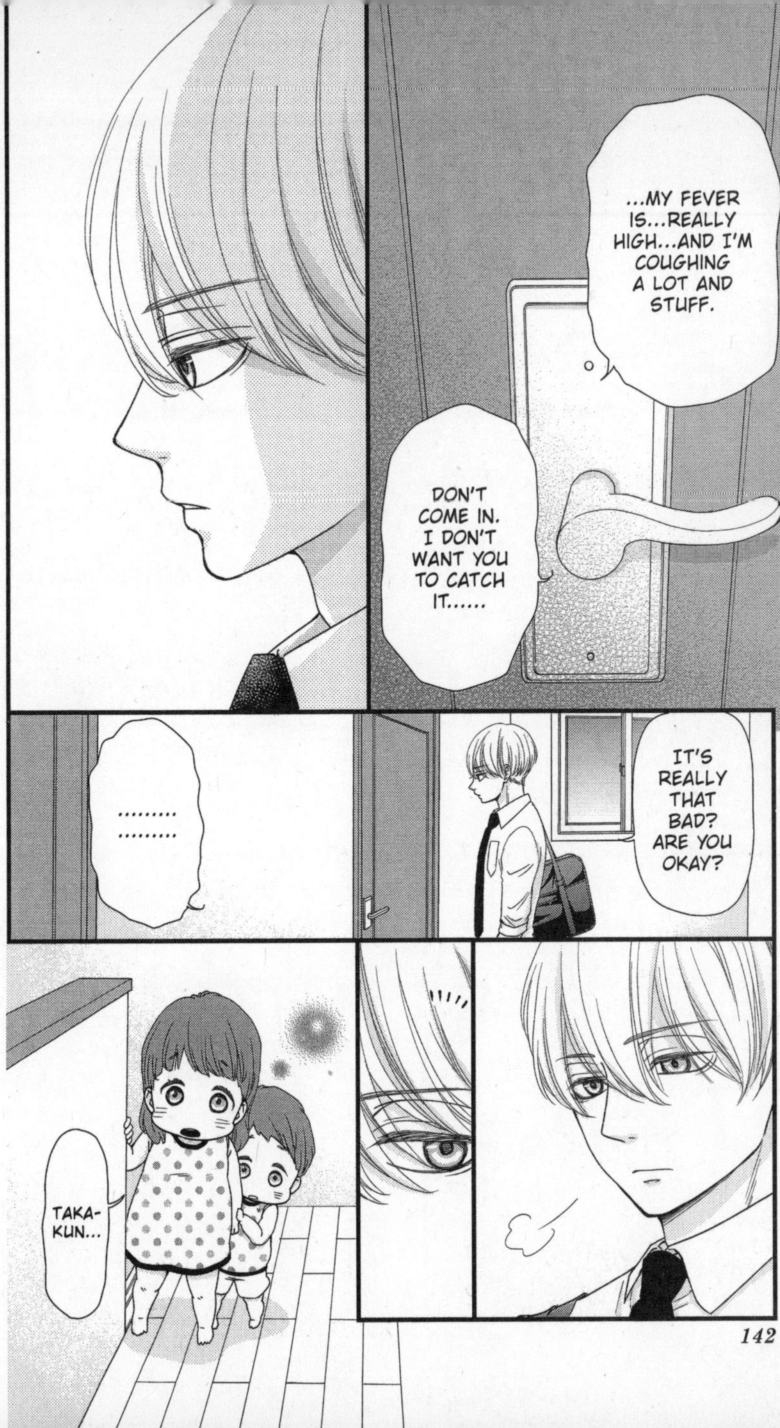
...MY FEVER IS...REALLY HIGH...AND I'M COUGHING A LOT AND STUFF.
DON'T COME IN. I DON'T WANT YOU TO CATCH IT......
IT'S REALLY THAT BAD? ARE YOU OKAY?
....
....
TAKA-KUN...

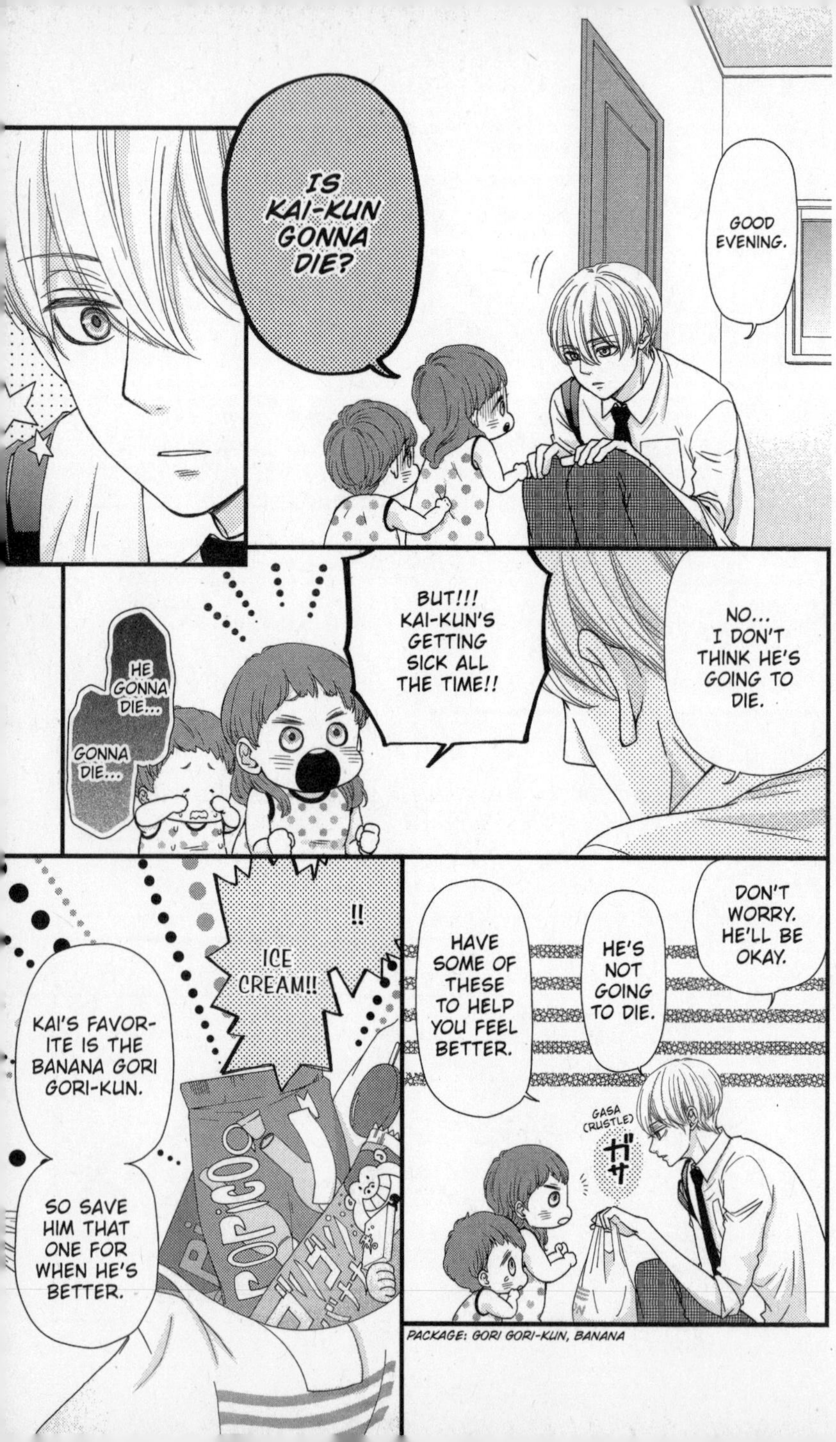
GOOD EVENING.
IS KAI-KUN GONNA DIE?
NO... I DON'T THINK HE'S GOING TO DIE.
BUT!!! KAI-KUN'S GETTING SICK ALL THE TIME!!
HE GONNA DIE...
GONNA DIE...
DON'T WORRY. HE'LL BE OKAY.
HE'S NOT GOING TO DIE.
HAVE SOME OF THESE TO HELP YOU FEEL BETTER.
GASA (RUSTLE)
ガサ
!!
ICE CREAM!!
KAI'S FAVOR-ITE IS THE BANANA GORI GORI-KUN.
SO SAVE HIM THAT ONE FOR WHEN HE'S BETTER.
PACKAGE: GORI GORI-KUN, BANANA

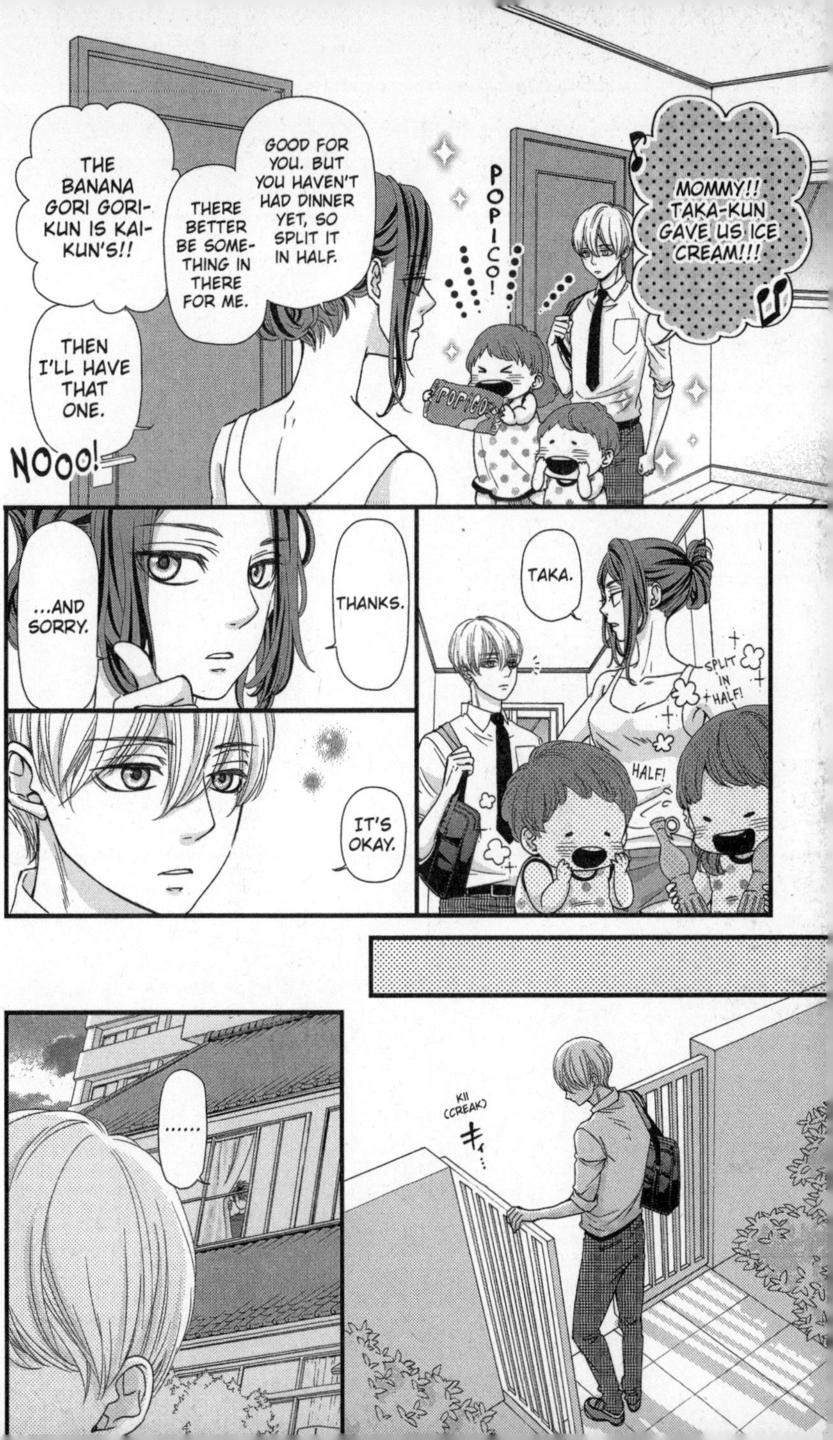
MOMMY!! TAKA-KUN GAVE US ICE CREAM!!!
POPICO!
GOOD FOR YOU. BUT YOU HAVEN'T HAD DINNER YET, SO SPLIT IT IN HALF.
THERE BETTER BE SOMETHING IN THERE FOR ME.
THE BANANA GORI GORI-KUN IS KAI-KUN'S!!
THEN I'LL HAVE THAT ONE.
NOOO!
TAKA.
SPLIT IN HALF!
HALF!
THANKS.
...AND SORRY.
IT'S OKAY.
KII (CREAK)
......

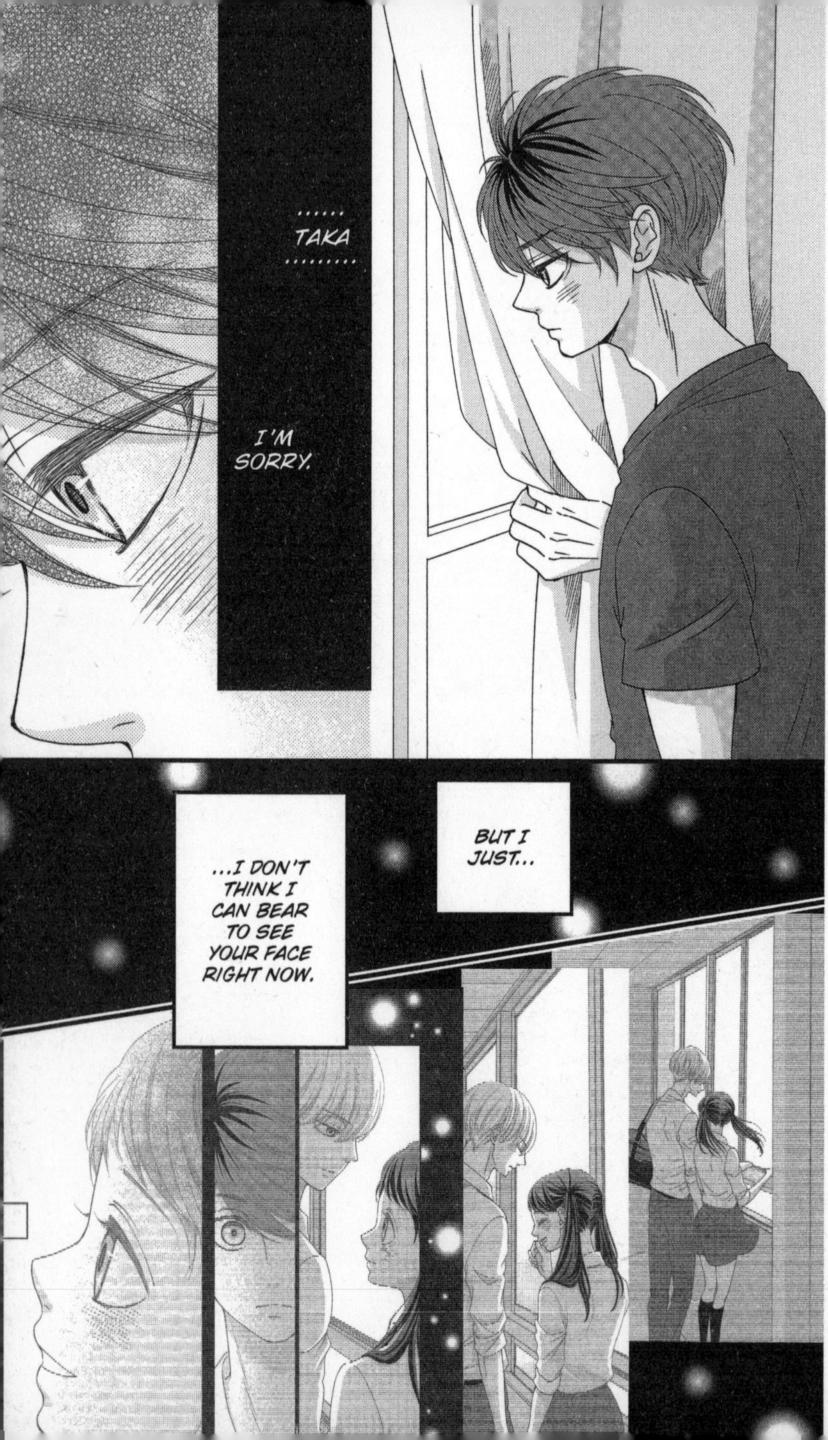
......TAKA.........
I'M SORRY.
BUT I JUST...
...I DON'T THINK I CAN BEAR TO SEE YOUR FACE RIGHT NOW.

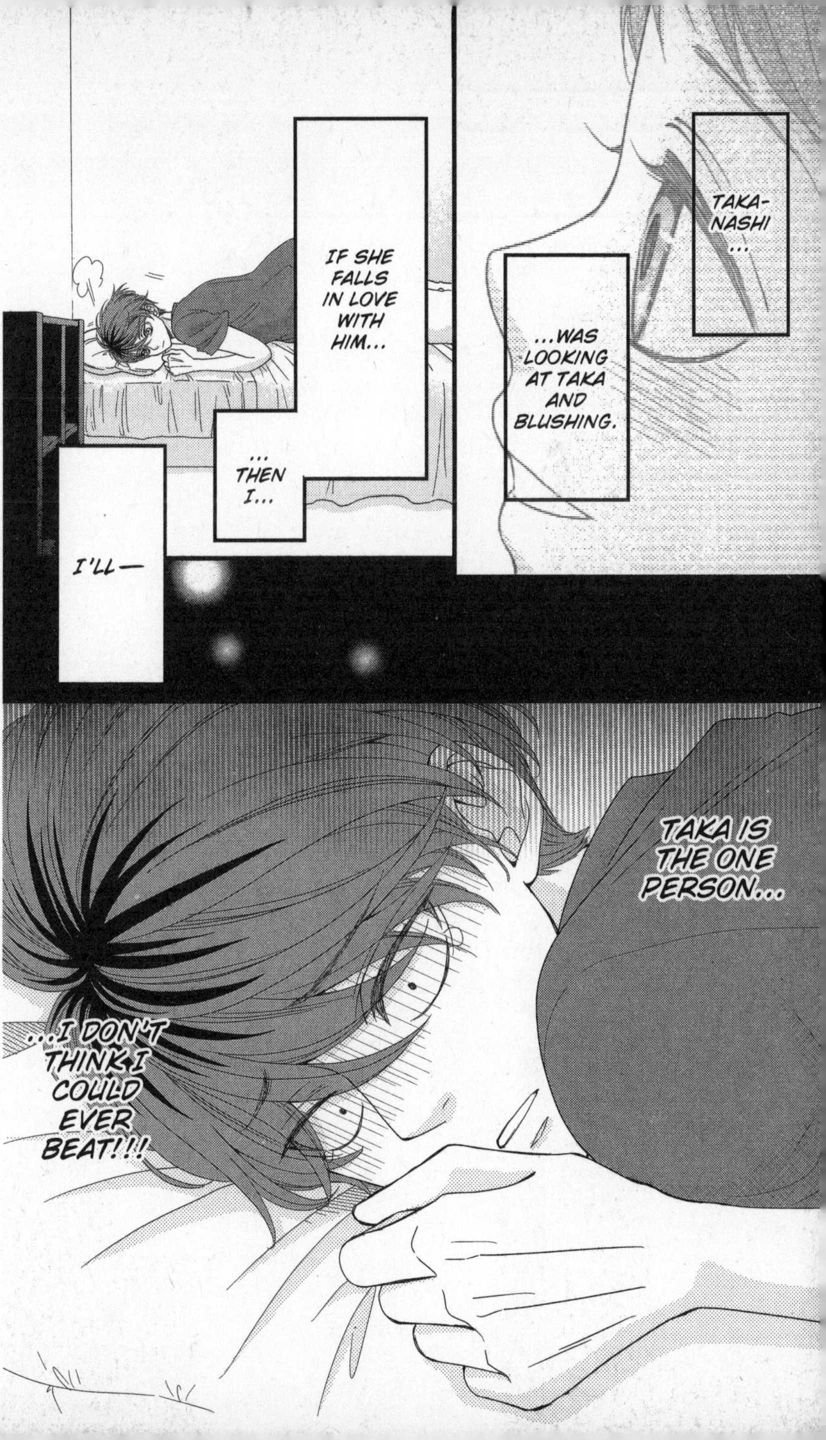
TAKA-NASHI...
...WAS LOOKING AT TAKA AND BLUSHING.
IF SHE FALLS IN LOVE WITH HIM...
...THEN I...
I'LL—
TAKA IS THE ONE PERSON...
...I DON'T THINK I COULD EVER BEAT!!!

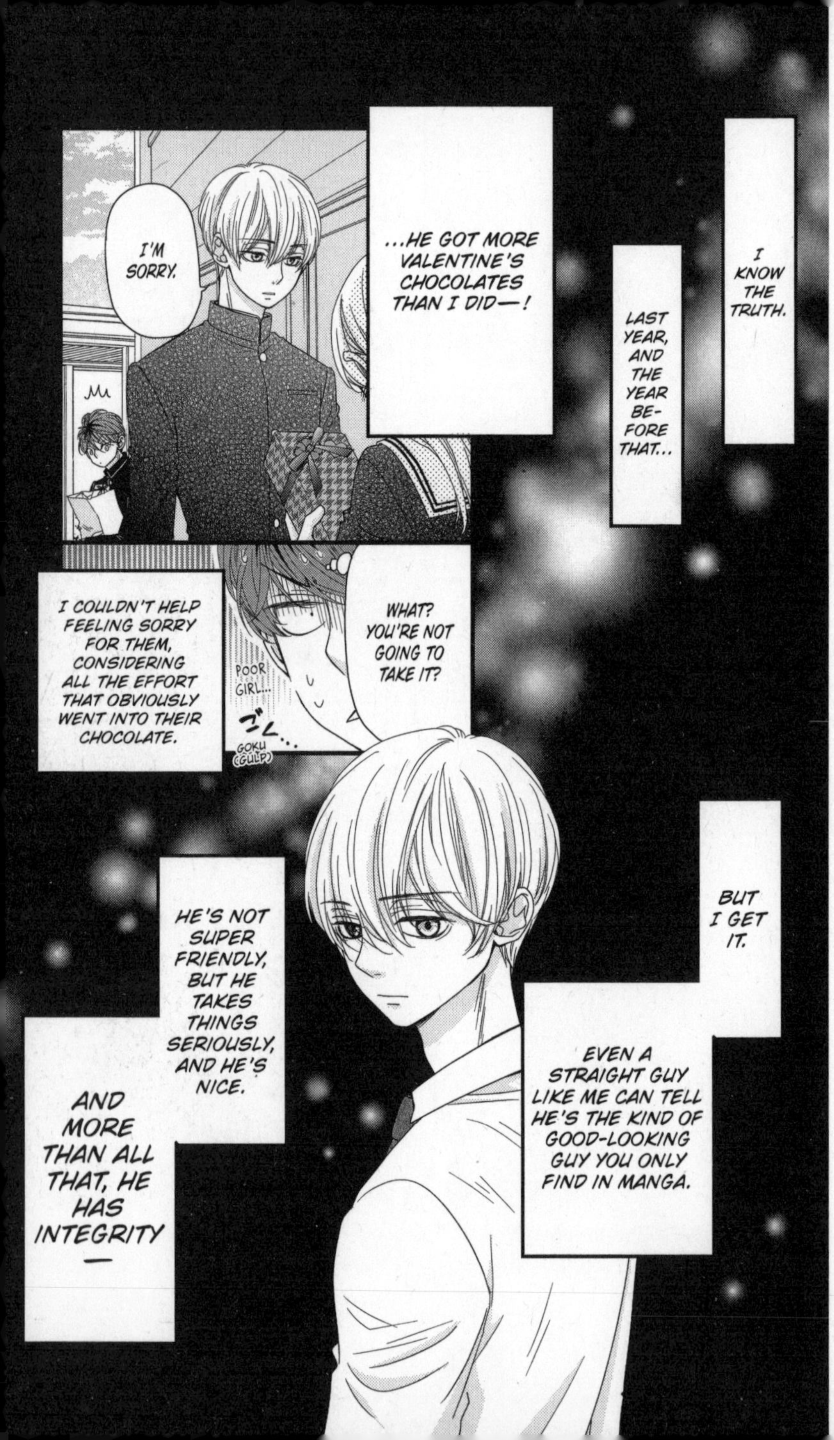
I KNOW THE TRUTH.
LAST YEAR, AND THE YEAR BEFORE THAT...
...HE GOT MORE VALENTINE'S CHOCOLATES THAN I DID—!
I'M SORRY.
MU
WHAT? YOU'RE NOT GOING TO TAKE IT?
POOR GIRL...
ゴく...
GOKU (GULP)
I COULDN'T HELP FEELING SORRY FOR THEM, CONSIDERING ALL THE EFFORT THAT OBVIOUSLY WENT INTO THEIR CHOCOLATE.
BUT I GET IT.
EVEN A STRAIGHT GUY LIKE ME CAN TELL HE'S THE KIND OF GOOD-LOOKING GUY YOU ONLY FIND IN MANGA.
HE'S NOT SUPER FRIENDLY, BUT HE TAKES THINGS SERIOUSLY, AND HE'S NICE.
AND MORE THAN ALL THAT, HE HAS INTEGRITY—

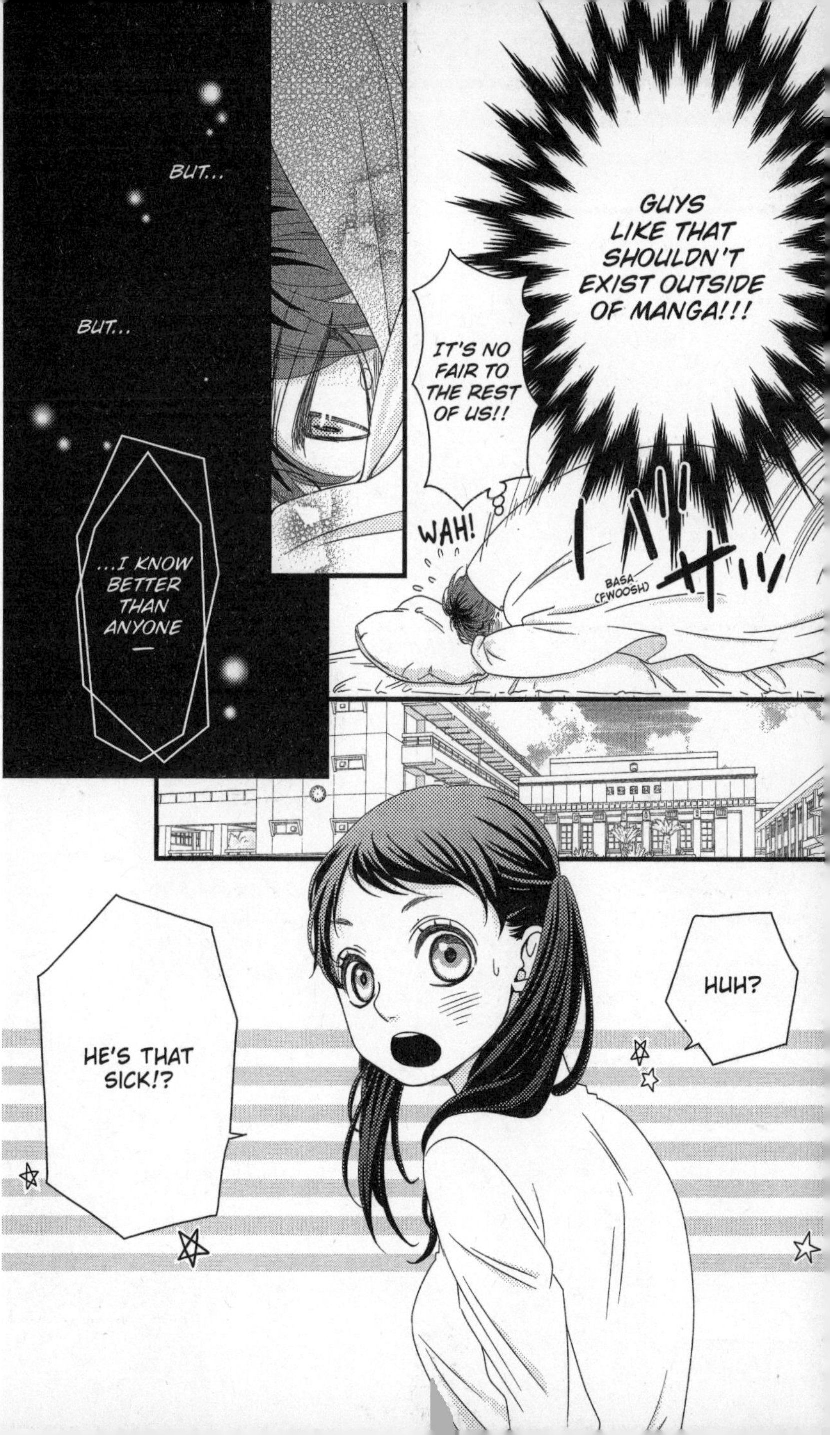
GUYS LIKE THAT SHOULDN'T EXIST OUTSIDE OF MANGA!!!
IT'S NO FAIR TO THE REST OF US!!
WAH!
BASA (FWOOSH)
BUT...
BUT...
...I KNOW BETTER THAN ANYONE—
HUH?
HE'S THAT SICK!?

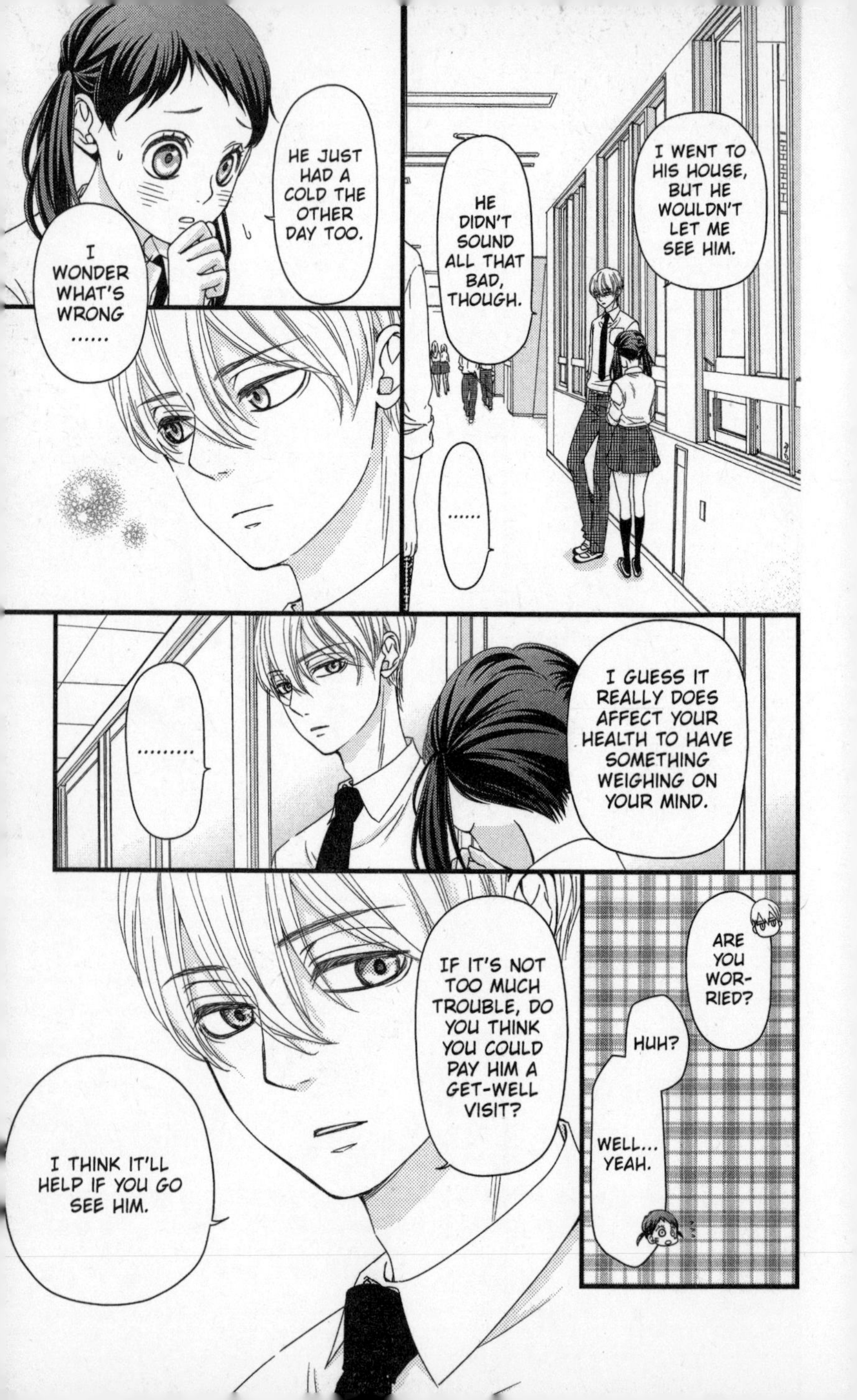
I WENT TO HIS HOUSE, BUT HE WOULDN'T LET ME SEE HIM.
HE DIDN'T SOUND ALL THAT BAD, THOUGH.
......
HE JUST HAD A COLD THE OTHER DAY TOO.
I WONDER WHAT'S WRONG ......
I GUESS IT REALLY DOES AFFECT YOUR HEALTH TO HAVE SOMETHING WEIGHING ON YOUR MIND.
....
ARE YOU WOR-RIED?
HUH?
WELL... YEAH.
IF IT'S NOT TOO MUCH TROUBLE, DO YOU THINK YOU COULD PAY HIM A GET-WELL VISIT?
I THINK IT'LL HELP IF YOU GO SEE HIM.

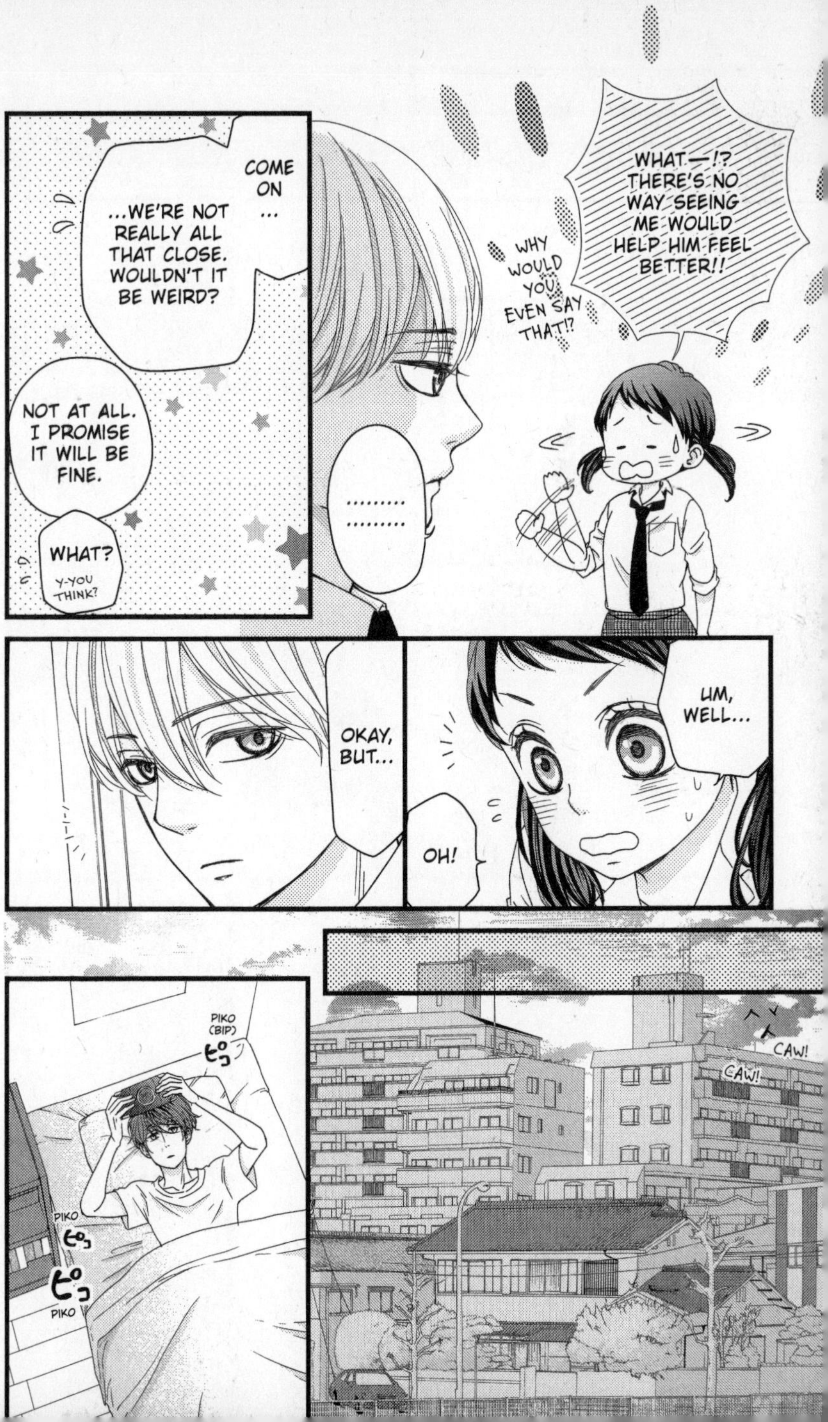
WHAT—!? THERE'S NO WAY SEEING ME WOULD HELP HIM FEEL BETTER!!
WHY WOULD YOU EVEN SAY THAT!?
....
COME ON ...
...WE'RE NOT REALLY ALL THAT CLOSE. WOULDN'T IT BE WEIRD?
NOT AT ALL. I PROMISE IT WILL BE FINE.
WHAT?
Y-YOU THINK?
UM, WELL...
OH!
OKAY, BUT...
CAW!
CAW!
PIKO (BIP)
ぴこ
PIKO
ぴこ
ぴこ
PIKO

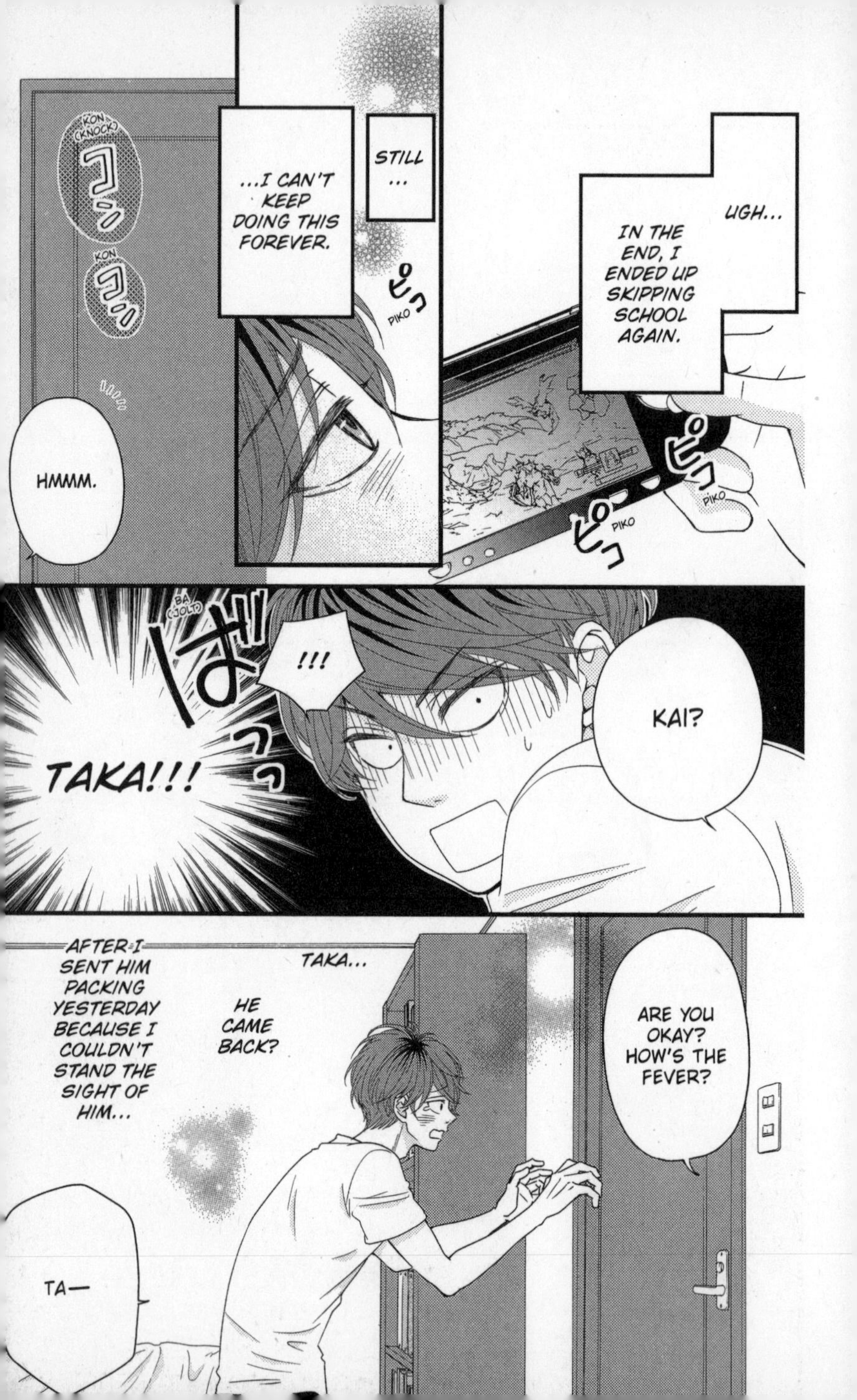
UGH...
IN THE END, I ENDED UP SKIPPING SCHOOL AGAIN.
PIKO
PIKO
STILL...
...I CAN'T KEEP DOING THIS FOREVER.
PIKO
KON (KNOCK)
KON
HMMM.
KAI?
!!!
BA (JOLT)
TAKA!!!
ARE YOU OKAY? HOW'S THE FEVER?
TAKA...
HE CAME BACK?
AFTER I SENT HIM PACKING YESTERDAY BECAUSE I COULDN'T STAND THE SIGHT OF HIM...
TA—

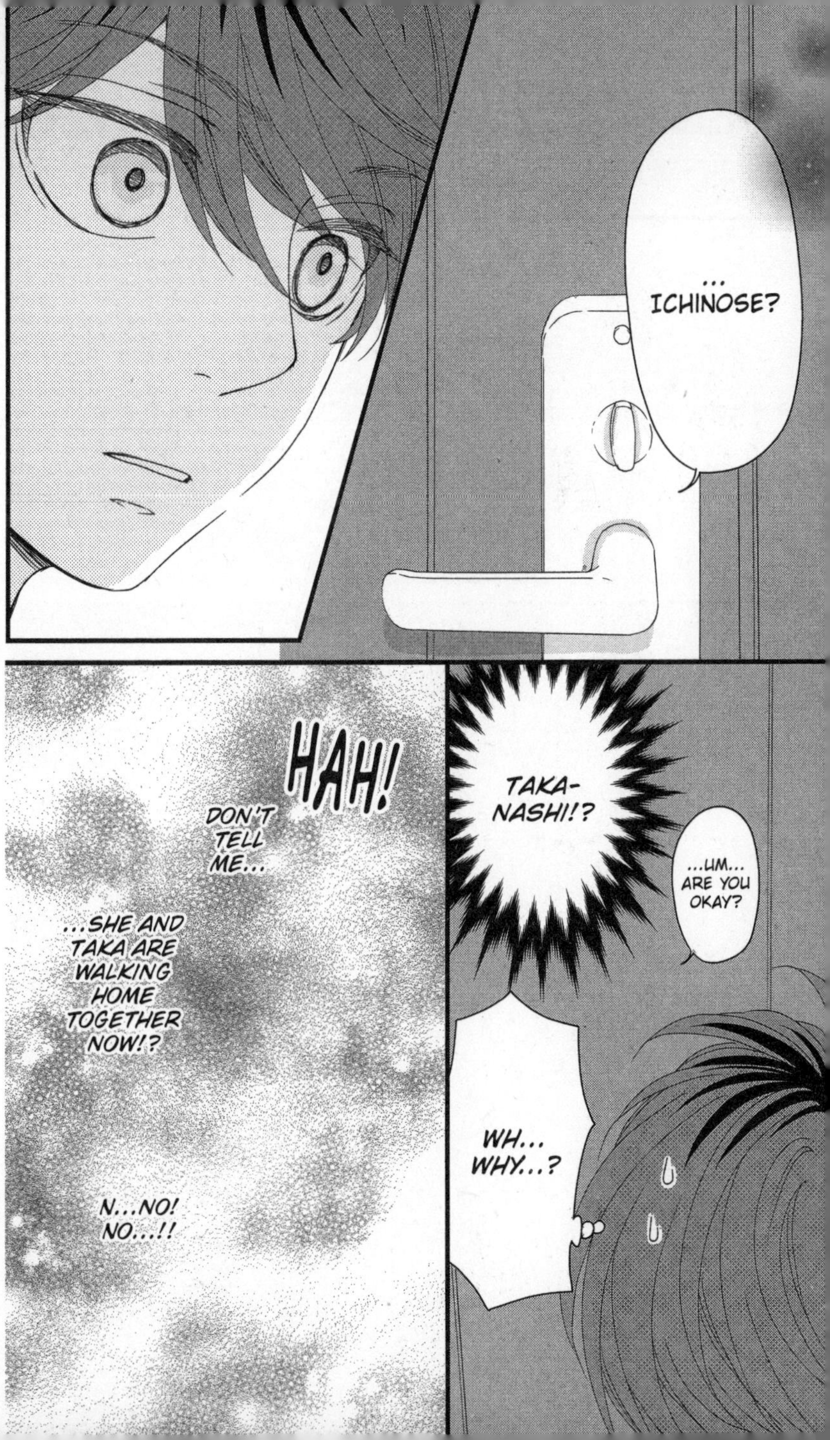
...ICHINOSE?
TAKA-NASHI!?
...UM... ARE YOU OKAY?
WH... WHY...?
HAH!
DON'T TELL ME...
...SHE AND TAKA ARE WALKING HOME TOGETHER NOW!?
N...NO! NO...!!

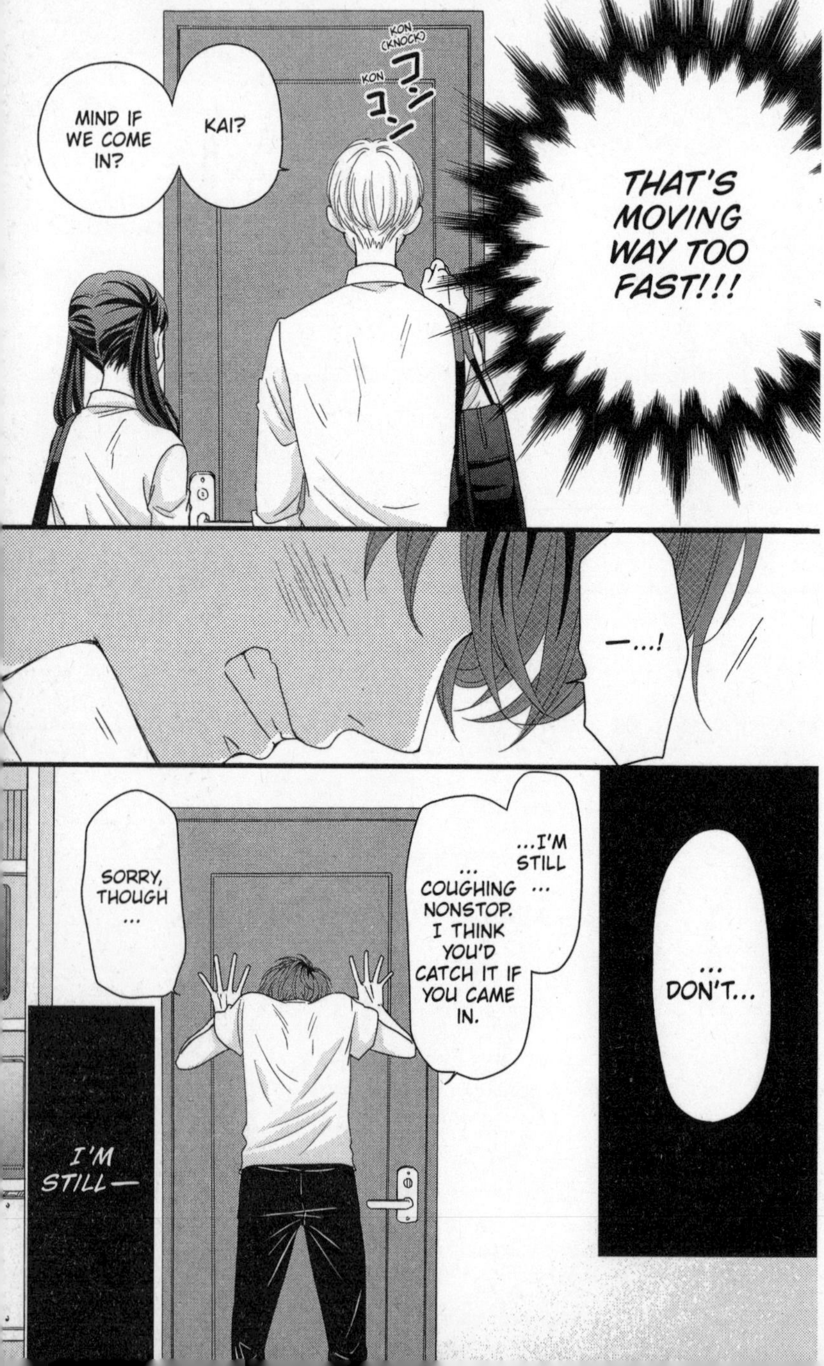
THAT'S MOVING WAY TOO FAST!!!
KON (KNOCK)
KON
KAI?
MIND IF WE COME IN?
—...!
... DON'T...
...I'M STILL ...
... COUGHING NONSTOP. I THINK YOU'D CATCH IT IF YOU CAME IN.
SORRY, THOUGH ...
I'M STILL—

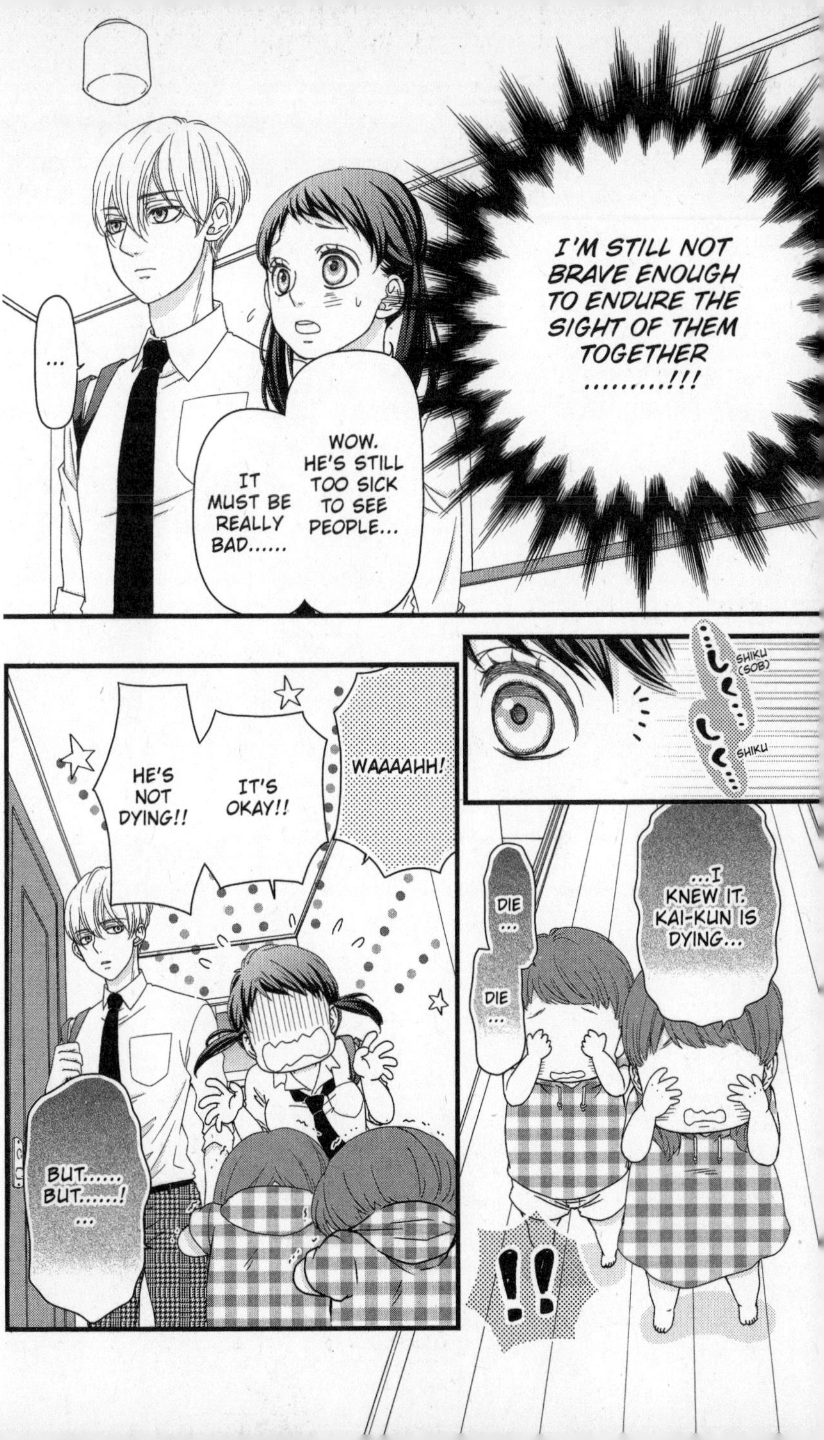
I'M STILL NOT BRAVE ENOUGH TO ENDURE THE SIGHT OF THEM TOGETHER ....!!!
WOW. HE'S STILL TOO SICK TO SEE PEOPLE...
IT MUST BE REALLY BAD......
...
...しく... しく...
SHIKU (SOB)
SHIKU
...I KNEW IT. KAI-KUN IS DYING...
DIE ... DIE ...
!!
WAAAAHH!
IT'S OKAY!!
HE'S NOT DYING!!
BUT...... BUT......! ...

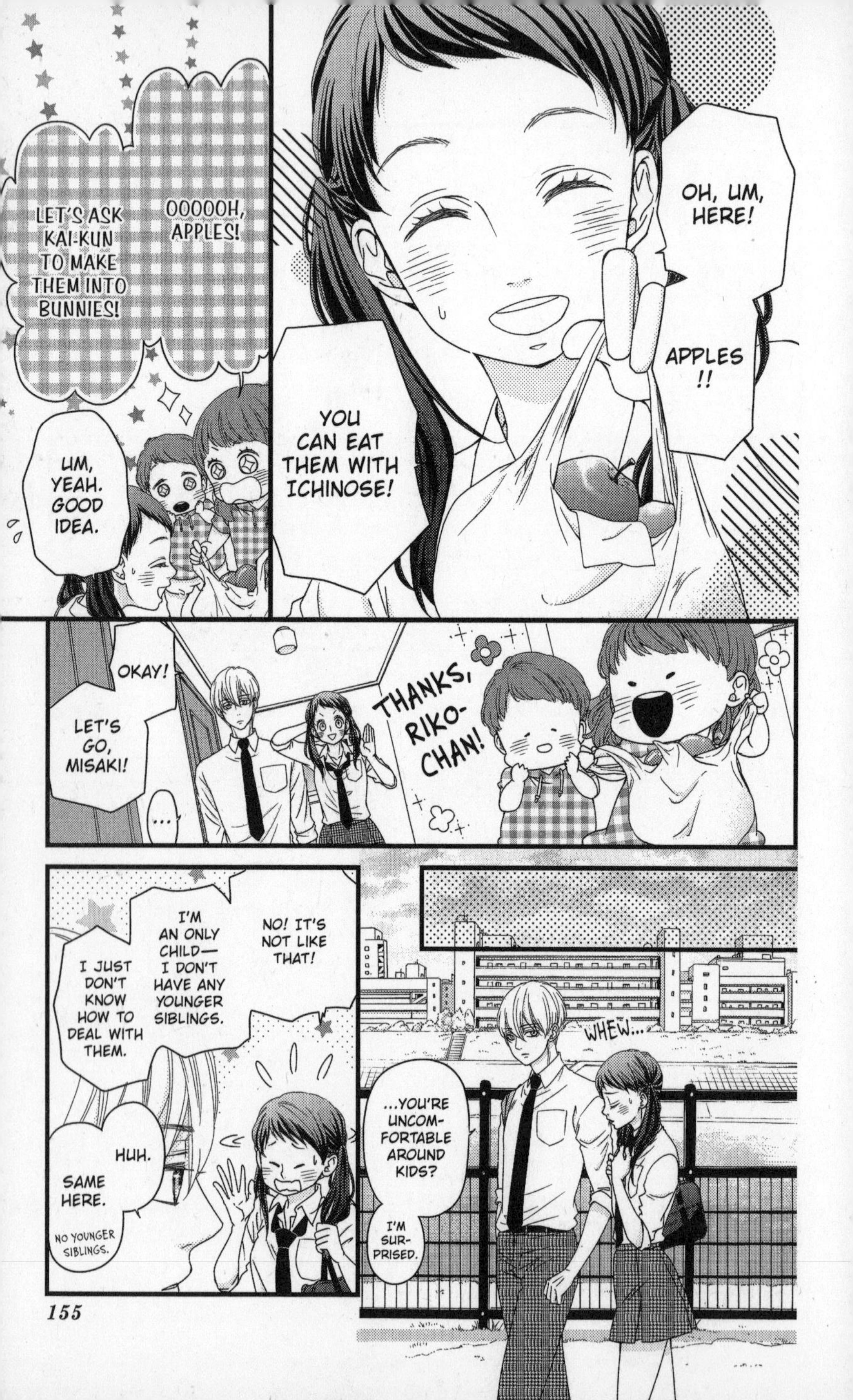
OH, UM, HERE!
APPLES!!
YOU CAN EAT THEM WITH ICHINOSE!
OOOOOH, APPLES!
LET'S ASK KAI-KUN TO MAKE THEM INTO BUNNIES!
UM, YEAH. GOOD IDEA.
THANKS, RIKO-CHAN!
OKAY!
LET'S GO, MISAKI!
...
WHEW...
...YOU'RE UNCOMFORTABLE AROUND KIDS?
I'M SURPRISED.
NO! IT'S NOT LIKE THAT!
I'M AN ONLY CHILD— I DON'T HAVE ANY YOUNGER SIBLINGS.
I JUST DON'T KNOW HOW TO DEAL WITH THEM.
HUH.
SAME HERE.
NO YOUNGER SIBLINGS.

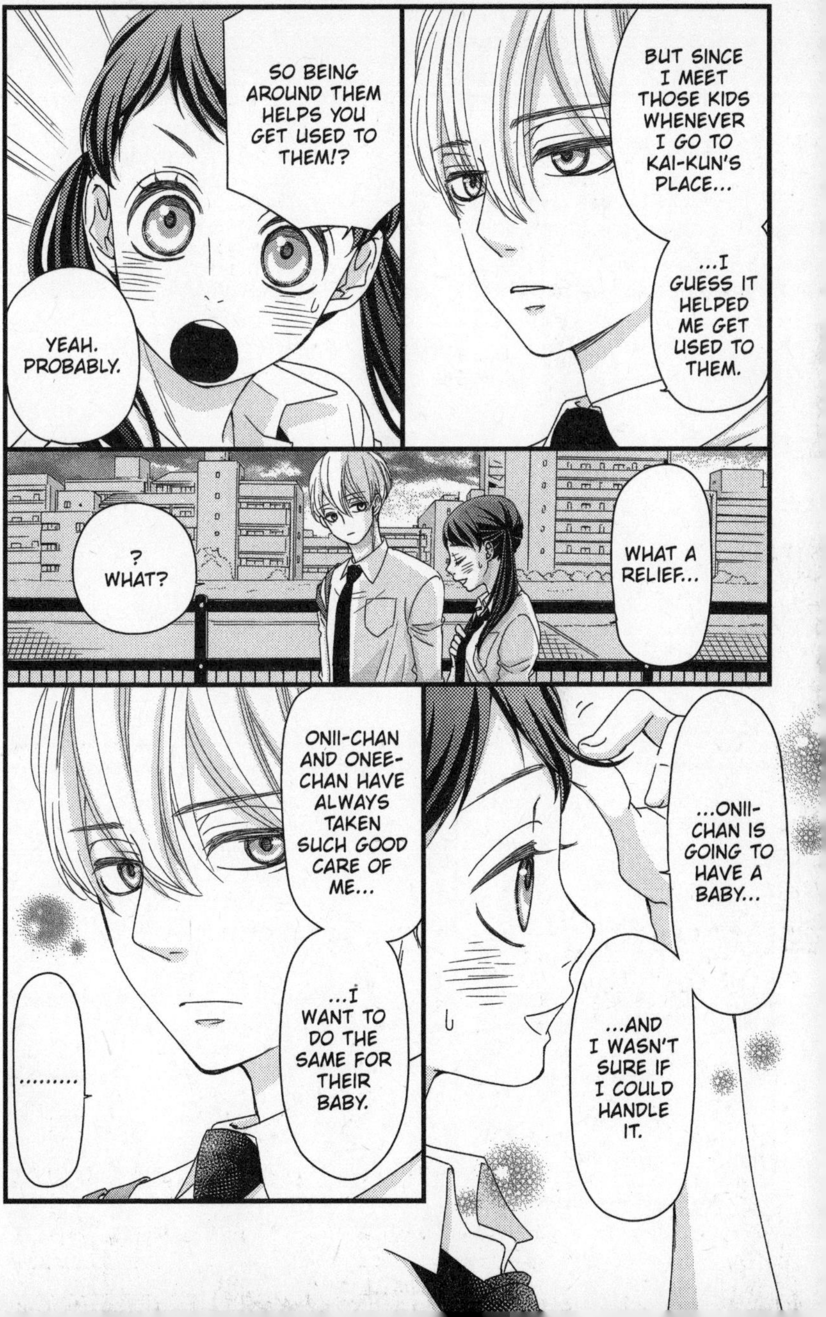
BUT SINCE I MEET THOSE KIDS WHENEVER I GO TO KAI-KUN'S PLACE...
...I GUESS IT HELPED ME GET USED TO THEM.
SO BEING AROUND THEM HELPS YOU GET USED TO THEM!?
YEAH. PROBABLY.
WHAT A RELIEF...
? WHAT?
...ONII-CHAN IS GOING TO HAVE A BABY...
...AND I WASN'T SURE IF I COULD HANDLE IT.
ONII-CHAN AND ONEE-CHAN HAVE ALWAYS TAKEN SUCH GOOD CARE OF ME...
...I WANT TO DO THE SAME FOR THEIR BABY.
....

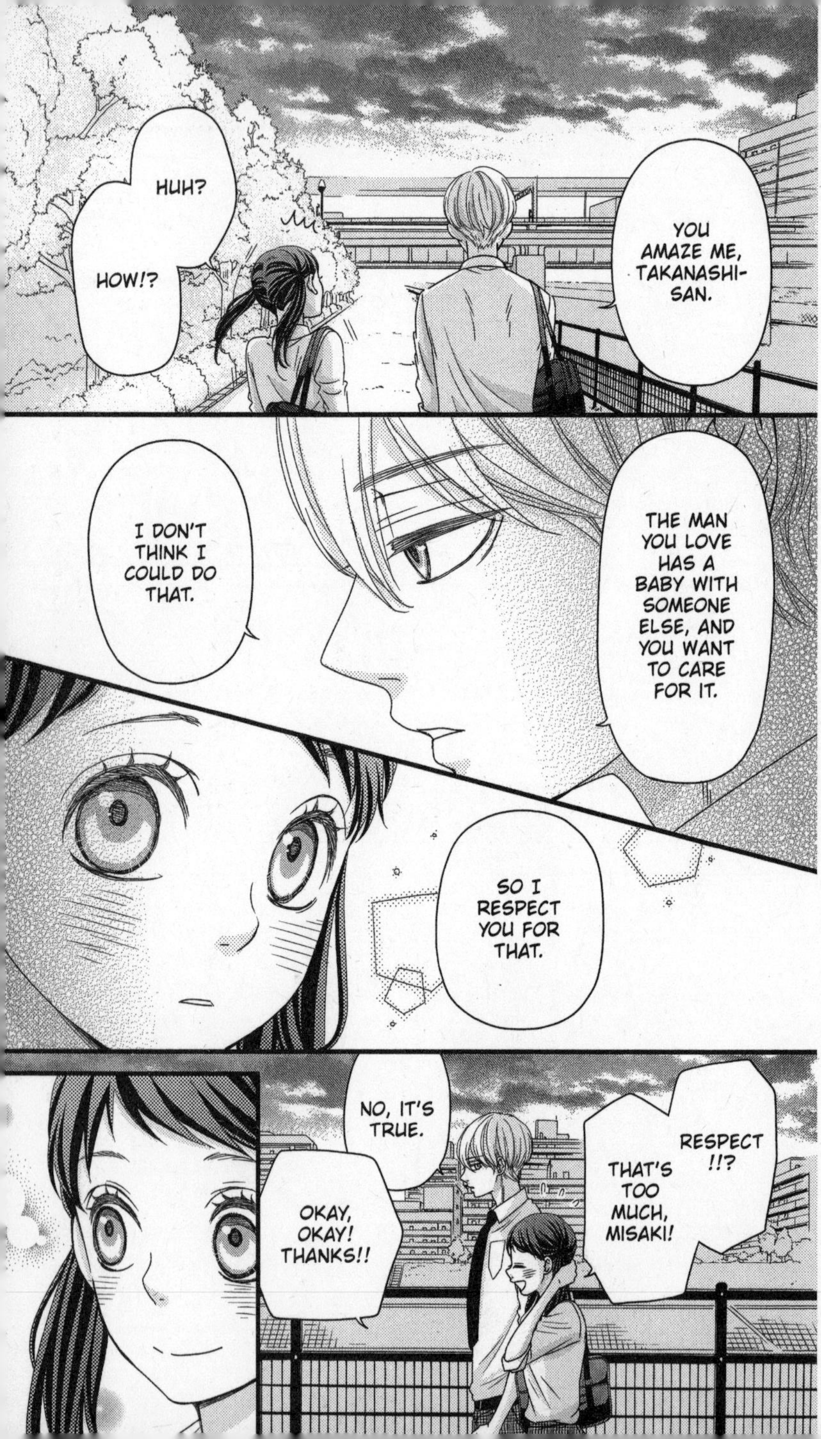
YOU AMAZE ME, TAKANASHI-SAN.
HUH?
HOW!?
THE MAN YOU LOVE HAS A BABY WITH SOMEONE ELSE, AND YOU WANT TO CARE FOR IT.
I DON'T THINK I COULD DO THAT.
SO I RESPECT YOU FOR THAT.
RESPECT!!?
THAT'S TOO MUCH, MISAKI!
NO, IT'S TRUE.
OKAY, OKAY! THANKS!!

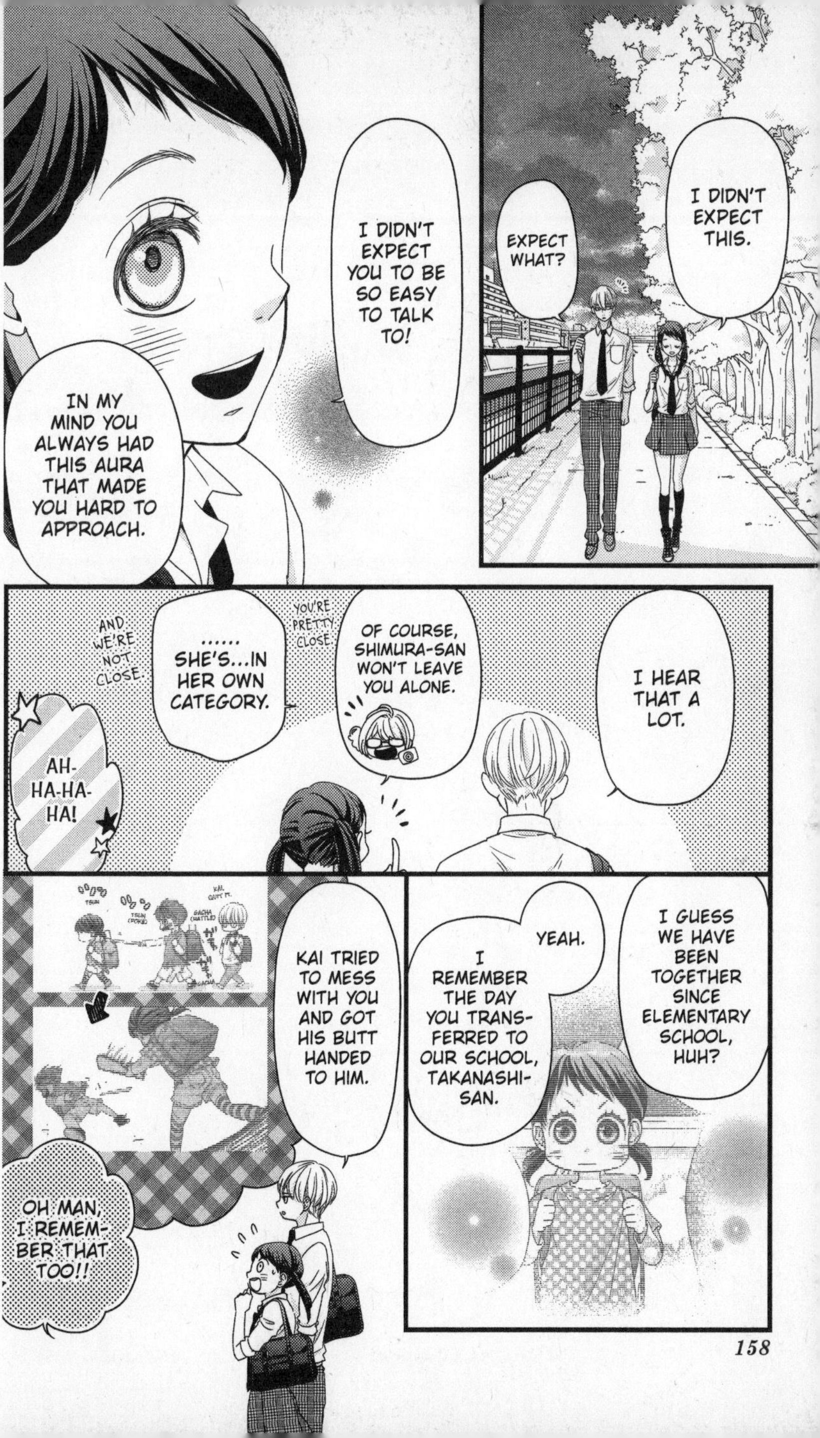
I DIDN'T EXPECT THIS.
EXPECT WHAT?
I DIDN'T EXPECT YOU TO BE SO EASY TO TALK TO!
IN MY MIND YOU ALWAYS HAD THIS AURA THAT MADE YOU HARD TO APPROACH.
I HEAR THAT A LOT.
OF COURSE, SHIMURA-SAN WON'T LEAVE YOU ALONE.
YOU'RE PRETTY CLOSE.
......SHE'S...IN HER OWN CATEGORY.
AND WE'RE NOT CLOSE.
AH-HA-HA-HA!
I GUESS WE HAVE BEEN TOGETHER SINCE ELEMENTARY SCHOOL, HUH?
YEAH.
I REMEMBER THE DAY YOU TRANSFERRED TO OUR SCHOOL, TAKANASHI-SAN.
KAI TRIED TO MESS WITH YOU AND GOT HIS BUTT HANDED TO HIM.
OH MAN, I REMEMBER THAT TOO!!

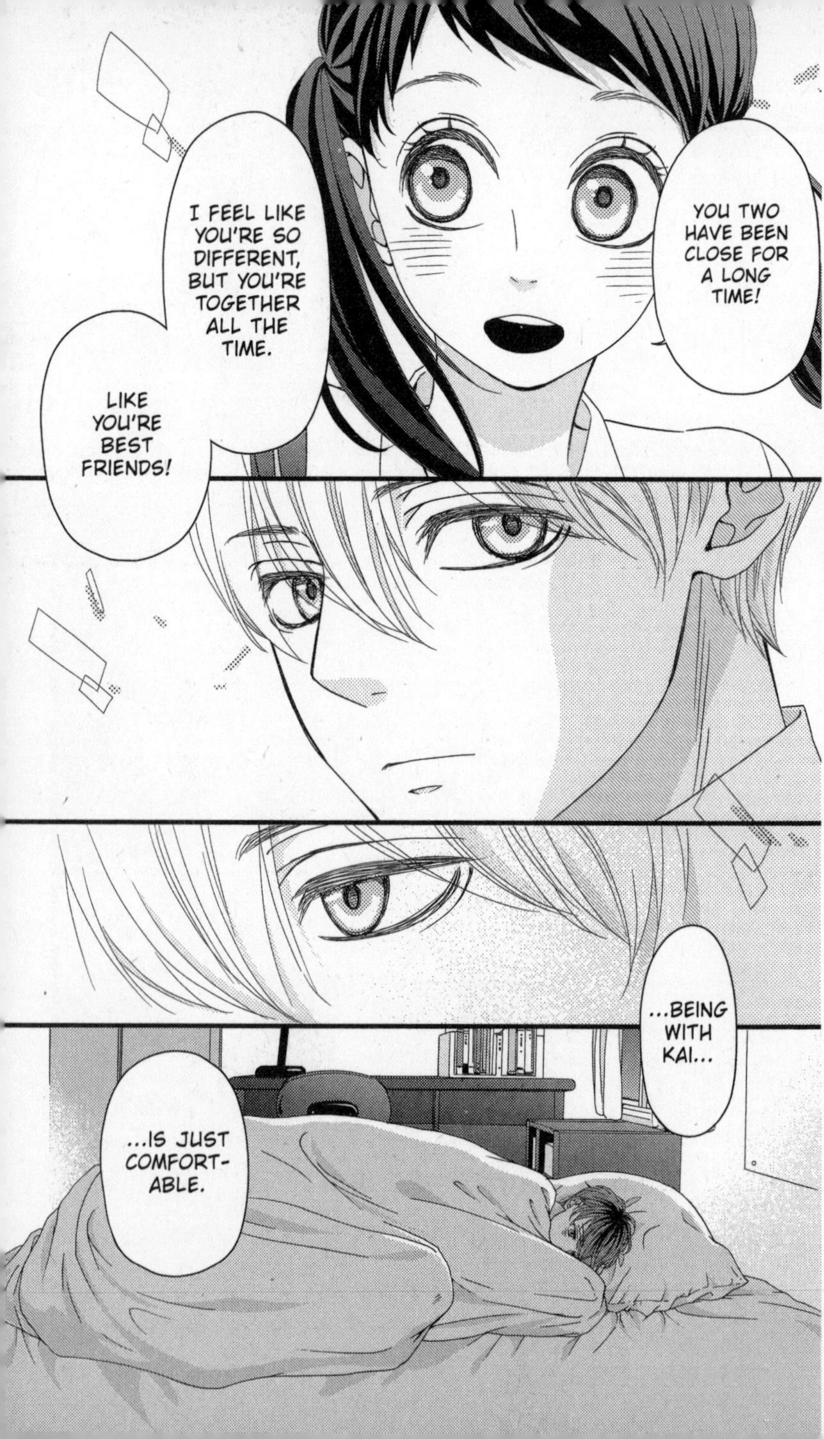
YOU TWO HAVE BEEN CLOSE FOR A LONG TIME!
I FEEL LIKE YOU'RE SO DIFFERENT, BUT YOU'RE TOGETHER ALL THE TIME.
LIKE YOU'RE BEST FRIENDS!
...BEING WITH KAI...
...IS JUST COMFORT-ABLE.

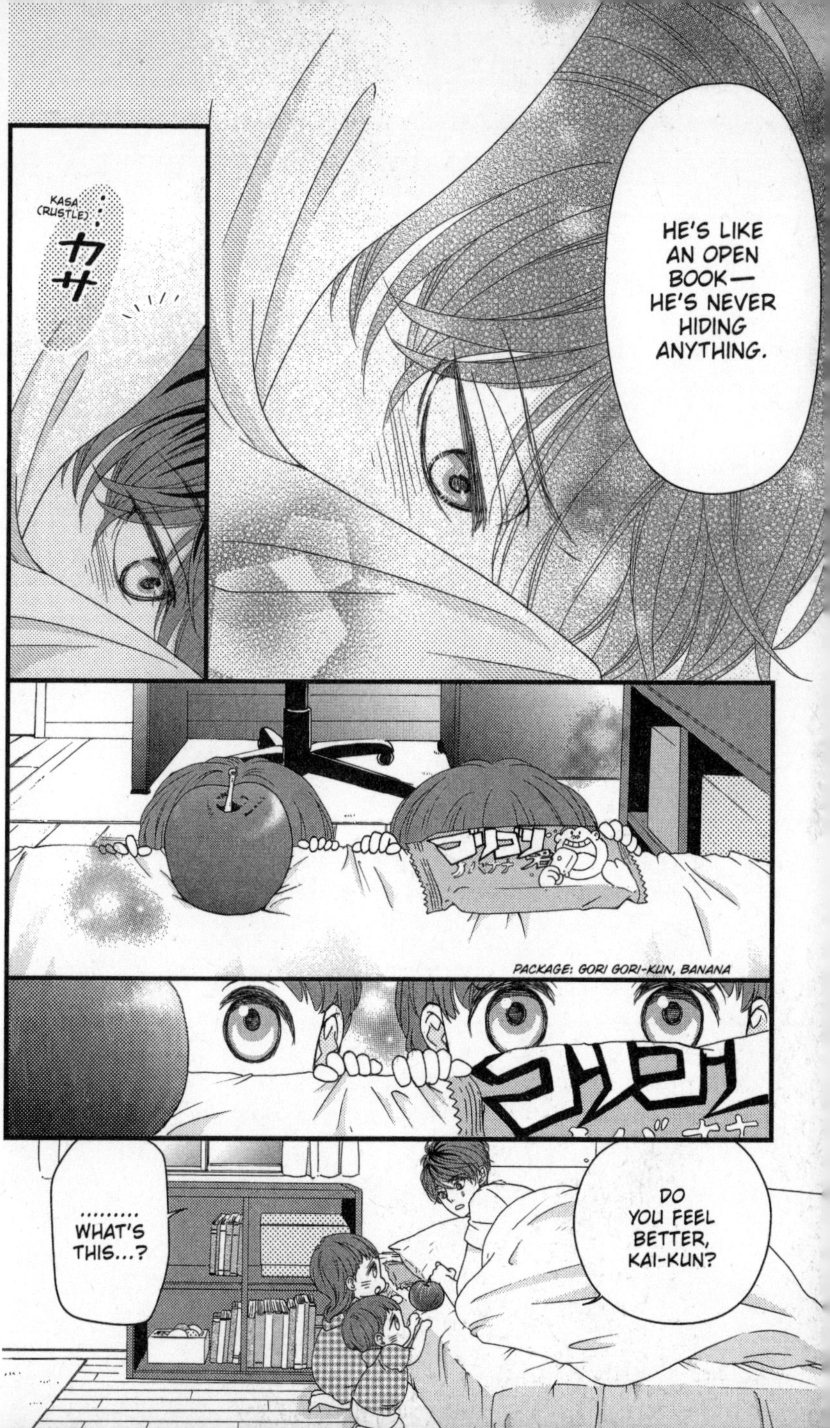
HE'S LIKE AN OPEN BOOK—HE'S NEVER HIDING ANYTHING.
KASA (RUSTLE)
カサ
PACKAGE: GORI GORI-KUN, BANANA
DO YOU FEEL BETTER, KAI-KUN?
....
WHAT'S THIS...?

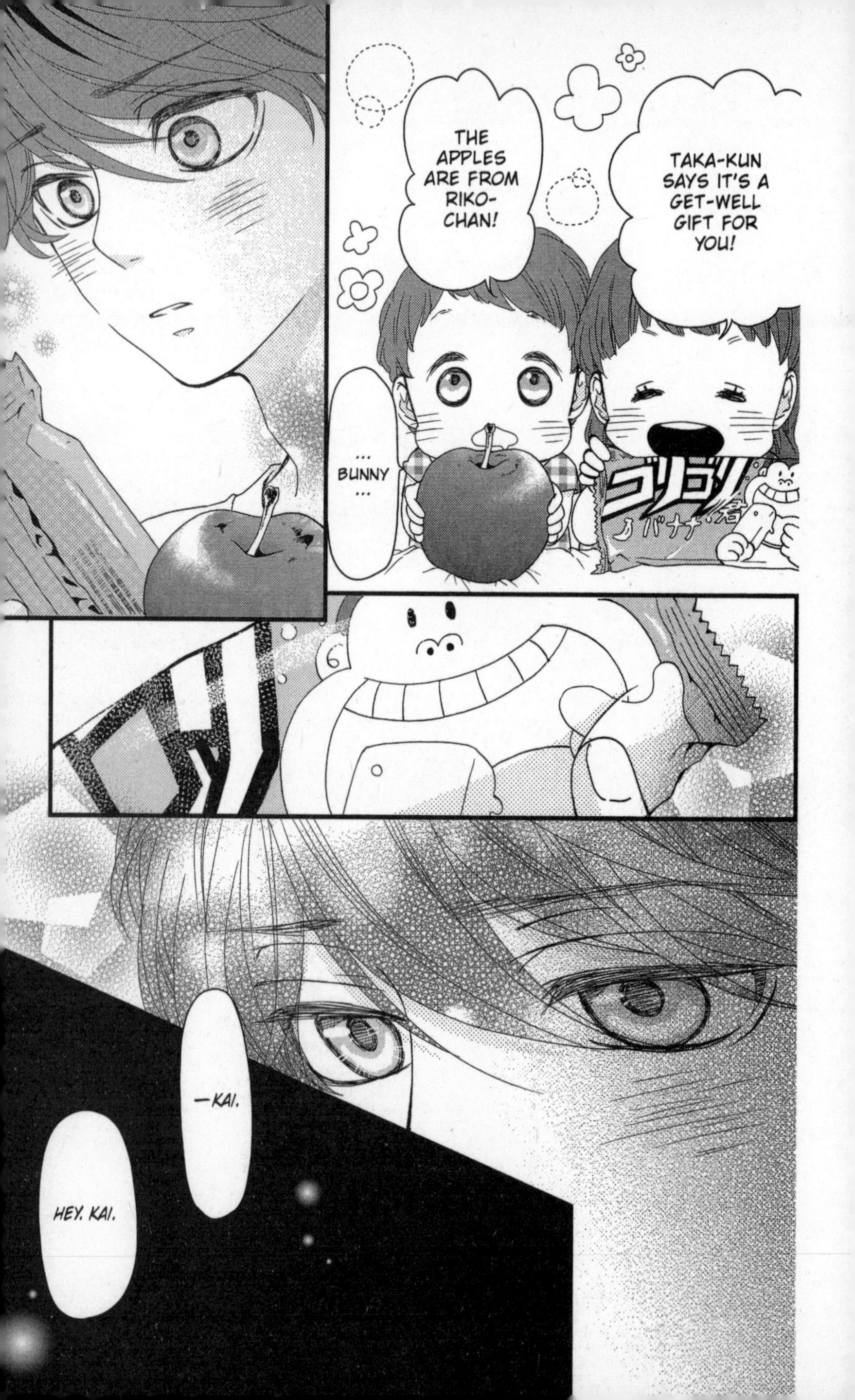
TAKA-KUN SAYS IT'S A GET-WELL GIFT FOR YOU!
THE APPLES ARE FROM RIKO-CHAN!
...BUNNY...
—KAI.
HEY. KAI.

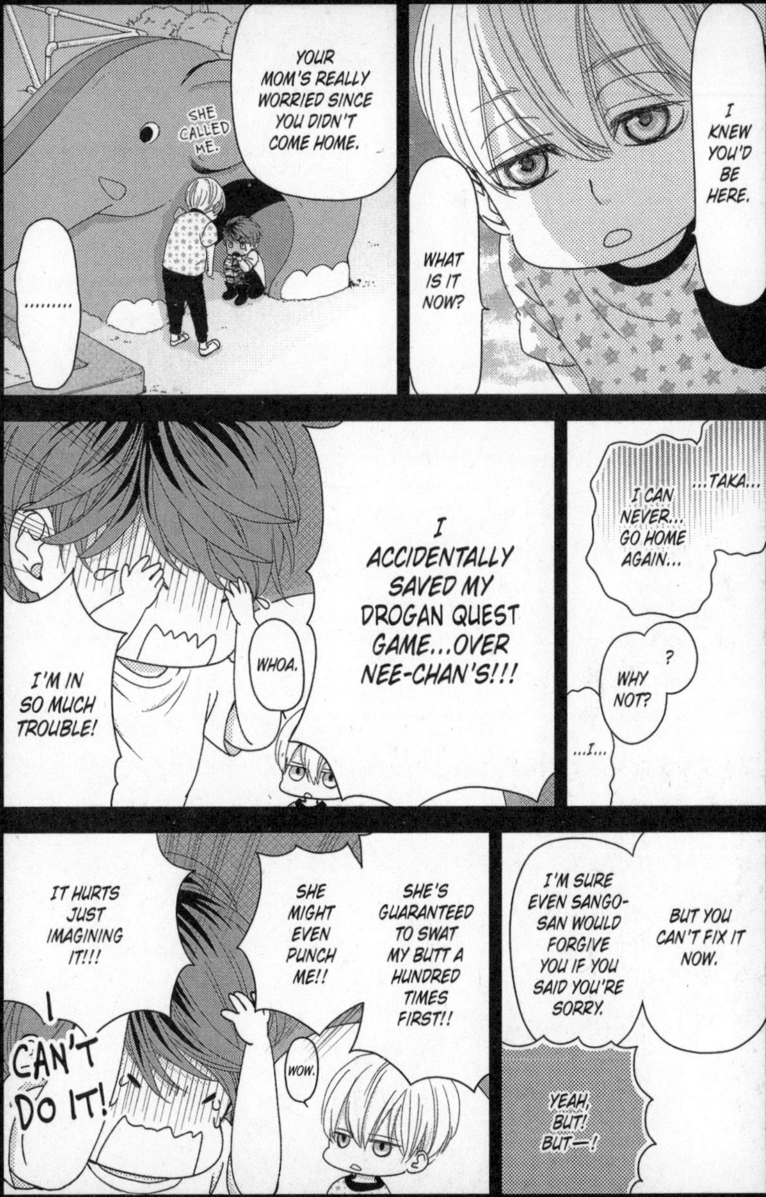
I KNEW YOU'D BE HERE.
WHAT IS IT NOW?
YOUR MOM'S REALLY WORRIED SINCE YOU DIDN'T COME HOME.
SHE CALLED ME.
....
...TAKA...
I CAN NEVER... GO HOME AGAIN...
?
WHY NOT?
...I...
I ACCIDENTALLY SAVED MY DROGAN QUEST GAME...OVER NEE-CHAN'S!!!
WHOA.
I'M IN SO MUCH TROUBLE!
BUT YOU CAN'T FIX IT NOW.
I'M SURE EVEN SANGO-SAN WOULD FORGIVE YOU IF YOU SAID YOU'RE SORRY.
YEAH, BUT! BUT—!
SHE'S GUARANTEED TO SWAT MY BUTT A HUNDRED TIMES FIRST!!
SHE MIGHT EVEN PUNCH ME!!
IT HURTS JUST IMAGINING IT!!!
WOW.
I CAN'T DO IT!

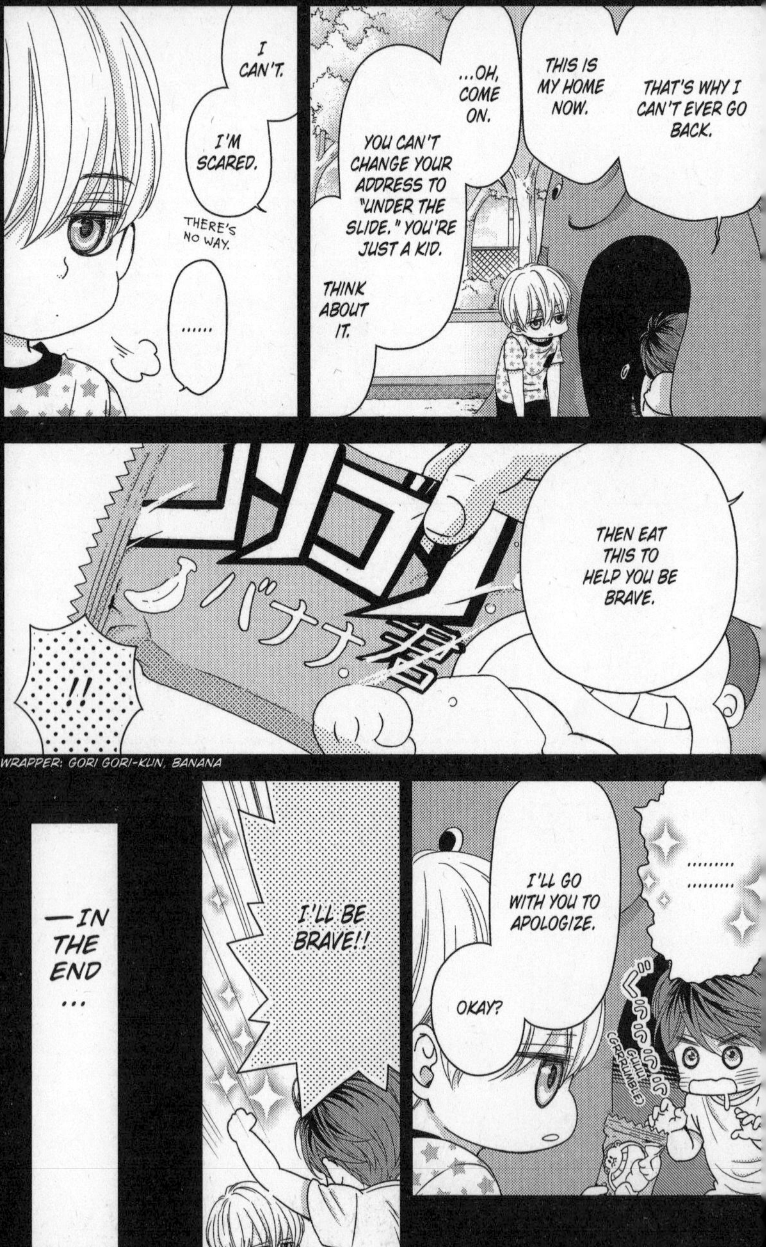
THAT'S WHY I CAN'T EVER GO BACK.
THIS IS MY HOME NOW.
...OH, COME ON.
YOU CAN'T CHANGE YOUR ADDRESS TO "UNDER THE SLIDE." YOU'RE JUST A KID.
THINK ABOUT IT.
I CAN'T.
I'M SCARED.
THERE'S NO WAY.
......
THEN EAT THIS TO HELP YOU BE BRAVE.
バナナ
!!
WRAPPER: GORI GORI-KUN, BANANA
....
I'LL GO WITH YOU TO APOLOGIZE.
OKAY?
GULP (GRRUMBLE)
I'LL BE BRAVE!!
—IN THE END ...

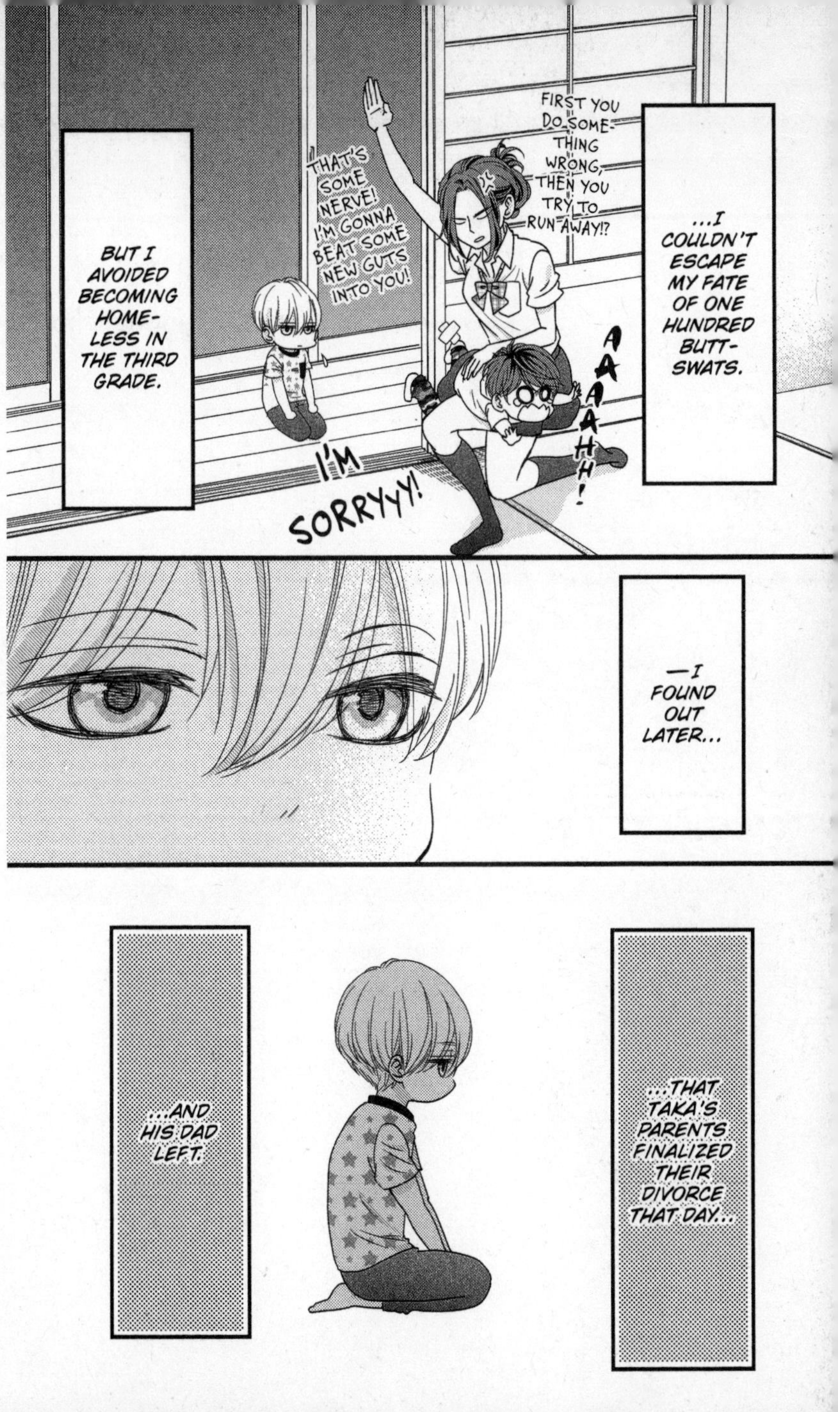
...I COULDN'T ESCAPE MY FATE OF ONE HUNDRED BUTT-SWATS.
FIRST YOU DO SOME-THING WRONG, THEN YOU TRY TO RUN AWAY!?
THAT'S SOME NERVE! I'M GONNA BEAT SOME NEW GUTS INTO YOU!
AAAAAHH!
I'M SORRYYY!
BUT I AVOIDED BECOMING HOME-LESS IN THE THIRD GRADE.
—I FOUND OUT LATER...
...THAT TAKA'S PARENTS FINALIZED THEIR DIVORCE THAT DAY...
...AND HIS DAD LEFT.

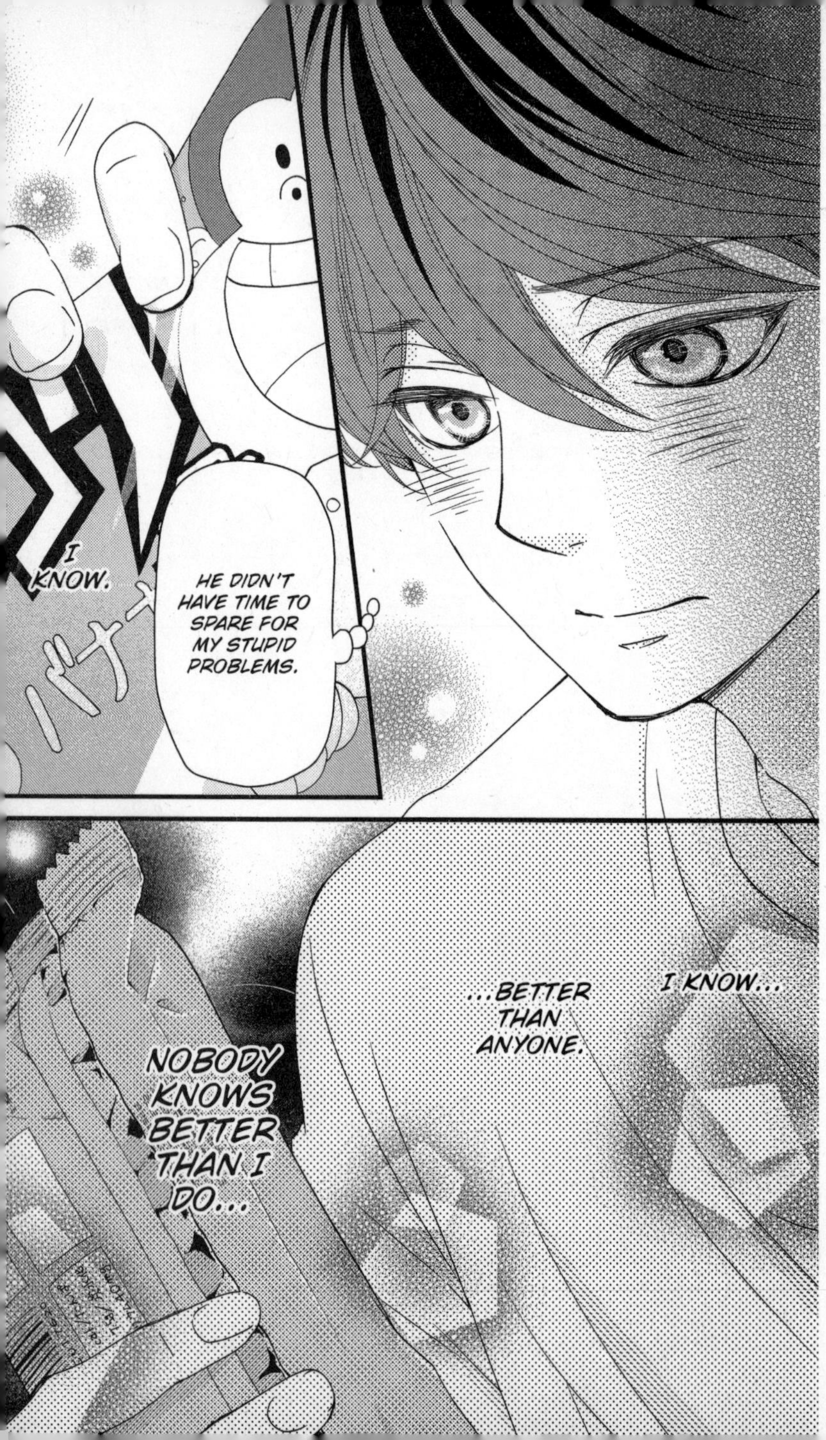
HE DIDN'T HAVE TIME TO SPARE FOR MY STUPID PROBLEMS.
I KNOW.
I KNOW...
...BETTER THAN ANYONE.
NOBODY KNOWS BETTER THAN I DO...

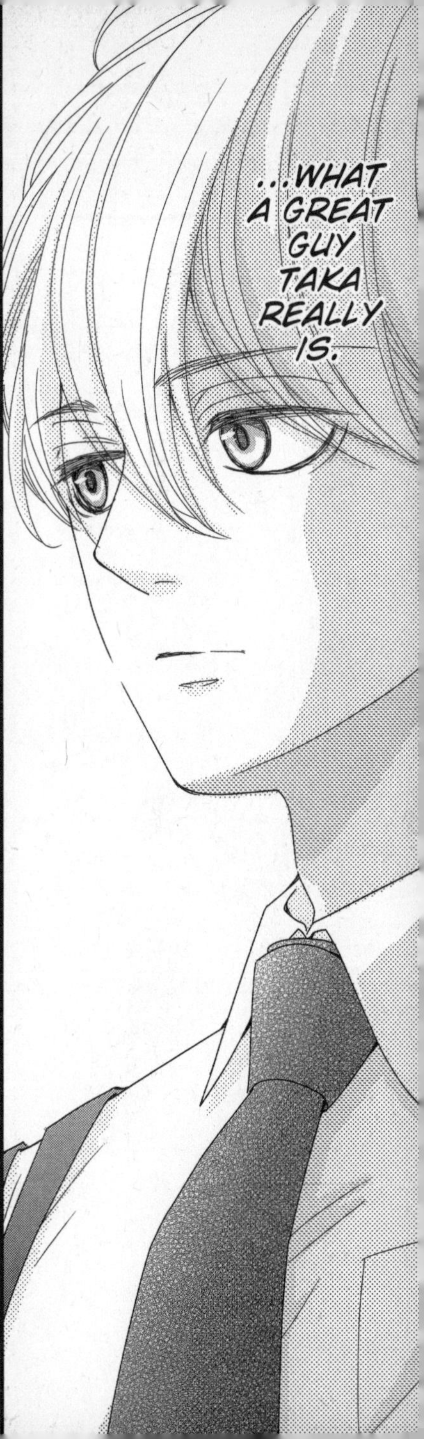
...WHAT A GREAT GUY TAKA REALLY IS.
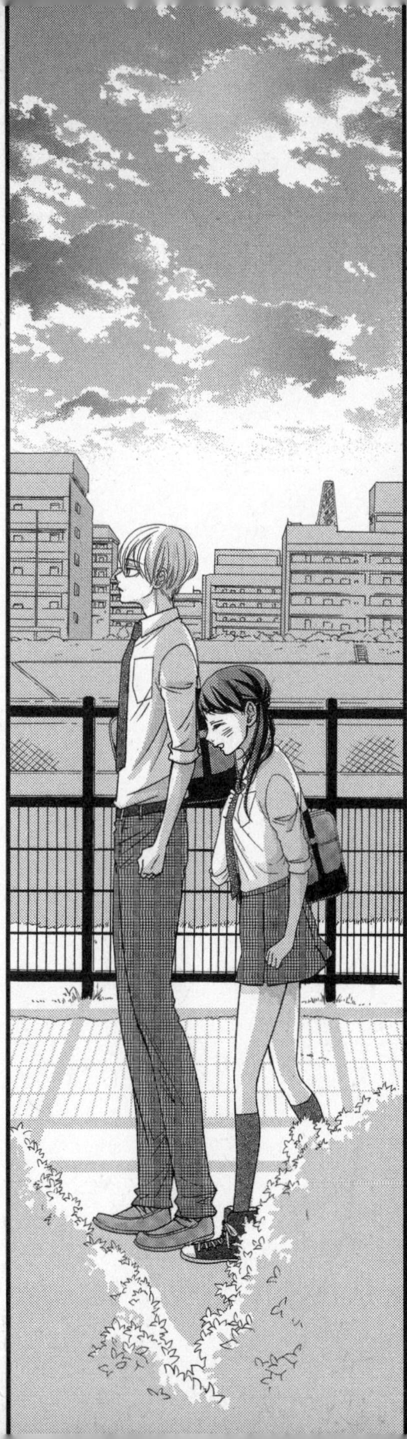

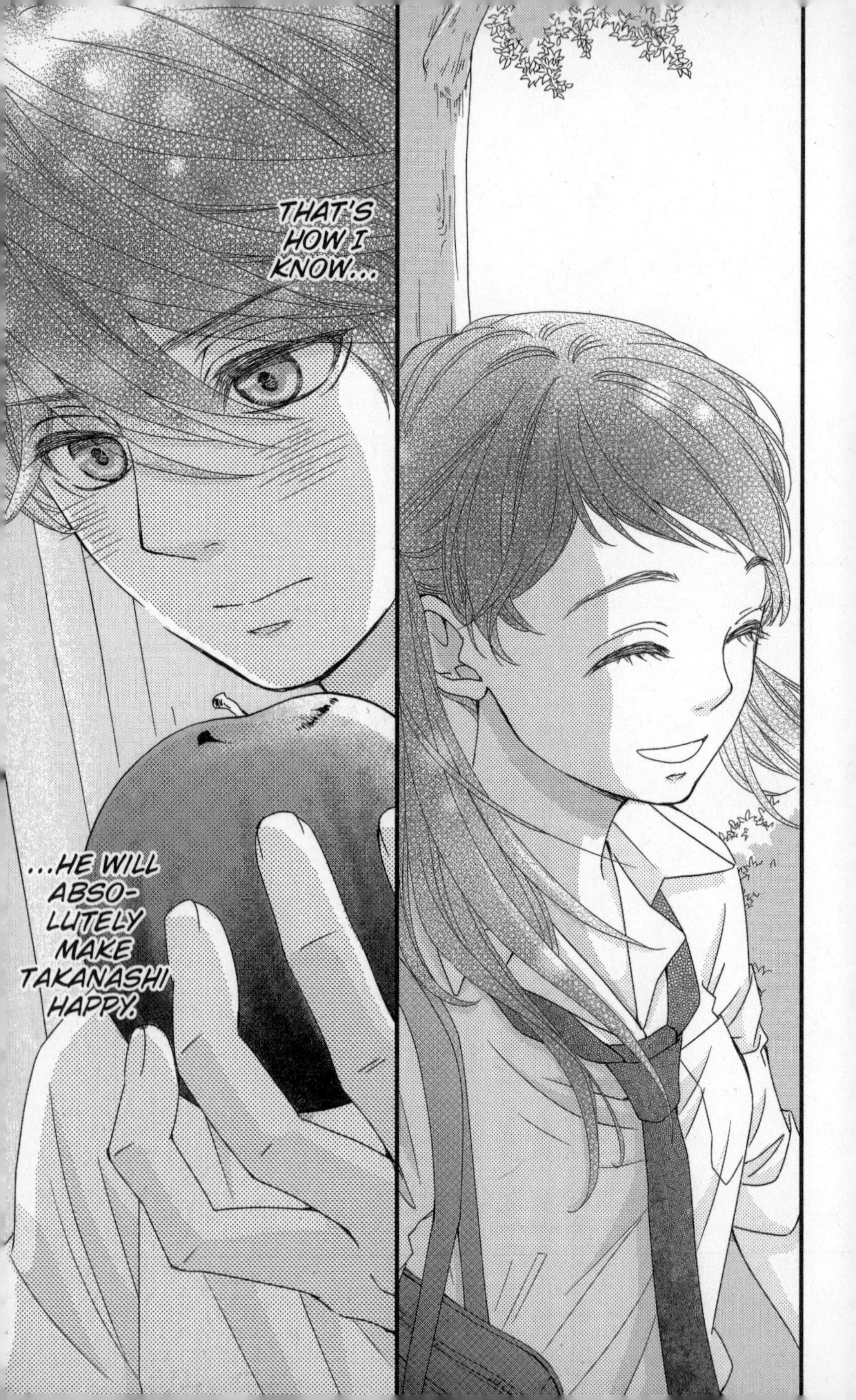
THAT'S HOW I KNOW...
...HE WILL ABSO-LUTELY MAKE TAKANASHI HAPPY.

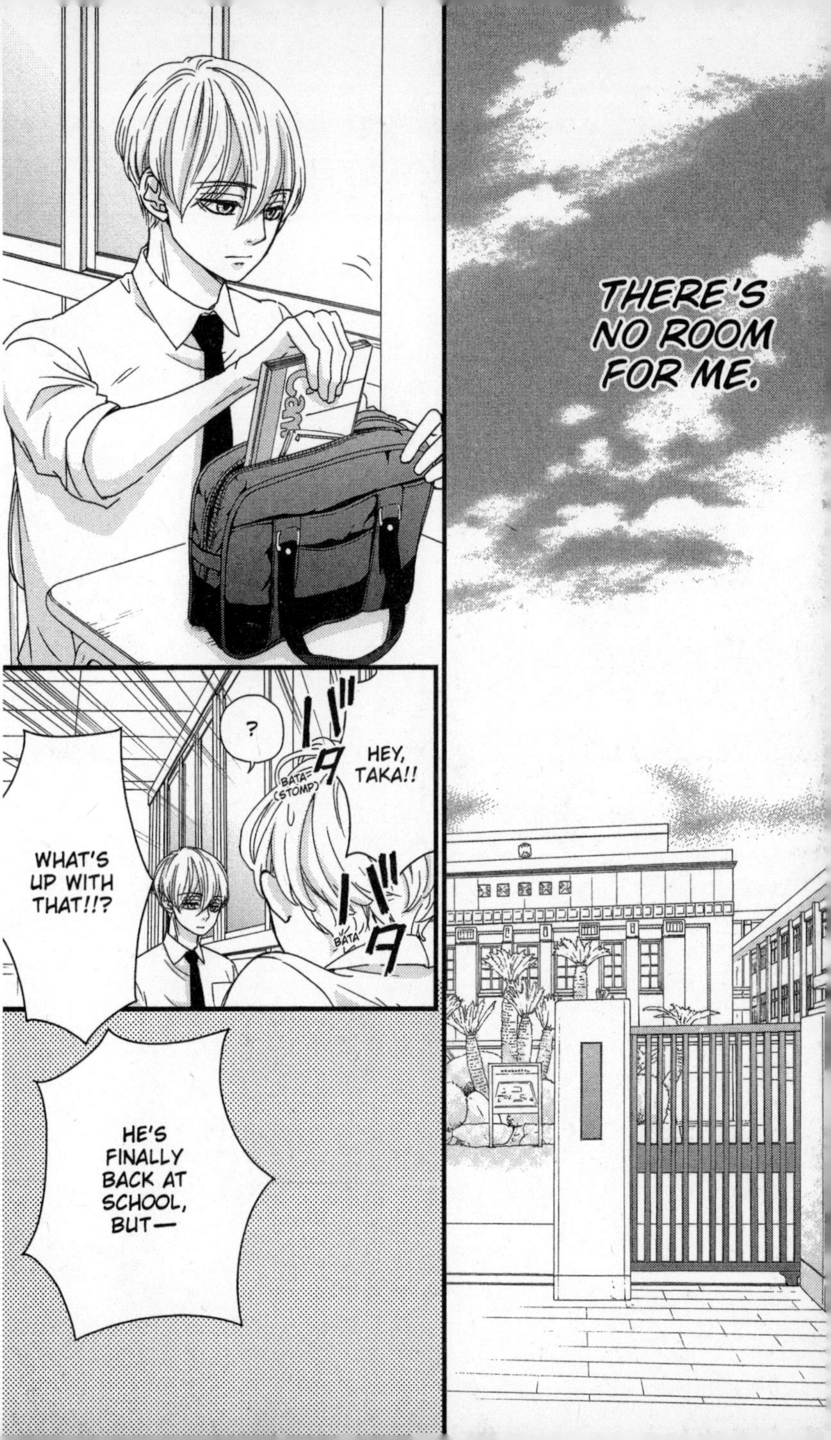
THERE'S NO ROOM FOR ME.
HEY, TAKA!!
BATA= (STOMP)
?
WHAT'S UP WITH THAT!!?
BATA
HE'S FINALLY BACK AT SCHOOL, BUT—

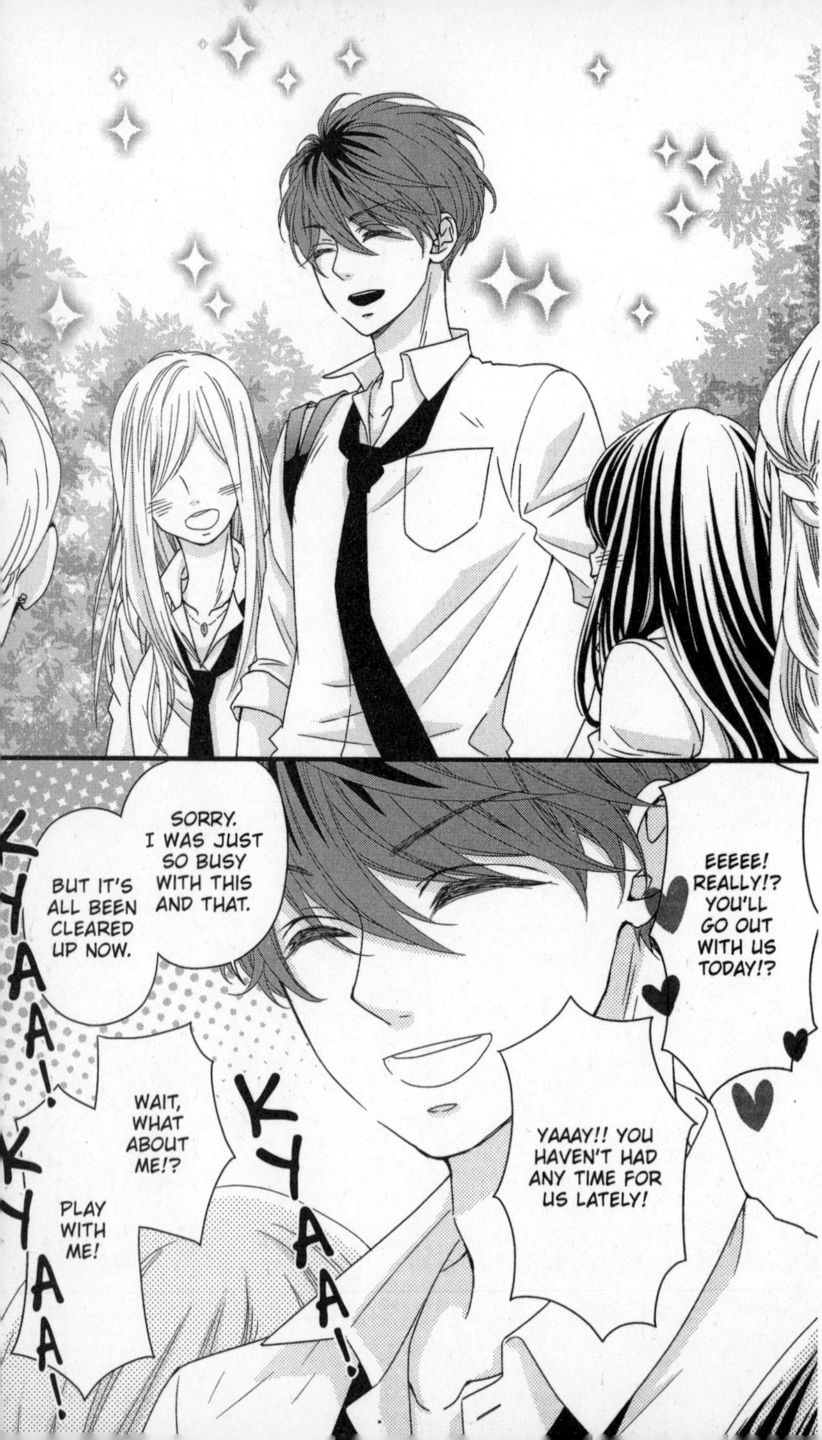
EEEEE! REALLY!? YOU'LL GO OUT WITH US TODAY!?
SORRY. I WAS JUST SO BUSY WITH THIS AND THAT.
BUT IT'S ALL BEEN CLEARED UP NOW.
YAAAY!! YOU HAVEN'T HAD ANY TIME FOR US LATELY!
KYAAA!
WAIT, WHAT ABOUT ME!?
PLAY WITH ME!
KYAAA!
KYAAA!

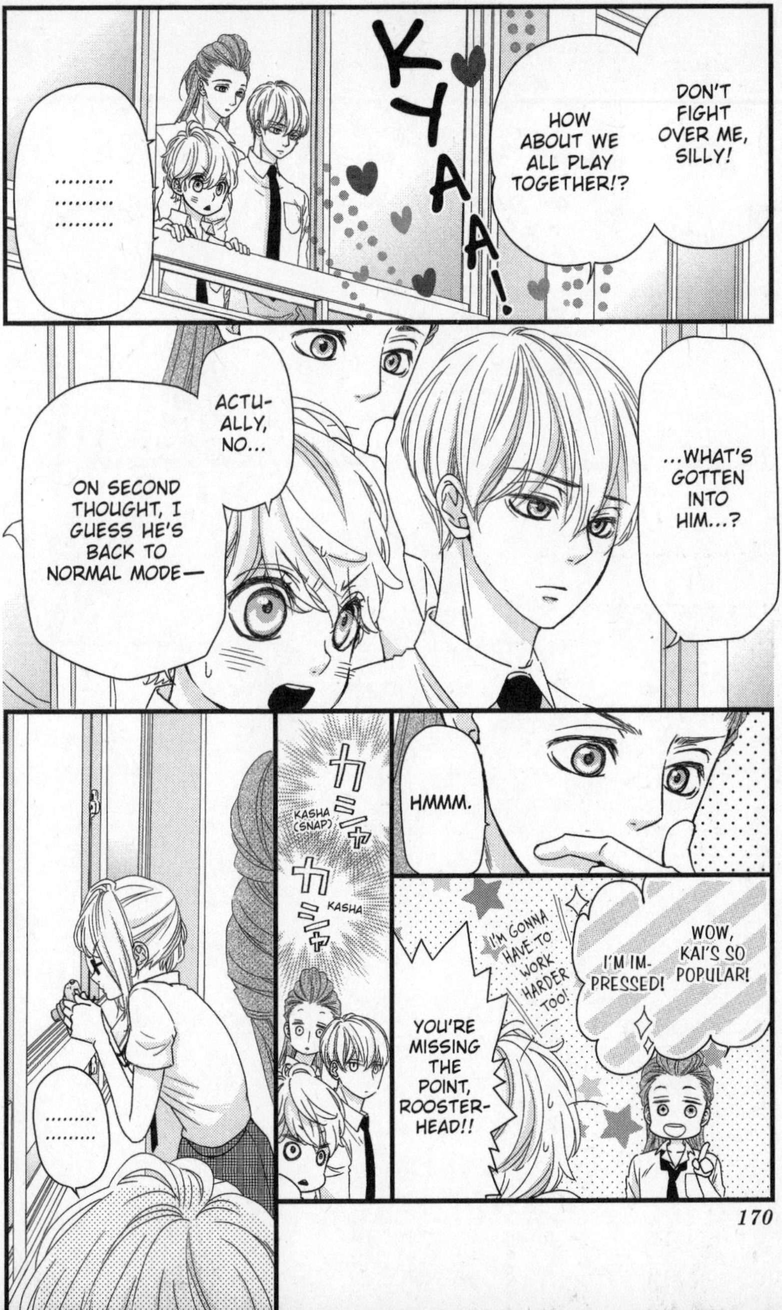
DON'T FIGHT OVER ME, SILLY!
HOW ABOUT WE ALL PLAY TOGETHER!?
KYAA!
....
....
....
...WHAT'S GOTTEN INTO HIM...?
ACTU-ALLY, NO...
ON SECOND THOUGHT, I GUESS HE'S BACK TO NORMAL MODE—
HMMM.
WOW, KAI'S SO POPULAR!
I'M IM-PRESSED!
I'M GONNA HAVE TO WORK HARDER TOO!
YOU'RE MISSING THE POINT, ROOSTER-HEAD!!
カシャ
KASHA (SNAP)
カシャ
KASHA
....
....

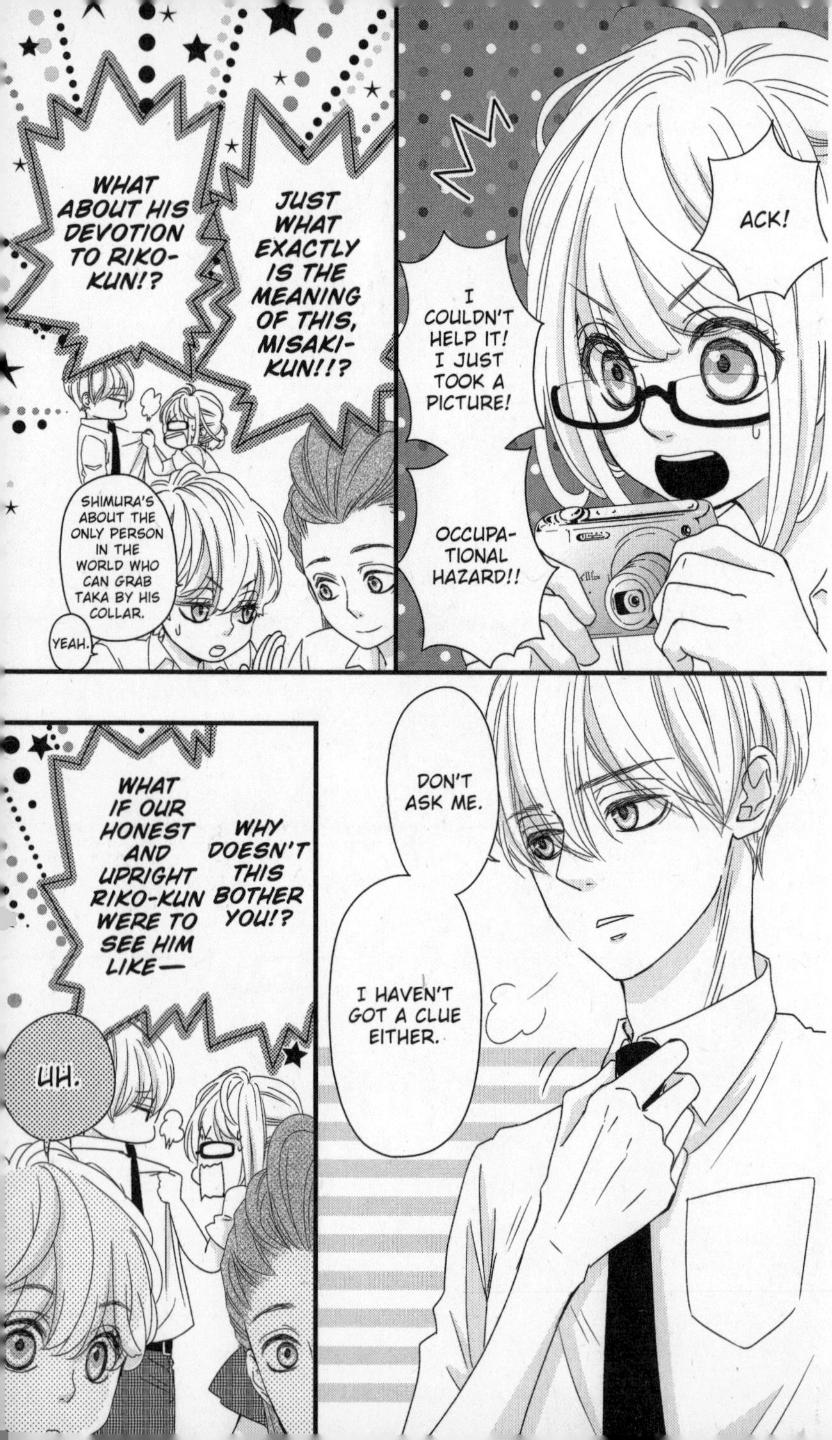
ACK!
I COULDN'T HELP IT! I JUST TOOK A PICTURE!
OCCUPATIONAL HAZARD!!
JUST WHAT EXACTLY IS THE MEANING OF THIS, MISAKI-KUN!!?
WHAT ABOUT HIS DEVOTION TO RIKO-KUN!?
SHIMURA'S ABOUT THE ONLY PERSON IN THE WORLD WHO CAN GRAB TAKA BY HIS COLLAR.
YEAH.
DON'T ASK ME.
I HAVEN'T GOT A CLUE EITHER.
WHY DOESN'T THIS BOTHER YOU!?
WHAT IF OUR HONEST AND UPRIGHT RIKO-KUN WERE TO SEE HIM LIKE—
UH.

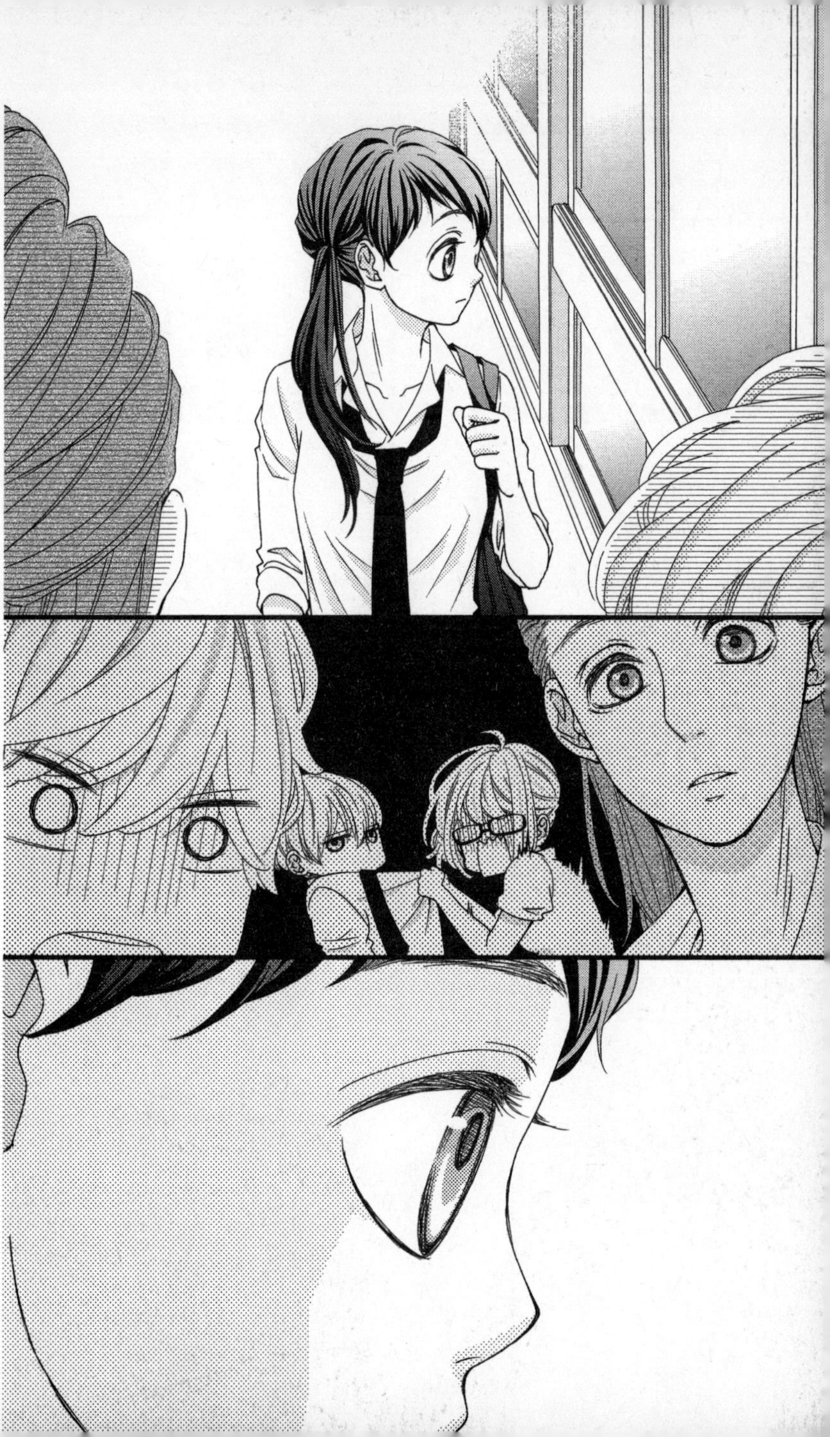

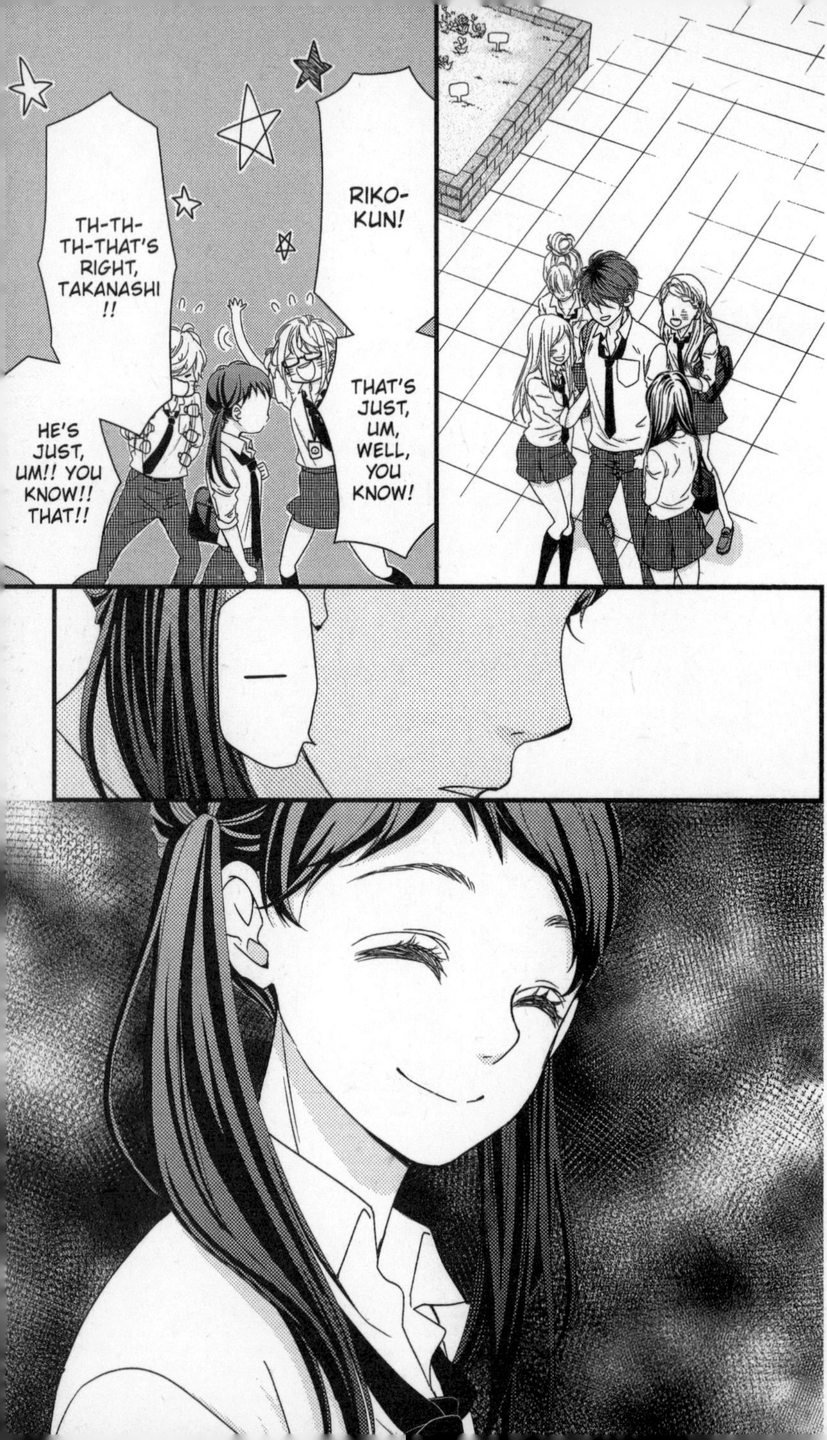
RIKO-KUN!
TH-TH-TH-THAT'S RIGHT, TAKANASHI!!
THAT'S JUST, UM, WELL, YOU KNOW!
HE'S JUST, UM!! YOU KNOW!! THAT!!

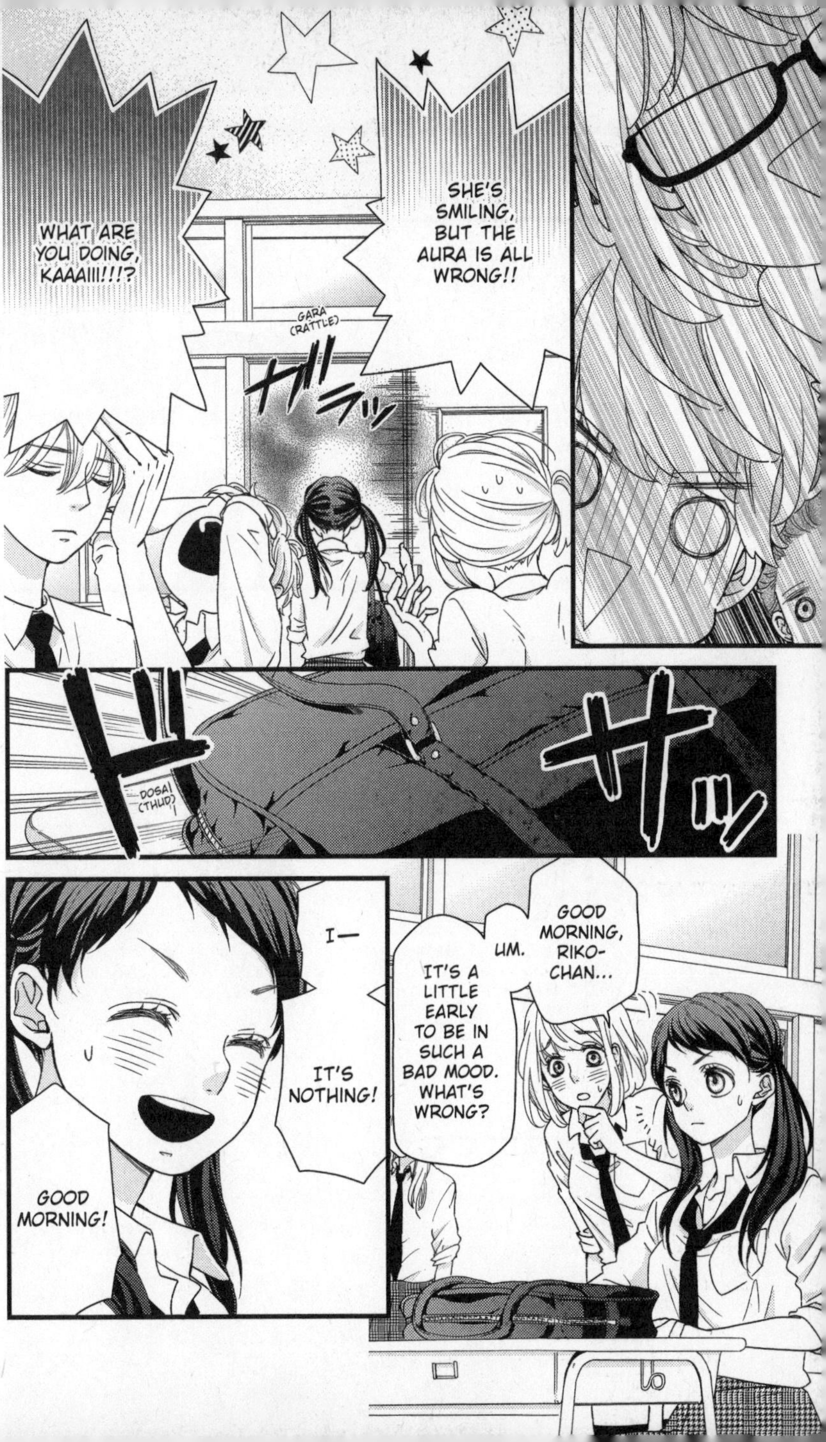
SHE'S SMILING, BUT THE AURA IS ALL WRONG!!
WHAT ARE YOU DOING, KAAAIII!!!?
GARA (RATTLE)
DOSA! (THUD)
GOOD MORNING, RIKO-CHAN...
UM.
IT'S A LITTLE EARLY TO BE IN SUCH A BAD MOOD. WHAT'S WRONG?
I—
IT'S NOTHING!
GOOD MORNING!

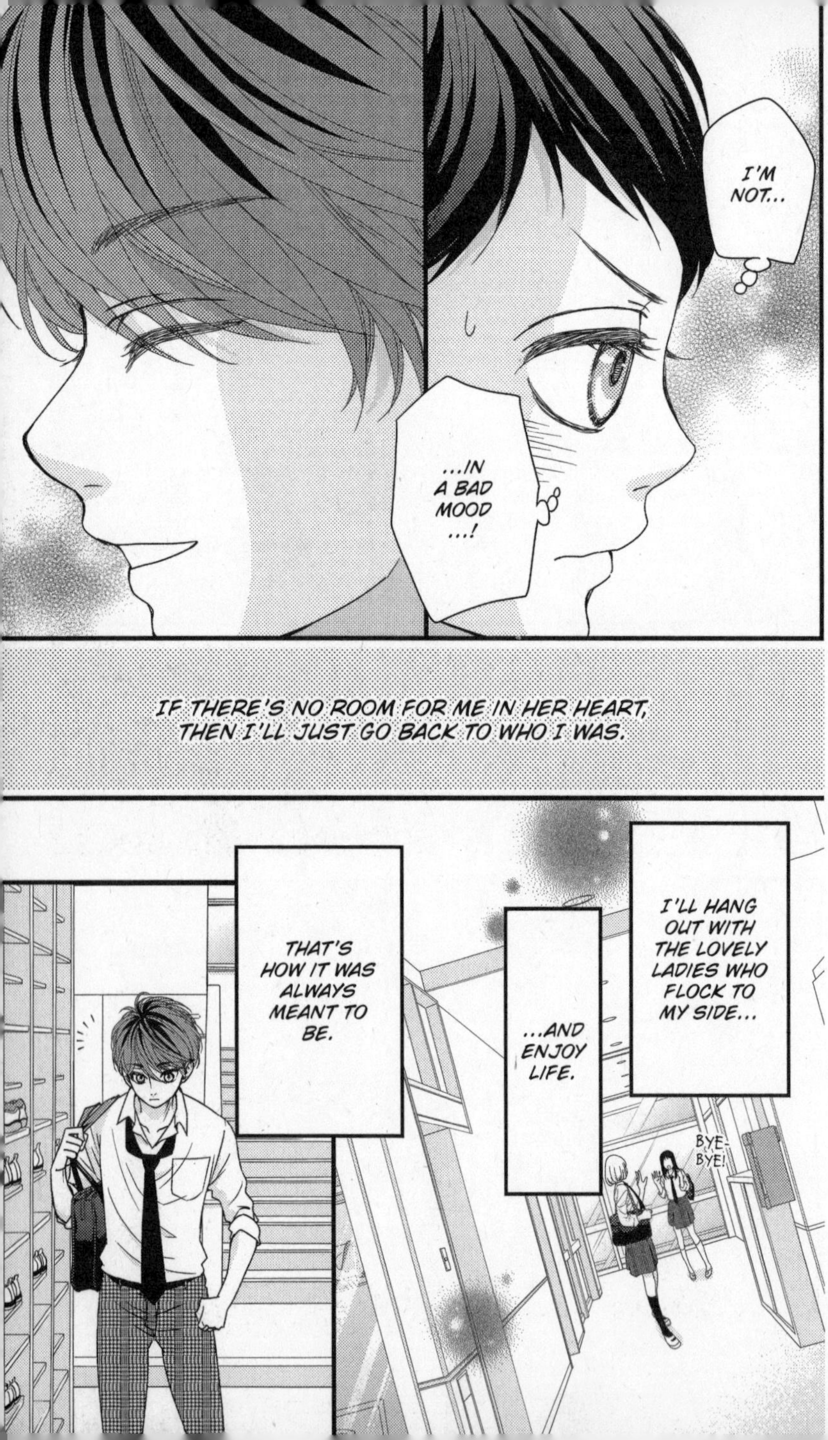
I'M NOT...
...IN A BAD MOOD ...!
IF THERE'S NO ROOM FOR ME IN HER HEART, THEN I'LL JUST GO BACK TO WHO I WAS.
I'LL HANG OUT WITH THE LOVELY LADIES WHO FLOCK TO MY SIDE...
...AND ENJOY LIFE.
THAT'S HOW IT WAS ALWAYS MEANT TO BE.
BYE-BYE!

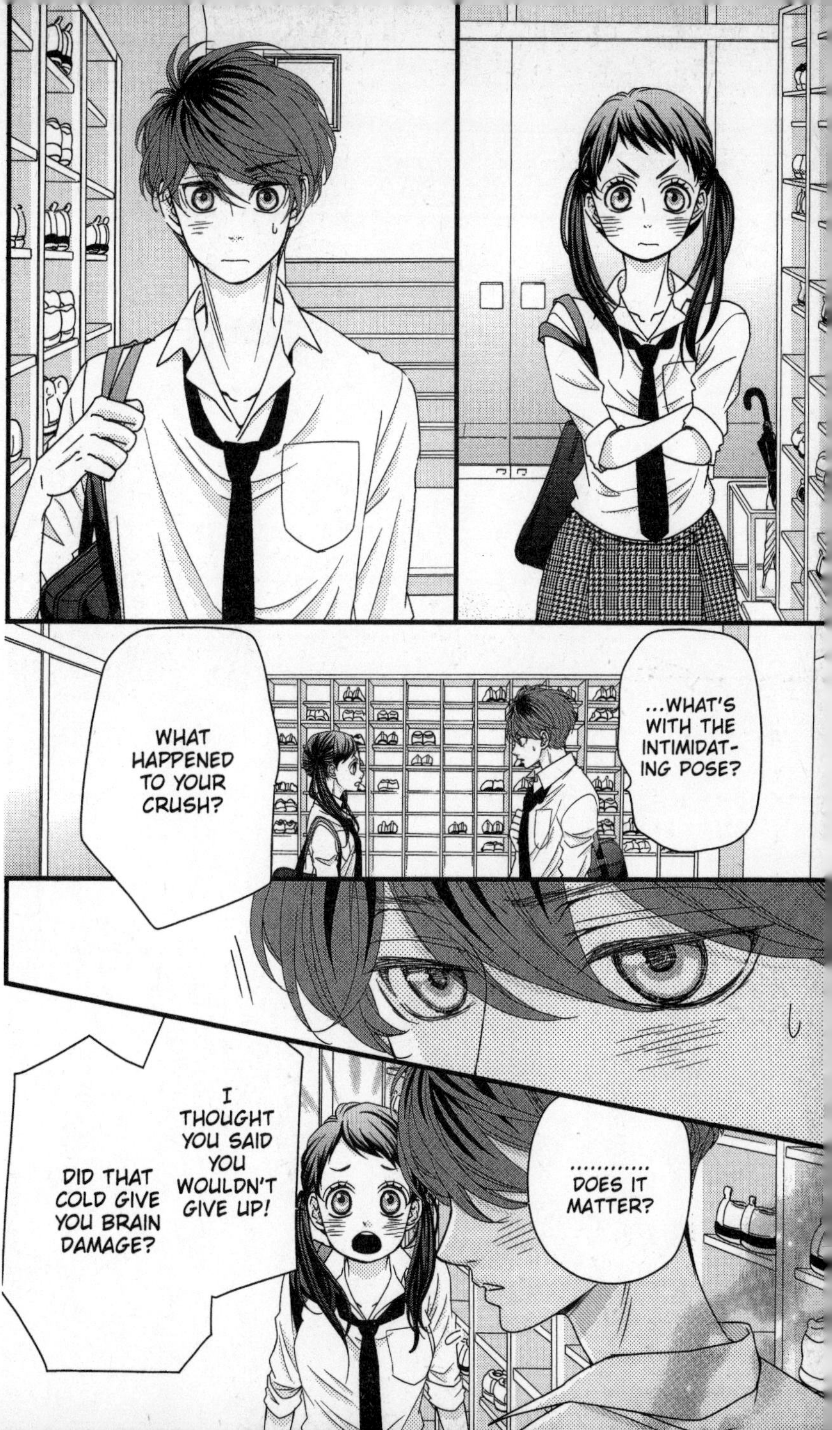
...WHAT'S WITH THE INTIMIDAT-ING POSE?
WHAT HAPPENED TO YOUR CRUSH?
I THOUGHT YOU SAID YOU WOULDN'T GIVE UP!
DID THAT COLD GIVE YOU BRAIN DAMAGE?
.... DOES IT MATTER?

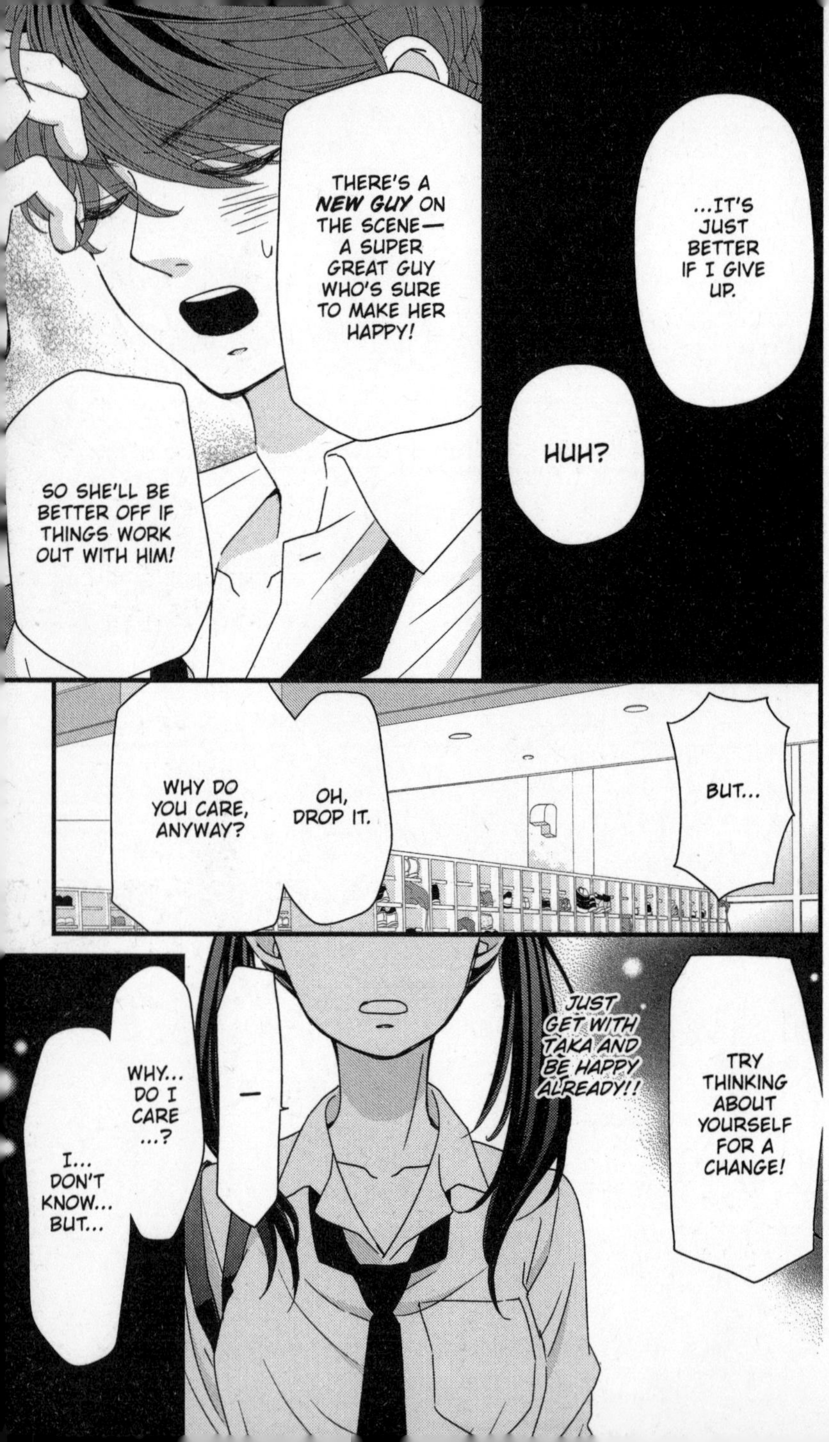
...IT'S JUST BETTER IF I GIVE UP.
HUH?
THERE'S A ***NEW GUY*** ON THE SCENE—A SUPER GREAT GUY WHO'S SURE TO MAKE HER HAPPY!
SO SHE'LL BE BETTER OFF IF THINGS WORK OUT WITH HIM!
BUT...
OH, DROP IT.
WHY DO YOU CARE, ANYWAY?
TRY THINKING ABOUT YOURSELF FOR A CHANGE!
JUST GET WITH TAKA AND BE HAPPY ALREADY!!
WHY... DO I CARE ...?
I... DON'T KNOW... BUT...

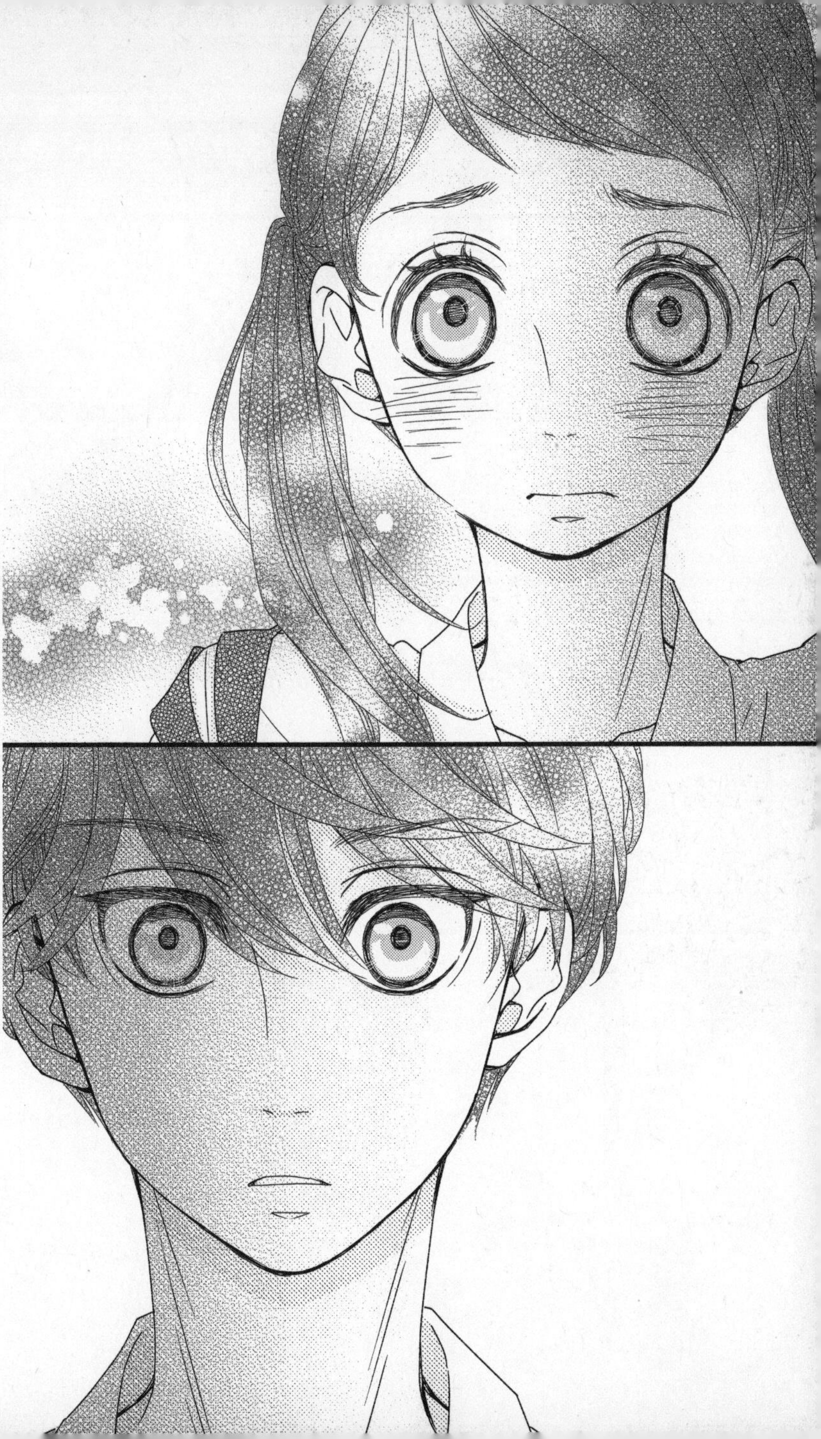

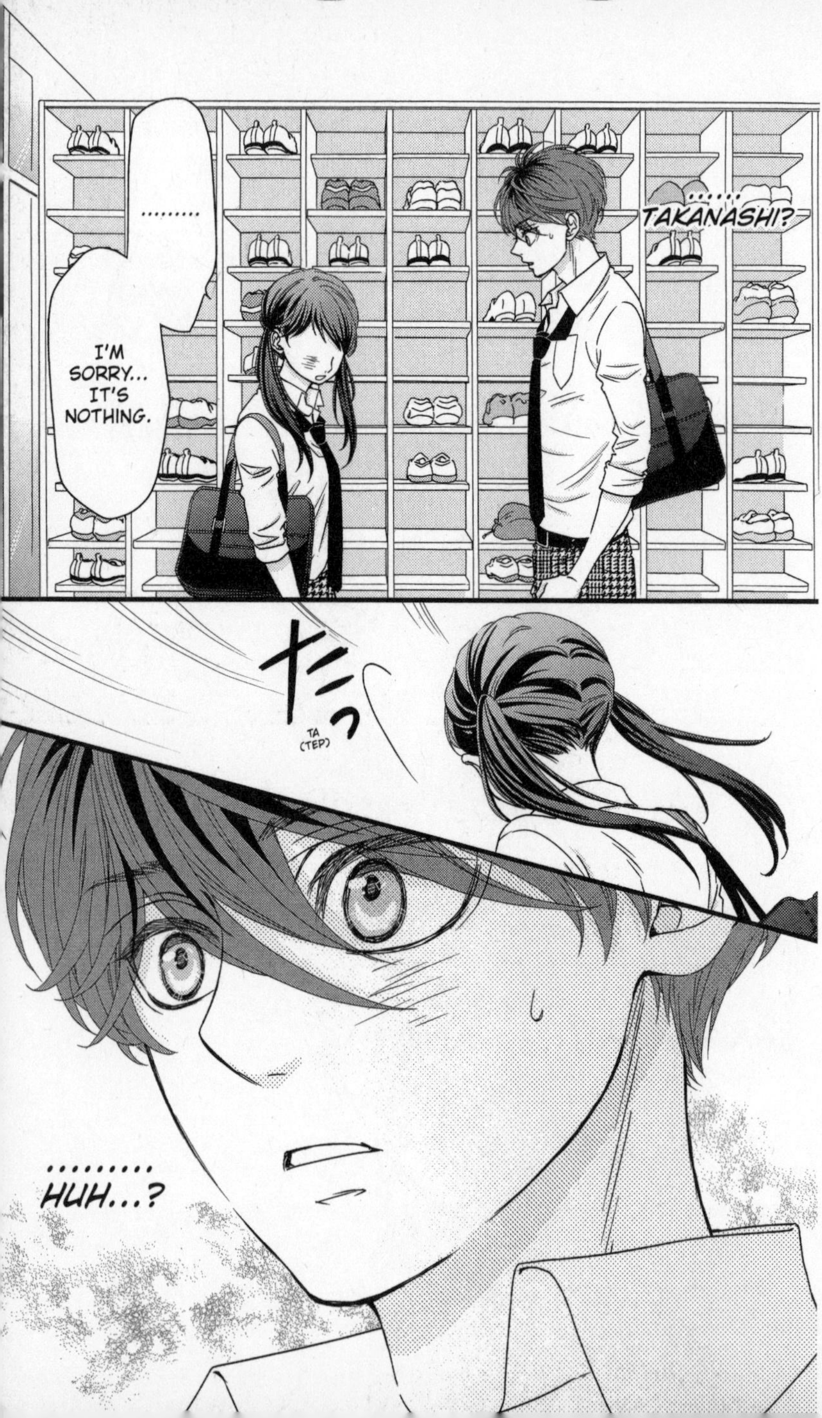
......
TAKANASHI?
....
I'M SORRY... IT'S NOTHING.
TA (TEP)
....
HUH...?

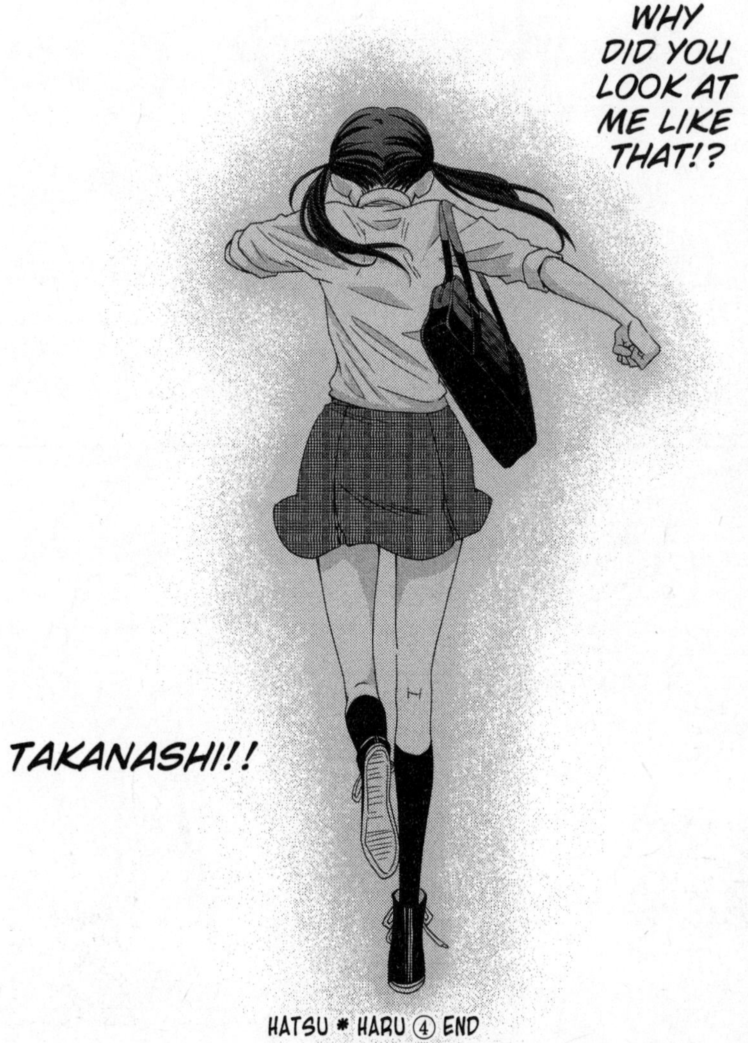
WHY DID YOU LOOK AT ME LIKE THAT!?
TAKANASHI!!

HATSU * HARU ④ END

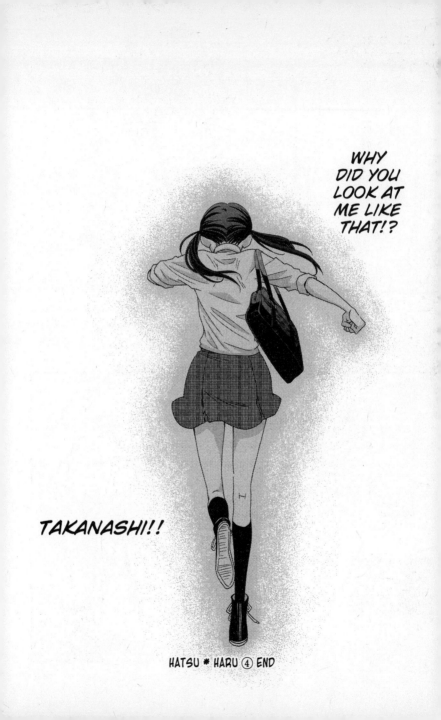

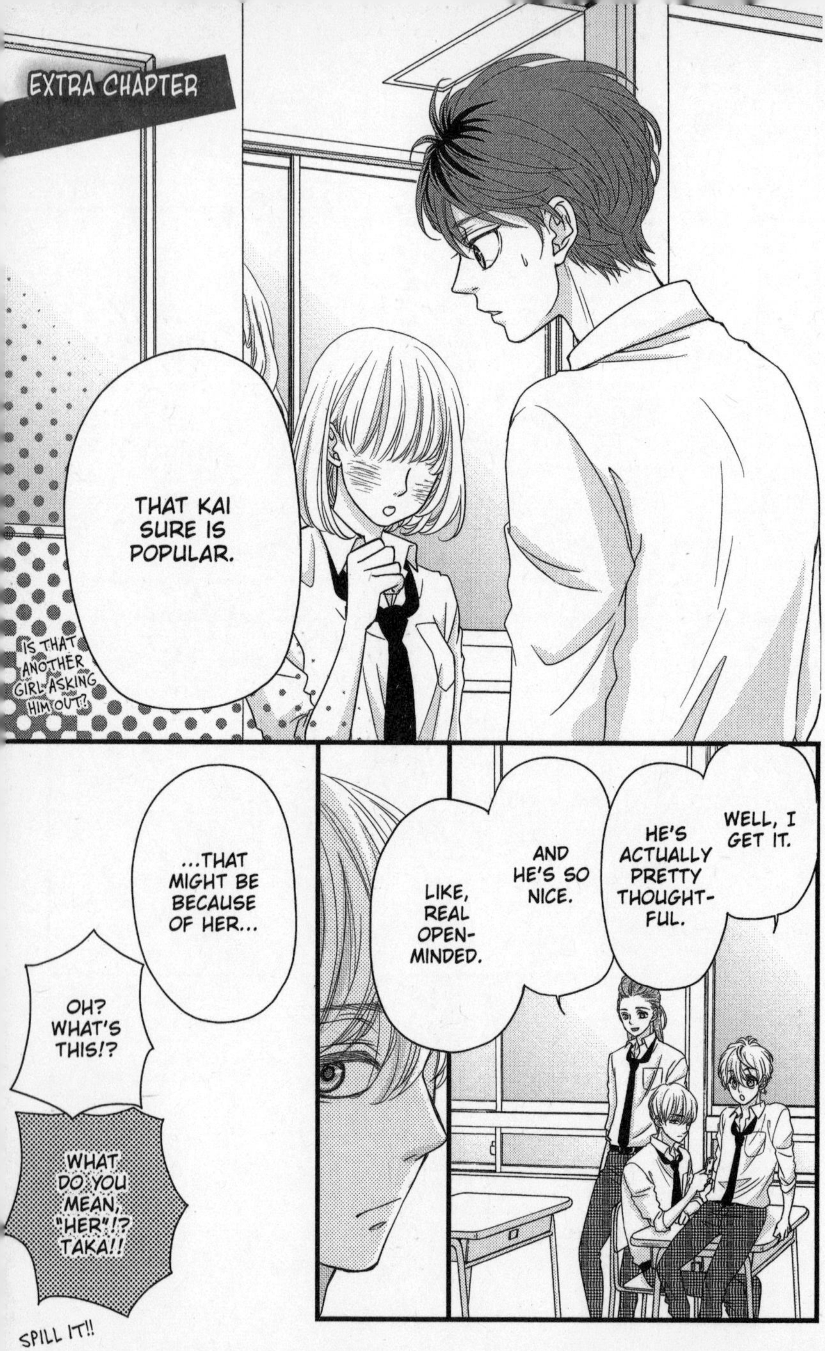
EXTRA CHAPTER
THAT KAI SURE IS POPULAR.
IS THAT ANOTHER GIRL ASKING HIM OUT?
WELL, I GET IT.
HE'S ACTUALLY PRETTY THOUGHT-FUL.
AND HE'S SO NICE.
LIKE, REAL OPEN-MINDED.
...THAT MIGHT BE BECAUSE OF HER...
OH? WHAT'S THIS!?
WHAT DO YOU MEAN, "HER"!? TAKA!!
SPILL IT!!

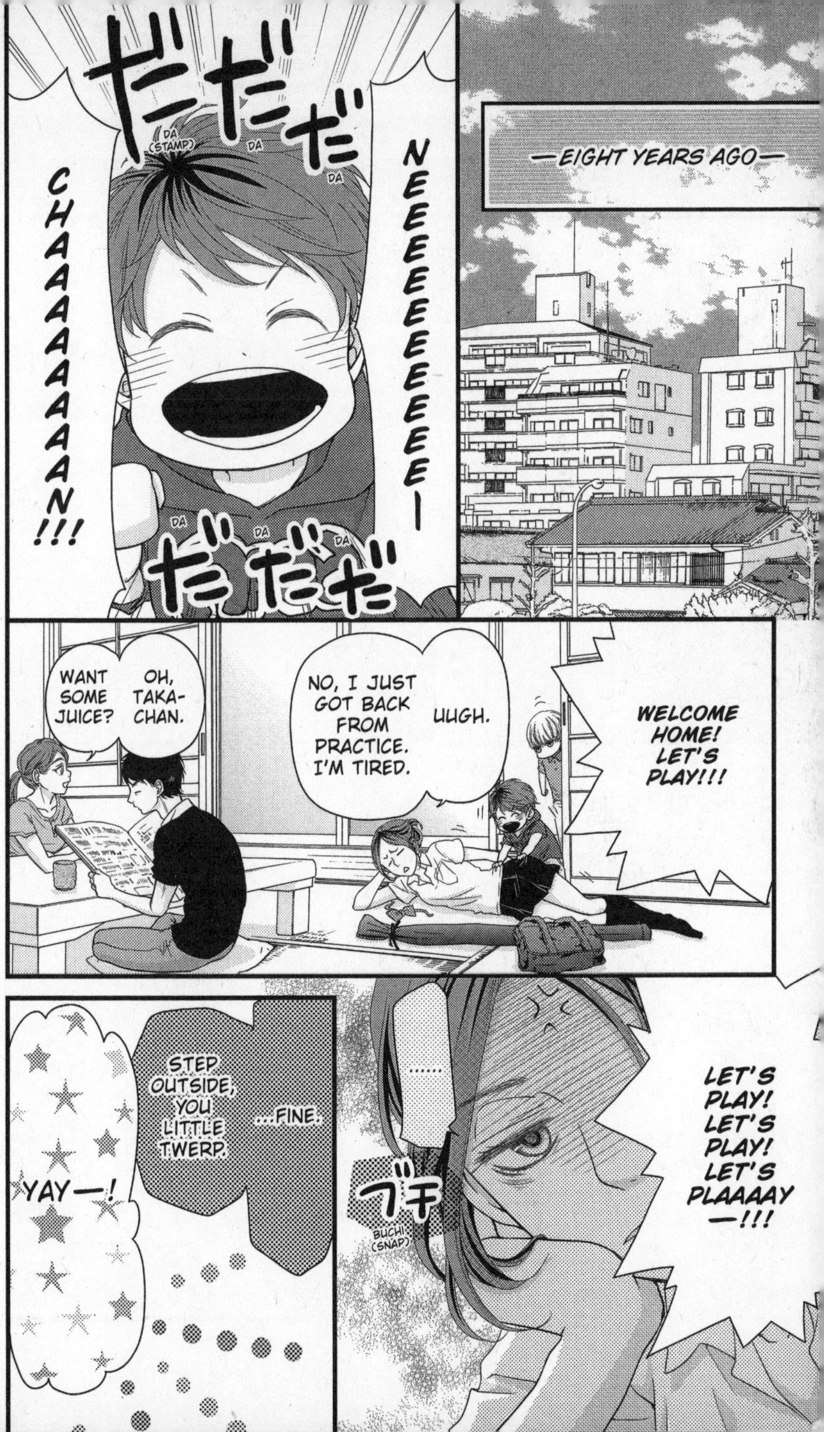
—EIGHT YEARS AGO—
だだだ
DA (STAMP)
DA
DA
NEEEEEEEEEEEI
CHAAAAAAAAAAN!!!
だだだ
DA
DA
DA
WELCOME HOME! LET'S PLAY!!!
UUGH.
NO, I JUST GOT BACK FROM PRACTICE. I'M TIRED.
OH, TAKA-CHAN.
WANT SOME JUICE?
LET'S PLAY! LET'S PLAY! LET'S PLAAAAY—!!!
ブチ
BUCHI (SNAP)
......
...FINE.
STEP OUTSIDE, YOU LITTLE TWERP.
YAY—!

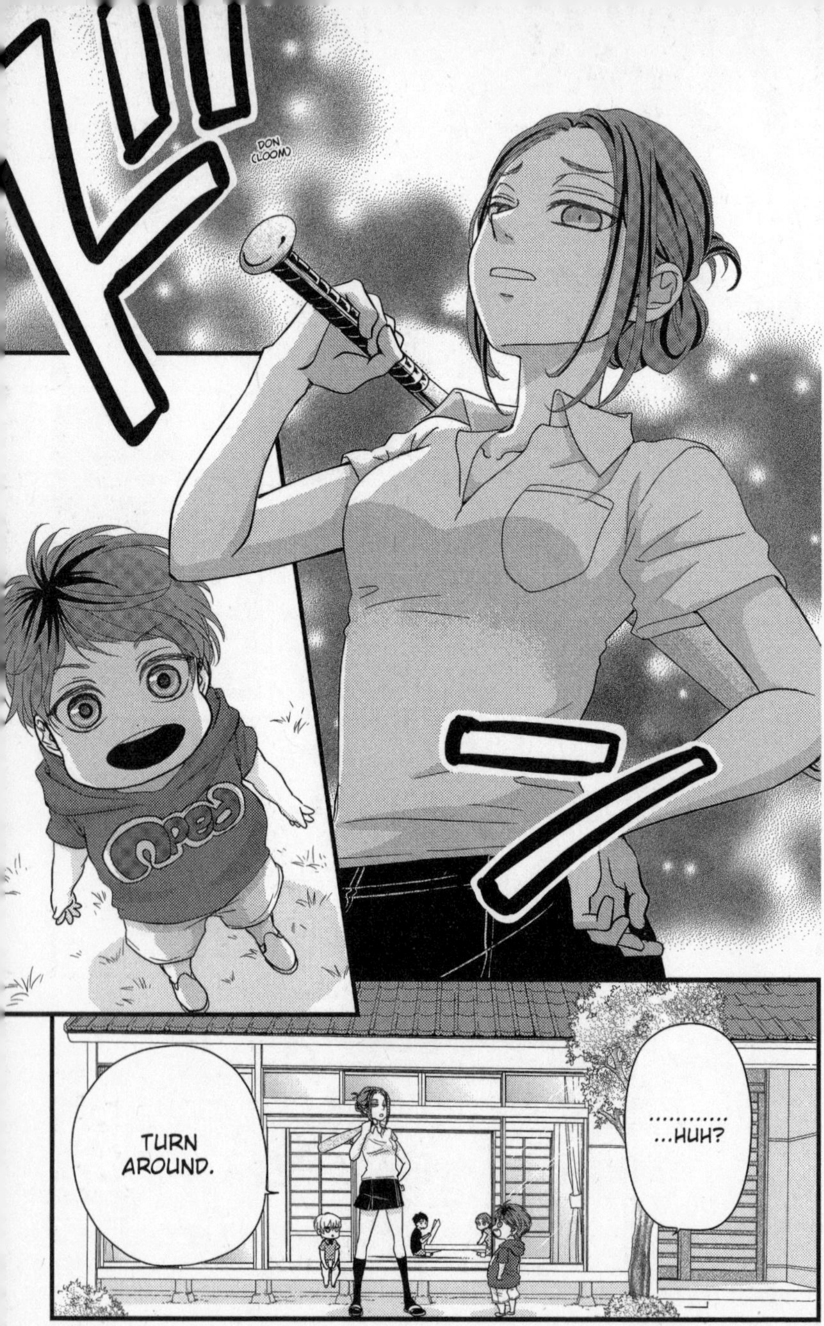
DON
(LOOM)
....
...HUH?
TURN
AROUND.

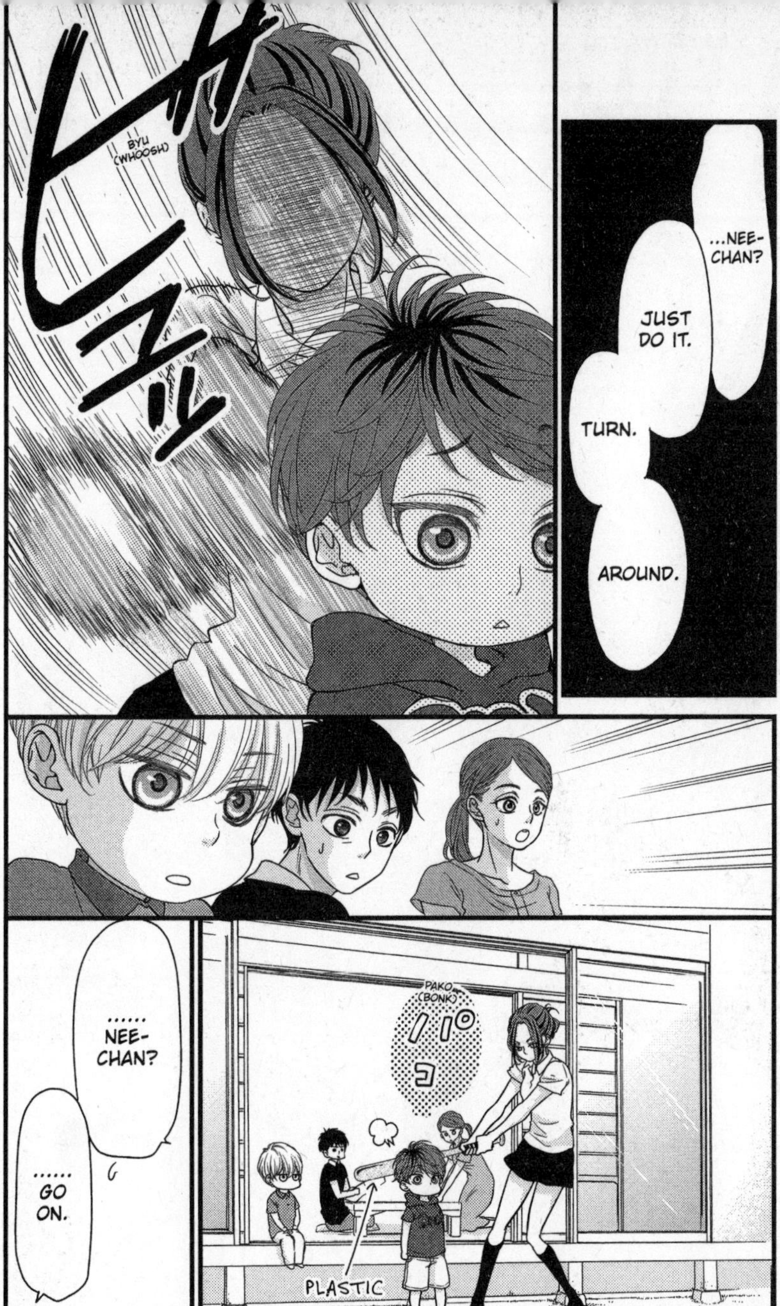
...NEE-CHAN?
JUST DO IT.
TURN.
AROUND.
BYU (WHOOSH)
PAKO (BONK)
PLASTIC
......NEE-CHAN?
......GO ON.

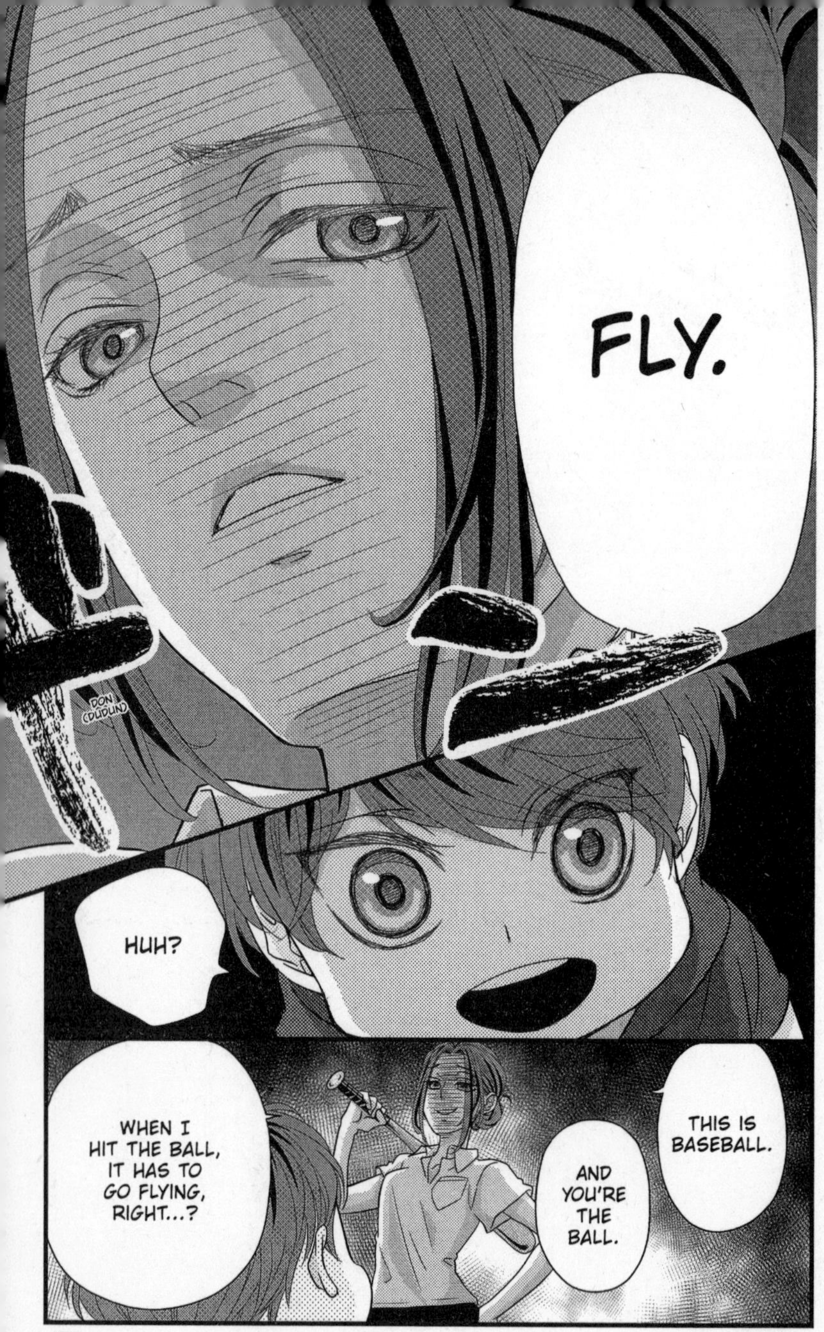
FLY.
DON (DUDUN)
HUH?
THIS IS BASEBALL.
AND YOU'RE THE BALL.
WHEN I HIT THE BALL, IT HAS TO GO FLYING, RIGHT...?

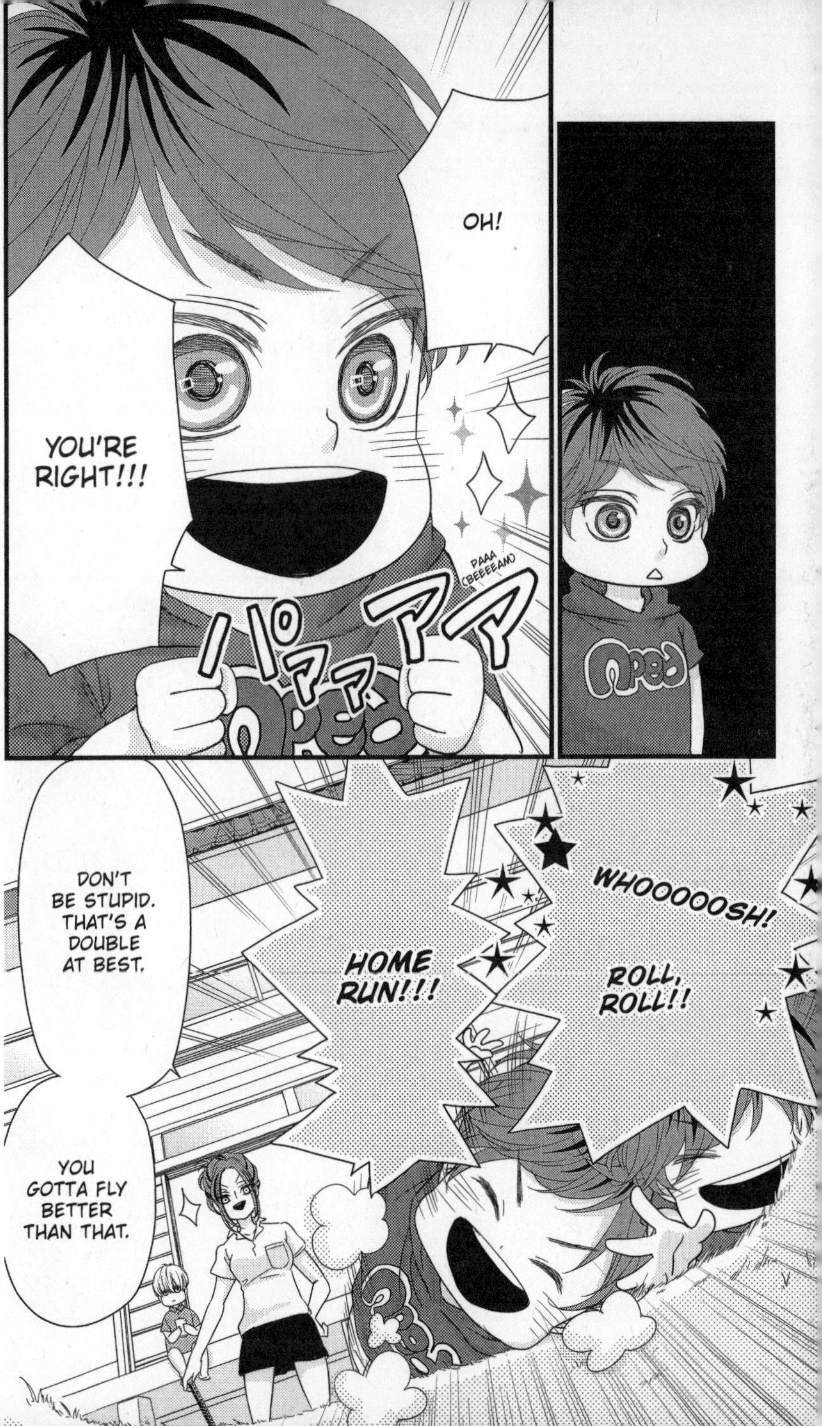
OH!
PAAA (BEEEEAM)
パアアア
YOU'RE RIGHT!!!
WHOOOOOOSH!
ROLL, ROLL!!
HOME RUN!!!
DON'T BE STUPID. THAT'S A DOUBLE AT BEST.
YOU GOTTA FLY BETTER THAN THAT.

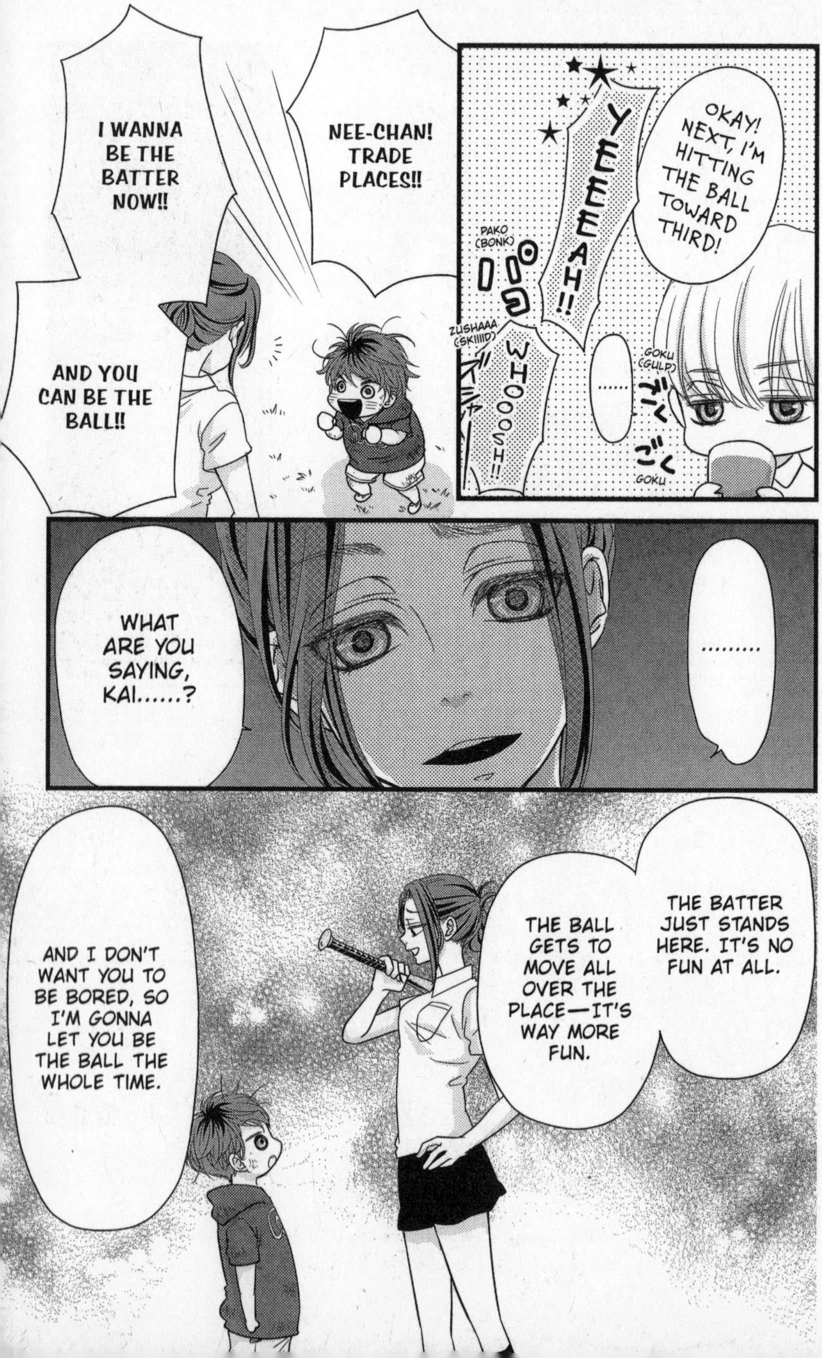
OKAY! NEXT, I'M HITTING THE BALL TOWARD THIRD!
YEEEAH!!
PAKO (BONK)
ZUSHAAA (SKIIIID)
WHOOOOSH!!
......
GOKU (GULP)
ごく ごく
GOKU
NEE-CHAN! TRADE PLACES!!
I WANNA BE THE BATTER NOW!!
AND YOU CAN BE THE BALL!!
....
WHAT ARE YOU SAYING, KAI......?
THE BATTER JUST STANDS HERE. IT'S NO FUN AT ALL.
THE BALL GETS TO MOVE ALL OVER THE PLACE—IT'S WAY MORE FUN.
AND I DON'T WANT YOU TO BE BORED, SO I'M GONNA LET YOU BE THE BALL THE WHOLE TIME.

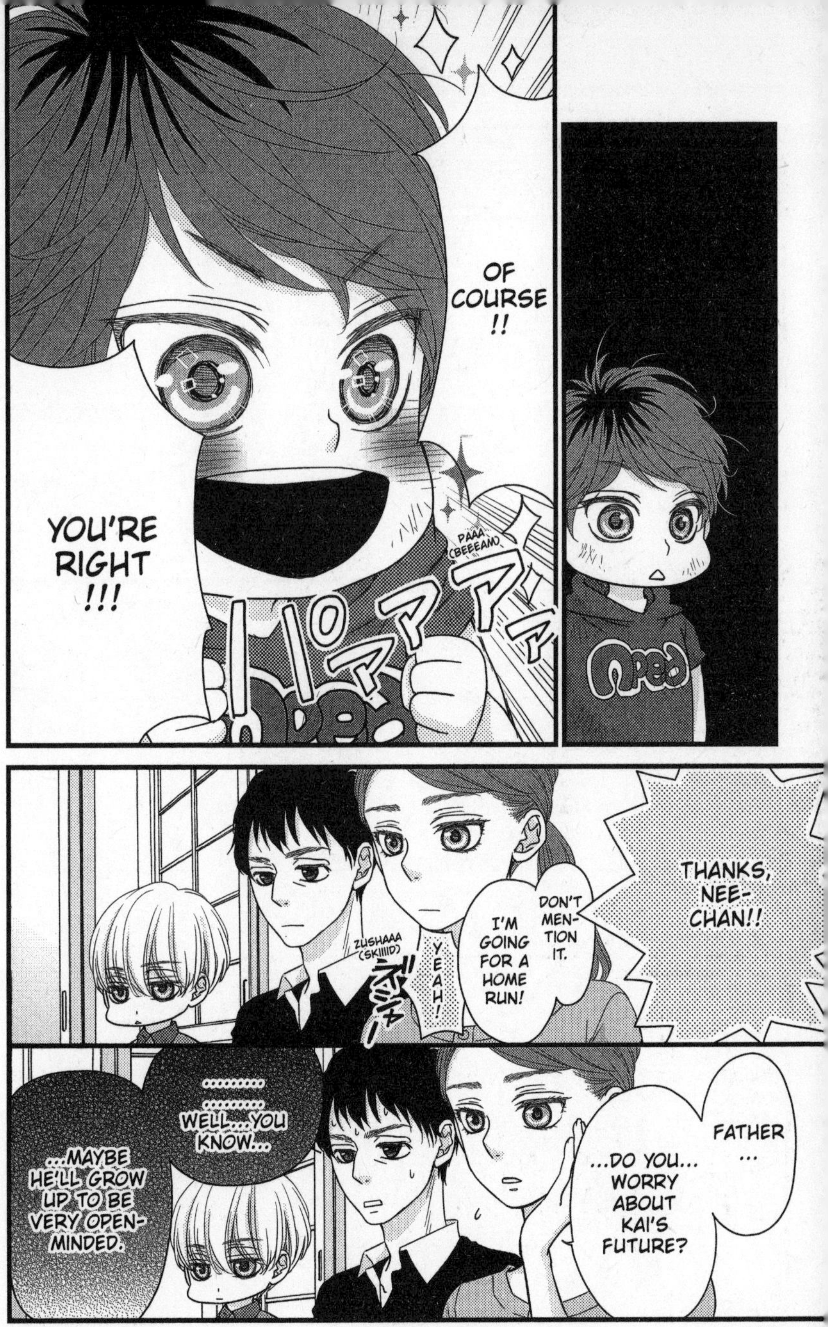
OF COURSE!!
PAAA (BEEEAM)
YOU'RE RIGHT!!!
THANKS, NEE-CHAN!!
DON'T MENTION IT.
I'M GOING FOR A HOME RUN!
YEAH!
ZUSHAAA (SKIIIID)
FATHER...
...DO YOU... WORRY ABOUT KAI'S FUTURE?
....
....
WELL...YOU KNOW...
...MAYBE HE'LL GROW UP TO BE VERY OPEN-MINDED.

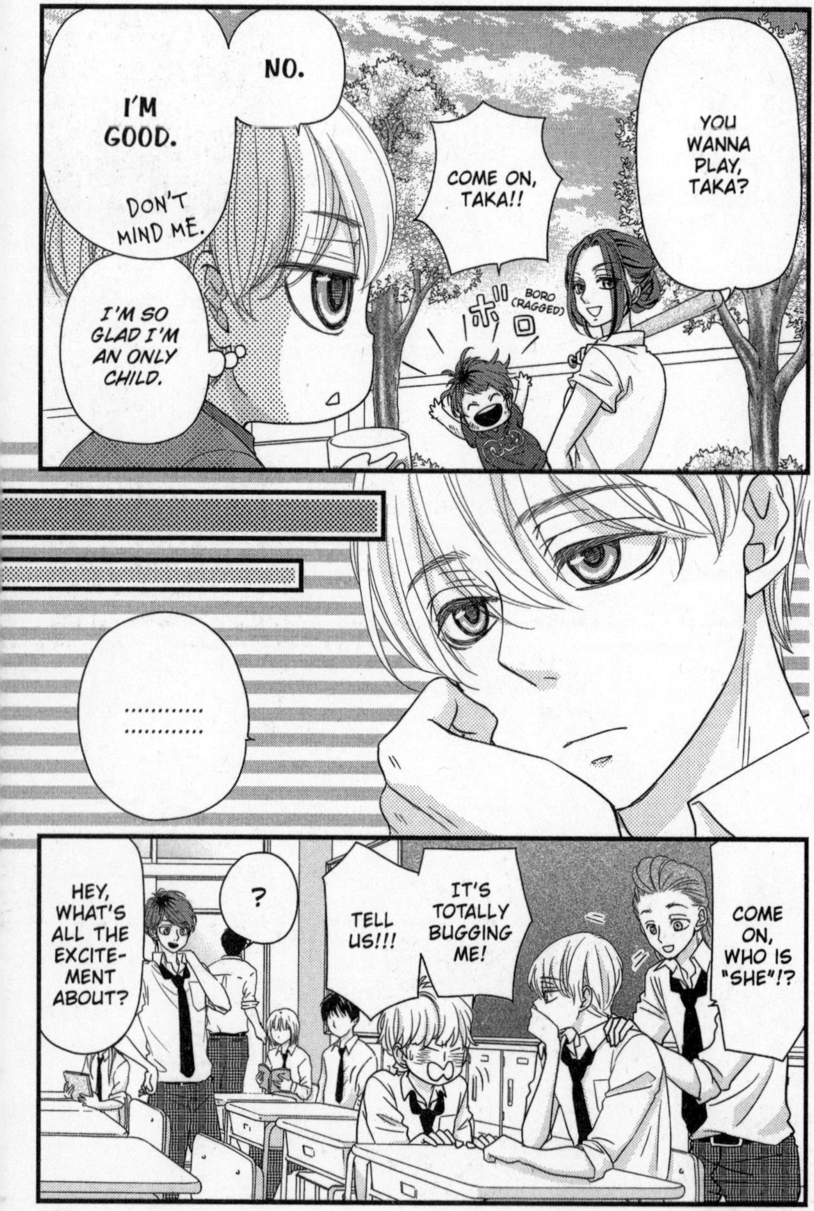
YOU WANNA PLAY, TAKA?
COME ON, TAKA!!
ボロ
BORO (RAGGED)
NO.
I'M GOOD.
DON'T MIND ME.
I'M SO GLAD I'M AN ONLY CHILD.
…………
…………
COME ON, WHO IS "SHE"!?
IT'S TOTALLY BUGGING ME!
TELL US!!!
?
HEY, WHAT'S ALL THE EXCITEMENT ABOUT?

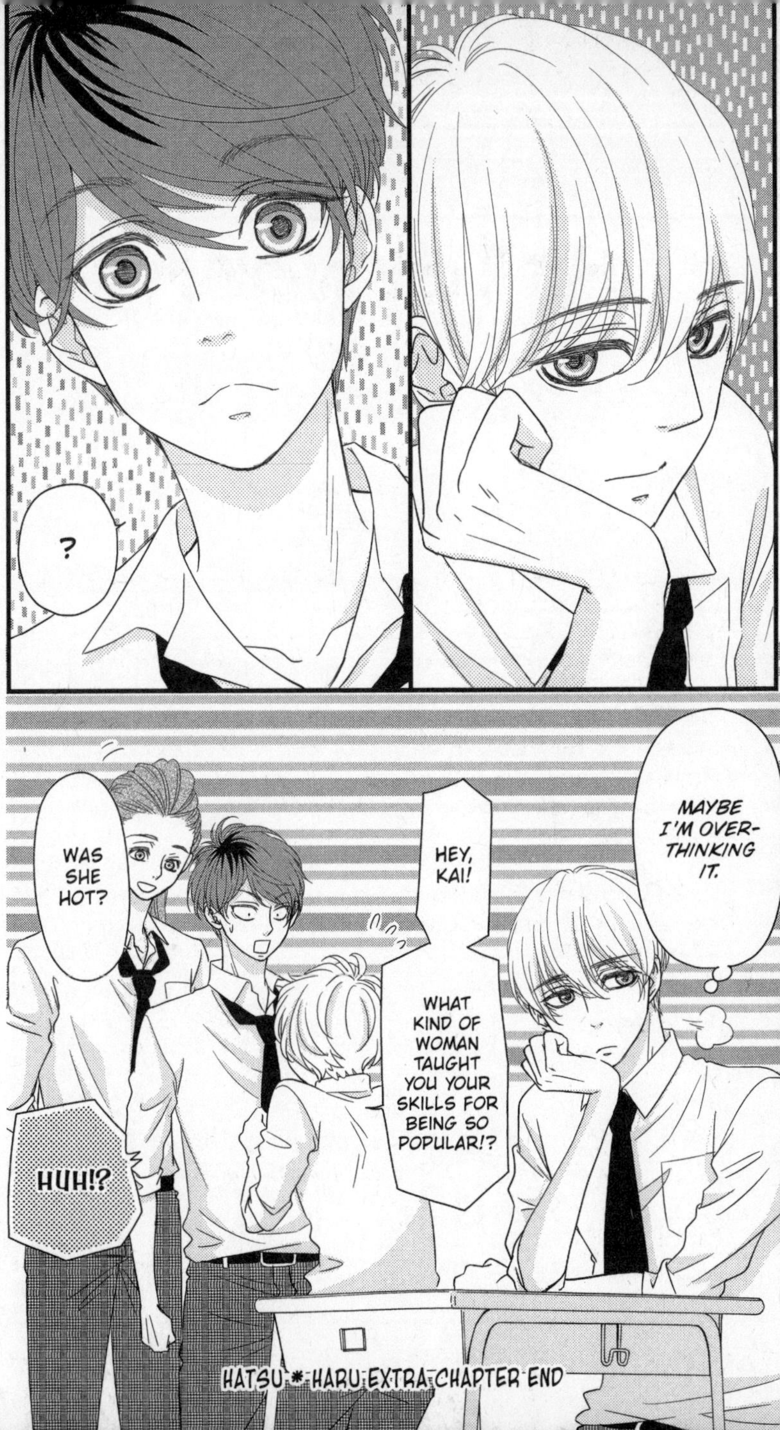
?
MAYBE I'M OVER-THINKING IT.
HEY, KAI!
WHAT KIND OF WOMAN TAUGHT YOU YOUR SKILLS FOR BEING SO POPULAR!?
WAS SHE HOT?
HUH!?
HATSU * HARU EXTRA CHAPTER END

Afterword

Thank you for reading!! I thought I'd put the girls' profiles in this volume, but there weren't enough extra pages, so I'll have to save that for next time.

*HATSU * HARU* has a lot of characters, so drawing them all can be pretty tough. But it's also a lot of fun drawing all their antics, so I always end up bringing everybody into the pages, and then I'm cursing myself every month. It's especially hard doing the scenes with this volume's cover girl, Ayumi-chan. Why? Because Ayumi-chan is always in very dynamic positions. She strikes poses for dramatic effect a lot too, the little troublemaker. Taka is hard too. Why? Because he's supposed to be a hot guy. There's so much pressure to make him handsome that he's really hard to draw even though he basically never moves. Kai is no problem.

Here I'm complaining about the hard stuff, but it's fun, so I'll keep going! I hope you'll read Volume 5 too!

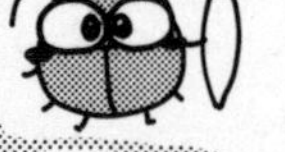

The friends who helped with the manuscript and hung out with me:

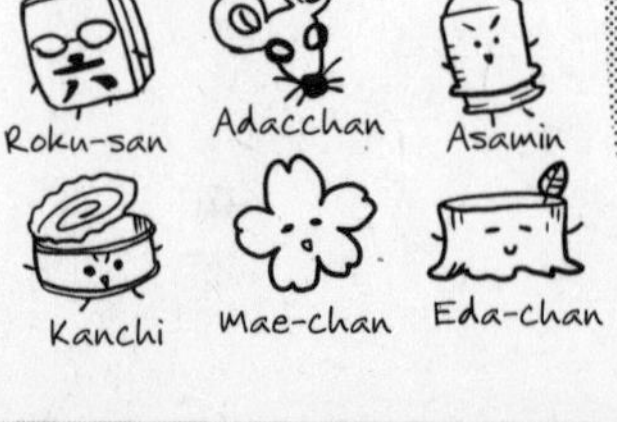

Roku-san
Adacchan
Asamin
Kanchi
Mae-chan
Eda-chan

I can't wait to hear from you!

Yen Press
1290 Avenue of the Americas
New York, NY 10104

• Blog → "Shizu Diary" shizukifujisawa.amebaownd.com
• Twitter ID → shizukifujisawa

hatsu

Shizuki Fuji

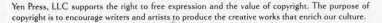

Translation/Adaptation: Alethea and Athena Nibley

Lettering: Lys Blakeslee

HATSU*HARU Vol. 4 by Shizuki FUJISAWA
© 2014 Shizuki FUJISAWA
All rights reserved.
Original Japanese edition published by SHOGAKUKAN.
English translation rights in the United States of America, Canada, the United Kingdom, Ireland, Australia and New Zealand arranged with SHOGAKUKAN
through Tuttle-Mori Agency, Inc.

English translation © 2018 by Yen Press, LLC

Yen Press
1290 Avenue of the America
New York, NY 10104

Visit us at yenpress.com ❀ facebook.com/yenpress ❀ twitter.com/yenpress
yenpress.tumblr.com ❀ instagram.com/yenpress

First Yen Press Edition: December 2018

Yen Press is an imprint of Yen Press, LLC.
The Yen Press name and logo are trademarks of Yen Press, LLC.

Library of Congress Control Number:
2018935618

ISBN: 978-1-9753-5352-0

10 9 8 7 6 5 4 3 2 1

WOR

Printed in the United States of America